RICHARD STRAUSS

VOLUME TWO

LUTON SIXTH FORM COLLEGE

Richard Strauss, 1917, from the etching by Emil Orlik

RICHARD STRAUSS

A CRITICAL COMMENTARY
ON HIS LIFE AND WORKS
BY
NORMAN DEL MAR

VOLUME TWO

BARRIE AND ROCKLIFF
LONDON

© 1969 BY NORMAN DEL MAR

FIRST PUBLISHED 1969 BY BARRIE AND ROCKLIFF

2 CLEMENT'S INN, LONDON WC2

SBN 214 16008 4

REPRINTED 1969

PRINTED IN GREAT BRITAIN BY

LOWE AND BRYDONE (PRINTERS) LTD., LONDON

CONTENTS

ILLUSTRATIONS

INTRODUCTION

THIS second volume carries the chronological survey of Strauss's life and works to the end of the collaboration with Hofmannsthal, perhaps the most celebrated co-authorship between two men of comparable stature in the realm of opera. Interest has recently been revived through the publication of their profuse correspondence in a new English translation which, especially with its admirable introduction by Edward Sackville-West, provides an indispensable source for all students of the subject. I am indebted to the publishers, Messrs Collins, for permission to quote liberally from this.

The partisanship of the world is at present inclined to be strongly in favour of the poet at Strauss's expense. In taking the opposite view I have to face the possibility that I have allowed the pendulum to swing a little too far the other way, although it will be seen that I am far from blind to my own hero's weaknesses. There is nothing harder than to be scrupulously fair while developing a thesis, particularly over so wide a period as this volume covers.

Volume II also takes world events to the brink of Nazi domination of Germany, and these combined circumstances are more closely connected in their relevance to a change in Strauss's life than at first appears; for had not death brought the partnership to an end the Nazis certainly would have done so on account of Hofmannsthal's partly Jewish ancestry. It is indeed hard to visualize the effect the new régime would have had upon the hypersensitive poet, if he had survived. However cruel the cause of his death, he was spared many even harsher experiences which may well have lain in store.

The line of demarcation in the story of Strauss's work is therefore as clear-cut as it was at the end of Volume I, and I have only crossed it in a few minor isolated instances for reasons of clarity and compactness. In this respect Volume II looks both forwards and backwards since I have, in between pursuing the main threads, taken opportunities to bring up alongside the considerable body of minor vocal and orchestral music. On the other hand, after some hesitation I have decided to leave Strauss's huge output of Lieder until the very end, and this will now therefore be dealt with at length only in the closing chapters of a third and last volume, the necessity for which could perhaps have been foreseen from the start!

I have many friends and colleagues to thank for help and advice of every kind; especially Mr Klaus Schloessingk-Paul, Mr Alan Jefferson and Mr Michael Rose, whose patience and kindly criticism have done so much towards keeping my perspective from becoming unduly distorted.

To Dr Willi Schuh, that doyen of Strauss biographers to whom every student of the composer is indebted, I extend my greetings and thanks for his courtesy in allowing me to quote material at present unpublished and his exclusive property.

The librarians of the B.B.C. have been immensely co-operative and I wish here to express my gratitude for their indulgence as also to my friends in the different departments of Boosey and Hawkes.

The index has again been prepared by John and Alix Farrell and to them I extend my warmest thanks and admiration.

In addition to Collins and to the publishers cited in Volume I, I am indebted to the following for permission to quote from copyright works:

> Bowes & Bowes, Publishers Ltd.
> Cassell & Co. Ltd.
> Forberg Verlag
> Collins Publishers
> Victor Gollancz Ltd.
> Hamish Hamilton Ltd.
> Heinrichshofen Verlag
> Hinrichsen Edition Ltd., copyright holders of Peters Edition
> Hogarth Press
> Hutchinson & Co. Ltd.
> Robert Lienau
> *Music & Letters*
> S. Fischer Verlag
> Universal Edition (Alfred A. Kalmus Ltd.)

Witchings, Hadley Common
December 1966   N.R.D.M.

LIST OF WORKS DISCUSSED IN VOLUME II

CHAPTER X

A THEATRICAL EXPERIMENT

(i) The Composite Work

I

WITH the world-wide acclaim of *Der Rosenkavalier* Strauss found himself at the height of his fame and success. Life had certainly been good to him both in his professional and in his private circumstances. He was now firmly established with his wife and 13-year-old son in their beautiful villa in the Bavarian Alps, where he spent an ever-increasing proportion of his time. Both as one of the leading German conductors and as the acknowledged master in the field of contemporary music, his position seemed secure and unassailable. All eyes were upon him to see in which direction he would turn for his next works, what new and varied experiences he would seek out, what fresh literary influence he would receive in the course, perhaps, of wide travelling for the refreshment and rejuvenation of his art.

But Strauss himself no longer saw his life in that light. He was 46, his prestige was enormous, and any avoidable effort was less attractive than it had once been. It was plain that his librettist of the past four years, Hugo von Hofmannsthal, was still eager to continue the collaboration. Perhaps *Der Rosenkavalier* might prove to be the operatic counterpart to the equally successful *Till Eulenspiegel*, an interlude between more serious undertakings. All that was needed was to coax out of Hofmannsthal some worthy successor to *Elektra* and Strauss felt confident that he need seek no further for the appropriate stimuli.

To set Hofmannsthal's mind working in the right direction, Strauss had already written to him on 8th October 1912, less than a fortnight after the last page of *Der Rosenkavalier* was complete, suggesting that they might now take another look at *Semiramis*, the Calderón drama which had briefly occupied their attention at the very outset of their work together. The character of the great Assyrian princess with her legendary sexual orgies was just what was needed to arouse Strauss's more erotic inventiveness, to enable him indeed to continue his adventures in modernistic composition. Hofmannsthal had just had a great success in Munich with a romantic version of the Oedipus legend which he had treated in much the same way as *Elektra*. The signs were propitious and Strauss eagerly congratulated the poet on his triumph with *Oedipus*, while at the same time slipping in a postscript reminding him of *Semiramis*.

In the light of later events it is hard to know whether, had he been encouraged to pursue the path of daring experimentalism, Strauss's natural geniality, and the easy routine existence into which he was fast falling, would have allowed him to continue long as an advanced progressive. Pioneers rarely live in affluent circumstances surrounded by luxury and adulation. He might perhaps have continued the trend of *Salome* and *Elektra* for a little longer especially in view of the vast strides music was undergoing in stylistic emancipation at precisely this time. For 1909 saw the composition of Schönberg's Five Orchestral Pieces and Scriabin's *Prometheus*, 1911 Bartók's *Bluebeard's Castle*, 1912 Schönberg's *Pierrot Lunaire* and 1913 Stravinsky's *Le Sacre du Printemps*. It is not too much to regard this period as crucial. The artistic world was bubbling and, in his professional life, Strauss was still very much part of it.

But Hofmannsthal had tired of the 'Romantic Agony'. Already during the collaboration on *Elektra* he had replied to Strauss's queries concerning proposals for the future (*Danton's Tod*, Sardou's *9 Thermidor*) by saying that, despite 'fairly liberal ideas' he held such horrific schemes to be 'absolutely no longer possible'.

From the author of *Der Rosenkavalier* this is understandable, but less so from that of *Elektra*, and Strauss had every reason to be taken aback. From the first he had pounced on the *Semiramis* project, and it must have been a sharp disappointment when an answer to his postscript arrived with a terse refusal to consider the matter. Hofmannsthal's views on suitable operatic subjects had become irrevocably fixed.

Oddly enough the idea of Strauss separating from Hofmannsthal never arose at all. Gabriele d'Annunzio, the great Italian poet and dramatist, made an approach to Strauss which was reported in the press, giving Hofmannsthal some momentary anxiety. The two collaborators were already as jealous as lovers over their artistic allegiance to one another. But Strauss only used d'Annunzio's offer as a lever to extract material from Hofmannsthal, never as a serious proposal. Since his entire interest in composing lay at present in the theatre, this threw his choice of subject-matter altogether into the hands of Hofmannsthal, who was not slow in seizing the initiative. From now on Strauss found himself obliged to follow in whichever direction Hofmannsthal led, even if over the years this took him away from his natural subject-matter and at times into regions in which he was constitutionally unable to comprehend the poet at all. It is thus not surprising that he sometimes had the greatest difficulty in summoning musical ideas of a corresponding depth and originality in the course of remaining true to the friend who had in the first place supplied him with *Elektra* and *Rosenkavalier*.

Significantly, in outlining his intended projects for their future together, Hofmannsthal never once considered providing Strauss with libretti on the more lurid subjects he craved. His only concession was to acknowledge that he had been deliberately side-tracking Strauss, and to propose that Strauss find his own outlet for such orgiastic tendencies through writing a symphony based on 'Orestes and the Furies', an idea which might conceivably prove valuable for some ballet scheme. In actual fact Hofmannsthal had entered into preliminary and abortive negotiations with Diaghilev, to the point of receiving a draft contract together with proposals for the personification of the Furies. However, not even the possibility of Nijinsky dancing the role of Orestes in some choreographic dramatization could arouse Strauss's interest. The truth is that the writing of symphonies was no longer congenial to him. During the past year he had actually begun one on his own account, descriptive of his beloved Bavarian Alps; but this amused him, as he put it, 'even less than chasing cockroaches'.[1]

2

Hofmannsthal had been intrigued by French literature of the eighteenth century ever since drafting the preliminary sketches for *Der Rosenkavalier*. For this opera he had taken some ideas from Molière, including, for example, the aria of the Italian Tenor in Act 1 which is quoted verbatim from the *petit ballet* which concludes the fifth act of *Le Bourgeois Gentilhomme*. He continued, therefore, to look wistfully at the rich un-

[1] See Chapter XI, p. 105.

tapped store of comedies by that greatest dramatist of the period, merely hinting to Strauss that he was toying with an idea for a little Molière piece.

At the same time another project was occupying Hofmannsthal. This was to be a comedy which he believed might take place in some Bohemian castle. The plot would centre round a young heiress, whose three suitors arrange for an Opera Seria company and a troupe from the Commedia dell'Arte to visit her castle simultaneously.

The action was already taking shape in his mind when, during a visit to Paris, the poet saw in a flash that if in some way he could combine Molière's *Le Bourgeois Gentilhomme* with the Bohemian comedy he might thus create an entirely new form of *divertissement*.

In March 1911 he wrote to Strauss opening the door to his latest proposals which by now included not only the little opera which was to form part of the new entertainment but a still further and very complicated project (later to become *Die Frau ohne Schatten*) which he described as 'standing in the same relation to *Die Zauberflöte* as *Rosenkavalier* does to *Figaro*'.

Already conscious that here he had a scheme of enormous profundity involving a considerable time to work out, and ignoring urgent pleas from Strauss for news of weightier plans, Hofmannsthal continued working on his small-scale venture in tragi-comedy. He had by now progressed well beyond the Bohemian castle and had chosen the Ariadne-Theseus myth as the subject of the opera to be coupled with *Le Bourgeois Gentilhomme*. The whole composite scheme had already advanced substantially and Hofmannsthal had also lighted upon a new and good idea for linking the two works.

Faced with a virtual *fait accompli* Strauss saw little choice but to acquiesce, and this he did with as much grace as he could muster. It might turn out very prettily; he might have a lot of fun with it, writing 'some pleasant salon music'; although it seemed dramatically rather slender it might amuse him to work on set numbers for a change.

In the event Strauss must have found it something of a relief that the shape of the work promised better than he had expected. He even made some important contributions to the organization of the contrasting elements of comedy and classical drama in the now agreed *Ariadne auf Naxos*. He was determined, for example, that the Columbine figure from the Commedia dell'Arte who began in the poet's sketches as Tartaglia and ended as Zerbinetta, no doubt as a result of Hofmannsthal's researches into Molière,[2] should be the occasion for a revival of the coloratura role. Hofmannsthal himself, however, viewed this idea with some misgivings as he recalled the ungainly appearance, let alone the acting qualities of such well-known virtuosi as Kurz, Hempel and Tetrazzini.

3

The first few set pieces of the Incidental Music for the *Bourgeois Gentilhomme* section did not delay Strauss for long. For the music of two of the dances (the Dancing Master and the Tailors) he drew from the abandoned sketches for the ballet *Kythere* and being very much in the mood for composition, soon polished off a few attractive numbers. He then wrote to Hofmannsthal asking for as much as possible of the *Ariadne* text in terms which not only antagonized the poet, but were ethically somewhat dubious. While insisting on a star singer for the coloratura role he said: 'there must be a few star singing-roles in it since the action as such has no interest. . . . Personally the whole thing doesn't overwhelm me with interest either.' He then went on to ask for 'Hymns à la Schiller' and 'Rückert-ish flourishes' to excite his inspiration for the sake of occasions like this where the action itself left him cold. 'Rhetoric full of *élan*', he wrote, 'can stupefy me adequately to keep writing music on quite uninteresting subjects', a pronouncement of considerable significance to the understanding and final assessment of Strauss's life-work as a whole.

If Strauss was tactless, Hofmannsthal was most unfair. 'I have during the last few days put everything aside for your sake in order to occupy myself intensively and exclusively with *Ariadne*. My purpose in the execution of this work was purely to please you (and in the second place Reinhardt too) and to do you a service.' This is a remarkable statement. He had virtually bludgeoned Strauss into collaboration on an artificial comedy of a kind by no means natural to the composer and which he had been largely prompted to accept on trust for better things to follow. No doubt Strauss put himself in the wrong by agreeing to the scheme merely because he wanted work for the summer. Yet Hofmannsthal had somehow lost all sympathy with the composer's point of view and was becoming insufferable in his nagging complaints whenever Strauss did not receive each new instalment as a masterpiece in its own right:

> 'I must say quite plainly your extremely paltry and cool words over the completed *Ariadne* . . . have vexed me

[2] Zerbinetta is a prominent character in Molière's *Les Fourberies de Scapin*.

2

somewhat. . . . You may of course have written your letter
or read the manuscript when you were not feeling quite up
to the mark . . . nor do I fail to take into account how much
worse this pretty subtle creation must appear in handwriting
instead of in clear typescript (unfortunately my typist was
away ill). So I am not without hope that closer acquaintance
will bring home to you the excellence of the text more
strongly. I may venture to say that pieces like the Intermezzo . . . cannot be excelled in their own genre by anyone
writing in Europe today. . . . Furthermore I doubt if you
could find in any other one-act opera libretto three songs
that can compare for delicacy, as well as characteristic
firmness, with Harlequin's Song, Zerbinetta's Rondo and
Bacchus' Song to Circe. Naturally I would rather have
heard you say all this than write it to you myself.'

He then proceeded to outline in considerable detail the psychological
implications of the drama. The contrast between Ariadne and Zerbinetta,
and their relationship *vis-à-vis* Theseus, Harlequin and Bacchus, were
subtleties which, clear and vibrant in Hofmannsthal's own mind, had so
far eluded poor Strauss in a very disappointing manner.

It says much for Strauss's good humour and courtesy that he took this
pompous and self-righteous outburst (let alone several more of a similar
character which followed shortly after) without indulging in a full-
blown quarrel. He had much to put up with at this time, for Hofmannsthal, possibly sensing himself basically at fault in expecting the wrong
kind of literary perceptions from the essentially down-to-earth Strauss,
was devastating in his dismissal of one after another of the composer's
own ideas.

The more Strauss criticized the dramatic lameness of the action at this
point or that, the more Hofmannsthal explained himself in long and
beautifully expressed analyses, reading ever more profound psychological significance into apparently simple passages. In vain might
Strauss protest: if even he proved unable to perceive the beauty through
the obscurity of the underlying thought how much less would the ox-
like spectators; only after reading Hofmannsthal's explanations had he
grasped the symbolism of the text; perhaps they should be published in
an open letter.

Feeling the need for intellectual support Strauss took the unwise step
of securing the agreement of his good friend and legal adviser Willy
Levin over the passages in question. Hofmannsthal immediately retali-

ated by reading the whole libretto through to a gathering of 'by no means erudite people'—his own wife, a dancer, a young painter, a countess—all of whom, it would seem, understood every inner meaning instantly, producing moreover quite spontaneously all the enthusiasm and sympathetic appreciation he had hitherto sought in vain. The implications that Hofmannsthal had no very high opinion of Strauss are sinister and uncomfortably prophetic of their future relationship.

4

The dispute over the clarity of the action continued for months. Even when the opportunity for a full explanation of the psychological background presented itself Hofmannsthal continued to insist that he had driven the meaning 'into the heads of the audience with a sledge-hammer, point for point', particularly by means of his transition scene. Strauss continued, however, to protest that he was mistaken in this belief and that he had been far too profound for the majority of listeners and especially the critics. In the end Strauss had his way at least to the extent that Hofmannsthal's original letter, though with the personal sections suitably edited (!), was duly made public.[3] Nor were the quarrels between composer and librettist confined to the writing of the work. It is no exaggeration to say that in its composite nature the *divertissement* is unique, and this fact carried with it from the outset problems of satisfactory mounting which gave rise to new bones of contention.

Hofmannsthal had conceived the work essentially in terms of one theatre only—Max Reinhardt's Kleines Deutsches Theater in Berlin. Max Reinhardt was beyond question the outstanding theatrical genius of his day, with a vision and drive that gathered around him all the young actors and directors who were stimulated by his revolutionary innovations both in the technique of stage-craft and of production.

Hofmannsthal's association with Reinhardt was long standing; indeed it was to him that he owed his very association with Strauss, since it was at the Deutsches Theater that his *Elektra* had been staged in its original purely dramatic form, soon after Reinhardt's production of Oscar Wilde's *Salome*. It is thus no exaggeration to say that the whole new venture was conceived more specifically for Reinhardt than for Strauss himself. As a result, Hofmannsthal planned so far beyond his own legitimate province as to envisage the very nature and placing of

[3] The letter appeared in the *Almanach für die musikalische Welt*, Berlin, 1912.

Strauss's orchestra which he saw as a small body of players placed actually on the stage, thus anticipating Stravinsky's *Histoire du Soldat* by seven years.

In Strauss's hands however, the original maximum of fifteen to twenty players soon grew to thirty-seven,[4] few enough in all conscience by comparison with his normal orchestral demands but far too many to tuck into the corner of any stage, quite apart from the intrinsic difficulty of dressing up so many musicians and requiring them to act, a problem which Stravinsky and Ramuz were to solve by the sheer informality of their entertainment.

As the work approached completion it rapidly became clear to Strauss that the orchestra of the Deutsches Theater was simply not equipped to cope with the musical exigencies and that alternative plans ought to be considered. Hofmannsthal began to foresee the possibility of Strauss actually putting off Reinhardt, the kingpin of the entire enterprise. At this point Reinhardt, seeing which way the wind was blowing, thought it politic to indicate his disappointment at the prospect of losing *Ariadne* and Hofmannsthal expressed his disapproval to Strauss in strong terms. The greatest fear in his mind seems to have been that of Strauss entering into negotiations with Count Hülsen, the Intendant of the Berlin Opera, where a new production of *Rosenkavalier* was in the process of being staged.

Actually it is doubtful whether Strauss ever seriously considered taking *Ariadne* away from Reinhardt, but he was naturally concerned whether the practical arrangements of the operatic portion of the work might not prove a stumbling block to that master-producer. After all, an opera house had to be selected in which not only were the space and equipment adequate, but local goodwill could be counted upon. City after city was considered and rejected; Berlin, Dresden, Munich, each was unacceptable for one reason or another. At last Strauss proposed Stuttgart, and to this suggestion, however reluctantly at first, Hofmannsthal was obliged to agree.

Strauss's position at this time was exceedingly strong throughout Germany. His word was virtually law, and a first performance of one of his works was an event carrying great honour to the hall or opera house in which it took place. For a relatively small locality such as Stuttgart this was a rare opportunity and, at least to Strauss's face, the authorities showed not the slightest hesitation in acceding to all his demands and

[4] Stravinsky employs no more than seven instrumentalists.

conditions, high-handed as these might be. It was however all very well for Strauss to say: 'In Stuttgart, where I'll have absolutely full powers, everything's going to be tip-top ... the whole artistic milieu is extremely friendly.' In point of fact many of his conditions produced situations of the utmost delicacy when it came to standing down the resident Stuttgart actors and singers in favour of their colleagues from Berlin, Dresden or Vienna, for the principal roles. Considerable bad feeling was aroused not only amongst the artists themselves but at the highest level, even the Director of the Stuttgart Opera House making it plain that he resented the intrusion of these 'foreigners'.

5

Nevertheless, in the face of all these difficulties the production went ahead. The integration of theatre and opera was skilfully managed under Reinhardt's expert guidance and the first performance took place on 25th October 1912, under Strauss's own baton. Frieda Hempel was to have taken the exacting coloratura part of Zerbinetta but unfortunately an American contract made it impossible and Strauss returned to Margarethe Siems who had, incredible as it may seem, created the roles of both Chrysothemis and the Marschallin. Strauss also failed at the last moment to procure Emmy Destinn upon whom he had counted for the title role, but the Czech soprano Maria Jeritza was found to be ideal, thus establishing the international career of one of the greatest Straussian sopranos.

Reinhardt's Berlin company performed the Molière comedy superlatively ('the piece comes off splendidly. Molière is indescribably funny', wrote Strauss). Yet the opening night cannot be counted a success. A number of factors contributed to this, not least of which was the exorbitantly protracted reception given by the King of Württemberg during the interval. The opera itself, *Ariadne auf Naxos*, thus began two and a half hours after the beginning of the play, with the audience already more than a little restive. There was a more basic reason, on the other hand, why Hofmannsthal's excellent idea was at first regarded as a failure. As Strauss wrote in later years: 'the playgoing public had no wish to listen to opera and vice versa. The proper cultural soil for this pretty hybrid was lacking.' Practical considerations have also through the years militated against this attempt at marrying the worlds of music and straight theatre.

It was not long before Hofmannsthal felt so intensely discouraged that he coerced Strauss into collaborating once more in drastic remedies. Before entering into these, however, it will be clearer to outline the shape of the work in its original form which, when all has been said and done, remains artistically, if not practically, by far the most successful.

6

Le Bourgeois Gentilhomme is one of the last and most mature plays by Jean Baptiste Poquelin, Louis XIV's Court playwright, known to the world under his *nom de plume* 'Molière'. Written three years before his death in 1673 it was an immediate success and has remained a popular favourite ever since.

In the course of the five acts, Molière works out three separate and distinct themes. The first is Monsieur Jourdain, the *nouveau riche* himself, who is amusingly brought to life in the initial series of rapid scenes. We see him in his relationships with his servants, his family, and the various tradesmen and specialists whom he has engaged as instructors in his desire to emulate the aristocracy in every detail.

Secondly there is the unscrupulous Dorante, an actual member of the nobility, although a somewhat rakish character, who makes use of the simple Jourdain in order not only to bolster his own finances but to pursue his dubious affair with the Marquise Dorimène.

Lastly, there is the love-match between Jourdain's daughter Lucile and Cléonte, her suitor, to which is coupled a subsidiary courtship between their respective servants, Nicole and Covielle. The plot is slender and the beauty of the play lies in the detail. The happy denouement is reached by means of a scene of pure burlesque in which, to win Jourdain's respect, Cléonte masquerades as the son of the Grand Turk.

Of these three dramatic elements, the first occupies the original comedy exclusively until the third act. Indeed none of the eight principals other than Monsieur Jourdain appear at all in the first two acts and no less than three of them are only seen for the first time more than half way through Act 3. This long and unusual initial preoccupation with the title role constitutes the best and most celebrated section of Molière's comedy and it was this which attracted Hofmannsthal, who felt with Strauss that 'after Act 3, Scene 8, it gets weak'. Strauss's comment went still further; he thought Molière's piece a bit silly, but hazarded that, developed by Hofmannsthal, 'it might become a hit'.

Since it was no more than the exposition of the basic idea of the *Bourgeois Gentilhomme* which interested Hofmannsthal, he decided to suppress the entire sub-plot of the love-match. With Lucile, Cléonte and Covielle cut out altogether he could with greater clarity throw the emphasis on Molière's other episode, the intrigue between Dorante and Dorimène, which could then be made into a spring-board for the operatic part of the scheme. Dorante could, for example, seek to further his courtship by secretly persuading Jourdain to mount an entire opera for Dorimène's benefit; the justification would then be found for Strauss's more serious contribution which would constitute the second part of the performance. Moreover, by contriving a piece of typically Philistine folly on Jourdain's part, a good excuse could be made for the members of the Commedia dell'Arte to find themselves simultaneously on the same stage as the performers of an Opera Seria.

This is indeed the very crux of the matter. During the period of operatic decadence during the seventeenth and eighteenth centuries it was frequently the custom to lighten an evening of serious or tragic operatic entertainment by the interpolation of a frivolous Intermezzo between the acts of the main drama. Preposterous as such a concession to the superficiality of the period may have been, it is to this that we owe the creation of such masterpieces as Pergolesi's *La Serva Padrona* and so, in direct line of descent, Mozart's *Le Nozze di Figaro*.

The Intermezzo was however, never deliberately presented simultaneously with the Opera Seria, and it was the grotesque situation which such an eventuality might have produced which was the starting point of the entire scheme in Hofmannsthal's mind. As for creating the necessary circumstances, he would, he assured Strauss, have no difficulty in supplying these in the new scene linking the Molière with the Greek tragedy which was to form the backbone of the opera. In any case, there would be no music required. All Strauss need concern himself with for the present was the Incidental Music to the Molière; he had by now sent him the copy with the proper cuts; except for a brief alteration in Scene 1 the places for music were obvious.

Obediently Strauss set to work without further ado.

7

In the opening bars of the Overture, Strauss establishes a period atmosphere by using only strings and continuo (actually the piano—the harpsichord had not yet begun to enjoy its spectacular return to favour).

The style of the music, although far from the seventeenth century in detail of composition, nevertheless reflects the classical manner in its use of scales and solfeggi. It begins immediately with one of Jourdain's main themes which, however, whisks away so quickly that, apart from the startling flat 7th of the first two notes it fails to register until a change of time and mood ushers in a grand augmented statement in the brass:

Ex. 1

Ex. 1a

This broader section gradually quickens and dissolves into a resumption of the original brisk movement. The trumpet now gives out Jourdain's second motif.

Ex. 2

Ex. 1 then returns and leads to a full close after which the music changes into a gentle Sicilienne based on a lilting oboe melody.

Ex. 3

("Du Venus' Sohn, gibst sü - ßen Lohn für un - ser Schnen und Schmach - ten,")

(The quotation gives the melody with its vocal text as at the beginning of the play.)

The first scene is enacted between the Music Master and the Dancing Master who discuss the relative merits and opportunities of their respective occupations. When Jourdain suddenly joins them (his appearance is heralded by the second number of the Incidental Music, consisting of a brief statement of Exx. 1 and 2) they try to persuade him that he must, in order to behave like a nobleman, be accomplished in both their arts. In the course of the scene the Music Master introduces his pupil who has composed an aria especially for Jourdain and to which they wish him to listen. Hofmannsthal put additional emphasis on this pupil, showing him seated at the clavichord as the curtain rises and actually in the throes of composition. The young man even speaks a few words to Jourdain shortly after the latter's bustling entrance. None of this is in the original Molière play and it will be important later to observe how this interest in the person of the young composer gradually grew in the minds of Strauss and Hofmannsthal when it became necessary to reshape the work.

Having established the identity of the composer Hofmannsthal is at once able to attribute to him the authorship of the opera *Ariadne auf Naxos* which is to be performed at Jourdain's house that very evening. As a sample, Jourdain is to hear the new aria which is sung for him by the artist who in the opera takes the role of Echo. At one time it was Hofmannsthal's intention to introduce the Prima Donna at this stage, but he later decided that it would be undignified for so exalted a personality to have to attend Jourdain's music lesson. In her place, therefore, three singers are brought on who in the opera play the three nymphs. At first Hofmannsthal even proposed that one of these should sing an extract from Ariadne's Monologue deputising, as it were, for the Prima Donna, but this doubtful idea was fortunately jettisoned in favour of an arietta which proves to be the Sicilienne which we have already heard as part of the Overture, Ex. 3. A comparable audition occurs in the original play but Hofmannsthal decided against Molière's little verses, and drafted a new stanza especially for Strauss's melodic requirements.

Jourdain finds the gentle music somewhat dreary and volunteers a popular ditty of his own. Molière's couplets are hilariously awful:

> 'Je croyais Jeanneton
> Plus douce qu'un mouton
> Hélas, Hélas . . .' etc.

Unfortunately they translate ill into German, although Strauss makes as much capital as he can, with Jourdain bellowing away in his attempts to hit the right note.

Ex. 4

[Jourdain]
Schnell

Ich glaube-te, mein Schätzchen ist doch so mild als schön

The Music Master presses his point about the essential nature of music and song by asking the three singers to give another short performance. Molière here attacked the artificial conventions of his day according to which members of the nobility dressed up as shepherds and shepherdesses in order to perform love dramas or music. Thus disguised they could indulge in the vicissitudes of true *affaires du cœur*, for it was considered ill-bred for the aristocracy openly to reveal their susceptibility to the pangs of human emotion.[5]

Accordingly, much to Jourdain's perplexity, he is asked to visualize the quite ordinarily dressed singers as rustics while they wade through a typical piece of contemporary superficiality. The 'Dialogue en musique' which they perform consisted in Molière's original text of a pastoral trio in the form of a conversation on the subject of love and faithfulness followed by a short ballet traditionally used to conclude each act. Hofmannsthal, bound by no such tradition and whose Act 1 had scarcely begun, decided to cut the ballet altogether. This Dialogue was also part of his plan to introduce the three nymphs, Najade, Dryade and Echo; since Echo had already sung the arietta, Hofmannsthal now used the two remaining singers, Najade and Dryade. As with the arietta he had felt sure that he could improve on the original text, but in the end conceded that 'try as I may, I cannot find any better verses for the *berger-bergère* duet than those in the Molière; there they form a trio; I am adapting them, of course, for a duet.'

Strauss's setting has that mock simplicity full of sly harmonic twists which were becoming an increasingly prominent feature of his natural style. The opening and closing bars show this very clearly.

[5] A similar satire on this subject occurs during the first part of Cervantes' *Don Quixote*, *vide* J. M. Cohen's Introduction in the Penguin Classics: 'Only the goatherds and shepherds are sentimentalized, for Cervantes was deeply affected by a convention of his own times ... which involved the pretence that only simple folk had deep and genuine sentiments, and sent the fashionable gentry for a century out into their carefully tended parks in the fancy dress of shepherds and shepherdesses.'

Ex. 5

It has become a characteristic technique of the musical comedy and motion picture that, a rehearsal or preview being shown of some entertainment, when the actual performance later takes place it proves to bear no resemblance to the passage so carefully prepared in the earlier scene. This naïve device, no doubt born of a fear lest repetition should become tiresome, is oddly anticipated by Strauss and Hofmannsthal at this point. Although the next lines of Molière's text are altered in such a way as to suggest that the duet is an excerpt from the opera *Ariadne* (which is to replace Molière's simple ballet combining Music and the Dance) this is in fact not the case. With the scheme to perform part of Ariadne's monologue abandoned, there is now no connexion of any kind, poetic or musical, between these specimen excerpts and the opera from which they are supposed to have been drawn.

Discussion over the instrumentation of the projected entertainment causes Jourdain to comment that he looks forward to hearing a tromba marina in the orchestra. Needless to say, this is a quite preposterous idea, as anyone who has heard this incredible instrument will recognize. Unfortunately, Hofmannsthal saw fit to substitute the Waldhorn at the mention of which the Composer is instructed to make a gesture of fury. The change was not a good one, partly because the horn had for the past 250 years been a well-established orchestral instrument, and partly because there are no less than two actually performing in the pit in Strauss's orchestra.

Jourdain now consults the Dancing Master, and Hofmannsthal takes the opportunity to introduce a first mention of the Intermezzo element of his own original scheme, the title of which is to be 'The faithless Zerbinetta and her four lovers'. In order to point its contrasting function this is allocated specifically to the Dancing Master, a delegation of responsibility which will later be brought into significance.

But Jourdain is determined that there should be a Minuet, his favourite dance he says, and the Dancing Master leaps into action to give his ridiculous employer a lesson in the correct steps. In Molière's own day the greatest of all contemporary French composers, Jean-Baptiste Lully, wrote the Incidental Music for performances of the play at court. His Minuet for this scene is one of his best known pieces and Strauss was at first greatly tempted to make use of it. He decided, however, to keep it in reserve (see below, Ex. 56) and for the present revived the Minuet from his own abandoned ballet *Kythere*, a graceful movement with elegant writing for two flutes.

Ex. 6[6]

Jourdain's dancing lesson is interrupted by the arrival of the Fencing Master who couples his entrance with an immediate and vivid demon-

---

[6] The recently published Leuckart miniature score contains a foreword in which the suggestion is made that the accents on the weak third beats of the bars (marked x in the example), illustrate Jourdain's maladroit attempts at the steps. Yet the accents in question are considerably less grotesque than in other dances where Strauss makes his intention clear. Moreover, in Kythere the movement had fulfilled an entirely different function, far removed from Jourdain and his gaucheries.

stration of his art. The music to which he prances about, parrying and thrusting with the bewildered Jourdain, consists of a series of bravura passages for, in turn, trombone, trumpet, piano and horn, mostly in fanfare character.

A rather pathetic passage follows, possibly descriptive of Jourdain who, though trying his hardest to comply with the demands of his formidable instructor, is by now more than a little demoralized.

Ex. 7

The number ends with a subsidiary movement, wholly military in style and based on terse trumpet-calls, to which the Fencing Master barks out peremptory commands.

In the next long scene, which is entirely without music, the Music and Dancing Masters attempt to defend the artistic way of life against the scornful attacks of the professional man-at-arms. As they inevitably come to blows they are interrupted by the arrival of the Master of Philosophy. After upbraiding the others for demeaning themselves by fighting, this silly old fellow is goaded into drawing his own sword, with almost fatal consequences.

At last the three other instructors retire, leaving the dishevelled and confused Master of Philosophy to recover what dignity he may in order to give Jourdain a lesson on the superiority of words over action. This long-drawn-out scene of unrelieved dialogue gave rise to such restlessness on the part of the opera-goers waiting for Strauss's music that, despite the excellent performances by the actors of Reinhardt's company, it was cut soon after the première, and was never restored in its original form, even in the full version later made of Molière's play.

Close on the heels of the departing Philosopher come the Tailors, with fantastic garments which they have persuaded the wretched Jourdain to commission. The designer of the original production, Ernst Stern, tells an excellent anecdote concerning this scene,[7] in which the Stuttgart authorities, eager to find fault with foreigners to the city such as Stern himself, committed a splendid blunder:

> Encouraged by the disapproval of the All Highest, his subordinates began a general campaign of complaints and

[7] *My Life, My Stage.* Gollancz, 1951.

grumbles; nothing was right. The wood from which the Berlin manufacturers had made the stage furniture was allegedly of inferior quality; the upholstery was poor, the tables and chairs were much too heavy, and so on. And the costume department was worst of all; they grumbled at the quality of the materials used; they grumbled at the cutting; they even grumbled at the way the buttons were sewn on. But at last they went too far and I had them on the hip.

One morning I was invited into the office to meet a collection of men and women obviously under the chairmanship of a portly gentleman with a massive beard and an air of great dignity and severity. At a sign from him, M. Jourdain's gala coat was laid out before me on the table. It was a most expensive and luxurious garment, liberally embroidered with gold thread and decorated with a striking pattern of flowers. With solemn finger the bearded one pointed to these flowers.

'Mein Herr', he began, 'I take it that you failed to notice that the flowers on this coat have been embroidered upside down. Instead of pointing upwards as they should, they point down.'

'No', I agreed, suppressing my delight as best I could. 'I did notice it.' For a moment there was an embarrassed pause whilst they all looked at each other. Then the bearded one continued his catechism: 'Are we really to assume, Mein Herr, that you noticed the error, and that you nevertheless . . . that you nevertheless . . .'

The shocking conclusion seemed to rob him of words so I sprang to his assistance: 'That I knowingly let it pass. Yes, that's quite true. By the way, is there a copy of the script available?' There was an icy silence until the script was produced. When it arrived, I turned up the requisite page and handed him the script. 'Would you care to read what M. Jourdain says to his tailor and what his tailor says in reply. Here it is in Scene Five of Act Two. And would you please read it out loud, so that everyone else can hear it.'

A little subdued he began to read the text I had indicated: 'M. Jourdain: "What's this. Your flowers are upside down. Look, their heads are pointing downwards."
The Tailor: "You didn't say that you wanted them pointing upwards."
M. Jourdain: "Good Heavens! Is it necessary to say things like that?"
The Tailor: "Certainly it is. All persons of quality wear them pointing downwards."

M. Jourdain: "All persons of quality wear their flowers upside down, you say?"
The Tailor: "Certainly, Sir."
M. Jourdain: "Oh well, that's a different matter."
The Tailor: "If you wish it, I can make them point upwards."
M. Jourdain: "Oh no, no, no . . . not at all".'
After which there was a deathly silence and I left the room.

The ceremony with which the Master Tailor produces Jourdain's new garments gives Strauss his next cue. The detail in which Hofmannsthal described this scene to Strauss is indicative of the primary role he had by now assumed in their collaboration:

'at first when the tailors come hopping on (goat motif?), and for the jerky attempts to put on Jourdain's court suit, we need something with very marked rhythm: then follows a pretty, stately minuet-like tune (of one or two minutes) for the first journeyman tailor, who shows him how to wear court dress, and with it some parallel-contrasting orchestral music for Jourdain himself as he clumsily tries to get the idea. Don't begrudge the labour spent on this scene; it will benefit the whole work and is indeed needed to establish it, let us hope for many years to come, as a complete piece of a bizarre kind.'

For the entry of the journeyman tailors Strauss once again called out of limbo a movement from *Kythere*, a light and graceful Gavotte.

Ex. 8

This leads to a Polonaise[8] in which the First Tailor dances a solo to the accompaniment of a spectacular violin solo.

Jourdain stumps about to the grotesque sounds of his Ex. 1 played both straight and in ponderous augmentation. The dance is in elaborated

---

[8] The choice of a Polonaise is said to have been a jocular allusion to the fact that tailoring in Vienna had been for centuries the virtual monopoly of the Polish section of the community.

rondo form with mock-pathetic episodes not unlike that in the Fencing Master's movement (Ex. 7).

Ex. 9

The coda of the movement returns to Ex. 8 which alternates both with the Polacca theme of the solo violin and with haunting strains of Ex. 9 now on the horn. The dance ends with a last descending version of Jourdain's Ex. 1.

8

In Molière a short ballet again marked the end of an act. Hofmannsthal, however, felt the need of a more decisive moment for lowering the curtain, and he therefore continues for one further scene characterized by the first appearance of Madame Jourdain and the servant-girl Nicole. Their relentless mockery of Jourdain is interrupted by the dissolute nobleman, Dorante, who enters with the avowed intention of returning to Jourdain the vast sums he has already borrowed from him. Instead, having thus apparently established good faith, he succeeds in extracting a further substantial loan from the simple-minded man who is over-joyed at receiving so distinguished a guest in his house. Dorante then draws Jourdain aside in order to speak with him about the fair Marquise, Dorimène, and also about the enormously costly and elaborate enter-tainment which he has persuaded Jourdain to mount on her behalf. Nicole creeps towards them, trying to overhear, so as to keep Madame

Jourdain abreast of their schemes, but Jourdain observes her antics and angrily takes Dorante away into another part of the house.

It is at this point in the original text that Cléonte and Covielle entered, but since these characters were to play no part in his version Hofmannsthal chose this moment to bring the first act to an end. In order that the curtain should fall to music, he arranged for Jourdain to open the door ostentatiously for Dorante, thereby allowing the orchestra to be heard rehearsing the Overture to *Ariadne*. This links up with Dorante's whispered references to the operatic portion of the entertainment, and the close of the act, if a little contrived, is sufficiently dramatic to prevent too serious a loss of tension.

9

Hofmannsthal's second act begins ten scenes later, at Molière's Act 3, Scene 16, in which Dorante returns leading Dorimène by the hand. Strauss characterizes the aristocratic couple by an introduction in *style galante*.

Ex. 10

A contrasting theme in gently dancing staccato triplets alternates with this suave melody,[9] and between them these ideas provide the whole material for the excellent little movement. At one point the music pauses on two held chords. The curtain has risen revealing Jourdain clumsily unprepared for his noble guests. During the chords a lackey announces their arrival, upon which the panic-stricken Jourdain bids him make the necessary apologies while he dashes off to complete his toilet. The orchestra then concludes the movement while Dorante and his Marquise enter and make a brief tour of the immense room, Dorimène confessing her embarrassment at receiving Dorante's protestations of love in such peculiar circumstances. The dialogue is interrupted by the reappearance

---

[9] The concluding cadence was quoted in Vol. I, p. 43 as an instance of Strauss's harmonic manner.

of Jourdain who thoroughly disconcerts the Marquise by a series of grotesque obeisances, a hilarious satire by Molière on the courtly behaviour of his time.

Dinner is then announced, giving Strauss the occasion for his *pièce de résistance*. It opens with a Grand March to which the waiters enter laden with a superb meal, and Strauss could not resist introducing an element of caricature with references (albeit in inverted form) to the Coronation March from Meyerbeer's *Le Prophète*. A grazioso linking figure then leads to the first course.

Hofmannsthal made every effort here to redraft the original text so as to provide Strauss with the maximum opportunity both for a substantial ballet as in Molière and for amusing allusions to the bill of fare. A comparison between the vastly elaborate dishes outlined by Dorante in Scene 1 of Molière's fourth act and the relatively straightforward courses announced by the flunkeys in Hofmannsthal's script might produce a certain feeling of gastronomic disappointment. But a young turkey-cock crowned with white onions blended with chicory might have been hard to describe musically, whereas Rhine salmon followed by saddle of mutton played straight into Strauss's hands.[10]

Hence the fish course is greeted by a quotation of the Rhine motif from Wagner's *Ring*, while the joint evokes the onomatopoeic sheep music from Strauss's own *Don Quixote*. Molière's background verses, originally sung by Jourdain's musicians, are entirely jettisoned and the guests now eat their salmon to the accompaniment of a watery piece for oboe, solo violin, pizzicato strings and harp, and their mutton during an idyllic cello solo (constantly suggestive of the solo part in *Don Quixote*).

The entrée is followed by a dish of larks and thrushes, Strauss contributing references to his own musical descriptions of these birds during the opening scene of *Der Rosenkavalier*, as well as a curious sly allusion to 'La donna è mobile' from Verdi's *Rigoletto*.[11] The movements are all lightly scored and allow for the essential conversation between the principal characters which takes place over the music.

The final course is an *Omelette Surprise*, the surprise being supplied by a kitchen-boy who springs out of the enormous dish and executes a wild

---

[10] Hofmannsthal to Strauss: 'I hope the menu: fish, mutton, song-birds, is in accordance with your ideas.'

[11] The Mantuan predilection for spit-roasted song-birds has been mooted as a possible explanation.

and erotic dance intended to symbolize Dorante's passion for the Marquise. Hofmannsthal again gave Strauss a detailed scenario for this dance:

> 'Dancing scene of the scullion (two or three minutes of music): At first, having got down from the little cart, he is timid at finding himself in such company. He snatches with furtive avidity a glass of sweet wine and sips it. Now he grows bolder and scrutinizes the noble company. Soon he sees everything through the golden haze of slight drunkenness. He is intoxicated by the beauty of the Marquise: he expresses in his gestures that she is driving him out of his senses, that she gives him the power to fly. Now he takes another bold and hearty drink. He kisses his own hand; the whole situation strikes him as most amusing, Jourdain's presence as increasingly droll; the atmosphere between the two lovers is an element which he seems perfectly capable of understanding, which intoxicates him more than the wine—finally he spins several times round the table like a madman and off.'

Oddly enough, however, Strauss did not match the intended mood of sensuality, and wrote instead one of the gayest and freshest of all his Viennese waltzes. As a result, Dorante's aside to Dorimène regarding the persuasive significance of the music, if heard at all, contains little relevance to what is actually being played. Indeed even the central lyrical episode has a buoyancy and light-heartedness of idiom which, like the *Burleske* of twenty-four years earlier, set the pattern for the livelier inspirations of composers such as Dohnányi.

Ex. 11

The dance ends with a brilliant whirling coda of such finality that it supplied a splendid conclusion when Strauss later formed an orchestral suite out of the music. In the theatre however, Hofmannsthal's second act has some difficulty in picking up the threads, since practically nothing is left of Molière's comedy. This moment is undoubtedly the weakest in Hofmannsthal's adaptation of the play.

After the Dance of the Kitchen-boy there remains only Madame Jourdain's ill-timed interruption of the dinner, her attack on Dorimène for her seeming designs upon the wretched Jourdain, and Dorimène's offended departure, before the curtain falls lamely on a moment of anti-climax. Since this was the point at which Molière had introduced the initial references to the farcical Turkish episode, it was the obvious cut to the opera and Hofmannsthal effected the transition by way of the linking scene which he had always insisted should be entirely his responsibility and without music. Strauss, who had in the first place intended to write a musical introduction to this dressing-room scene, readily agreed; as he put it: 'I would like the music to be silent for a good while to keep the ear fresh before the beginning of *Ariadne*.'

It is easy to see, therefore, what havoc the King of Württemberg's extended reception on the opening night must have wrought at this already dangerously flaccid moment in the scheme. Strauss had many pangs over this second and important curtain but although he begged Hofmannsthal to consider some manoeuvre to give it greater dramatic weight the poet refused, insisting characteristically that:

> 'To strengthen the curtain . . . either by new dramatic ideas or through music, does not appear to me called for by the situation. Anything that is not organic invariably looks studied and weak. But if one were merely to change round the last sentence a little, an experienced comedian could surely get a laugh out of it, and it is always safe to bring down the curtain on a laugh . . .[12] (even if Jourdain) stops there with his silly, pompous face, that will be enough to make us laugh, and it will at the same time point firmly towards what is to follow, the chief event of the evening.'

Yet Strauss was right, and producers and translators still find considerable difficulty in finding an adequate substitute for this weak tableau.

[12] The last sentence ran as follows: Jourdain: 'Come here, I need you! Call the others' (the footmen take their places one on each side of him). 'I've got something very serious and important to order, but I still don't know what it is.'

10

The connecting scene begins by establishing the contrast between the two groups of performers who are disconcerted at each other's presence. The members of the Opera Seria regard the comedians of the Intermezzo disdainfully, while the latter consider their high-minded colleagues to be dull and priggish intellectuals. Hofmannsthal (by no means historically) identifies the Music Master with the opera and the Dancing Master exclusively with the antics of the Commedia dell'Arte. Each takes his respective principals secretively into different corners of the stage with whispered words of flattery over their own function and disparagement of their rivals in the opposite camp.

All is ready for the entertainment to begin when a lackey suddenly announces a change of plan. In order to leave sufficient time for a firework display, Jourdain has decreed that the comedy and the tragedy are to be performed not merely on the same stage but simultaneously. Apart from the new convulsions of despair into which the artists are thrown, this brings into prominence the Composer, who can see no possible result but the imminent ruin of his masterpiece. A lively discussion ensues, during which the action of the opera is explained to Zerbinetta in order that she may improvise upon it during the performance. By this means, Hofmannsthal is able to present his psychological thesis on the subject of 'Fidelity in Womanhood' which to him lay at the root of the entire piece.

Strauss had never been able to apply such high-falutin philosophy to so slight a *divertissement*. To Hofmannsthal, however, this was an essential part of the very stimulus of literary creation, as he tried to explain to Strauss in the celebrated letter which, at Strauss's insistence, he consented to make public. In it Hofmannsthal first explained the basic themes of the play in terms of a crucial opposition in outlook between Ariadne and Zerbinetta:

> 'What it is about is one of the straightforward and stupendous problems of life: fidelity; whether to hold fast to that which is lost, to cling to it even unto death—or to live, to live on, to get over it, to transform oneself, to sacrifice the integrity of the soul and yet in this transmutation to preserve one's essence, to remain a human being and not to sink to the level of a beast, which is without recollection. It is the fundamental theme of *Elektra*, the voice of Elektra opposed to the voice of Chrysothemis, the heroic voice against the human.

In the present case we have the group of heroes, demi-gods, gods—Ariadne, Bacchus, (Theseus)—facing the human, the merely human group consisting of the frivolous Zerbinetta and her companions, all of them base figures of life's masquerade. Zerbinetta is in her element drifting out of the arms of one man into the arms of another; Ariadne could be the wife or mistress of one man only, just as she can only be one man's widow, can be forsaken only by one man. One thing, however, is still left even for her: the miracle, the god.

But what to divine souls is a real miracle, is to the earthbound nature of Zerbinetta just an everyday love affair. She sees in Ariadne's experience the only thing she can see; the exchange of an old lover for a new one. And so these two spiritual worlds are in the end ironically brought together in the only way in which they can be brought together; in noncomprehension.'

It is this profound and complex divergence of mentality which emerges from the dialogue between the Composer and Zerbinetta. The burning sincerity of the handsome but immature young musician-philosopher, and the assurance of the coquette who knows the world for what it is, presented a decidedly promising situation which, extraordinary as it may seem, was scarcely exploited. Strauss and Hofmannsthal recognized this once the work was in production, taking the opportunity of bringing the scene to fruition when working on the revised version a few years later. Strauss had already had the idea at the back of his mind that 'Zerbinetta might have an affair with the Composer, so long as he is not too close a portrait of me'.

Nevertheless, the basic state of affairs is clear and the stage is now made ready; the Music Master gives the Prima Donna a few last words of encouragement; the inner curtain is lowered; Jourdain, Dorimène and Dorante enter and take their places (the last-named seizing an eleventh-hour opportunity to arrange his surreptitious escape with Dorimène near the end of the drama); and the opera at long last begins.[13]

---

[13] This was the first time Strauss used the term 'Opera' since *Guntram*. *Feuersnot* was entitled 'Singgedicht'; *Salome*, 'Musikdrama'; *Elektra*, 'Musik Tragödie'; and *Der Rosenkavalier*, 'Komödie fur Musik'. No greater contrast between the two specifically designated operas can possibly be imagined. Perhaps Strauss was conscious of this when he described the revised version of *Guntram* as a 'Handlung in 3 Aufzügen'.

II

Ariadne was the daughter of Minos, King of Crete. She had fallen in love with Theseus, and when Minos gave the hero the formidable task of entering the labyrinth and killing the Minotaur she helped him to accomplish the deed and subsequently enabled Theseus and his men to escape from Crete. For her reward in thus aiding the Athenians she asked no more than that Theseus should take her with him away from Crete. This he did, but shortly afterwards abandoned her on the island of Naxos. The legends vary over his reasons for doing this, none giving a very satisfactory explanation. It is possible that, as so often, gratitude was no strong foundation for love and an even weaker one for constancy. Yet Theseus seems to have taken a callously early opportunity for ridding himself of the lady to whom he owed not only his escape but his life.[14]

In due course the marooned Ariadne was discovered on her island by the god Dionysus (now more generally known by the Thracian name, Bacchus) who carried her off, married her, and over the years had a large brood of children by her. As a rather touching mark of affection and admiration he also set her coronet, which Theseus had given her, among the stars, where it is known as the Corona Borealis.

This was by no means Bacchus' first exploit, although he is generally considered to have remained unmarried until his arrival on the island of Naxos. There seems to be no plausible explanation why after his adventure with the pirate ship[15] he made for Naxos, since he certainly had no idea of Ariadne's presence there.

None of these details of the authentic myth supplied Hofmannsthal with quite the psychological symmetry that he needed. If Ariadne's constancy was to be the foil to Zerbinetta's flightiness, there would need to be a balancing contrast of flirtation and fidelity within Bacchus' own experience. The poet accordingly decided to redraft the myth for his own purpose, making Bacchus very young and fresh from some previous adventure, which might, for example, have been with the sorceress Circe. Milton had already supposed such a liaison, his Comus being the son of Circe and Bacchus. It is reasonable to consider that Circe's sorceries, while failing to turn the young god into an animal, like any mere

[14] An interesting theory of the factual origins of the myth is brilliantly worked out by Mary Renault in her novel *The King Must Die*. According to her interpretation, Theseus was far more justified in his seeming harshness than is at first apparent.

[15] He caused a vine to sprout and encircle the mast; the pirates in terror jumped overboard and were turned into dolphins. Hence the power of these creatures to 'talk'.

mortal, would still have had some powerful effect upon him. Thus Hofmannsthal saw Bacchus emotionally transfigured from the experience and ripe for the coming encounter with Ariadne. He tried to explain this aspect of the drama to Strauss in the same letter in which he had already analysed and contrasted the characters of Ariadne and Zerbinetta:

> 'In this experience of Ariadne's, which is really the monologue of her lonely soul, Bacchus represents no mere *deus ex machina*; for him too, the experience is vital. Innocent, young and unaware of his own divinity, he travels where the wind takes him, from island to island. His first affair was typical, with a woman of easy virtue you may say, or you may call her Circe. To his youth and innocence with its infinite potentialities the shock has been tremendous: were he Harlekin, this would be merely the beginning of one long round of love affairs. But he is Bacchus; confronted with the tremendous significance of this erotic experience, all is laid bare to him in a flash—the assimilation with the animal, the transformation, his own divinity. So he escapes from Circe's embraces still unchanged, but not without a wound, a longing, not without knowledge. The impact on him now of this meeting with a being whom he can love, who is mistaken about him but is enabled by this very mistake to give herself to him wholly and to reveal herself to him in all her loveliness, who entrusts herself to him completely, exactly as one entrusts oneself to Death, this impact I need not expound further to an artist such as you.'

In the myth Ariadne is entirely alone on her island until Bacchus arrives accompanied as always by his conventional train of satyrs and maenads. Hofmannsthal once more altered this arrangement, bringing Bacchus onto the scene without any of his riotous followers, while Ariadne is from the start surrounded by attendants, symbolized by the three token figures of classical antiquity: Naiad, Dryad and Echo.

It is with these traditional negative semi-characters that the period-opera *Ariadne auf Naxos* begins, after a miniature Prelude based on a group of pathetic little motifs descriptive of Ariadne's melancholy solitude:

Ex. 12

Ex. 13

Ex. 14

Ex. 15

Ex. 16

These thematic fragments reappear at various times during the work but are especially developed during Ariadne's first lament. Exx. 13 and 14 can be said to refer to Theseus and Ariadne respectively, though less as personalities than as a cherished, but none too clearly remembered, partnership of the ever more receding past (Theseus never appears in the opera as an individual, only as a memory). Ex. 15 is later transformed to become the opening theme of Ariadne's big aria, while Ex. 16 gives the beginning of the final group which contrasts impetuously with the melancholy character of both the Prelude and the scene which follows.

The Prelude ends with a flourish and passes directly into the opening Trio for Najade, Dryade and Echo, a tiny self-contained number in two sections. The first of these is based on Ex. 12(x) with its characteristic opening drop of a seventh[16] as the nymphs sing of Ariadne's bitter lament, while in the second section they carol gently in the major key, though even here a periodic return is made to the lament which is the main theme of their song and which concludes it. The shape, even the mood and style of this Trio, was suggested by Hofmannsthal in marginal remarks on the draft libretto which he sent to Strauss: 'the last three lines to be repeated *ad lib*; an elusive, continuously flowing vocal line, to express the smiling indifference of Nature towards human suffering. Something of the fluttering of leaves and the undulating of waves...'

As the nymphs finish, the voice of Ariadne is heard in a *cri-de-cœur* answered appropriately enough by Echo.

---

[16] Although the sevenths are not identical it is interesting that Strauss should have begun both Ariadne's theme and Jourdain's Ex. 1 with such an initial drop.

Ex. 17

Ariadne's lament follows immediately, in which she is accompanied at first by solo viola and harmonium. After a climax Ex. 17 returns, its rising tritone now leading symphonically to earlier motifs from the Prelude, and the lament soon develops into an extended Scena and Aria, though with various interruptions. The voices of the Commedia dell'Arte can be heard off-stage fretting about the difficult task ahead of them with so dreary a young girl, pretty as she is. In addition to these off-stage asides, which are worked into the musical texture, the voice of Jourdain can also be heard cutting across orchestra and singers, as he complains of the monotony of Ariadne's singing and makes the remark about the Waldhorn already discussed.

Ariadne's lament now passes to a short passage in quicker tempo which recapitulates the more dramatic closing section of the Prelude, Ex. 16. A brief link, in which she philosophises on her name and on that of her departed lover, leads to a third statement of Ex. 17, though this time instead of Ariadne's 'Ach' the three attendants call her by name, an intrusion which she rejects vehemently before embarking on the first part of her aria.

At this point Jourdain again interrupts, and although Dorante tries to pacify him by explaining the plot, he protests that his orders for the light comedy are not being obeyed, and looks around for the Dancing Master. At last Dorante and Dorimène firmly hush him and we hear no more of him until shortly before the end. It is of course apparent that the device of these interpolations derives from Christopher Sly in *The Taming of the Shrew*.

Strauss found the libretto here distinctly puzzling and it was perhaps on this account that he chose just this section for the distraction of Jourdain's comical expostulations. Hofmannsthal raised no objections and in one of his letters devoted a whole paragraph to clarifying his meaning:

> As for the obscure passage in the text, Ariadne endeavours to recall in her bewildered brain the picture of her own inno-

cent self, of the young girl she once was—(and this young girl she fancies is now living again here in the cave)—but the name of Ariadne she refuses to employ for the sake of this recollection—the name is for her all too closely bound up, grown together with Theseus—she wants the vision, but nameless—it is on this account that when the three nymphs call her by name—she turns away in distress saying: 'Not again' (Don't let me hear that name again!)

Such elaborate explanations had become the very *modus operandi* of Strauss and Hofmannsthal's relationship over this new work, so unlike its predecessors. Indeed, at every stage of the Ariadne Monologue the poet inserted marginal guides to Strauss both to explain the heroine's state of mind and the kind of music he imagined for the passages: 'here a radiant, glowing phrase for the voice . . . a sudden, nervous new thought going through [Ariadne's] poor confused head, which the music can practically ignore and treat in purely melodramatic fashion . . . ' and so on. Strauss strove hard to obey, but in so far as he had difficulty in keeping abreast with Hofmannsthal, he was unable to bring Ariadne to life in the same way as he had succeeded with Elektra and the Marschallin.

The first portion of the main aria is built on a variant of Ex. 15. Its new air of innocence, portraying Ariadne's childhood purity is, like that of the Marschallin also recalling the innocence of her childhood, amusingly reminiscent of *Till Eulenspiegel*.[17]

Ex. 18

The parallel with the Marschallin's Monologue is extraordinarily close, with a little figure (Ex. 19) resembling Ex. 34b (Chapter IX), in addition to Strauss's use in *Rosenkavalier* of a chamber orchestra which now fully comes into its own.

Ex. 19

The aria is barely under way when new interruptions can be heard from the Commedia dell'Arte. At first Ariadne, far from showing annoyance at these asides, even incorporates them into her spoken thoughts, although they are entirely outside the framework of the drama she is presenting. She is accordingly instructed in the stage directions to sing her next lines, 'without turning her head, to herself, as if she has heard the last words in her dream'.

The impingement of the comic upon the tragic element had always constituted one of the principal *raisons d'être* of the entire entertainment, yet this is one of the few places where such an interaction occurs. Apart from interruptions, the two dramas, the serious and the flippant, work themselves out alternately without affecting each other's progress to any degree.

Ariadne's attempts at continuing her aria are now temporarily halted when Harlequin, on Zerbinetta's instructions, comes forward to 'try a little song with music'. Harlequin naïvely recommends Ariadne (who remains motionless) not to take life so seriously:

Ex. 20

Harlekin: "Lie - ben, Hassen, Hoffen, Zagen, al - le Lust" etc.

Strauss's setting is an example of his spiced classicism, sweet enough, but of no depth or substance. Considering that from the first it was one of the planned musical numbers, in company with 'Ariadne's Recitative and Aria' and Zerbinetta's 'Great Coloratura Aria and Andante' (as Strauss listed them in an early letter) it is surprising that 'Harlequin's song' turned out to be so slight. After all, tentative as the first appearance of the Commedia dell'Arte might reasonably be expected to be, it might also have been contrived to make a greater impact both on the audience and on Ariadne herself. Its opening phrases are repeated wordlessly three times by the nymph Echo ('without soul, like a bird'), a curious, unrealistic device. Thereafter Harlequin and Zerbinetta have a brief quarrel and disappear once more.

The quarrel itself is not without significance, establishing as it does the jealous attitude of the comic lovers to each other despite their light-hearted view of life itself.

Ex. 21

The second and main part of Ariadne's aria is based on a new motif.

Ex. 22

The origin of this theme (apart from its striking similarity to the slow movement of Haydn's Symphony No. 93 in D) can, like two of the movements of the *Bourgeois Gentilhomme* music, be traced back to the projected ballet score *Kythere*, where it appeared in Act 2 scene 4 as a *Feierlicher Hymnus—Ankunft von Venus und Adonis*.[18] Here it represents Ariadne's vision of Death, and especially the god Hermes in his role of Messenger of Death.

Ariadne now sings rapturously of her longed-for release from life:

Ex. 23

'Du wirst mich be - frei -   -   -   -   -   -   en'

[18] Solemn Hymn—Arrival of Venus and Adonis.

Exx. 22 and 23(x) alternate with a throbbing motif of repeated notes recalling the despairing hopelessness of 'Der Wegweiser' from Schubert's *Winterreise*. An ecstatic climax is then quickly built up with that yearning use of the soprano voice which Strauss could now call upon at will. This is one of the great moments of beauty in the opera containing a sudden and unforeseen surge of passion, and it is therefore the more curious to discover in the orchestral texture close resemblances to Strauss's earlier operas, such as a suggestion of Octavian's love theme and, at the very end of the Monologue, a passage admittedly derived from Ex. 22 but unmistakably like *Salome* (Vol. I, p. 256, Ex. 15) followed immediately by the after phrase of the same motif, quoted almost exactly.

Abruptly Zerbinetta's followers have invaded the stage and an entirely new and brittle scherzando movement has replaced the gorgeous texture of Ariadne's heart-searchings.

12

From this point until the nymphs' heralding of Bacchus' approach in the last scene of the opera, the Commedia dell'Arte holds uninterrupted sway over the action, the silent Ariadne retreating more and more into the background as the clowns seize the limelight. Their burlesquing falls into three distinct sections—two ensembles separated by Zerbinetta's great aria. The first of these ensembles is in no way concerned with the working out of the tiny sub-plot of Zerbinetta's relationship with the four clowns, which is left until after the aria. In the meantime they sing of their healthy attitude towards love, and refer deprecatingly to Ariadne's tragic introspection. The four male comedians, Brighella, Scaramuccio, Harlequin and Truffaldino appear first without Zerbinetta and sing a vocal quartet accompanied by pizzicato strings, occasional woodwind passages and, above all, piano. This instrument is used throughout the work in the same relationship to the comedians as the harmonium to the tragedy. The individual characteristics of the clowns are not yet musically underlined, though Brighella and Truffaldino can be readily identified by the extreme high and low tessituras of their respective parts. On the stage, of course, they are distinguished by their traditional gait and costumes; Harlequin in his diamond embroidered shirt[19] and black skull-cap, with the galumphing Truffaldino behind carrying a string of sausages.

The Quartet begins with a passage based motivically on a theme of the species which Strauss had already invented for the Fool in *Guntram* and for Sancho Panza.

Ex. 24[20]

This alternates experimentally with two or three other ideas before Ex. 21 suddenly reappears and leads straight into the principal theme of the whole section.

Ex. 25

Ex. 25 also alternates with other material but there is no longer a sense of groping. The opening bars of Harlequin's song appear fleetingly and Zerbinetta comes from the wings to join her companions. Unexpectedly the theme of her dance is more melancholy in character. The figure ⌐ x ⌐ from Ex. 24 is worked into the texture and mocking statements of Ex. 21 lead repeatedly to returns of the main subject, Ex. 25.

At first Zerbinetta is amused by the singing and dancing of the four clowns though she cannot as yet choose between them. Before long, however, she becomes aware of Ariadne. She sees that instead of entertaining the Princess she and her colleagues are merely distressing her and,

[19] I am indebted to Randall Swingler for the fascinating origin of Harlequin both from Hermes, 'or Mercury, whose wand he still carries' and from Bacchus himself, 'of whose leopard skin he now wears a formal memory in his spangled and chequered suit.' *Lilliput*, December 1948.

[20] Cf. ⌐ x ⌐ with Ex. 23 from Chapter IV and Ex. 36 from Chapter V.

as the music gradually takes on the characteristic harmonies of a coda, Zerbinetta steps between the dancing comedians and bids them withdraw. Nevertheless they are slow to take the hint and the coda proves to be of considerable length. Strauss is by now enjoying himself and he repeats Hofmannsthal's lines as often as the music requires. For some time Zerbinetta's admonitions possess no kind of urgency or authority while she carols away to Strauss's soaring phrases. After a slightly humdrum beginning the section has turned into an excellent piece in the composer's lighter style.

At last, the material having been fully worked out through a number of distant keys with ingenious chromatic modulations, Zerbinetta succeeds in routing her companions and, still singing fragments of Ex. 25, they disappear, leaving her in sole command of the situation. The pianist strikes a chord of F major and Zerbinetta performs an exaggeratedly deep curtsy to the still silent and bewildered Ariadne as she embarks on her great Recitative and Aria.

13

Strauss had all along been resolved that the Zerbinetta aria should be the central show-piece of the whole entertainment. He laid it out, therefore, on the largest scale with an opening recitative, two linking ariettas and an immense concluding rondo in which the coloratura vocal writing is of unprecedented brilliance and staggering virtuosity. In the recitative, Zerbinetta addresses Ariadne directly, sympathizing with her sufferings which are—she says—common to every woman. She sings of her own experiences (the music anticipating the theme of the second arietta), she upbraids Ariadne for remaining aloof and unwilling to listen (Ex. 22 on woodwind) and, as she finds her words making no impression, delivers a mock serious tirade against all men. But Ariadne has been retreating further and further towards the mouth of her cave and now disappears altogether leaving Zerbinetta to turn quite frankly to the audience.

The musical style of this recitative carries the chamber music idiom of the work to its ultimate conclusion. The accompaniment begins with piano alone, giving the impression of one of the composer's characteristic Lieder, for Strauss had by this time already composed over a hundred of the kind. In the eleventh bar, however, three string players join in, answered shyly by the flute. Next the oboe inserts a coy phrase and gradually each of the wind have had a turn. With Zerbinetta's outburst against the male sex, the string quintet has begun to take a stronger part in the structure of the music, but it is not until the beginning of the first arietta that the piano relinquishes its role of principal accompanist, taking on instead the more conventional orchestral guise of anti-harp.

Zerbinetta sings of how with each lover she really believes that she belongs solely to him until sooner or later, and despite herself, she deceives him. The music is a gently flowing $\frac{3}{4}$ movement in the warm key of D flat, full of Strauss's favourite harmonic side-slips and interspersed with entries of a gay coquettish figure. A number of flourishes spring up—scales and arpeggios—in which the voice joins happily; the music becomes richer, Zerbinetta soars ever higher until, with a dazzling top C sharp, she wrenches the music right out of key into the bright new tonality of E, ready for the second arietta.

The flourishes are now formed into actual motifs, Zerbinetta enumerating the different flirtations which she has experienced. There was Pagliazzo, there was Mezzetino, Cavicchio, Burattino, Pasquariello, and so on, most of which members of the troupe are wholly unfamiliar and rarely come by today.[21]

Ex. 26

[21] Mezzetino and Burattino were servant-figures, Pagliazzo a simple clown, Pasquariello an elderly gardener, and Cavicchio a peasant. All were, of course, type figures in common with the whole Commedia dell'Arte.

Important as it is (it is quoted several times later in the work) this arietta is quite short. Zerbinetta's scales and roulades finally dissolve into an extended unaccompanied coloratura cadenza actually reaching a top F sharp. The main movement of the aria then follows immediately with Zerbinetta herself, undaunted by her acrobatics, announcing the principal subject:

Ex. 27

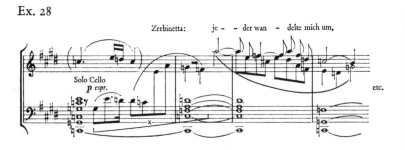

This is treated as a fully worked out rondo with two episodes, cadenza and coda. The first episode introduces two new thematic ideas which are strongly contrasted with Ex. 27 and also with each other. One of these, with its upward flinging arpeggios, is first cousin to the theme of the second arietta (Ex. 26(x)), but the other supplies an element of calm lyricism:

Ex. 28

The correct formal return of Ex. 27 follows, though this contains an amusing parody of classical practice. Star singers of the seventeenth and early eighteenth centuries were wont to omit part of their vocal line in order to re-enter with greater effect at the cadenza. Strauss satirizes this tradition with delightful wit: Zerbinetta misses an entry and, then observing that the clarinet is prompting her, maliciously leaves the part entirely to him with a great show of good humour, merely joining in for the last half-dozen notes of the final cadence. The orchestra then plays a modulatory link to the next episode, while Zerbinetta draws as much

attention to herself as possible by means of coquettish by-play, describing
how she alternately enters into passionate liaisons and then completely
renounces them.

The second episode of the rondo contains little new material and is
largely concerned with developments of Ex. 28(x) superimposed with
endless *fioriture* by the indefatigable Zerbinetta. Some of these, imitated
by the flute in the manner of Bellini or Donizetti, are typical of the kind
of embroidery used by Strauss in the concertos of his Indian Summer
period.

There is a brief return to Ex. 27 on the orchestra, after which the coda
begins in Strauss's best behaved innocent-Mozart style. The music then
builds up together with the earlier arpeggio figures, Zerbinetta warming
to her own effusiveness as, yet again, she soars higher and higher.

Unfortunately the orchestra is as much carried away as the singer and
waxes ever louder and mightier. For a short time Zerbinetta battles
bravely but finally gives up in despair. The orchestra, observing her
dismay, hurries on to a conventional $^6_4$ chord and pauses expectantly.
At this, Zerbinetta makes an extravagant 'thank you' gesture to the conductor and embarks on her great cadenza.

The whole escapade indulges in much self-conscious play with the
'business' of entertainment. Zerbinetta steps right out of her role, making
it plain that she is neither a character on Ariadne's desert island, nor a
member of the Commedia dell'Arte in the course of the conventional
drama of her troupe. She is now purely a coloratura soprano performing on a stage in unequal competition with the orchestral resources of the
composer.

Musically, the cadenza, which is fully accompanied throughout, is by
no means without interest. Its opening plays with the lyrical theme Ex.
28(x) in a way for which Strauss was soon to find an even happier place,
in 'Amor' from the Brentano Lieder, op. 68. This leads to a development of the skittish violin figure ⌐ x ⌐ from the main rondo subject
Ex. 27 which is in turn followed by a series of embroidered figurations
similar to those of the second episode. At last a climax is built up with
imitations and elaborate orchestral displays of virtuosity equalling those
of the voice (Strauss seems inadvertently to have ignored the amusing
parody of this rivalry of only a few bars earlier) and Zerbinetta reaches
the end of her cadenza on a last top E *in alt*.

Thereafter dying references to the principal rondo subject Ex. 27
with its skittish violin figure allow Zerbinetta to conclude graphically

with the words 'hingegeben war ich, stumm— stumm -----' ('I surrendered—dumb') the third and last 'stumm' being literally dumb-show.

14

Since Strauss had earmarked the fantastically difficult Zerbinetta aria for the focal point of the opera, it is curious what pains he took to stifle the spontaneous enthusiastic applause which would certainly greet its triumphant conclusion. The fortissimo final snap chord is indeed there, but is not played until after Harlequin has interrupted from the wings with the words 'A pretty sermon!' Moreover, the chord has hardly had time even to register before he leaps prattling on to the stage, Zerbinetta gives some dry reply, and the moment of potential appreciation is past.[22]

It has always been a feature of the Commedia dell'Arte that their whole repertoire being universally known in every detail, little time is spent on preliminaries for fear of enraging the impatient spectators eagerly awaiting their favourite moments of comedy and denouement. Accordingly Harlequin tosses aside Zerbinetta's protestations about the unsuitability of a desert island for love-making, and without further ado adopts his conventional role of seducer.

Equally in traditional style, his three rivals interrupt him before he can make any headway. This whole section, which links Zerbinetta's aria with the second ensemble of the Intermezzo, is set to a rapid accompanied recitative in which reference is made repeatedly to the quarrel-some theme Ex. 21, as well as to Exx. 26 and 27 from the aria itself. Finally a new motif is heard which looks forward to one of the main subjects of the succeeding ensemble (Ex. 34). Zerbinetta's outburst ends in yet one further coloratura display and the second and most substantial contribution by the comedians follows without a break.

During the course of this new ensemble Zerbinetta and her followers work out the whole of their sub-plot. Zerbinetta flirts with each in turn, losing a shoe during the dance and allowing Scaramuccio to refit her with it while she is perched on the back of the obliging Truffaldino. The

---

[22] In the original libretto Hofmannsthal had arranged for Echo, even before Harlequin's interruption, to repeat Zerbinetta's rondo theme in a wordless *vocalise* in the same way as in Harlequin's own little air, but Strauss omitted this additional complication.

latter is heard making the classic remark: if he had a horse he would take the little one out alone in a horse and cart if he had a cart.[23]

The music is built for the greater part out of a set of entirely new melodic ideas:

Ex. 29

(a)

Ex. 30

(b)

Ex. 31

(c)

Ex. 32

(d)

Ex. 33

(e)

Here for the first time Strauss attempts some characterization of the clowns: Brighella's naïve stupidity; Scaramuccio, the crafty one; the clumsy but jovial Truffaldino and lastly the successful lover, romantic Harlequin himself, who for the moment remains patiently in the background awaiting the outcome which he and the audience know to be a foregone conclusion. Zerbinetta, however, has as yet no new themes and is characterized by the florid Ex. 26 from her aria, which now re-enters and is combined with the themes of the lovers as she dances with each in turn. Ex. 29 is used as a refrain, a general dancing tune which recurs at key points during the ensemble.

A further even more striking dance theme of a general nature appears as the comedy progresses.

[23] cf. Groucho Marx 'I'd horsewhip you if I had a horse', a clever extension of the same line of wit. Groucho with his characteristic style can indeed be considered as the contemporary development of a kind of super-Truffaldino.

Ex. 34

Although written out in ⅜ this ditty has the strongest Viennese waltz flavour. It is in fact more in the manner of Strauss's later waltz writing, such as in the opera *Intermezzo* of 1924, than of *Feuersnot* or *Rosenkavalier*, and this gives an interesting glimpse into the gradual change in Strauss's style which began at this time.

Ex. 34 is built up symphonically to a climax: Zerbinetta has chosen a moment during which the three ill-fated lovers have their backs turned to leap upstage into the arms of the waiting Harlequin, upon which the united pair disappear. A scurrying theme describes the excited agitation of the abandoned trio who, not having seen Zerbinetta's elopement, believe her to be planning a secret *tête-à-tête* with one of themselves.

Ex. 35

Although this passage is used here to accompany the comical antics of the unsuccessful suitors it is later used most aptly to describe the hilarious behaviour of the troupe of comedians as a whole.

After a majestic restatement of the first dance-theme (Ex. 29) the three go off in search of her. A typical piece of traditional slapstick ensues with Scaramuccio and Brighella secretly re-entering from either side of the stage and backing into one another. Truffaldino also enters without noticing the others and the three comedians collapse in a heap in the centre of the stage just as the voices of Zerbinetta and Harlequin are heard singing a duet behind the scene. Harlequin sings to his own theme (Ex. 33) but although at first Zerbinetta's words still come from her aria, she now has a new melody in which Harlequin later also joins her.

Ex. 36

pp _espr._

The themes of the discomforted trio are heard alternating with the scurrying Ex. 35 while the chortling backstage lovers continue their triumphant love song. Zerbinetta has been content to concede to him, at least for the present, an unequivocal victory. As for the other wretched comedians, they dance off to a last great statement of Ex. 29, and with fragments of Exx. 32–34 the ensemble fades away altogether.

<h2 style="text-align:center">15</h2>

There are a number of signs that Strauss at least sketched out the next passage before he had completed the music which leads up to it. The transition from a perfect cadence in the key of D to a fanfare in C sharp is so abrupt, the change of idiom so complete, that virtue could be made of complete contrast irrespective of what music he actually composed for the closing bars of the comedians. Moreover it is entitled _III Scene_, whereas no demarcations exist for the previous scenes. Strauss would presumably have already visualized that the first scene would centre round Ariadne, the second feature the comedians, while the third would be concerned with the arrival of Bacchus and the huge closing duet. Taken in the broadest sense this still remains the overall form of the opera.

Before Bacchus appears, however, Najade, Dryade and Echo have a second trio to themselves. They sing to each other somewhat in the manner of the Three Norns,[24] outlining at times only by allusion, at times in some detail, Bacchus' career from birth until his arrival on the island. As we have seen, Hofmannsthal took what liberties he chose with authentic Greek legend, but much of what is hinted in the tantalisingly mysterious utterances of the nymphs is classical in origin.

Bacchus' mother Semele, daughter of King Cadmus of Thebes, was wooed by Zeus. Unwisely she was persuaded to beg repeatedly for a glimpse of her divine lover in all his glory. Worn out by her importunity Zeus ultimately complied, with the consequence that she was instantly consumed by the fiery spectacle. The child in her womb was, however, saved from the ashes by the god who nursed it within his own

[24] Dryade: 'Ihr wisst,—was er war?' cf. _Götterdämmerung_ Prelude: 2nd Norn: 'Weisst du, was aus ihm wird?'

thigh until ready for birth. It was then raised through childhood by nymphs and in due course received full status as a god.[25]

The three nymphs give so sketchy a résumé of this elaborate legend, that only a listener already in complete possession of the facts could possibly reconstruct it. Hofmannsthal's version now goes off at a tangent as the nymphs tell how Bacchus sets sail with wild companions on his first adventure, landing his sailing-ship at nightfall on Circe's island. He is received ceremoniously with torchlight processions and is led to the banqueting hall of the palace. Here he is met on the threshold by Circe herself, who gives him food and the magic potion. Somewhat brief allusion is made to the effect this drink usually has upon Circe's guests, transforming them instantly into swine in which undignified form they serve Circe for the remainder of their lives. No such fate befalls Bacchus, however; pale and shaken he stands before her in the full panoply of a young god. The psychological aspect of this was explained by Hofmannsthal in the letter quoted above (see p. 28).

So elaborate and Wagnerian a method of outlining past events presented Strauss with a certain difficulty. Narratives, whether handled by a single character or bandied about between two or three, are generally of a low emotional temperature. Strauss's theatrical sense was conscious of the fact that up to this point the Ariadne drama had been wholly static and that a return to such a mood after the gaiety of the Commedia dell'Arte would put classical tragedy into too unfavourable a light. He accordingly set this informative trio in a movement of the utmost rapidity in which both the gestures of the nymphs and the style of the music would constantly suggest an excitement scarcely to be controlled.

They rush on from every side, calling out in extreme agitation about the splendour of the young god:

Ex. 37

---

[25] As the child of a god and a mortal Bacchus should have been only a hero.

Both the fanfare ⌐ x ⌐ and the ascending melody ⌐ y ⌐ refer to Bacchus, the fanfare suggesting perhaps his striking appearance, the melody his attractive personality. This complex of themes is rounded off by a warm cadential figure which, although at first purely musical in function, later refers to his divine character.

Ex. 38

This moves directly to the next important Bacchus theme which reflects his background, his origin and birth, development from child to manhood, and super-human upbringing.

Ex. 39

Hence in essence,

Ex. 39a

[26] 'His mother died in childbirth' (not in fact an accurate interpretation of the myth).

or indeed countless similar variants: here is a motif dating back to Strauss's early works, the Piano Quartet and the *Wanderers Sturmlied* (cf. Vol. I, pp. 31 and 33, Exx. 7 and 10b).

Two strands of melody, similar in general contour and character, are flung out by the nymphs. To begin with, only the second (Ex. 41) is specifically associated with Bacchus' initial experiences of love, but he himself later strings them together when recalling his adventure with Circe.

Ex. 40

Ex. 41

To Circe Strauss devotes a new complex of motifs containing more than a tinge of melancholy:

Ex. 42

(The wailing theme from *Elektra*[27] is strongly in evidence in the figure ⌐ y ¬.) A further motif evokes Circe's sorceries and is consistently developed during the description of her vain attempt to bewitch the ingenuous looking young god.

Ex. 43

[27] cf. Vol. I, p. 319.

Strauss being scarcely one to lose an opportunity, when the nymphs tell of the 'Trank' held out to Bacchus by Circe they are accompanied by an appropriate quotation of the Magic Potion motif from *Tristan*.[28]

As they come to the end of their narration the nymphs call upon Ariadne, telling of Bacchus' approach. Although she has not caught the meaning of their summons she emerges from her cave once more, just as the voice of the god can be heard from the extreme rear of the stage. He is instructed to be visible to the audience, standing on a rock by the sea, but out of sight of Ariadne and the nymphs. His song is in three verses, after each of which Ariadne, as if in a trance, sings of her reactions to the newcomer whom she takes to be the long-awaited messenger of Death.

Bacchus sings rhetorically to Circe from whom, bewildered, he has fled. He realises that he has miraculously escaped some fearful evil but cannot fathom what fate she had intended for him. This heart-searching is sung to his own and Circe's themes while the refrain of his song provides the combination of the two melodic strands Exx. 40 and 41.

Bacchus' second stanza also begins with a new melodic outburst which is shortly to achieve some motivic importance representing the psychological change he has undergone as the result of Circe's potion.

Ex. 44

Doch da___ ich un - ver - wan - - delt von dir ge-gan-gen bin,

Ariadne's visionary comments bring no wholly individual themes; the little trumpet call Ex. 37(x) continues to sound throughout the first verse of her duet with Bacchus, and Circe's melancholy chromatic theme Ex. 42(x) dominates the passage. Ariadne fails to comprehend the disturbing feelings with which the sound of his voice fills her. In her outburst after the second verse of Bacchus' song she expresses her unshakeable belief that he is Hermes, the god of sleep, whom she hails at first with a wistful memory of Ex. 23(x) from her Monologue, but the music passes prophetically to the theme of Bacchus' own god-hood, now strikingly

---

[28] Apt as it is, the reference by Strauss and Hofmannsthal (whose planting of the opportunity was certainly intentional) seems a little soon after the similar instance in *Rosenkavalier* (see Chapter IX, Vol. I, p. 354). This must be the most quoted theme in music (Berg, Britten, Debussy, etc.).

transformed. Although mistaken over his identity, Ariadne already sings of the divine nature of the being who is approaching, in whose veins balsam and ether flow in place of mortal blood.

Ex. 45

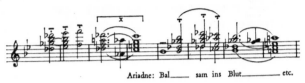

Ariadne: Bal_____ sam ins Blut_____ etc.

Not only is this great theme derived from Ex. 38 but it is also an augmentation of the theme of Circe's witchcraft Ex. 43. The motivic connexion between the sorceries themselves and the being whom they cannot affect is subtle but perfectly logical.

During Ariadne's third address to the god she cannot yet see, she shuts her eyes, opens her arms and in a mighty statement of Ex. 45 prepares to deliver herself to Death, begging the supposed Hermes to deal gently with her weakness of spirit—so long has she been waiting for him.

Ariadne's prolongations of Bacchus' first and second verses each led in their turn to parallel verses of a tranquil, simple song delivered partly in unison, partly in close harmony by the three nymphs.

Ex. 46[29]

Nymphs: Tö____ ne,   tö____ ne   sü - - - -ße   Stim - - - me,

PP   etc.

The third verse however gives the nymphs no chance of a corresponding third stanza of Ex. 46. Ariadne's apostrophe has led up to a great climax the resolution of which, it seems, could only be the long prepared entry of the god. At this precise moment the malicious Zerbinetta springs out of the wings and executes an elaborate curtsy at Ariadne's feet. The spell is broken and in a musically rather flippant little scherzetto Zerbinetta tries in her own way to prepare the princess for Bacchus' arrival.

[29] Strauss was perfectly aware that this charming little melody comes straight from Schubert (from the *Wiegenlied* 'Schlafe, schlafe'), much as the little duet for Sophie and Octavian at the end of *Der Rosenkavalier* which it recalls.

Some degree of mockery might reasonably have been expected in her eulogistic descriptions of this new lover who has indeed, in the words of her aria, 'come as a god' (Ex. 27). There are no signs of this in the text, however, in which Zerbinetta pictures Bacchus as a man like a god—a man but without the man-like faults she had earlier been enumerating, in fact a paragon. She goes into the most elaborate poetic similes during her paean of praise, some lines of which the nymphs repeat ecstatically. As she sings, appropriate motifs are heard in the orchestra: Bacchus' Exx. 37(x) and (y), as well as his song Ex. 44. In addition there are allusions to Ex. 27 from Zerbinetta's aria, as well as to themes from the second comedians' ensemble (Exx. 34(x) and 36). All these motifs are heard simultaneously with a new pair of motifs indigenous to this scene:

Ex. 47

The bell-like figure ⌐ y ¬ with its characteristic clusters of fourths is later exploited in various ways, in ascending passages and in undulation viz:

Ex. 47a

In this latter form the motif becomes of great importance during the succeeding duet on account of its subtle approach to the similar undulations of Bacchus' theme Ex. 39a.

The climax of this extra, perhaps unnecessary little scene[30] comes with the passionate return of the god-hood theme Ex. 45. In a state of complete spiritual exaltation Ariadne calls to her mother to witness her long-awaited departure from Naxos, and indeed from life itself. The nymphs

[30] Hofmannsthal however saw it as 'important in itself . . . Zerbinetta's pronouncement giving the orchestra predominance in a hymn-like march theme.' [!]

dress and adorn the bewildered, semi-conscious Ariadne while Zerbinetta adds a few words of encouragement. In the background, Ex. 45 builds up once again in order to re-establish the mood of excited expectation previously interrupted by Zerbinetta's intrusion.

An extended orchestral interlude follows (the characters on the stage remaining in breathless anticipation) in which Bacchus' Exx. 37(y) and 44 are offset vehemently against the theme of consecutive fourths, Ex. 47(y), which takes on more and more the appropriate character of a Bacchanale. Powerful striding can be heard coming ever nearer; Ex. 47(x) appears for a last time as Zerbinetta returns to the wings and with a grand cadence in C major Bacchus at last enters, his Bacchanale pealing jubilantly in celebration of his arrival.

16

The final scene of the opera consists entirely of the great duet between Bacchus and Ariadne. If Zerbinetta's aria was intended for the central show-piece, then this scena was equally planned as the main substance of the opera towards which everything would converge. Strauss accordingly used this culminating duet to weld together all the motivic strands of the Opera Seria into a vast symphonic recapitulation and coda. In doing this, he also draws for the first time on his full instrumental resources, including the two harps, celeste, harmonium and piano. In using the latter he was, of course, acting inconsistently since until now the piano had been exclusively associated with the Intermezzo, but for this culminating section he clearly wanted to employ every available colour in his palette of stringed or keyboard instruments.

The introduction to the duet begins with a dramatic outcry from Ariadne subsiding gradually into a lyrical passage of peaceful beauty very much like the great passage in *Elektra* if on a smaller scale. Strauss set this section in the manner of a 'Little Recognition Scene', despite the paradox of Ariadne's disconcerting *lack* of recognition. Against a bell-like ostinato of the parallel fourths (Ex. 47(y)) Bacchus' themes peal out with the greatest vehemence, but Ariadne scarcely glances at the god standing before her, puts both hands in front of her face and calls out 'Theseus!' After this momentary aberration, born of her long and wishful brooding, she cries out, equally erroneously, 'No, it is the beautiful silent god', meaning the messenger of death, Hermes. Accordingly she welcomes her visitor in a soaring phrase under which the now peacefully undulating fourths of Ex. 47a can still be heard in their basic colours of harps and piano. Simultaneously in the background are the god-head themes of Bacchus, who the newcomer really is (Ex. 45(x)), and of Hermes (Ex. 22), who he is not.

Bacchus answers this extraordinary greeting from a ravishing princess who is bowing low before him in tones of equal humility and wonderment. Everything about Ariadne seems to the young god so strange that for a time he believes himself to have fallen into the hands of a second Circe who will perhaps also sing magic songs and offer him food and a magic draught (Exx. 42 and 43). Her reply tells him nothing, for she merely reiterates her readiness for death and stresses how long she has been waiting for him. The music gradually retracts during this naïve pronouncement until it reaches a comparable simplicity in which the music of the Prelude (Ex. 12) is quietly played by a quintet of wind instruments, an exquisite use of formal recapitulation.

In the following section of the duet Ariadne elaborates her vision while Bacchus tries vainly to fathom who it is that this amazing creature believes him to be: she called to him by a strange name. Wistfully he woos her and his courtship is built upon a new variant of his ascending motif Ex. 37(y) which grows in importance until it becomes the salient melody of the entire musical structure.

Ariadne waves aside his reference to her confusion. Now she knows; he is the Lord of the Dark Ship. The orchestra points her belief that he has come to bear her to Charon's Boat by a quotation in the minor key of the appropriate theme from her Monologue, Ex. 23.

Intrigued, Bacchus stands nodding while the orchestra quietly repeats the little fanfare which heralded his coming (Ex. 37(x)). Yes, he has a ship. Does she wish to go in it? But Ariadne pursues a new line, equally incomprehensible: perhaps he is trying to prove her worthy, is he about to effect some transformation with either his hands, a wand or a drink— he spoke earlier of a draught? Confused and wholly enraptured by her appearance Bacchus no longer knows what he spoke of, and the 'Trank' motif Ex. 43, which had crept in, is left alone on the harmonium, descending into the bowels of the instrument, an extraordinarily original and magical effect.

Bacchus' bewilderment is taken by Ariadne to be only natural. Since he must have come from the Land of the Dead he can bring just such forgetfulness as will provide a peaceful solution to her sufferings. The orchestra accompanies her misinterpretation of Bacchus' confusion not only with his love melody, Ex. 48, but with a further new and gentle theme:

Ex. 49

Bacchus, seeing Ariadne close her eyes in total surrender, pulls himself together and with great solemnity reminds himself of his true stature and origin. He recalls his godhead, his mother's death in the flames caused by his father's fiery appearance in godly form, and the failure of Circe's magic owing to the strange mixture which flows through his veins in place of mortal blood. This is all declaimed against a splendid development of the appropriate themes: Ex. 39 (origin of Bacchus), Ex. 43 (Circe's magic) and Ex. 45 (Bacchus' divine constitution). He then tries to impress upon the expectant Ariadne that his embrace is unlikely to cause her death. It is now her turn for perplexity and taking up the strains of Ex. 39, though in ethereal tones and harmonies, she sings of the wonder and forgetfulness she already feels. The music then passes into a glorious outpouring of pure melody expressive of Ariadne's relief at having shed the burden of her sufferings:

Ex. 50

(Note the combination of the new melody with Bacchus' Ex. 44 during the second sentence.) Despite the relationship of this beautiful theme to the great *Elektra* melody (Vol. I, p. 302) it has a marked character of its own. Both melodies, moreover, are typical of how the mood of words frequently suggested to Strauss an instrumental melody to which the voice part had subsequently to be fitted, a curious trait in so experienced a composer of Lieder.

Bacchus tries to calm Ariadne's agitation in passages of reassuring stability in which the themes of his first coming, Ex. 37(x) and (y), are accompanied by renewed undulations of Ex. 47a. Ariadne meantime refers timidly to herself 'lying pressed against the floor of her cave like a wretched dog' in terms so strongly reminiscent of the words Hofmannsthal used of Elektra that it is hardly surprising that Strauss also found himself inventing phrases recalling their earlier joint masterpiece.

As Bacchus speaks of the new life about to open for both of them the daylight fades and the stars begin to glow in the sky. Each of the lovers believes the other to be a magician and the music now increases rapturously in intensity until the first great unison statement of Ex. 48 is reached, transformed by Bacchus into a mighty declaration of love. The orchestra continues the ecstatic sweep of melody which sinks easily and naturally into the nymphs' third verse of their Schubertian trio 'Töne,

Töne' (Ex. 46), delayed with shrewd theatrical sense for this affecting moment. Soft breezes have wafted the lovers to the mouth of the grotto, and Ariadne sings against the background of her now invisible attendants a sweet song of surrender to her divine wooer. The song over, she adds an extra phrase of her gentle theme, Ex. 49, begging that with the blissful drowning of misery her very sorrows should not be wholly forgotten.

During a soft magical orchestral interlude, dominated by the bell-like fourths on celeste, harps and piano, vine leaves and ivy drop gently from above, hiding the enchanted couple from view as the lights fade. The last section then quietly begins with Ex. 48 on solo cello and viola alternately. In the total darkness the voices of Bacchus and Ariadne can be heard singing the *Elektra*-like melody, Ex. 50 (still complete with its answering phrase, Ex. 44). This resolves on to a mighty orchestral tutti in which no less than three of Bacchus' themes (Exx. 37(x), 37(y) and 44) are played simultaneously and also combine with the stately Hermes theme, Ex. 22. To the end Bacchus is never able to explain the truth to Ariadne; as Hofmannsthal wrote in the same letter already quoted:

> 'To him she gives herself, for she believes him to be Death; he is both Death and Life at once; he it is who reveals to her the immeasurable depths of her own nature, who makes of her an enchantress, the sorceress who herself transforms the poor little Ariadne; he it is who conjures up for her in this world another world beyond, who preserves her for us and at the same time transforms her.'

The last thing to be heard from the jubilant god is his strong comforting assurance, sung to the second declamatory statement of Ex. 48, followed in the manner of a triumphant refrain by a repeat of his extravagant claim that the eternal stars will sooner die than she in his arms.

This great warm D flat major coda makes an eminently satisfying climax both to a beautiful and lyrical duet and to the whole opera which, with its wide contrasts of mood and style, greatly needed the unifying influence of such an extended movement.

17

The little opera is over, but the last word cannot be allowed to remain with the tragedians. Throughout the evening they had remained aloof from their gayer colleagues and, so far from attempting to defend their own aesthetic viewpoint or challenge that of their rivals, had barely even acknowledged their presence. For the last twenty minutes the Prima Donna and chief tenor have had the stage to themselves. In just retribution therefore, the clowns steal back under cover of darkness while the orchestra is still quietly reiterating the motif of Bacchus' Godhead (Ex. 39a). Najade, Dryade and Echo also momentarily appear from the opposite wings, but seeing the approaching clowns they vanish, never to be seen again.

This is also the moment when Jourdain's noble guests had planned to make their escape and noiselessly the two distinguished visitors, for whose benefit the whole entertainment has been mounted, disappear unnoticed.

Fragments of the Commedia dell'Arte motifs creep in: Zerbinetta's rondo (Ex. 27) and the principal subject of the first ensemble (Ex. 25) accompany her triumphant and mocking reference to her aria, 'a new god comes along and mutely we surrender'. The parallel between her poetic view of what happens to every woman and what has actually just happened before her very eyes is irresistible. She warms to her theme as the stage gradually lightens once more, and the melodic episode from her aria (Ex. 28) joins the build-up. A twisting figure which in the aria pointed the words 'sind verwandelt um und um' (are transformed through and through) is extended and swings the music into a jubilant return of the mood and rhythm of the comedians' music, in the course of which Harlequin's theme, Ex. 33, and the motif of Zerbinetta's flirtations, Ex. 26, are brilliantly combined. A climax is reached with a return of the waltz, Ex. 34, in which the four comic lovers join Zerbinetta, singing and dancing and at last cavorting off the stage amidst peals of laughter suitably imitated in the orchestra by Ex. 35 rising to the upper regions where it dissolves into Zerbinetta's little twisting figure.

This time, however, it is Jourdain himself who has found his world transformed. The effort of trying to follow an opera has proved too much for him and he had fallen into a profound slumber from which one of the lackeys with difficulty rouses him. The lackey draws his attention to the open door through which his noble guests have vanished. His theme, Ex. 1, enters violently and is then repeated in soft perplexity as he performs the reverences required by court etiquette in the direction of the empty doorway. The lackey pertinently enquires whether despite the turn of events the firework display should still take place, but in his distress Jourdain does not answer. Instead, against a spaced-out statement of his Ex. 1 he delivers his last poignant *credo* concerning his views on the nobility: people reproach him, he says, for his association with persons of rank, but his admiration for their behaviour and courtly ways knows no bounds: he would have given the fingers of his hand to have been born a nobleman and to have the knowledge how to invest one's every action with so grand a manner.[31]

The complex work ends brusquely with a rapid flourish of Jourdain's trumpet tune, Ex. 2, extended by an emphatic cadence. The opera *Ariadne* has not only ended in comedy with the dancing clowns but has further been fully enclosed within a framework drawn from Molière's comedy, the humour and lightness of which remains in the spectator's mind as the outstanding characteristic of the whole.

(ii) *The Opera without the Play*

18

That the first performance cannot be counted amongst Strauss's successes has already been mentioned. Despite Reinhardt's imaginative production and the excellence of his cast, the Molière was played to an impatient audience and the criticisms were largely hostile. In fact, as was surely to have been anticipated, the startling novelty of the scheme misled its first audience altogether. The work conformed so little to what they had expected from a new work by Strauss that they were unable to perceive where the faults and qualities lay.

If the work was misunderstood even when presented as at Stuttgart, under the eye and direct jurisdiction of its creators, how much worse was it to fare when it had, in the natural course of events, to make its way in the outside world. Hofmannsthal received with mortification the news of this or that production in which the Jourdain was turned into a mere clown, Ariadne massacred, the conductor no more than a repetiteur,

---

[31] The implied censure of the noble guests' contemptuous treatment of Jourdain, vital as it is, is so subtly hinted at in the text as easily to pass unnoticed unless stressed in production. In 1911, confronted by the great courts of Germany and Austria, Hofmannsthal may indeed have felt it impossible to allow Jourdain to speak openly; more recently however, Miles Malleson caught the intention to perfection in his witty translation of the libretto. 'Everyone laughs at me,' complains Jourdain, 'because I want to be a man of quality but, for my part I envy them, Oh yes! I admire them. Their aloofness, their composure, their superiority! Oh what wouldn't I give to have been born a great one, a Count; or a Marquis, or a Duke, and be able to behave as badly as they do . . . and think so little of it . . . !'

crazy cuts, no glimmer of humour and so on. To what extent his censures can be taken seriously has to be carefully considered in view of the fact that the conductor, in some cases, was none other than Bruno Walter. Nevertheless, Strauss agreed that he was not without reservations over the way this unusually delicate piece was being handled, especially (to air an old grievance) in Munich. For a composer to watch the progress of his work through every performance and production once it has left the parent fold is, of course, to court distress; yet, sensitive as he was to adverse opinion, Strauss this time showed less serious concern than Hofmannsthal.

Already on 19th January 1913, barely three months after the first performance, the poet was outlining to Strauss a transformed *Ariadne*, an entirely redrafted version with a new Vorspiel to be set in *recitativo secco*, the idea for which seems to have been mooted by Strauss himself in conversation.

Such drastic thoughts so early in the life of the work were the direct result of Hofmannsthal's reaction, not just to the lack of public acclaim, but to the attacks of the critics:

> '. . . the almost unbelievable degree of antagonism this light and poetic work of art has aroused among the scribbling race. . . . Is it that people sense in it what they apparently hate more than anything else; this turning away from merely ephemeral effects, from the mere semblance of reality, this search for transcendental meaning? Is that what arouses their hatred and antagonism?
>
> P. S. Fürstner, i.e. Oertel, wrote to me a while ago that the sale of the piano score also falls short of his expectations; this makes it more puzzling than ever, for after all, it cannot be due to my libretto and to Molière; and all the world is agreed that the music is among the most beautiful you have ever written!'

This show of self-confidence disguised his actual bitterness, for during the following June Hofmannsthal wrote to say that he was 'nauseated by the whole affair', that it was useless to think of patching and cutting, what should he care if the piece was ruined; despondency would only ensue if he wasted any time on a lost cause.

He then inconsequentially went on to say that he had found 'the real remedy', a rewritten version of the dressing-room scene, which had been on his desk for a week and would in a few days be in Strauss's hands fully typed. He had, if truth be told, for the past six months been doing these very things he decried—tinkering, patching, 'wasting his time on a lost cause', if lost it really were. Indeed it becomes apparent that his arrogant assurance had all been a façade, the elaborate philosophy a smoke-screen to hide a basic feeling of insecurity over the piece.

Its real virtues had always been essentially its novelty of theatrical format together with the lightness and delicacy of its style. But it is of course self-evident that these problems must always make any performance something of a special occasion. Even so, left alone it would certainly have found its natural level in the operatic repertoire without any 'tinkering or patching', and this, in his agony of mind, Hofmannsthal was unable to see. Without giving the delightful work a chance to establish itself, he had, almost immediately after its first performance, decided that it was a failure, that he had misjudged the taste and subtlety of the artistic world and that he must simplify and redraft the entire conception, jettisoning the ill-fated Jourdain once and for all;

> '. . . It will take a real load off my mind, and believe me, off yours too, once that unnatural connexion between the living and the dead has been severed (I thought the stage would enable me to galvanize the defunct, but the instrument failed me!). . . . Imagine how crystalline and complete, how harmonious our beautiful Ariadne will emerge once she is placed on this pedestal. Believe me, please.'

But Strauss did not believe him, and expressed himself vehemently in words which show his theatrical sense and artistic understanding in the finest light:

> 'I cling obstinately to our original work, and still regard it as so successful in structure and conception that this new version will always look to me like a torso . . . to my judgement, the idea of the whole piece was excellent and will undoubtedly be resurrected in this form.'

There was, however, an additional factor in Strauss's distaste for the new rewritten scene. Hofmannsthal had always disliked the Zerbinetta coloratura aria. It reminded him, as he later told Egon Wellesz, 'of a mere musical automaton, a doll who could not possibly awaken any feeling in the spectator'. He even went so far as to give this as his real reason for writing the new version with its

> 'prologue with the scene between Zerbinetta and the young Composer, in order to create a figure capable of some human

warmth, "like Philine in Goethe's *Wilhelm Meister*". It was through this change that Zerbinetta became a real character in the opera.'

But this change was effected through the figure of the Composer who, already raised in the original linking scene to a position of some importance, now became the very central character; as Hofmannsthal put it: 'He is, symbolically, a figure half tragic, half comic; the whole antithesis of the action (Ariadne, Zerbinetta, Harlequin's world) is now firmly focussed on him'. Even more symbolism, more obscure philosophical concepts, were to be introduced. Strauss went so far as to describe it as the most dreary task now lying before him. He wrote irritably to Hofmannsthal:

'to be quite frank, I have so far not found the scene to my liking at all. Indeed, it contains certain things that are downright distasteful to me—the Composer, for instance; to set him actually to music will be rather tedious. I ought to tell you that I have an innate antipathy to all artists treated in plays and novels, and especially composers, poets and painters.'

This is perhaps a little violent, in particular when one remembers the little love affair with Zerbinetta which Strauss himself had suggested for the Composer not two years before. Moreover, within three years Strauss was to draft his own libretto for a comic opera in which he, as Strauss the composer, was to be the hero.[32]

Nevertheless, at the time the point seemed real and Strauss set himself firmly against this redrafting of a work which he had been pushed into in the first place but which had in the end turned out to be surprisingly interesting. In the face of such determination Hofmannsthal resigned himself to letting matters rest for the time being. A good performance in Munich, after all the troubles there, even stimulated him into writing back enthusiastically to Strauss, 'You are quite right; we shall change nothing, not one thing.' And so matters were left for some two years, during which Strauss marked time, waiting for the promised and long-hoped-for large-scale drama which he had every reason to believe Hofmannsthal would soon deliver.

Yet even now fate was against him. *Die Frau ohne Schatten* was making slow progress which was hampered still further by the unsettling effect of the outbreak of war. The annoying truth was that Hofmannsthal had

[32] See Chapter XIII.

for some months delayed applying himself to this formidable conception in order to work out an idea for a ballet on the biblical subject of Joseph, suggested to him by Count Harry Kessler.

Strauss had thus reluctantly found himself committed to working on this new red herring, the production of which was to be his last before the war effectively put a brake on all major ventures. When in 1915 the draft sketch of *Die Frau ohne Schatten* was finished there were no prospects whatever of its being brought to the stage. To begin work on yet another opera in these circumstances was not to be considered, and Strauss, at no time the most adaptable of men, to whom the cataclysm of world war represented nothing but a monstrous nuisance, found himself at a loss. How should he fill in the months which he was in the habit of devoting to composition? Admittedly a huge task of orchestration lay before him, but there was now more than enough time for this.

Gradually Strauss came to perceive that he could do worse than agree to set Hofmannsthal's revised Vorspiel to *Ariadne auf Naxos*. On the one hand he would be faced with a new creative task; on the other with the limited resources which would now be required for that unique work in its truncated form, he could surely not fail to obtain a new production of what would be, for all practical purposes, a new piece. Accordingly, in the January of 1916, he reopened the subject with Hofmannsthal who was as keen as ever. A meeting was quickly arranged followed by a plan to attend a performance of the original *Ariadne*, after which they would adjourn with Reinhardt as well, to discuss what could be done 'to rehabilitate this hapless child.' The plan was successful and the decision taken to go ahead. The première was offered to Vienna, and Strauss without further ado embarked on the composition. By late May the tinkering was well advanced and on 20th June the score was complete.

This is not to say that the scheme was without its headaches. The figure of the Composer, even after Strauss had accepted his appearance in principle, still remained a bone of contention. In order to remove this controversial character as far as possible from the commonplace aspects of his own real-life existence Strauss decided to make his Composer another *travesti*; he already had the ideal performer in mind, Lola Artôt de Padilla, a Franco-Spanish soprano who had made a great reputation in the Berlin Opera where she had been the first Rosenkavalier.[33] Strauss visualized her as representing 'a young Mozart, say, at the Court of

[33] She was born to the life of a singer, being the daughter of the famous soprano Desirée Artôt and the baritone Mario Padilla.

Versailles or among the Philistines of the Munich Court, for whom, at the age of sixteen, he composed *Idomeneo*.' Although Strauss was adrift in his dates—*Idomeneo* was composed in 1780 when Mozart was twenty-four—the conception was sufficiently credible and attractive to be insisted upon in the face of Hofmannsthal's outraged opposition. For another of the poet's furious self-righteous effusions promptly arrived, rejecting the idea out-of-hand as an example of Strauss's 'opportunism in theatrical matters . . . to make something pretty-pretty of this very char-acter who should have a spiritual quality, some greatness about him, and turn him into what will always be a slightly Pantomime *travesti* figure —this, forgive my bluntness, is to me simply odious. . . . Oh God, if only it were given to me to make really clear to you the essence, the spirituality of these characters.'

Apart from his justifiable indignation at this high-flown tirade, Strauss's reply was essentially practical and commendably firm. After going through the possible voices for the role (tenor impos-sible with three already in the cast, and he wasn't having a First Baritone singing the young Composer) he concluded: 'What is left to me except the only genre of singer not yet represented in *Ariadne*, my Rofrano, for whom an intelligent female singer is available anywhere'.

Here was the ideal casting and that was that. In the face of such deter-mination Hofmannsthal gave in without another word and one of the most endearing figures of the operatic stage was born.

19

In the original linking scene, which had been wholly without music, Hofmannsthal had been able to establish in a few lines the *mise en scène* together with the whole foundation for the presence of the contrasted theatrical groups. Jourdain's vast and pretentious palace, his complete lack of taste or understanding of the arts, indeed the very *raison d'être* of the evening's entertainment as a mere pretext for Dorante's seduction of the Marquise Dorimène, these things had been firmly planted as the back-ground for all that was to follow.

For his part Strauss had also contributed to the general impression by subtly infusing an air of Period into the style of his Incidental Music, despite the unmistakably personal idiom of every bar. With this preparation cast aside both scenically and musically, poet and composer faced an audience who knew nothing, to whom everything had to be explained from the beginning, and to whom the lightness and quasi-pastiche of the music once associated with Jourdain's mansion would have no significance whatever.

The authors attempted to solve some of these formidable problems firstly by moving the scene from seventeenth-century Paris to Vienna. Historically, in order to establish a parallel situation in a comparable noble house in Vienna, the action had to be advanced in time by at least half a century. The wretched Jourdain, mocked alike by servants and friends, becomes instead a nameless personage of extreme eminence, designated merely by his Major-domo with pride as 'the richest man in Vienna'. Hofmannsthal describes him as some 'Maecenas . . . allegorical, in the background, represented only by his footmen who transmit his bizarre commands.'

The most serious anachronism caused by the alteration is the conster-nation of the Music Master on learning that his troupe is to share a stage with a pack of comedians. The interpolations of this kind, which already in the early years of the eighteenth century were by no means uncommon in the Court opera houses of Europe, had at the period now in question become everyday occurrences.

Strauss, freed of the associations with Paris and the world of the harpsichord, quickly relaxed into his natural warm and ebullient style. For a new Vorspiel of such considerable proportions, fresh principal subjects would draw together the many diffuse elements in a complex scene:

Ex. 51a   Ex. 51b

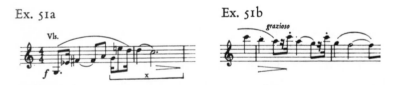

Neither of these two salient ideas, which strung together form the ex-tended opening sentence of the Vorspiel, belongs to the material already composed for *Ariadne*, yet the relationship of rhythm or melodic contour is unmistakable. (Compare, for example, ⌐ x ⌐ with Zerbi-netta's Ex. 28(x), or the rhythmic shape of Ex. 51b with Ariadne's Ex. 22(x).)

The new themes prove to be associated with the young Composer who is now to dominate the scene, Ex. 51b representing his instinctive protest against the buffo characters, while Ex. 51a delineates the impetuosity of the boy himself. In this respect it is amusing to discover how in portraying another *travesti* figure Strauss invented a phrase more than a little reminiscent of Octavian's great leaping motif (cf. Ex. 1, Chapter IX).

A medley of motifs from the first version of the opera quickly follows. Bacchus' Ex. 37(y) is introduced against the new phrase Ex. 51b and gradually leads the music into a broad and complete statement of the great *Elektra*-like melody, Ex. 50. Two themes of the comedians are now abruptly interspersed, after which Ex. 51 (a and b) lifts the music to the exaltation of the Bacchus-Ariadne duet. A coy entry of Ex. 51b on the horn then takes us back to the comedians with Ex. 34, upon which is superimposed Ariadne's Ex. 22. So the polyphony continues with constant references to and fro between the classic drama and the Commedia dell'Arte until the music reaches a climax and the curtain rises. The stage is empty and the elaborate reworking of so many contrasted motifs represents the arguments and antagonism between the two opposing factions which has caused the Music Master to run through the house in search of the Major-domo.

When the two men meet the one is harrassed and flustered, the other icy calm and haughty of manner. The disdain with which he treats so inferior a servant, a mere musician, is intensified by the fact that the Major-domo is a speaking role, the coldness of calm unaccompanied speech contrasting amusingly with the rapid recitative of the Music Master.

It is through their discussion that the audience is informed about the full-scale reception being prepared in the great mansion. As in the entertainment provided by Jourdain for Dorante, the opera *Ariadne auf Naxos* is to be followed by a Singspiel in the Italian buffo manner[34] as well as by a display of fireworks. One is to understand that the interpolation of the Opera Buffo has only just been made, and that the consternation of the classical performers is being manifested behind the scenes. The Music Master protests that the Composer, his own pupil, will never allow such desecration to take place. The Major-domo retorts that no one other than his master has the right to allow or disallow anything. In return for his generous commission he naturally expects his orders to be

[34] There is here a contradiction in terms which can only have been deliberate. The Singspiel made use of spoken dialogue whereas the Italian Intermezzo was strung together with *recitativo secco*.

obeyed without question and to the letter. This blind obedience to commands which may be grotesquely unreasonable is the thesis of the piece. In the meantime, the Music Master ponders gloomily how he is to break the news to his poor young pupil, and the two men depart in opposite directions. The whole conversation has been carried on in a form of fragmentary melodrama, in the writing of which Strauss had had a certain experience some years earlier in *Enoch Arden*.[35]

20

The Composer[36] now enters and his inferior status and boyish personality are emphasized immediately. Hofmannsthal's intention was that he should exemplify more strongly than before the focal point of the piece, the musician's destiny: '. . . the composer as a man in love, fooled, as guest, child, victor and vanquished in this world.' The moment we first see him he suffers humiliations from the lowest servant of the household. A young subaltern arrives to keep an assignation with Zerbinetta. Impatiently he sends packing a lackey who tries to impede his entrance. In return the lackey is rude and sneers at the Composer, who has just rushed in to ask that a last-minute rehearsal be called for the violins. These, it would seem, are at table, and Strauss takes the opportunity of quoting from the Dinner Music of the *Bourgeois Gentilhomme*, which he combines with the first notes of the Comedians' theme, Ex. 25, revealing that the one idea is, unexpectedly, the inversion of the other.

The Composer next tries to go into the Prima Donna's dressing room in order to discuss a few points in Ariadne's aria, but again the lackey prevents him rudely, his sniggers showing the spectators that a very different Prima Donna is occupying the room: the Composer, who has tried to assert a little pride in his position, is in for a rude shock since he has no inkling of the existence of Zerbinetta, least of all the role she intends to play in the evening's entertainment.

The first glimpse we had of the young Composer was originally in the act of writing the little arietta 'Du Venus' Sohn', Ex. 3. The melody had

[35] The technical device known as 'Melodrama', in which spoken dialogue is punctuated by longer or shorter sections of music, is not to be confused with the modern popular use of the term. See also Chapter XVII, pp. 357/8.

[36] Like the other members of the company—Music Master, Tenor, Prima Donna, Zerbinetta, etc—the Composer is never given a name. All are simple type-figures.

already formed part of the overture and was later sung complete by Echo for Jourdain's benefit. Although the arietta could have no possible place in the new scheme, Strauss and Hofmannsthal were loath to abandon this first impression of the Composer in the throes of creation, regardless of the fact that his opera is not only already complete, but due for its first performance within fifteen minutes. Lip-service to this difficulty is paid by his remarking 'Oh, I would like to change many things at the eleventh hour', as the flute gently plays the opening of the arietta. We are to imagine the theme taking shape in his mind, and as the oboe picks up the phrase he sings a few bars, quickly trying to jot down the ideas as they come to him. From the 'Knabe . . . Kind . . . allmächtiger Gott' his thoughts turn to Bacchus and are immediately soured by memories of the self-important *Hanswurst* of a Tenor who is to sing the role. Here Strauss speaks from the heart.

At the moment when the Composer, clinging fast to his new-found melody, brings the arietta Ex. 3 to a climax, the door of the Tenor's changing room is flung open and the wigmaker tumbles out. The somewhat confused scene which follows serves the purpose of introducing, however briefly, several more of the principal characters: the ill-humoured and conceited Tenor himself; Zerbinetta, as flighty in real-life as on the stage, complacently telling a military admirer all about her part in enlivening the wearied audience after the tedium of the opera; the haughty Prima Donna sending imperiously for some Count, presumably her protector; the Dancing Master, who occupies the same position in charge of the Intermezzo as in the original version, and who is disclosed telling Zerbinetta in an undertone that her task will be a simple one in an opera so boring and unmelodious.

The Music Master equally remains in control of the Opera Seria and the attacks of each group upon its rival are similar to those in the original linking scene, except only in the greater prominence of the Composer. Again as before, he is immediately impressed by Zerbinetta, whom he finds enchanting, only to be horrified when told by the Music Master who she is. His derogatory gibes at the 'dancing and trilling' of the Nachspiel calls from Strauss a reference to Ex. 34, which is contrasted with Ariadne's tragic theme, Ex. 12, reiterated on the violins.

There follows the first considerable outburst on the part of the Composer, as a result of which a clearer impression is formed of Hofmannsthal's new elaboration of this rather touching, if improbable character. He is at first impetuous and passionate in his despair; never again will a melody come to him, his soul is eternally poisoned through contact with such a commonplace troupe. Then he relives his experiences of the last few minutes until he reaches the magical moment when his spirit was smitten by the pangs of love. The memory sparks off his muse once again and he completes the arietta, Ex. 3, then and there. As the last soaring phrase dies away he boyishly looks at the faces around him and quaintly asks for a piece of manuscript paper.

The four buffoons now appear, during a little march to which they goose-step out of Zerbinetta's dressing-room. She introduces them to her officer-admirer and then commands them to fetch all the trappings for her make-up. The four obediently run to do her bidding and are thus presented during an off-duty scene as behaving in much the same formalized manner as during their act. Although Truffaldino, Scaramuccio and Brighella had in the original version helped Zerbinetta with make-up and toilet preparations—holding the mirror, lighting candles, lacing her stays and so forth—there was never any suggestion of so artificial an atmosphere as is now created, and it is revealing to discover Hofmannsthal feeling such a need for formality when preparing this new introductory section.

21

Up to now, the libretto of the Vorspiel had comprised largely fresh material. At this point, however, Hofmannsthal reverted to the spoken linking scene from the original version, which he considered might be set to music almost exactly as it stood. The character of the Composer had by now been sufficiently established to justify the lyrical *entretien* with Zerbinetta which he had devised as the new musical climax. Such minor alterations as might be necessitated by the exchange of Jourdain for the anonymous Viennese plutocrat could, he saw, be effected by a few simple cuts.[37]

[37] Hofmannsthal seems to have had reservations over which of Jourdain's artistic indiscretions his usurper might have been guilty and which not. He retained the idea of peopling Ariadne's uninhabited island with a company of comedians on the splendid grounds that it would be *infra dig* in so noble a house to represent anything so dreary as a desert island; on the other hand he suppressed the lackey's charming remark (which might have come straight out of Molière) that 'all instruments should be sounded at the same moment, and the whole affair be gone through quickly, for the Master cannot bear slow music for anything in the world. He has already entered the Art Gallery with his guests and it would be impossible for them to stay there longer than five minutes for it is only an empty room with nothing in it but pictures on the walls.'

The libretto switches to the original text, therefore, immediately after the Composer has attacked his Music Master for knowing all along what was brewing, and the situation links effortlessly to that of the original opening lines in which we once saw for the first time the Prima Donna calling for her Count. As it has become a repeated summons Strauss adds majestic splashes on two harps. Zerbinetta's complaint over the difficulty of her task is now accompanied by a miniature Piano Sonata while the long speech of the Dancing Master, putting the case for the Comedians in a favourable light, is turned into an arietta[38] based firstly on another motif from the Dinner Music of the *Bourgeois Gentilhomme* (references to the guests at table) and passing on to the Comedians' theme, Ex. 25, passages which are still closely related in idiom and style.

Amusingly appropriate as the Dinner Music obviously is, there is an element of the incongruous in these quotations of musical themes or passages from the wholly excised Incidental Music to a play concerning which there is not a single reference in the text. Strauss then continues by incorporating Mendelssohn's theme of the rustics from the Intermezzo of the *Midsummer Night's Dream*, which also proves to be closely related by inversion to Strauss's motif.

The counterpart to Zerbinetta and the Dancing Master is next given by the pompous Music Master, who briefly assures the Prima Donna that she and Ariadne will be all the audience will remember. He is interrupted by a lackey who runs in, announcing that the noble guests have risen from the dinner table. The Music Master accordingly breaks off his tirade and calls to the company to go at once to their place in readiness for the performance.

At the crucial moment, however, there is a cymbal clash and an arresting drum figure. The Major-domo has re-entered during the general frenzy and delivers to the dumbfounded assembly the decree concerning the simultaneous representation on a single stage, at one and the same time, of both the serious and the comic portions of the evening's programme.

It still seems not to have occurred to the authors that in the end this all-important combination is never fully exploited in either version. The buffoons or Zerbinetta comment from time to time on Ariadne's behaviour—Zerbinetta even addresses Ariadne directly; but

---

[38] The passage is actually labelled 'Ariette' in the score although it has less valid independent existence than the Composer's 'Du Venus' Sohn' which no longer receives the appellation.

the two plots, i.e. the abduction by Bacchus of the deserted Ariadne and Zerbinetta's choice of Harlequin from amongst her four admirers (each plot, it will be noticed, a simple resolution of a single issue) are worked out entirely separately and while each is in progress the personages of the other are absent from the stage. Considering how important the conception had been to the poet from the very beginning, and what splendid situations could have emerged had it been whole-heartedly carried out, this is both puzzling and disappointing.

With the reappearance of the non-singing Major-domo, the music, which had become increasingly continuous and symphonic in style, is once again broken into fragmentary ejaculations matching the prevailing atmosphere of flabbergasted consternation. From here on, the music very gradually builds up a second time to the great lyrical scene between the Composer and Zerbinetta, after which there remains only a short and brilliant coda bringing the Vorspiel to an end. Thus the second entry of the Major-domo divides the scene more or less evenly into two balancing sections. In the original version there had barely been time to establish the state of annoyance of the different characters at having even to appear on the same stage before this new bombshell. Thus almost the whole of the action in Hofmannsthal's original scene had been devoted to the reactions of the players to only one, though the greater, of the two emergencies.

It was when Hofmannsthal found himself faced with the need to rethink and expand his first scheme that he decided to shift the balance by adding an equally important early section featuring the young Composer, whose character could be drawn in considerably greater detail. As a result, when he arrived at the later scene, the young man could be set in opposition to the intriguing Zerbinetta in a way which had previously only been suggested.

22

The Music Master and the Composer are thrown into despair by the disastrous change of plan, but the Dancing Master assures them that to his own more resourceful company the matter presents no difficulty. The Composer, he insists, must be instructed to reduce the indisputable longueurs of his opera, while Zerbinetta, whose improvisations on any given situation are masterly, will be brought quickly into the picture.

The Composer, his ideals shattered, is eventually forced into compliance and thus taught the hard lesson that until one's reputation is established it is often necessary to make the bitterest compromise with the world in order to gain any hearing. He is led gently to the work-table by his Master, the score of his beloved opera is laid before him, lights are brought and gloomily he applies himself to Strauss's own *bête noire*—the task of making cuts. The Prima Donna and the Tenor intensify the Composer's disgust when both secretly press him to cut down to the minimum the role of the other while preserving their own intact.

The music has once again acquired continuity and Strauss writes a brilliant scherzo for the passage in which the Dancing Master outlines to Zerbinetta the story of the Ariadne myth, factually if gaily. Although largely based on new material this section contains occasional soft allusions to different motifs (Ex. 22, Zerbinetta's own Ex. 26, the melody of the duet, Ex. 48, Ex. 39b, and so on) and in addition, at one moment marked 'parodierend, heroisch' in the score Strauss interpolates the children's dancing tune 'Brüderchen komm' tanz mit mir' from Humperdinck's *Hänsel und Gretel*.

Zerbinetta quickly understands the gist of the classical drama of which she naturally takes a matter-of-fact, common-sense view. The Composer, who has overheard, reacts spontaneously with some heat, and as he tries to persuade her and her sceptical companions of Ariadne's immutable faithfulness the gay scherzo theme alternates with substantial extracts from the closing scene of the opera. Zerbinetta has too few illusions of the world to take the young man's objections seriously, but finds him personally most attractive.

The growing intensity of music and situation is interrupted briefly while, simply and without derision, Zerbinetta outlines in rapid *recitativo secco* the *mise en scène* to her companions. In the original spoken dialogue this was undoubtedly justified, but in the musical version it holds up the flow of the scene's lyrical crescendo which is once more gathering strength.

The Composer takes up the thread of his philosophizing, however, as if the whole interruption had not taken place, and soon voice and orchestra are swept upwards in that warm flow of ecstatic melody which was becoming ever more Strauss's speciality. Zerbinetta joins in and it is difficult to realize that she and the Composer are not singing a love duet. On the contrary Zerbinetta's remarks are extremely cynical and provocative. Perhaps Strauss was at fault in allowing his melodic vein to take

6

over; yet the work needed some such expansion at this point. It is rather that Zerbinetta's words belie the music she sings, and Strauss might have suggested a change of text at this salient point where an important insertion was in any case being made. The transition, a long and coquettish solo for Zerbinetta, sinks nostalgically from a glowing climax to a mood of serenity for Zerbinetta's 'Ein Augenblick ist wenig, ein Blick ist viel',[39] a highly ingenious transformation of her Ex. 26 accompanying her on the solo violin:

Ex. 52

The interpolated phrase ⌐ x ⌐ plays an important part in the beautiful passage which follows. Zerbinetta portrays herself as a serious-minded girl who, behind her jovial stage personality, hides a lonely and bewildered heart. The Composer is won over (Ex. 51(x) also metamorphosed into a broad melody), and seeing this she plays her trump card by suggesting that in real-life she is searching for the single being to whom she can be true to the end of her days. This affecting suggestion evokes from Strauss an expressive motif plainly descended from the mournful theme which we have traced through his works from *Tod und Verklärung*, via *Elektra*, to the reference to Circe in Ex. 42(y).

Ex. 53

[39] 'A moment is little, a glance much'—the play on words is naturally lost in translation.

(Perhaps Circe's seduction of Bacchus was hardly fundamentally different from Zerbinetta's of the Composer in the present scene, and was certainly no more sincere.) The entranced Composer sees in Zerbinetta a kindred spirit; she shrewdly plays on his loyalty, exacts his enduring faithfulness and makes her escape.

Hofmannsthal here incorporates a passage from the original version in which the Music Master calls the whole company on stage. The Prima Donna voices her indignation in a restless passage based on one of the themes from the Prelude to the opera, Ex. 16. The Music Master summons all his tact to reassure her that the presence of Zerbinetta will enhance by contrast, rather than damage, her prestige.

This marked the end of the original text, the Prima Donna leaving with the others while Jourdain entered with his distinguished guests. Now, however, a further important interpolation is made. The Music Master turns anxiously to the Composer who unexpectedly embraces him. Exx. 51a and 51b leap about in high spirits as the boy tells him how he has been made to view everything with entirely fresh eyes. Zerbinetta's new melody, Ex. 53, swings up to a passionate return of a rising phrase from the arietta 'Du Venus' Sohn' (Ex. 3) and the love-inspired Composer pours out his joy of the world in a surge of melody. This leads directly into Hofmannsthal's Ode to Music: 'Musik ist eine heilige Kunst' ('Music is a Holy Art') which, conceived as long ago as January 1913, was one of the chief *raisons d'être* of the entire revision. Strauss set it as a short but glowing song in the richest colouring. His enthusiastic letter to Hofmannsthal is very understandable:

'The scene between Zerbinetta and Composer has all in all turned out *very* prettily and belongs to my very best ideas. I really believe that the whole thing is thoroughly well planned and built up. . . .'

Ex. 54

Hofmannsthal himself had set great store by this passage which he described not only as the lyrical climax but as 'a kind of little Prize Song . . . here,' he wrote, 'the words ought to inspire you to find a new beautiful melody, solemn and ebullient'. He added that they struck him as the kind of text Beethoven might have liked to use.

No sooner has the Composer reached the cadence of his song than there is a piercing whistle. Zerbinetta has danced backwards out of her dressing-room and, together with her companions who have just finished making-up, runs on to the stage to the theme of their most hilarious behaviour, Ex. 35. In a flash the Composer sees through her duplicity and, his elation vanished like a pricked bubble, he rages at the comedians. With passionate reiterations of Ex. 51 he rushes off demented, and while the Music Master watches him, shaking his head, the curtain falls.

23

So altered a layout of the work naturally meant total re-publication, and this gave Strauss the chance to have second thoughts over the opera itself. In the first place, with the elimination of Jourdain as a specific personality, both authors agreed that the two interruptions on the part of the spectators (see above, p. 30) were no longer desirable or necessary. Indeed there are no longer any spectators on the stage to make such comments or complaints, for the stage within a stage has for the purposes of the opera been relegated wholly to the imagination. The 'Richest man in Vienna' does not, like Jourdain, come on with his guests to witness and perhaps fall asleep during the opera which he has commanded. There is considerable loss here, both with respect to the basic conception and in the actual remarks originally interjected by Jourdain, Dorante and Dorimène. It is not just that these comments were amusing, but that they were as much a part of an objective view of the drama as those contributed within the inner stage by the Buffo characters. With their excision, there is a greater feeling of self-importance given to a dramatic fragment, a redeeming feature of which had been that one was constantly being prevented through a series of circumstances from taking it too seriously. With the opera now occupying the whole stage as in any other music-drama, the comedians often seem left out on a limb.

One of the most important passages which Strauss revised was Zerbinetta's aria. Considering how much excellent music this contained it had been a pity that Strauss in his enthusiasm had allowed the piece to become discursive and almost formless. Now, however, he was in the position to reconsider it, having witnessed its effect in performance. But with an eye to the future he also concluded that it might be as well to soften its alarming difficulties not merely by reducing its length but by dropping its pitch a whole tone over the greater part of its principal sections. The opening is identical and the jump into D instead of E major is made just before the second arietta 'So war es mit Pagliazzo' at the sacrifice of the entire climax (including the top C sharp) of the previous $\frac{3}{4}$ movement. This now 'breaks off abruptly' (Strauss's own directions in Zerbinetta's part, in an attempt at making a virtue of necessity) and after a couple of arabesques on flute and clarinet Zerbinetta now enters in D major (cf. Ex. 26), the modulation successfully accomplished. From this point the two versions proceed side by side for the first sections of the Rondo, through the main episode and until the first formal return of the principal theme. At this point Strauss makes a cut of some thirty-nine bars, omitting the by-play with the clarinet and the entire florid middle section. The closing section thus follows immediately, but after a mere half-dozen bars Strauss again cuts some forty bars, though replacing them this time with an entirely new coda, less than half the length of the original passage.

This second cut not only does away with the cadenza but also robs Zerbinetta of her remaining piece of mockery at the conventions and hazards of opera, including her farcical contretemps with orchestra and conductor. Although in theory these burlesques were *ben trovato* and amusing, in practice their humour must have seemed somewhat heavy unless carried off by a consummate artiste. With their disappearance the aria is not only more concise and thus more practical in the opera house, but has survived in addition as a highly successful piece on the concert platform.

The new coda is still full of trills and arabesques, and even contains a brief Donizetti-like duet for voice and flute. It is also far better shaped and leads logically into the grand cadence, which Strauss rewrote[40] leaving the voice unaccompanied at the supreme moment when Zerbinetta takes her last top D. The final eight bars of dying references to the rondo subject, Ex. 27, are the same as in the original score (apart from key), but the last snap chord is transferred to the more conventional

---

[40] The cadence itself has a curious false entry for the trumpet which is sometimes omitted. There is no reason to believe, however, that Strauss wrote it in error.

position before, instead of immediately after, Harlequin's leap onto the stage.

No doubt here, too, Strauss had run into difficulties with previous Zerbinettas over the subtle but less gratifying original scheme. At all events the way is now clear for well-deserved applause and the custom has quickly come into being in which the performance is broken here for this purpose.

24

The fluid tonalities of the recitative which follow Zerbinetta's aria made it a simple matter for Strauss to effect the transition back to the original key, and the music now returns for some considerable distance to the first version. Two minor cuts of eight and eighteen bars respectively occur during the scene in which Zerbinetta's unsuccessful suitors are discomforted, ridding the passage of some unnecessary repetitions. Otherwise the work remains exactly as it was until the point during the third scene when Zerbinetta suddenly interrupts Ariadne's apostrophe to her invisible and unrecognized liberator.

Although Hofmannsthal had once set such store by this intrusion, when Strauss later suggested cutting the entire scene the poet acknowledged that it held up the action. Thus when the time came to make revisions Hofmannsthal himself welcomed the proposed cut, describing it as 'excellent', although it entailed the exclusion of one of the only two passages in which any direct interaction existed between the rival factions of Opera Seria and Intermezzo. The cut itself makes a neat transition and omits not only the whole entrance of Zerbinetta but the greater part of the orchestral interlude which follows it. Interesting as this was orchestrally, it had undoubtedly left a very serious hiatus on the stage which the 'Starkes Heranschreiten' ('strong sound of striding footsteps approaching') did little or nothing to fill. Bacchus' entry gains enormously in dramatic effect from the tightening of the action.

Finally came the insoluble problem of the ending, a matter which was responsible for considerable hard feeling between Strauss and his librettist. Hofmannsthal's protests over Strauss's first ideas were so vehement and derogatory that one is strongly inclined to sympathize with Strauss writing back pathetically:

> 'Why do you always get so bitterly angry if for once we can't understand each other straightaway? ... my suggestions

concerning the end of *Ariadne* were only quite unconsidered ideas which you could have thrown into your wastepaper basket without another thought; their only purpose was to induce you to reconsider seriously the closing words of the Composer—and how was I to know that you might not think of something particularly brilliant for the ending if I told you that Artôt was to do it?'

Certainly a perplexing situation was caused by the absence of Jourdain on whom the final curtain so utterly depended. Strauss's proposal, which had caused the storm, consisted of replacing Jourdain by the Composer, thus providing an additional solo scene for this now infinitely more important personage. Such an idea would need much thought, but in itself was excellent. Hofmannsthal's objection, when reduced to essentials, proved to hinge on the mere duration of the Composer's return to the scene. Admittedly Strauss's idea that the Major-domo could pay the distraught Composer his salary was unduly prosaic, but when Hofmannsthal's indignation had died down he viewed the overall suggestion rather more favourably, and a few days even elapsed during which both men took it for granted that the Composer might reappear for the final curtain. This solution would have had the virtue of lightening the mood of grandiose over-inflation, always dangerously near the surface at the end of the Bacchus/Ariadne duet, as well as rounding off the whole work in the same way as in the original composite version.

It is thus the more disappointing to find the scheme once more abandoned with no alternative whatever to replace it. Hofmannsthal found it justifiably difficult to light on the correct phrases to put in the Composer's mouth:

'[these] final words which belong to the very fringe of the framework. Coming from Jourdain, the man of prose, that Monsieur tout-le-monde who hasn't an idea of what he has been up to and what he has set afoot, the words were organic. But coming from the Composer! For him to complain where the opera has after all succeeded in forging harmony out of the two components, that would be absurd; for him to rejoice would be more absurd still. There is a risk that this will make nonsense of the whole thing. A curse on all revision! I shall try my best to find a possible solution. What if the Major-domo were to speak these final words, with an air of smug satisfaction, to the Composer? In prose, like Jourdain?'

This line of reasoning had the unfortunate effect of persuading Strauss that the task should be given up as hopeless, even though it meant that the Composer, whom one would gladly have welcomed once more, never appears outside the Vorspiel. Hofmannsthal for his part agreed to this with a sigh of relief, making only the proviso that Zerbinetta be allowed to keep some brief last appearance in order that the symbolism of her role as 'human counterpart' to Ariadne should be retained in the closing scene, however momentarily. Strauss saw no problem here, making the insertion by simply superimposing Zerbinetta and her theme above the once so magical orchestral interlude before the final section of the duet (see above, p. 54). Visually Hofmannsthal found any adaptation unnecessary, the curtain merely closing upon Ariadne and Bacchus after the disappearance of the cave. He even rejected Strauss's suggestion of a tableau showing Bacchus' flower-laden ship, on the grounds that 'ships on the stage are pretty awful; even the fearless Reinhardt fights shy of them'.

The reappearance of the clowns could now be jettisoned *in toto*, together with the entire closing section which had once been specifically and shrewdly contrived to enliven the atmosphere after the long pre-occupation with the Divine Lovers. At the same time the comical ending had served to round off the encircling plan, still extant in the Vorspiel but easily forgotten in the opera, of a play within a play. All was abandoned and replaced impatiently by a mere three pages of majestic D flat major for the full instrumental ensemble in Strauss's richest style, combining as many of the relevant themes as possible. As Strauss quickly wrote FINE at the bottom of the last page he must have uttered a fervent prayer that, perfect or imperfect, this problem-child might at long last have found some definitive form.

25

The first performance of the new version of *Ariadne auf Naxos* took place in Vienna on 4th October 1916[41] and was followed a month later by the Berlin première. Though it had an adequate reception it was clearly no

[41] It is of particular interest to discover that the part of the Composer was taken by a young singer by the name of Lotte Lehmann. (Artôt gave the first performance in Berlin, where she was one of the regular singers in the Royal Opera.) Towards the end of his life Strauss wrote of this discovery of his: '. . . with the splendid Lotte Lehmann (who was later to sing Ariadne, Färberin, Arabella, Octavian [!]: an unparalleled Christine and unforgettable Marschallin) as Composer. She combined a warm voice and excellent diction with inspired acting ability and a beautiful stage appearance, all of which made her a unique interpreter of my female roles.'

furore. In Berlin, in particular, Strauss complained that the Vorspiel was not properly understood despite the care lavished on it by the Intendant, Count Hülsen. Even so, it quickly went the rounds of the German cities (Dresden, Breslau, Leipzig, Düsseldorf, etc.) until it steadily supplanted the original work in the repertory of opera houses.

The point was ultimately reached at which the first version was never performed except on isolated, and generally somewhat special, occasions. Sir Thomas Beecham discussed the reasons and merits of this state of affairs in his autobiography:[42]

> 'During the late spring [of 1913], by way of an interlude, I gave the *Ariadne auf Naxos* of Strauss at His Majesty's Theatre in conjunction with Sir Herbert Tree, who himself played the part of Monsieur Jourdain in the comedy. The work was given in English, translated from the German through the French by Somerset Maugham, whose equanimity was on more than one occasion disturbed by the actor-manager's propensity to forget his lines and substitute an improvised patter for the polished prose of that distinguished master of the vernacular. Otherwise Tree, who in this line of broad and fantastic comedy had hardly a rival, was capital, and the whole production was adjudged superior to the original given at Stuttgart in the previous year. In this, the earlier version of *Ariadne*, I have always considered that the musical accomplishment of Strauss attained its highest reach, yielding a greater spontaneity and variety of invention, together with a subtler and riper style, than anything that his pen had yet given to the stage. . . . It has to be admitted that it is neither an easy nor practicable sort of piece to give in an ordinary opera house, as it postulates the employment of a first-rate group of actors as well as singers; and for this reason, no doubt, the authors re-wrote it at a later period, making a full-blown opera of the old medley and thinking probably that they were making a very good job of it. The result has been doubly unfortunate, for the later version has not only failed to hold the stage, but has dimmed the public recollection of the far superior and more attractive original. Our only consolation is that here we have a rare and refreshing instance of the inability of Commerce to read a lesson to Art, with a nice touch of Nemesis thrown in.'

Despite the essential element of truth in Beecham's verdict, all is not loss. For the reasons already stated, the first version must inevitably be only rarely staged, but it continues to remain available for performance

[42] *A Mingled Chime*. Hutchinson, London, 1944.

should the opportunity occur. Meantime, *Ariadne auf Naxos* has certainly become widely known and appreciated through the ability of opera houses to mount the readily practicable revised version. In this respect Beecham goes too far: if the truncated *Ariadne* has failed to hold the stage in the sense of *Der Rosenkavalier* or even *Salome*, it is revived with sufficient regularity to make the music amongst the more familiar of Strauss's operatic scores; and without that familiarity it is unlikely that the considerably more artistic but costly original would ever be revived at all.

Although not perhaps the unqualified masterpiece it is often taken for, *Ariadne auf Naxos* in either version stands high in Strauss's artistic development. As an antithesis to Beecham's assessment here is Rolland's entry in his Journal for 1924:

> 'the comic part is pretty and well played; the vocal polka of
> the buffoons does not fail in its effect, but the impression of
> the whole is a deception. I have heard this work spoken of as
> Strauss's masterpiece! . . . It seems to me cold and hybrid.'

As always, there is perception here, and he rightly deplores the ending in the later version as 'a pompous and icy tragedy for two high-flown characters'. He wrote to Strauss with great wisdom:

> 'I have the feeling that Hofmannsthal begins each of his
> pastiches of olden times with an ironic design, but that his
> admirable virtuosity enables him to succeed so well that he
> always ends up by taking them seriously. And this is a pity:
> the whole value of a pastiche subject like *Ariadne* lies in its
> irony; and this irony must above all blossom out at the end,
> . . . I regret . . . that in the definitive version the buffo
> figures have been eliminated from the ending.'

26

(iii) The Play without the Opera

Whatever the failings or virtues of *Ariadne II*, as it has come to be called, its greatest disadvantage was undoubtedly the sacrifice of the Incidental Music to the Molière portion of the original score, which now stood in considerable danger of total neglect. Hofmannsthal had himself long maintained that this was music of an especial quality, particularly with regard to consistency of style.

His affection for it was corroborated by a chance remark of Hermann Bahr, a dramatist friend[43] who described Strauss's character as a mixture of 'hearty Bavarian with a witty, subtle mind', commenting that the music for the *Bourgeois* was the most beautiful thing he had ever done.

Hofmannsthal was sufficiently stimulated by such praise to wonder whether there might not be some way in which so much good material could be saved. A highly successful revival of another Molière comedy *Le Malade Imaginaire* in Reinhardt's Deutsches Theater strengthened Hofmannsthal in his belief that a complete version of *Le Bourgeois Gentilhomme* with the same principal comedian, Pallenberg, in the title role might have a similar success.

Accordingly, in July 1916, even before the première of the revised *Ariadne*, Hofmannsthal proposed to Strauss yet another reworking in which this time the Molière was to be rehabilitated.

> 'Please, dear Dr Strauss, do not rashly waste these pieces of music; I am sure I shall succeed in inventing a second delicate action for this comedy (centred on the daughter) which lends itself to music, to replace that conventional subsidiary plot. I will make the whole thing into a genuine half fantastic, half realistic *Singspiel*, with a burlesque ceremony at the end where Jourdain as Pasha finally launches out on the pond in a Turkish carnival bark while the lovers remain behind in the moonlight—just the thing for Reinhardt.'

This entailed still further rehashing of the now five-years-old material, and even resuscitating more of the Molière, including those parts which had been written off as 'pretty feeble stuff'. It must have been a curious experience for Strauss to watch Hofmannsthal waxing enthusiastic not only over the very stage boats he had just ridiculed in connexion with the finale to *Ariadne*, but a restoration of precisely the most absurd section of Molière's comedy, the Turkish ceremony, which he had been the first to dismiss as utter nonsense.

Yet when the early months of 1917 arrived, and the end of the full score of *Die Frau ohne Schatten* was in sight, no new project had been mooted by Hofmannsthal. The war was still dragging on and Strauss dreaded the empty summer which loomed ahead with no work on hand

[43] Bahr became closely involved with the gestation of *Intermezzo* (see Chapter XIII).

to occupy him. He accordingly allowed himself to be persuaded to enter into negotiations with the Reinhardt brothers (Max's affairs being always dealt with through Edmund) and to plan the first performance of the reconstituted *Der Bürger als Edelmann*. The date was fixed for 9th April the following year, with a two months' run to follow.

27

It was now Strauss's turn to stir Hofmannsthal into more vigorous action by means of a good-humoured note to the effect that 'Edmund R. [is being] extremely generous, so I think you can get down to work without any worries. Meantime, I am slowly training my charger to a Turkish trot; I've also got old Lully handy, but there's hardly anything in him that's any use, except a little distilled mustiness as a stimulant, like Schiller's apples!' In fact, Strauss did draw to quite a considerable extent on material which he unearthed from Lully's score and which he used both to supply period atmosphere to the work and to carry his imagination over so unstimulating a task.

In the meantime, Strauss actually began drafting some ideas for the Turkish ceremony, while Hofmannsthal soon put his mind to what could be made of the Molière adaptation from his own point of view. After working for a month the poet came to feel that it was causing him more trouble than he had expected, but nevertheless when towards the middle of May he found himself near the end he grudgingly admitted that he had in fact enjoyed it.

> 'I believe that without any harm being done to the basic structure, it has become enchanting, richer, more glowing than the original play, where the author's genius comes out chiefly in the central character, while a lot of the rest gives the impression of having been put together in a hurry and scribbled down, so to speak, with the left hand.'

Hofmannsthal's criticism of Molière's play, though damning, was an understandable viewpoint, and indeed both he and Strauss had been very conscious of the slender nature of the last acts when they had decided to make use of only the earlier portions. Yet in their new-found eagerness they had now fallen into the error of believing that elaboration and rewriting could build something of interest out of the remainder.

Hofmannsthal again treated Strauss very high-handedly over the shape the revised work was to take. He seems to have been on the offensive immediately he put pen to paper, partly perhaps because of a realization that he would derive little or no credit from a great deal of skill and hard work. He had already, only a few months previously, completely rewritten another Molière (*Les Facheux*) for Reinhardt, in which he had the malicious satisfaction of watching the critics' failure to realize that every line had been his work rather than that of the French comedian. He was now determined again to remain anonymous, and indeed both on the theatre billings of the first production and to this day in the score no names appear other than those of Strauss and Molière.

There is here an element of the ridiculous, since Hofmannsthal imposed on Strauss a number of features which the composer did not care for in the least. The first act, for instance, was to end with a new scene between Lucile and Jourdain which was to be entirely without music.[44]

It is true that Strauss had not understood the radical nature of Hofmannsthal's interpolations, but in any case a curtain without music seemed to him inconceivable, and he proposed instead bringing the act to an end much as in the first version (see p. 21), though perhaps with Dorante and Jourdain bowing each other out *à la* Ford and Falstaff in Verdi's opera. In a musical work such as this, he pointed out, each act must be introduced and effectively concluded with music.

In line with this requirement, Hofmannsthal found an ingenious way of preserving Jourdain's last speech of all by transferring it to the end of Act 2 (see p. 89), but now Strauss felt the overall effect of the act itself to be weak: 'pretty as it is, I don't expect it to have an over-great success with the audience.'

As for Act 3 with all its Turkish tomfoolery, in contrast to his original indictment, we find Hofmannsthal describing it as consisting of a series of delicate melodramas 'between Jourdain and some sylphs or spirits . . . in which seriousness and jest, sentiment and caricature are mingled.' This seems wishful thinking, for indeed it is difficult to imagine anything more artificial. Even before seeing Hofmannsthal's draft Strauss wrote in despair that it seemed to him extremely risky and terribly unrewarding musically. He begged Hofmannsthal to recall the ghastly fiasco at Stuttgart in which the humour was so embarrassing and the curtains at the end of each act so lame that he could have crawled under the music desk.

[44] In Molière, true to seventeenth-century custom, Lucile never confronts her father directly at all.

He was convinced that the play must end with some large-scale ballet with singing, making use of all the performers who had appeared during the course of the evening.

Hofmannsthal's replies to these most genuine and relevant points were high-handed and patronizing, and Strauss wrote straight back begging to be left out altogether. The best plan would be for Hofmannsthal and Reinhardt to produce the new version with no more than 'a mere thin varnish of rearranged music from Lully.' Hofmannsthal had to woo him back with the same argument he had used with respect to *Ariadne*—that his only purpose in working on the project at all was to serve Strauss and his music.

Nevertheless, within a few weeks he was again bullying Strauss unmercifully on the grounds of his own superior sense of style and more reliable taste. He even felt sufficiently sure of his power over Strauss to be able to write:

> 'Your proposals I consider ... beneath discussion. They demonstrate to me that your taste and mine are miles apart. ... Pray let me have in due course your decision whether I am free to dispose otherwise of this Molière adaptation, of which I do not intend to alter one iota ... your critical remarks reveal such absolute incomprehension ... of what I have tried to do, and have accomplished by devoting to it for two months every effort of my imagination, my artistic sensitivity, my tact and self-effacement [!]; there was something so devastating in the vista opened up by your finding it possible, after reading this play three times, to put forward proposals of this kind which make nonsense of the whole thing, that it was my first impulse to wire and ask you to leave it alone and never speak to me, or write of it again.'

Since he had, of course, no intention of breaking with Strauss, he continued to explain in profound, philosophical detail why everything he had written was right and unchangeable and why all Strauss's ideas were tasteless and impossible.

So Strauss, apart from a few increasingly feeble and apologetic protests on the main points, crumpled and produced by the sweat of his brow, and without a trace of inspiration, the additional settings for the text Hofmannsthal pushed at him, precisely as it stood, taking considerable comfort in the fact that Fürstner, his publisher, had at least managed to make very attractive financial arrangements out of the whole dreary assignment.

28

Although the first act was intended to correspond for much of its course with the original opening, the young Composer had been brought into such prominence in the revised version of *Ariadne* that Hofmannsthal decided to exclude him altogether from *Der Bürger als Edelmann*.

As a result there was no longer a place for the arietta, Ex. 3, and this in turn meant the jettisoning of the closing section of Strauss's overture. The curtain rises, therefore, immediately after the trumpet solo, Ex. 2. The Music Master and the Dancing Master then speak their opening lines over music and the number ends with slight alterations of tempo and dynamics at the point which previously had led into the arietta.

One of Hofmannsthal's main objects in his revision of Molière's text was to transfer the emphasis to precisely the subject which he had previously omitted, that is to say, the two pairs of lovers: the master and mistress (Lucile and Cléonte) and their servants (Nicole[45] and Covielle). He accordingly interpolated a scene here at the very beginning in which Covielle outlines to the two girls the hazards and problems besetting Cléonte in his courtship of Lucile.

In these circumstances it might have been thought that Hofmannsthal would have provided an opportunity for Strauss to write a little piece with perhaps some motifs for these new characters. On the contrary, Hofmannsthal even removed large sections of the original text, embodying musical cuts as well, to make room for his own new scene. The arietta had already gone: next to go were Jourdain's *couplets*, no great loss in themselves perhaps, but entailing still more pages of uninterrupted dialogue without music. Strauss fought a rearguard action over this number but, as always, Hofmannsthal was adamant,[46] and, apart from the few bars accompanying Jourdain's entrance, the first musical number is now the *Musikalisches Gespräch* of the Shepherd and Shepherdess, Ex. 5.[47]

Apart from the omission of various references to the opera and its characters (Zerbinetta, etc.) the text then continues as in the original for the Minuet (Ex. 6) and the scene with the Fencing Master (Ex. 7). The

---

[45] Nicole had appeared in the original version, though with a greatly reduced role.

[46] Nevertheless Strauss did, some time after the publication of the vocal score, slyly have the *couplets* restored into the full score, as an 'Insert No 2a'!

[47] The voice parts in the score still contain the indications 'later Dryade' and 'later Najade'.

farcical entrance of the Master of Philosophy was excised and his scene
drastically cut and revised, removing Molière's comic passages in favour
of new lines bringing the Philosopher into the main drama of Lucile's
oppositions to her father's wishes.

Strauss regretted the loss of Molière's lines here, but while Hofmannsthal conceded that 'opinions may well differ on the absence of the
spelling lesson' he went on petulantly:

> 'Reinhardt and I find it clumsy and tedious (although it does
> raise a laugh or two; this is quite irrelevant, since the secret of
> comedy is in the rhythm and not in occasionally titillating the
> sense of the ridiculous) and so, without discussion we agreed
> that it had to go. The essential gain of my treatment of the
> Philosopher has unfortunately escaped you like *everything*,
> *everything* else in my work.'

Again the revisions provided no new opportunity for music which
only returns for the scene of the Tailors (Exx. 8 and 9). This remains as it
was except for cuts in the dialogue, including Molière's dig at the
idiocies of fashion as exemplified by the upside-down floral embroidery
(see p. 17). Indeed it was by now amply clear that Molière's style of
humour had become distasteful to Hofmannsthal, perhaps on account
of its failure with audiences during the war years, during which the
excerpts contained in the first version had been playing in the various
opera houses of Germany and Austria with variable success.

Even the scene with Dorante which still follows the ballet of the
Tailors is played without Madame Jourdain and Nicole. It is this time the
turn of the down-to-earth, slightly vulgar Madame Jourdain to be
removed from the Dramatis Personae of Hofmannsthal's rewritten
version, and with her goes most of the comic by-play which the sophisticated Viennese poet had come to find so crude.

The Dorante scene accordingly had to be entirely reconsidered and
Hofmannsthal decided to sandwich the episode of his extravagant loans
between endless discussions concerning Dorimène and an elaborate
ceremony involving the use of a new coach which Jourdain is to put at
her disposal. Here again there is no opening for Strauss who wrote
imploring for 'a dash of really pleasant music, not just a few stop-gap
squeaks . . . I know exactly what, if I'm to have a share in this business,
the public expects of me. In fact, everybody is saying to me about the
two acts of Molière we've got now: "Why so little music?"'

Hofmannsthal, however, was already planning quite independently that there was to be no further music for the remainder of the act, and Strauss, who already felt that the Dorante scene was too long, even had to press for his curtain music. At the end of the closing scene Lucile and Nicole laugh at Jourdain, and Lucile reproachfully quarrels with her father over Cléonte and her prospective marriage. The bemused, day-dreaming Jourdain then pre-enacts in dumb pantomime (and to Lucile's despair) the coach ceremony planned for Dorimène.

There is obvious opportunity for music here, but the curtain itself was only finally decided upon after various alternatives had been mooted and rejected, including re-entrances of Dorante or even of the Tailors. At last Strauss received a conditional go-ahead from Hofmannsthal provided there was no singing, which was a relief as he 'had already sketched some rather pretty music for it'.

Nevertheless, pretty as it might be, it cannot be compared with the splendid original movements. Essentially it consists of a couple of dozen bars of colourful orchestration and sliding harmonies combining the motif of Dorimène and Dorante (Ex. 10) and Jourdain's, Exx. 1 and 2, before bringing the curtain down with a rumbustious flourish.

The characteristic progressions, on the other hand, are interesting because they are typical of Strauss's increasing nonchalance with regard to the vertical sound of passing notes. Many such instances occur in, for example, the ballet *Schlagobers*:

Ex. 55

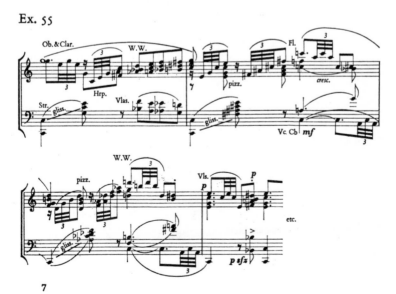

7

Hofmannsthal now divided his second act into two parts, relegating the entrance of Dorante and Dorimène and the supper scene to the latter half. A new Prelude to Act 2 was accordingly needed since the original movement (Ex. 10) would now be taking over the function of intermezzo. Having searched once more through Lully, Strauss decided to use the Minuet—which he conceded to be charming—for his new Prelude. He dressed it up in gently modern harmonic and instrumental guise, abandoning any thought of classical tradition such as the use of continuo; even the piano, which he had introduced into the earlier numbers five years before, was excluded both here and in most of the subsequent arrangements he made of Lully's music.

The Minuet appears in Lully's own Incidental Music to *Le Bourgeois Gentilhomme*, written on a single line for the Dancing Master to intone while delivering frenzied instruction to the maladroit Jourdain, viz:

Ex. 56

Nevertheless, although the strain has become so familiar through its comic appearance in *Le Bourgeois Gentilhomme*, Lully was himself quoting from his music to another Molière comedy, *Les Amants Magnifiques*, composed in the same year, 1670. In this work it appears fully harmonized and in perfect seriousness as a 'menuet pour les Faunes et les Dryades' during the elaborate ballet music which is so substantial a feature of the piece.

The new first part of Act 2 is almost entirely fresh matter. It presents the lovers, with Cléonte's servant Covielle as a Master of Intrigues, Organiser of Machinations, the Figaro, so to speak, of the group. A misunderstanding between Lucile and Cléonte is resolved just in time for Cléonte to escape before the rapid arrival of Jourdain. Together with Jourdain, unexpectedly enough, is the Master of Philosophy, for Hofmannsthal had the idea of confronting Lucile with him in order to link up at least one of Jourdain's instructor-figures with the remainder of the plot.

Covielle now reappears in full disguise, masquerading as Ambassador to the Son of the Grand Turk, the only scene from Molière included so far in this act.

The essence of Molière's sub-plot is that since Cléonte can never hope to be accepted by Jourdain as a son-in-law in his own right, not being of noble birth, he carries forward his suit of Lucile by means of this preposterous impersonation. In so doing he not only drives Jourdain's obsession to its ultimate absurdity but succeeds during the closing lines of the comedy in securing Jourdain's consent to his marriage. The whole of this denouement occurs at the end of Molière's play[48] and as a result the proposed marriage is mooted without delay by the disguised Covielle, after which Cléonte's entry with the hordes of Turks close upon his heels follows immediately.

Hofmannsthal, however, decided to divide the Turkish ceremony, Cléonte's entrance as a Turk being brought forward to Act 2 at a point before the dinner scene to give it increased stature and significance. By this means Jourdain can be made to receive his 'distinguished visitor' on two separate occasions, the first visit preparing the ground for the elaborate ceremony of the second. The next music cue therefore accompanies the entrance of Cléonte dressed up to represent the Grand Turk's son himself.

Here Strauss once again drew from Lully and, by resetting some appropriate movements, supplied the background music to the scene accompanying the dialogue in which the reluctant Lucile is hastily brought into the plot against her father by the disguised Covielle. The movements Strauss chose for the purpose proved to be only partially from Lully's *Bourgeois Gentilhomme* music, the opening Sarabande being the 'Air pour les Bergers' from the ballet *George Dandin ou le Grand Divertissement Royal de Versailles* which Lully composed by royal command in 1668.

This is succeeded by a rapid little dance in triple rhythm, Lully's 'Troisième Air' from the Turkish ceremony. Strauss transposes it a fourth higher and sets it for a sextet of woodwind with triangle, in contrast to the *George Dandin* Sarabande which was given to a string octet. After further unaccompanied dialogue the Sarabande returns for the majestic entrance of Cléonte dressed up as a Turkish potentate. Here it is rescored for the full available forces, including an independent trumpet fanfare and with the percussion department stepped up to five players

---

[48] Act 4, Scenes 5 et seq. and the whole of Act 5.

(two more than in the original score, on account of the Turkish element in the new sections).[49]

The music finishes shortly before the end of the scene and the curtain falls on a departing Cléonte. After the Intermezzo (the original Prelude to Act 2, Ex. 10, as already mentioned) the entire scene of Dorante and Dorimène follows together with the supper, which is largely unchanged.

Next to his suppression of Madame Jourdain, the most striking change in Molière's comedy which Hofmannsthal made was his addition of four entirely new characters to the cast, extremely dubious persons called Mascarille, Nerine, Lucette and Charles. Mascarille claims to be an old army colleague whom Dorante has taken the liberty of inviting to Jourdain's house, together with two of his doxies who masquerade as noble ladies from Madrid. Charles is an enigmatic figure who appears to have been brought along as a kind of bogus chaperone to the two girls but clearly occupies a menial position in Dorante's household. After supper these intruders force Jourdain to gamble and are only prevented from stripping their unfortunate host of huge sums of money by the timely intervention of the conscience-stricken Dorante.

Before they take their leave, the guests dance a Courante, and this time Strauss had a return of inspiration which resulted in a very attractive dance movement in a similar pastiche to the opening numbers, though still wholly individual in idiom. It is based on a series of canons (indeed Strauss actually emphasized the fact in the title of the piece 'Courante, in Canonform') of considerable ingenuity and contrapuntal dexterity:

Ex. 57

and later:

[49] The Turks have always been regarded as specialists in the percussion field. Whenever they have impinged on the musical scene, as in Mozart's *Die Entführung aus dem Serail*, Beethoven's *Ruins of Athens* or Weber's *Abu Hassan*, triangle, cymbals and bass drum have been present in the score. It is interesting, moreover, that to this day the finest cymbals and tam-tams are made by a justly celebrated family in Istanbul.

The canons continue throughout the length of the movement, save only
the opening and closing bars. For these Strauss wrote a typical surging
phrase which, acting equally well as introduction and coda, rounds off
the movement with both *élan* and delicacy.

The guests depart and Jourdain is left contemplating the scene which
has just drawn to a close, a meditation which is the more puzzling owing
to certain enigmatic remarks made to him by the Marquise. There is a
suggestion here of a charade enveloping Jourdain which is never fully
explained but was perhaps intended to provide some further justification
for Hofmannsthal's use of Jourdain's ironical lines concerning the aristocracy, which he had saved from the final bars of the first *Ariadne* score.
They accordingly find here a not inapposite resting place in very much
their original musical setting, though with a soft ending, as the curtain
of this revised second act.

30

Strauss's first intention had been to write a Prelude to Hofmannsthal's
Act 3 based on material which was to have been composed around the
lovers. But when it came to the point he had neither the opportunity nor
inclination and therefore simply improvised a gentle *alla Sicilienne*, both
as a curtain-raiser and for the new scene of the spirits which Hofmannsthal had written for the opening of the act. The music, if pleasant, is
undistinguished although interesting for the ingenious way in which
Jourdain's Ex. 1 appears and reappears in the texture, as well as for the
indications it affords, as in Ex. 55, of Strauss's new ballet style of non-
chalant harmonic clashes and false relations.

Ex. 58

The movement is worked as a melodrama during which, as Covielle explains to Nicole in the opening lines, Jourdain is to be hoodwinked into believing that his blood may be transformed into the true blue blood of the nobility. To this purpose minerals and waters from the centre of the earth will provide his daily bath, in which he will be ministered unto by magic spirits, enacted by the gardener's daughter and Jourdain's own stable-boys all dressed up.

This far-fetched nonsense was perhaps intended by Hofmannsthal to stimulate Strauss into inventing some colourful orchestral effects. It is indeed very similar to several passages in *Die Frau ohne Schatten* for which Strauss had just completed some of his most imaginative scoring. In much the same way as the Färberin in that opera, Jourdain is handed a magic potion by the sylphs, after which a mirror is brought for him to see the transformation. This time, however, Strauss found himself too restricted to comply; Ex. 58, which contains in figure ⌐ x ⌐ the principal theme of the section, is used exclusively throughout, the gently flowing passage-work being at times interrupted by the dialogue, at other times left to continue while the dialogue is superimposed—a prevalence of melodrama which had already given Strauss some concern when Hofmannsthal first outlined the scheme of his new third act.

The absence of singing further thwarted Strauss's ingenious plan of allowing the singers of the Shepherd and Shepherdess Duet (No. 3 of the Incidental Music) to reappear as sylphs. Had they done so, they would not only have established themselves to far greater advantage but would have enhanced the general effect; even the opportunities for dancing in this scene cannot compare with earlier examples of the kind such as the Tailors or the Dinner.

With the disappearance of the sylphs, Covielle returns to the important matter in hand, the projected uniting of Lucile with the son of the Grand Turk. Hearing the approach of Turkish music Jourdain sends

hastily for his daughter and, simultaneously, for a notary. The Turkish
ceremony follows with the entrance of the Mufti and his dervishes.

31

We have already seen that Strauss had intended to complete this most
extended section of the score before embarking on any of the rest. It
consists, however, of Molière's Act 4 virtually unchanged, and this was a
scene which he had always felt to be lamentably foolish; to set it to music
proved to be something of a chore. Nevertheless he managed to concoct
a spiky theme aimed at being Turkish in idiom, set in appropriately exotic
orchestration.

Ex. 59

Strauss found it hard to maintain this movement at any great length without slipping into music more reminiscent of Harlequin and his colleagues than of the idiotic Turkish Chorus who intone their 'Allah! Alli, Allah eckbar' as the piece proceeds.

Ex. 60

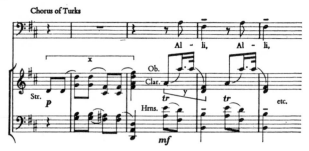

Jourdain's embarrassing re-entrance dressed as a Turk, his head shaved, is the cue for his Ex. 1 to be combined with Ex. 59, but beyond this even Strauss's imagination could stretch no further; accordingly he now decided to draw liberally from 'old Lully'. The Mufti's air is taken almost note for note from Lully's score, though its phrases are punctuated by the figure Ex. 60(y). Moreover, after a Dance, in which another of the little Turkish motifs (Ex. 59(y)) is combined with the seventeenth-century pastiche both directly and in inversion, Lully's second air for the Mufti is transcribed with again little alteration. In between these last two movements there is a brief quotation of the passage from the Overture to Act 1 in which Jourdain's Ex. 1 appeared in augmentation.

The second air of the Mufti is now arranged for baritone with a chorus of dervishes. The orchestra adds embroidering counterpoints, at the climax of which Ex. 59 is further superimposed on the whole structure. During the course of this episode Jourdain has been taken off as an Unbeliever by two dervishes, and the Turks headed by the Mufti pray to Mohammed, in Molière's Italianate Lingua Franca.

A new movement now starts, based on Ex. 60(y), in which Jourdain, after returning, is made to go down on his hands and knees so that his back may serve as a reading desk for a huge Koran. When the Mufti is satisfied that Jourdain intends to adopt the true faith he raises him to his feet and equips him with sabre and turban as insignia of noble rank, upon which his promotion is confirmed by blows which are rained on him by the sabres and sticks of the dancing Turks. The ceremony being now completed, the Mufti is surrounded by dervishes and led away with immense pomp as the music whirls to a brilliant and exciting end. The thematic material at Strauss's disposal may have been contrived, even commonplace, but he had no trouble in building up an extended symphonic movement. By the time the Lully air had covered the moment of flagging inspiration Strauss had got his second wind and was able to whip up Exx. 59 and 60 into a satisfactory formal design of the requisite length and vivacity. This was, of course, crucial since on this movement hinges the musical interest of the act and hence of the piece as a whole.

32

Molière made the uniting of Lucile and her lover dependent on the support of Madame Jourdain who, distressed at seeing her husband made a laughing-stock on every side, is determined that his foolish notions with regard to the nobility shall not be allowed to ruin their lives and that of their daughter. With the suppression of this all important character Hofmannsthal had no recourse left but to bring about the wedding without even exposing the preposterous burlesque of which Jourdain has been the victim. Molière himself had only added it in the first place under pressure from the Court on the grounds that the Roi Soleil, Louis XIV, had conceived the desire to take part in the performance dressed up as a Turk.

Although Molière had perforce to indulge his monarch's grotesque whim, there was never any question of his allowing the farcical finale to acquire undue importance, or for the performance to end on a false note of seriousness. Yet, as in *Ariadne II*, it is just such a serious mood which Hofmannsthal's version labours. Jourdain's earnest self-importance is preserved to the very end through the interpolation of a closing speech, similar—though weaker in pathos—to that with which the original composite scheme had ended and which had, moreover, been additionally rescued for the curtain of Act 2.

The new ending inescapably called for yet more use of melodrama, and Strauss, in drafting the finale, struggled hard to avoid the fragmentary character which such a scheme threatened to produce. He was in any case far from convinced by Hofmannsthal's solution. Humbly he wrote:

> 'Now the main point: but please don't kill me. It seems to me that the piece ought to have a fourth act. The third act with the simple wedding of Lucile and Cléonte is absolutely no

ending for a play that is entitled *Der Bürger als Edelmann* and
represents a comedy of manners, fitted almost exclusively
around that one figure. Besides, Dorante and Dorimène now
just fade out and all connexion with the other comedy, which
is hinted at very prettily in Molière, at least towards the end,
is lacking in your version.

To my mind the piece ought to end quite grotesquely,
either with a merry eye-opener and cure for Jourdain, like
Don Quixote, or as a tragi-comedy with the eye-opening
being followed by Jourdain's complete collapse and possibly
madness. Do think it over, please! Don't be angry with me!'

But Hofmannsthal was angry, very angry. It is regrettable that he
could not follow Strauss's reasoning objectively because there was
much truth in his criticism even if his solutions, ventured off the cuff,
were unsatisfactory. The idea of yet another act would prolong an
already slender work beyond endurance; for Jourdain actually to lose his
reason would produce a sudden element of tragedy out of keeping with
the frivolity of the work as a whole. Yet Hofmannsthal's scathing reply
(already quoted above, p. 82) precluded discussion or compromise on the
controversial issues at any level, both by its tone—for which, to do him
justice, Hofmannsthal tried later to show regret—and by its utter rejection of Strauss's very artistry. By setting himself up as Strauss's superior
in intellect and taste he even allowed himself in a fit of temper to liken
Molière's original comedy to an old ill-constructed summerhouse and
Strauss's proposals to 'a high wall shutting out the main view', a 'brick
thrown at a mirror in passing' and 'a dung-heap put in place of a fountain'.

Sad reading as this makes, there are nevertheless further paragraphs
which are in the best sense revealing of Hofmannsthal's literary judgement and erudition, for which Strauss had the highest respect.

Yet even these qualities show the poet's way of conjuring up ever-new
corners to think round. Thus his decision to rewrite Molière required
the new premise that the original is basically poor and 'incomprehensible
by present-day standards'. Once he had managed so to convince himself
the remainder of the argument followed swiftly: it was no more than his
duty to supply new scenes which with 'subtle transposition and so on'
would make his work far surpass the original, 'rapidly thrown off, as it
was, and obviously improvised in construction'. Moreover, since his
version was completely successful in overcoming the inadequacies of
Molière's denouement he could brook no criticism or suggestions from

so patently inferior an artistic mind as the world-famous composer whose collaboration he had once sought so eagerly. Strauss's objection that the *demi-monde* figures, as Hofmannsthal described Dorante and Dorimène, must appear in the closing scene for formal balance (Molière has them married by the same notary who performs the ceremony for Cléonte and Lucile) was dismissed out of hand.

> 'It was the adaptor's task to make these figures more specific and definite, and to concentrate them into one distinct episode. I have made them definite (morally and socially), have placed Dorimène the highest (she is far more dupe than accomplice) Dorante in the middle as a confidence man, but a dashing and not altogether repellent figure, and to throw him into a stronger relief have surrounded him by worse sharpers still; yet I have packed the whole thing and finished it in one clear-cut episode (Act 2 second half). This episode is finished and done with and that alone is reason enough to keep these two characters out of the ending. But their exclusion is vital for two reasons above all; first so as not to complicate the various strands of the ending to an intolerable degree, and secondly for a moral reason far more significant still, because any connexion . . . between this group of base scoundrels, and the story of the lovers would inevitably debase the young couple.'

There was clearly no help but for Strauss to fall in with Hofmannsthal's fixed ideas without further argument. A plan for the finale had already been laid down in detail: 'begin your whole musical finale . . . at the point where the lovers re-enter, continue it with melodrama passages which now form the end and finish up with the vaudeville, a few lines sung by the nymph (who would come on the stage once again with a mirror), a few lines by Jourdain, and ensemble. . . .' and this scheme Strauss obediently followed in all essentials.

Since to him it did not ring true, however, it did not suggest any new musical ideas and Strauss accordingly fell back on Lully once more. The entrance of the plighted pair Cléonte and Lucile (Cléonte still masquerading as the Turk) is made to the famous Minuet, Ex. 56, and, as Jourdain repeats to himself the bogus Italian phrases used by the chorus during the Turkish ceremony, Strauss ingeniously combines Ex. 56 with the bass line of Lully's 'Air du Mufti'.

Jourdain next delivers his blessing on the pair while swinging his sabre over them and repeating further lines of the Italian burlesquerie, one of Hofmannsthal's less happy ideas but which Strauss dutifully set

to the theme of the Turkish Chorus, Ex. 60. The Minuet and the Turkish
motif are then worked together while Lucile and Cléonte pronounce
their oath of obedience and loyalty, after which Jourdain calls for a
mirror, on the grounds that he can only believe in the truth of what
seems to be happening if he can see himself simultaneously with the
other participants in the scene.

His demand provides the excuse for the return of the nymphs, who
dance on holding the mirror to a recapitulation of the ballet music from
the beginning of the act, Ex. 58. This leads to the lines sung by the three
nymphs—the opportunity for which Strauss had been waiting to allow
the erstwhile shepherds of Act I to sing again. For the purpose he
transcribed the choral *Seconde chanson à boire* from Lully's original music
for the Dinner Scene, 'Sus, sus, du vin partout', as a madrigal for three
voices, piano and strings.

Strauss oddly retained Lully's third voice as a bass even though Jourdain's musicians had all been transformed into sylphs. His explanation for
this has at least the virtue of expediency: 'We have three female sylphs
from the beginning of Act 3, of whom one can now act as a dancer and
the other two as singers (soprano and contralto, as in the duet in Act I).
For a third singing sylph I shall then take the earlier Mufti.'

Hofmannsthal had his doubts over the madrigal, especially in view of
the draft text which Strauss improvised roughly over the notes in the
manner of Lully's original. But Strauss knew exactly what kind of verses
he needed for the little piece and gave the poet a clear indication which
Hofmannsthal, however reluctantly, was able to follow up adequately:

Yet for all its period charm on which Strauss depended, the madrigal remains a stilted interpolation, and one heaves a sigh of relief when the music swings out of it by way of Jourdain's Ex. 1 into true Straussian orchestral gestures of Ex. 60 which match the grotesque obeisances with which the Turks and dervishes take their leave of Jourdain. There is an instrumental postlude as the ridiculous throng make their escape (embodying a descending sequence of phrases from Ex. 61) leading into a quiet ⁶⁄₈ movement for the exit, hand in hand, of Cléonte and Lucile.

The mood is ready, and the orchestration right, for the appearance of the Sicilienne, Ex. 3 'Du Venus' Sohn', but with an effort one realises that this has no place in the present scheme and instead, fragments of Ex. 1 are put forward tentatively, interspersed with silences. Gradually the music gathers confidence and returns to the sylphs' dance themes with which the act began, Ex. 58. As this flows peacefully along Jourdain, now left alone but for Nicole and Covielle, looks around him bewildered at the departed magic. He gives Nicole his sabre, Covielle his turban to hold, and then in a last sentence spoken over the dying phrases of music expresses his regret that the notary had not taken an official record of the events just concluded. Only this, he is sure, would convince the many jealous people who will refuse to believe the truth. The passage closes with the ingenious cadential phrase Ex. 58a, a last nostalgic reference to Lully's Minuet, Ex. 56, and a quiet cadence, each bass note of which is preceded by Jourdain's characteristic descending seventh, Ex. 1(x).

33

The whole soft ending in the aftermath of the preceding hurly-burly ought to be immensely affecting, especially as this is a device at which Strauss normally excels. If it fails to be so it is partly because the emotional temperature of the music has been too low throughout but also to a large extent because the dramatic situation does not touch the heart. Even Jourdain has lost our sympathy by this time and his lamentable closing speech is but a weak echo of the phrases which ended the original scheme. In Molière Madame Jourdain remains as a strong prop for her misguided husband, while meantime the triple marriage (Lucile/Cléonte, Nicole/Covielle, Dorimène/Dorante) and its attendant festivities provide a grand climax to the evening's entertainment. In Hofmannsthal's version, Jourdain is indeed left alone and with even his pathos misfiring the work ends with a whimper.

It is thus hardly surprising that despite all Max Reinhardt's care the production, which opened in the Deutsches Theater Berlin on 9th April 1918 was a flop. After only a few performances *Der Bürger als Edelmann* was quickly dropped out of the repertoire and has had only a single revival in 1924 in Vienna under the composer himself. In view of the omission of Hofmannsthal's name from the venture, Strauss was wholly saddled with the débâcle, and he must have found it galling when Hofmannsthal, while pretending to shoulder the blame, at the same time attributed the failure to the music rather than to his own reworking of Molière's comedy.

Characteristically the salt was rubbed into the wound with the utmost subtlety in a positive masterpiece of a letter:

> '... the fault is, if anyone's, mine; I ought to have realized that the public ... will take to anything elaborate and complicated, because it impresses them, as well as to the vile and commonplace, but will not put up with old-fashioned works like this one which are meagre and, for all their delicacy, naïve and puppet-like. And so I went wrong when ... acting more from wholly unselfish motives I brought up the Molière play once again in order to rescue those enchanting fragments of incidental music—though in this case I must say I was encouraged and confirmed in my mistake by the great and lasting success at the same theatre, with the same comedian, by an equally naïve prose comedy of Molière's, *Le Malade Imaginaire*. It was only this success which, in the spring of 1916, decided me to arrange *Le Bourgeois Gentil-*

homme for you. And so we arrive at the paradoxical result that the interposition of your music, music which receives the highest possible praise, has turned a Molière play, with Pallenberg in the title part, into a definite failure. . . .'

Hofmannsthal goes on to suggest yet a further redrafting in which with the use of *recitativo secco* the Molière might actually be turned into an opera. Never does he show a glimpse of understanding exactly where his share of the failure lies; in tinkering ruthlessly with the text of one brilliant man of the theatre, Molière, and in trampling upon the suggestions of another instinctive master, Strauss, he had actually taken away the sparkle and lifelike qualities of the characters of the comedy. Without those qualities Strauss's imagination proved unable to work upon them and his music was still-born. Fortunately, Strauss had really had enough and absolutely refused to reconsider the subject for yet a fourth time. The chapter was closed and was not to be reopened ever again.

(iv) *The Orchestral Suite and Summing Up*

34

It has been a long and complicated tale, and some résumé may not come amiss. Out of all Strauss and Hofmannsthal's working and reworking three distinct pieces emerge together with excerpts from these pieces:

(a) *Ariadne auf Naxos—zu spielen nach dem Bürger als Edelmann des Molière.* i.e. the combined play and opera.

(b) *Ariadne auf Naxos—oper in einem Aufzug nebst einem Vorspiel von Hugo von Hofmannsthal.* i.e. the opera without the play.

(c) *Der Bürger als Edelmann—Komödie mit Tänzen von Molière, Freie Bühnenbearbeitung in drei Aufzügen.* i.e. the play without the opera.

Of these (a) was, with all its faults, a masterpiece but one which can by its very nature only be given occasionally under special circumstances; (b) is variable in quality and a mixed success; despite the artificiality of its libretto it holds its place in the operatic repertoire owing to the undeniable beauty and enchanting felicities of much of the music; (c) is a total failure and has entirely disappeared as a stage work.

An orchestral suite was, however, drawn from (c) (though the opening movement is in fact given according to (a)) and presented by Strauss for the first time on 31st January 1920 in Salzburg. This did indeed have the effect sought after by Hofmannsthal of preserving in the permanent concert repertoire the best of those movements which Strauss threw off so successfully, as he expressed it himself in Hofmannsthal's words, 'as it were with his left hand'. The Suite, which ranks as one of his finest works, contains nine movements as follows:

1. Overture to Act I (Jourdain—the Bourgeois)
   (as given in (a) with the music of the arietta, Ex. 3)

See above, pages 11–12

2. Menuett—The Dancing Master	,,	,,	,,	16
3. The Fencing Master	,,	,,	,,	16–17
4. Entrance and Dance of the Tailors	,,	,,	,,	19–20
5. The Menuett of Lully	,,	,,	,,	86
6. Courante	,,	,,	,,	88–89
7. Entrance of Cléonte (after Lully)	,,	,,	,,	87–88
8. Prelude to Act 2 (Intermezzo)	,,	,,	,,	21

8. (Dorante and Dorimène—Count and Marquise). (The title is misleading, being composite: the movement is the Prelude to Act 2 in (a), but serves as Intermezzo in (c).

9. The Dinner   ,,   ,,   ,,   22–24
   (Table music and dance of the kitchen boy).

Of these movements only numbers 5–7 come specifically from (c) and are sometimes omitted as being less interesting than the remainder, the style and virtuosity of which is of the very highest quality in Strauss's lightest manner. It is a pity that Strauss felt his prestige too high for the supplying of mere incidental music—witness his repeated complaints that he was being allowed too few opportunities for music in (c)—that, in his own words, 'I know exactly what, if I'm to have a share in this business, the public expects of me.' For this Suite reminds us of how, ever since *Till Eulenspiegel*, Strauss had shown himself able to create sparkling orchestral character pieces in between his weightier conceptions. On one occasion he was indeed tempted to make a proposition of a literary kind to Hofmannsthal, on the lines of *A Midsummer Night's Dream* or *Manfred*. Unfortunately Hofmannsthal was far from encouraging and at the time Strauss seems to have too far lost his earlier self-confidence to take the initiative by himself without guidance or corroboration.

Strauss's villa at Garmisch

Of (a) and (b), that is to say from the opera *Ariadne*, less has entered into the repertory of a permanent nature in the way of extracts. The Prelude and Dance Scene of the Comedians was recently published as an orchestral item but without making any impression, and the items most often heard are Ariadne's Monologue and the Zerbinetta Aria, the latter in its revised form from (b). Hofmannsthal never lost his qualms that even this version was too taxing and might prejudice the future of *Ariadne* as a whole. As late as the summer of 1918 he was urging Strauss to rethink and recompose the whole aria: 'take the words of this aria which builds up a whole feminine type, perhaps the archetype of the feminine, and write new music of the smooth melodiousness of *Le Bourgeois* for its various phrases with their distinct variation in rhythm ...' Strauss replied, however, 'I suggest we stop doctoring it. ... I should find difficulty in applying the surgeon's knife to Zerbinetta again. ...' In the event successive generations of coloratura sopranos have mastered its difficulties and it has become, as Strauss had intended, extremely popular.

35

For the role of Bacchus Strauss allots the tenor voice to the hero for the first time since Guntram. Like Mozart, Strauss was more at his ease when the tenor occupied a character role (Basilio, Ottavio: Herod, Aegisth), the hero more often being a baritone (Figaro, Don Giovanni: Mandryka, Orest, Kunrad). Much as a tenor might seem the logical choice for the young Bacchus, Strauss's decision and his patent lack of true sympathy with the character may have been to some extent co-related.

In Molière and opera alike he was clearly enjoying himself once it came to the handling of his unusual orchestra. The use of solo instruments, already an increasing tendency within even a large orchestra, stimulated his polyphonic imagination in the same sort of way as smaller forces inspired Mahler in the Fourth Symphony and Stravinsky in *Renard* or *L'Histoire du Soldat*, after the handling of gargantuan orchestras in preceding works. In Strauss's case we have already seen in the discussion of *Der Rosenkavalier* how, in the Marschallin's Monologue for instance, he made use of individual instrumental colours with striking success, and this technique was naturally exploited to an unprecedented degree in the new work with its unusual limitations of personnel. It did not, even so, always come easily to him, and although he achieved this chamber music idiom with remarkable success in specific movements (for example, the Prelude to Act I of *Bourgeois Gentilhomme* with its ingenious opening Toccata for piano and string octet; the cadenzas for trombone, trumpet and piano in the scene of the Fencing Master; in the introduction to Act 2, in the oboe and cello solos from the Dinner Music; in the Overture and Zerbinetta's aria from *Ariadne* itself) his love of warm sonorities quickly led him to juxtapositions of instruments and complex mixtures of colour not dissimilar, if on a smaller scale, to his habitual manner with the orchestra.

The extent to which he missed his beloved full band of wind and brass is revealed by the remarkable and novel handling of the harmonium. Throughout the work Strauss preserves it for the Opera Seria, while the piano is largely kept as the accompanying continuo for the Intermezzo group. In this connexion he visualized the harmonium as something considerably more than the wheezing Moody and Sankey machine normally associated with the word. It was not the first time Strauss had used the instrument, which had already featured in *Feuersnot* and *Salome*, though hitherto always kept discreetly behind the scene. Now it appears in the orchestra pit and Strauss inserted an elaborate explanatory essay into the part describing both its function and its very nature in some detail.

> 'The Harmonium', he writes, 'has in this work an entirely new and much more far-reaching function to fulfil than has previously been customary. The attempt has been made for the first time, carried out—it is true—according to new principles, to introduce a keyboard instrument simultaneously with, and as a substitute for, whole groups of instruments, such as: 5th and 6th horns, trombones, bassoons, flutes, oboes, clarinets, etc.'

He then goes on to describe the different ways in which the practical aspects of this problem are to be solved—dovetailing of the various colours, insistence on an instrument with stops imitative of the orchestral wind, absolute avoidance of couplings which recall the conventional sound of an organ or harmonium, observance on the part of the player not merely of orchestral dynamics such as *cresc.* and *dim.* but the less natural *subito sf* and so on. Strauss then discusses the position of the harmonium in the orchestra pit (right in the middle with the player's face towards the conductor), and ends with a detailed catalogue of the necessary stops.

Unfortunately none of these fascinating instructions appear in the full score at all. Moreover, the complicated registrations worked out all through the opera with such exceptional thoroughness[50] also appear only in the part, with the result that the onus of approximating as nearly as possible to the effects so scrupulously planned is thrown entirely upon the player according to the instrument at his disposal, the conductor being generally ignorant of Strauss's intentions.

Despite this ingenious substitution of the harmonium for the large wind band which Strauss had come to regard as indispensable, when he reached the closing Ariadne–Bacchus duet he still felt cramped by his 35-piece ensemble and for a time seriously considered changing at this juncture to a full orchestra, even bearing in mind the possibility that the players might have to be accommodated elsewhere than in the pit. It was only at the fervent intercession of Hofmannsthal that he finally relinquished the idea, though in later years he conceded it to have been foolish.

Audacious experiment though it had been, Strauss always had faith in the original work and he repeated to Homannsthal more than once that it '. . . is so attractive in form and content that I cannot believe that a more cultured public than exists today will not sometime appreciate its value more fully'. It is sad that Hofmannsthal was at the time too directly influenced by temporary success or failure in the theatre to share Strauss's confidence, but his beautifully expressed lines of ultimate praise are founded on a sure realization of the worth of his achievement:

> 'Looking at the whole thing, I draw lasting pleasure from the thought that I forced upon you something so unusual and important. Of all our joint works this is the one I never cease to love best. Here alone you have gone wholly with me and—what is more mysterious—wholly even with yourself. Here for once you freed yourself entirely from all thought of effect; even what is most tender and most personal did not appear too simple, too humble for you here. You have lent your ear to the most intimate inspiration and have given great beauty . . . the music is as enchanting in the memory as anything could be; like fireworks in a beautiful park, one enchanted, all too fleeting, summer night.'

For all the tribulations of its engendering *Ariadne* is a masterpiece and Hofmannsthal could justly claim the credit for the vision behind its creation.

[50] They are, however, only in German and many of the terms, referring as they do to a rare and costly instrument, can often only be guessed at.

CHAPTER XI

MARKING TIME

I

ON 18th May 1911 Gustav Mahler died of overwork and a strained heart at the age of only fifty-one. Strauss's comment, if terse, reveals an unexpected depth of sympathy: 'Mahler's death has affected me greatly,' he wrote; 'now you'll see even in Vienna he'll be a great man'. The characteristic dig at the Viennese musical world refers to Mahler's eventual departure from the Court Opera, which as Director and Conductor-in-Chief he had raised to unprecedented heights, though not without making many enemies.

Yet much as Strauss revered Mahler's standing as an executant, he entirely failed to understand the importance of his creative work. As he later said to his colleague Fritz Busch in typical Bavarian dialect: 'Sö, Busch, der Mahler, dös is überhaupt gar ka Komponist. Dös is blos a ganz grosser Dirigent.' (That's really no composer at all. Just a very great conductor.)

Characteristic as this is of Strauss's attitude, it is also typical of the prevailing view of Mahler at that time. Max Reger used almost the same words when talking to Busch.

To some extent the cause for this lay in the quasi-amateur time-table of Mahler's creative outbursts. His career as a composer could never be pursued except during the brief intervals between his regular seasons in intense interpretative and administrative work which his conducting career inevitably carried with it. To the end Mahler greatly resented the fact that life had made of him a mere holiday composer, he to whom composition had in fact always been the very religion of his existence.

As a result every new work became a confession of faith, an outpouring of his soul the importance of which it would be impossible to exaggerate. To have tossed off a minor work, let alone to note-spin without care or conviction, would have represented a form of blasphemy, apart from the excruciating waste of priceless time.

It would perhaps be unfair to overstress the extravagant contrast of this passionate, desperate dedication with Strauss's methodical but un-fussed approach to his creative output. His career had developed with such ease, both as conductor and composer, that he had at an early age taken his artistic gifts for granted, to be exercised regularly and auto-matically. He himself compared his need to compose to that of a cow giving milk. It was not in his nature to fight too strenuously during his tenure of office in this opera house or that, with one orchestra or another, to the detriment of his daily ritual of turning out so many impeccably neat pages of score at the specially designed curved writing desk in his elegant music-room. Nor could this work itself be allowed to be inter-rupted merely because there was no very interesting project on hand.

It is thus not hard to understand how he came in the meantime idly to sketch out an orchestral fantasy on the subject of the beautiful mountains amongst which he had so recently built the luxurious villa which was to be his home for the rest of his life. Such a conception was no new one; Strauss had long before had the idea for it after a boyhood experience of mountaineering during which the party lost its way during the ascent, while on the return they were overtaken by a storm and drenched to the skin. Writing to his friend Ludwig Thuille at the time of the adventure he had said how extremely interesting he had found it, that he had at once set down his impressions onto the piano, and that 'naturally it had conjured up a lot of nonsense and giant Wagnerian tonepainting.'

Again in 1900, shortly after the completion of *Heldenleben*, he was writing to his parents of a symphonic poem which was slumbering deep in his breast, 'which would begin with a sunrise in Switzerland. Other-wise so far only the idea (love tragedy of an artist) and a few themes exist.'

Yet when he came to address himself seriously to the *Alpensinfonie*, it had become hardly more than a diversion, Strauss going so far as to make the well-known comment already quoted—that work on it amused him even less than chasing cockroaches. He toyed with it only intermittently and but for the war it is conceivable that he would never have bothered to finish it at all. Even so palpable a time-marker as *Josephslegende* was able to interrupt its progress with the result that composition was spread over four years, from 1911 to February 1915.

Nevertheless, once his mind was made up to go ahead in earnest, he managed to enjoy it and in the end progress was quick. The orchestration, begun on 1st November 1914 and completed in little over three months, can scarcely have presented any serious problems to Strauss, for all its complexity and the extremes of compass he employs for most of the instruments. Gone are the light touches and chamber orchestral textures of *Rosenkavalier* and *Bourgeois Gentilhomme*. Gone too are the technical extravagances and wild experimentation of *Till* and *Elektra*. 'At last I have learnt to orchestrate', he said at the *Generalprobe*, and sadly one acknowledges that the piece cannot fail to sound securely warm and mellifluous. At the same time the curious blending of the large orchestral forces has a colour all its own which is undeniably apt for the subject matter of the work.

Although once more entitled a Symphony, it is far less so even than its predecessor, the *Sinfonia Domestica*. There are some twenty-two continuous sections, all carefully labelled in the score, which follow the thesis of the work covering twenty-four hours from night to nightfall in the life of a mountain and its successful assailants. As in *Heldenleben*, these sections can, with an effort of ingenuity, be grouped together to simulate a gigantic Lisztian symphonic form, with elements of introduction, opening allegro, scherzo, slow movement, finale and epilogue; but the lasting impression remains of a free descriptive fantasia, more concerned with graphic pictorialism than of adherence to a formal outline. The following list gives in full the scheme of the work:

Nacht	Night
Sonnenaufgang	Sunrise
Der Anstieg	The ascent
Eintritt in den Wald	Entry into the wood
Wanderung neben dem Bache	Wandering by the side of the brook
Am Wasserfall	At the waterfall
Erscheinung	Apparition
Auf blumige Wiesen	On flowering meadows
Auf der Alm	On the alpine pasture
Durch Dickicht und Gestrüpp auf Irrwegen	Through thicket and undergrowth on the wrong way

Auf dem Gletscher	On the glacier
Gefahrvolle Augenblicke	Dangerous moments
Auf dem Gipfel	On the summit
Vision	Vision
Nebel steigen auf	Mists rise
Die Sonne verdüstert sich allmählich	The sun gradually becomes obscured
Elegie	Elegy
Stille vor dem Sturm	Calm before the storm
Gewitter und Sturm, Abstieg	Thunder and Tempest, descent
Sonnenuntergang	Sunset
Ausklang	Waning tones
Nacht	Night

2

The Symphony opens in deepest night on a unison B flat from which a scale slowly descends, each note as it is sounded sustaining until every degree of the scale is heard simultaneously. No sooner is this opaque mass of string tone established, than a solemn chordal motif is delivered by the heavy brass:

Ex. 1

It is not hard to trace the origins of this Wagnerian theme in Strauss's music from as far back as *Aus Italien* via the 'Bund' theme from *Guntram*, Kunrad's motif in *Feuersnot*, and Orestes' in *Elektra*. It is also immensely typical in its sudden change of tonality in the middle against which the sustained notes of the B flat minor scale persist relentlessly, an instance of polytonal effects rarely to be found in Strauss's music outside *Salome* and *Elektra*.

After this basic presentation of the mountain, massive and imposing in all its stern majesty, Strauss concerns himself for a time with background murmurings and shadowy scales over a long tonic pedal.[1] Frag-

[1] In order that the wind instruments should be able to sustain these long pedal points Strauss recommends the employment of 'Samuel's Aerophon'. This alas long-extinct device seems to have supplied oxygen to the distressed player by means of a foot-pump with a tube stretching up to the mouth.

ments of Ex. 1 appear on the wind and brass as the complex orchestration gradually builds up to a glowing climax depicting sunrise over the Alps. Inevitably one's mind is cast back to the previous occasion on which Strauss began a tone-poem with a pictorial demonstration of a mountain sunrise—in *Zarathustra*. If the earlier example was more dramatically striking, the latter excels in respect of realism. We shall see again and again in the *Alpensinfonie* Strauss's curiously detached attitude to the Nature subject of this last of his tone-poems, giving it a de-humanized majestic quality reminiscent, in a unique way, of Bruckner.

Motivically this Sunrise section is based on the descending scale of the Symphony's opening, though transformed into a melodic outburst:

Ex. 2

and followed by a new theme of rich, generous sonority:

Ex. 3

There is a further brief build-up, the orchestra cuts off abruptly, and with the entry of the main marching theme on the lower strings and harp the work passes from the introduction to the first allegro proper.

Ex. 4

This is worked out in a full symphonic sentence suggesting the climbing party as they set forth vigorously on the lower slopes. The shape of the theme, Ex. 4, is reminiscent both of the coda from the finale of Beethoven's C Minor Symphony and of the mountain horn-call in the first Nocturne of Mahler's Seventh Symphony. Even the treatment is not dissimilar to the latter, though Mahler avoids the jauntiness which is one of the more noticeable characteristics of Strauss's manner. This particular symphony of Mahler's is often considered as coming nearest in style to the work of Strauss and there is little doubt that Strauss, for his part, knew this period in Mahler's output. Moreover, such thematic similarities to the music of other composers continue to occur during the course of the work and are perhaps due to Strauss's regular appearances as conductor at this time.

The section comes to a full cadential close which is followed immediately by a triumphant fanfare:

Ex. 5

Despite its declamatory first statement, suggesting perhaps the impact upon the climbers of the magnificent rugged scenery around them, Ex. 5 is developed in a manner showing that it refers also to the sheer climb itself, especially with respect to its more arduous and dangerous aspects.

Hunting horns are heard in the distance, represented by an off-stage orchestra of twelve horns together with a pair each of trumpets and trombones.[2] The fanfares are wholly non-motivic and neither the hunting horns nor their phrases are heard again throughout the work. One is strongly reminded of the parallel passage in Smetana's symphonic poem

---

[2] Huge as Strauss's orchestra undoubtedly is, this apparently grotesque extravagance (a total of twenty horns, including the eight in the orchestra) is in fact less a sign of increasing unreasonable demands in his symphonic instrumentation than of Strauss's preoccupation with the Wagnerian opera house and the resources he could there take for granted. *Tannhäuser* and *Tristan*, for example, both call for twelve off-stage horns, while *Lohengrin* employs not only twelve off-stage trumpets but a further twenty-four instrumentalists for various ensembles of wind and percussion. The *Alpensinfonie* in fact throws an interesting light on the conditions which Strauss was now in a position to assume for the performance of his new symphonic compositions.

Vltava, an exciting moment in a popular work which Strauss must certainly have had in mind. The snapping figure ⌜ x ⌝ from Ex. 5 builds up in unison on the strings until it finally overwhelms the receding horn-calls, and with a burst of rich orchestral colour the mountaineers plunge into a wooded part of their climb. The instrumental tones deepen as thick foliage obscures the sunlight and a new meandering theme appears on horns and trombones:

Ex. 6

Against a continuously rustling background this new melodic idea alternates with the marching first subject, while fragments of further new motifs enter surreptitiously either as melody or birdsong during the course of some typical modulations:

Ex. 7

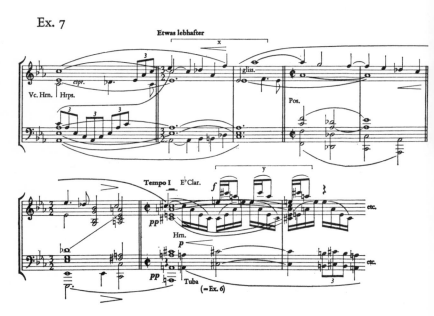

The Mahlerian bird-call ⌜ y ⌝ appears here as only one of a succession of different birds which contribute to the Murmurs of Strauss's Forest.

Later, however, it acquires considerable motivic importance, during which it is handled in a way strongly suggestive of yodelling (see Ex. 10 below).

This section also comes to a clearly defined close on one of Strauss's favourite cadences of shifting tonality, and a development section begins with a quiet return of the marching theme, Ex. 4, now played smoothly by the strings with only the softest background of lower woodwind. The climbers are at an agreeable part of their journey and Strauss too takes it comfortably, contenting himself with inventing agreeable polyphony. The orchestral treatment of these counterpoints varies from a solo string quartet to the full string orchestra with doublings of different degrees on groups of woodwind. Yet in a curious way the effect is like that of an organ and a strong impression is given of Strauss himself sitting at the console improvising while adding different stops on the Swell manual as the mood takes him.

In course of time the mountaineers come to a stream—nothing is omitted from the entire range of Alpine scenery—and Strauss adds the appropriate rushing passage-work to the texture. The motivic interest, however, continues to lie with Ex. 4, though block chords similar to Ex. 1—the theme of the mountain itself—can be heard rearing through the polyphony. The suggestion is clearly of ever higher cliffs surrounding the stream, and indeed before long a spectacular waterfall is reached. Here Strauss is in his element and the orchestral treatment lacks nothing in brilliance. After a few bars, beneath the glittering instrumental writing, fragments of an ingenuous little melody can be distinguished, presented phrase by phrase on the oboes.

Ex. 8

Strauss adds the heading *Erscheinung* (Apparition) at this point and we are to imagine the Fairy of the Alps appearing beneath the rainbow formed by the spray of the cascading water. This popular superstition of an Alpine Sprite, which dates back to ancient times, was used by Byron (though he referred to her as a witch) in his great poem *Manfred*, and

Tchaikovsky had already chosen to represent this same vision musically in the scherzo of his *Manfred* Symphony.

Brief references to Ex. 5 occur from time to time on the horn, suggesting, perhaps, attempts on the part of the climbers to struggle nearer to the glorious apparition. Gradually, however, the irridescence fades and a new melody pours out on the horn and violas, strongly reminiscent, as is well known, of the Max Bruch G minor Violin Concerto[3]:

Ex. 9

The music then passes into the next section in which the members of the party find themselves 'on flowering meadows'. Their easy progress is outlined by Ex. 4 on the cellos while the meadow is suggested by soft, high chords on the violins, against which pin-points of colour on woodwind, harps and pizzicato violas provide the flowers. This kind of orchestral pictorialism amused Strauss, who made the extravagant claim in conversation at about this time that he could, if necessary, describe a knife and fork in music.

3

The climbers do not linger in these amiable surroundings but press on (Ex. 9 combines melodically with the walking tune, Ex. 4) and quickly reach the *Alm*—the high verdant pastures on the mountain slopes where Alpine herdsmen put their cattle to graze during the summer months. Strauss accordingly introduces cowbells into the score, and so apt is their appearance that one might think this to be their first employment in the symphony orchestra. Surprisingly enough, however, Strauss took the idea from Mahler's Sixth Symphony, in which they are used with magical effect but entirely without programmatic significance, a device which Webern also incorporated into his Five Orchestral Pieces, Op. 10.

[3] This is not the first time that the ever popular concerto found an echo in Strauss's work (see Vol. I, pp. 13 and 18). Specht, on the other hand, belittles the similarity, claiming on the contrary the strong Straussian flavour of the melody and drawing an especial connexion with the song 'Anbetung', Op. 36 no. 4 (not Op. 37, as he cites). The idiomatic parallel is undeniable but his conjecture of a deliberate allusion on the grounds of the words 'Ah, wie schön' ('how beautiful') seems more like special pleading.

The idyllic calm and beauty of these pastures is conjured up most poetically by Ex. 3 alternating with a new motif derived from the bird-song Ex. 7(y), but now transformed so as to suggest yodelling or a herdsman piping[4]:

Ex. 10

A new and startling theme is screamed out abruptly by the woodwind;

Ex. 11

after which the horn introduces yet another new idea, this time a lovely flowing melody suggestive of soft undulating slopes:

Ex. 12

Ex. 12 is immediately developed in an elaborate contrapuntal passage of shifting chromatic tonalities during the course of which it is joined by the two earlier climbing themes, Exx. 4 and 5. The party has left the correct path and has got into difficulties trying to retrieve the error by cutting through the undergrowth. The tempo hurries forward as the mountaineers become more and more desperate until suddenly they

[4] The embellishments of trills and fluttertonguing throughout this section of the score show that the composer of the 'Sheep' Variation of *Don Quixote* has not lost his skill.

push clear of the entanglement and find themselves on the glacier. The
brass declaim the chordal motif of the great mountain itself which has
suddenly appeared once again in all its grandeur and, inspired and invigorated, the climbers press forward over the ice-field with a tremendous
surge of Exx. 4 and 5. For a time the rippling semi-quaver figure of the
stream can be heard beneath the stark statements of the rugged fanfare-
like Ex. 5, perhaps denoting the waters gushing from beneath the edge
of the glacier. Before long, however, these die away; there is a mighty
upsurge of Ex. 4 and of the sweeping cadence ⌐ z ⌐ of its closing bars,
the music fades completely and fragments of Ex. 5 are left tentatively
jabbing over a soft drum-roll. Chromatic figures on pizzicato strings add
to this passage which is headed 'Dangerous moments', and the idea of
insecurity is cleverly suggested in the fragmentary nature of the texture.
The jagged theme, Ex. 5, in particular receives extraordinary treatment
on the trumpet and upper clarinets shortly before the summit is reached.

Ex. 13

4

The conquest of the peak is of course the corner-stone of the work and
might have been expected to have evoked a splendid orchestral climax,
in the construction of which Strauss, of all composers, had long specialized. But whatever his faults Strauss rarely succumbed to the obvious;
although some climax of achievement there certainly is (built out of the
closing bars of Ex. 5), the orchestration is very restrained as the trombones declaim the Peak motif, a typical Macbeth-Guntram-Zara-
thustra Naturthema:

Ex. 14

The sounds then fade right away to a soft violin tremolo, beneath which the oboe stammers out a strange hesitant utterance:

Ex. 15

The effect is weird and unearthly; the climber seems transfixed by the spectacle which greets him on the actual summit. Indeed it is at first scarcely possible to take in the grandeur of the scene for the utter—even appalling—desolation. Only gradually, as realization of the overwhelming beauty of the view from every side takes the place of this profound sense of awe, does a surge of warm orchestral colour infuse the music. The oboe solo, Ex. 15, of which there are two extended sentences, is directly taken from the startling and graphic utterance of the woodwind, Ex. 11, which had plunged so steeply from the extreme heights as to suggest the precipitous appearance of the mountain side (cf. the note formations of the two respective phrases marked ⌈ x ⌉). There is in fact a temptation to attribute the birth of both these themes to an attempt at outlining in the very notes the visual impression of the mountainous profile. (In the same way in more recent years Villa Lobos based an orchestral composition on the famous New York skyline by plotting the skyscrapers onto graph-paper.) Certainly if it were so, and the idea is by no means inconsistent with Strauss's other sources of inspiration for this work, Ex. 15 might well be as true to the view from the summit as Ex. 11 would be of the giant rock-face.

The *Naturthema* Peak motif, Ex. 14, rears up once again on the trombones, the opening chord-formation of the mountain theme, Ex. 1, is declaimed in a bright C major tonality, and the horns pour forth the second Apparition theme (Ex. 9) followed enthusiastically by upper strings in a broad unison. This time, however, the shape of the theme—and especially its continuation—is different, recalling an earlier passage from the Woodland section, Ex. 7(x).

Ex. 16

This outpouring of glowing melody is, of course, the long-awaited emotional climax of the Symphony and leads to an impressive C major cadence which is rendered even more emphatic by the mighty cadence of the rock theme, Ex. 5. The effect is comparable with the centre-point of *Ein Heldenleben*, as is also, to some extent, the style of the continuation. Here is undoubtedly the moment for formal reprise, but, as in the earlier work, Strauss is enjoying himself too much to fall back on conventional devices. The Sun theme, Ex. 2, streams out in combination with the Summit motif (Ex. 14) and with a new cantabile countertheme supplied by the horns and cellos. This in its turn embodies a development of the little figure, Ex. 16(x), the latter sounding more and more like a familiar theme from Wagner's *Meistersinger*, especially during its treatment in diminution. The polyphony now becomes more elaborate with much rapidly flowing figuration accompanying a return of Ex. 3, the warm triplet horn theme which has not been heard since the climbers' brief idyll on the *Alm*, the high pasture-land.

The tonality shifts to F sharp, and a somewhat stark section begins entitled 'Vision'. It is as if Strauss has been trying to scan downwards into the far-off green valleys with his binoculars, but now raises them to the gaunt scenery at eye level. The peak motif and the second Apparition theme (Exx. 14 and 9) are combined in a weird development section which gradually incorporates many of the main subjects of the Symphony. The flowing passage-work, Ex. 12(y), and the *Meistersinger*-like Ex. 16(x) enter together followed by the Sun theme (Ex. 2) and the majestic chordal Mountain theme (Ex. 1), all of which material alternates, appears and reappears in this fascinating central working-out section.

The workroom in the Garmisch villa

The profusion of trills (often every note of a quickly-moving passage is supplied with a trill), the addition of original and irrelevant counter-points of deceptive interest, since they prove to be non-motivic and unimportant, and the unthinking virtuoso writing for the brass, com-bine to make this unemotional piece of symphonic construction oddly arresting.

Amongst the new material lavishly spread over the pages of score by the ever fertile and resourceful Strauss (extended melodisings on oboe and horn, elaborate *arpeggiando* passages for harp, jagged note-forma-tions with sweeping up-beats for the united violins of the orchestra, and so on), a strange, chromatically-rising sequence on the full wood-wind band proves to be of more than passing significance. Indeed, at its return a little later it is reinforced not only by strings but by additional desks of flutes, oboes and clarinets held hitherto in reserve and instructed to double with their regular colleagues in any large-scale orchestra employed for performance. The entry of these further forces to the already gargantuan instrumentation coincides with a particularly shrill statement of the Sun motif on four trumpets, followed closely by the first entry of the organ, supplying a deep pedal point in unison with two tubas. The chromatic ascending figure suggests a rising heat below which the Mountain theme (Ex. 1) is declaimed by the brass at full strength, and in the original key of B flat minor. The sense of fulfilment is complete, the recapitulation has begun, and the structure of the symphony has, in Bruckner-like manner, found its logical climax.

5

There is an abrupt change of mood. The murmuring and shadowy scales of the Symphony's opening are reintroduced to suggest the formation of mists rising up the mountain side. As before, this leads to the Sun theme (Ex. 2) but now given in strange colouring mixed with organ reeds. Gradually the sun is becoming obscured by the gathering haze and an oppressive stillness pervades the atmosphere. This is perhaps the most brilliantly clever section of the work; Strauss has caught with remarkable success the uncanny moment in the mountains when the weather is just beginning to break. In a section described as 'Elegy' veiled entries of the Sun theme alternate with a new idea, the setting of which (muted strings in unison against shifting harmonies on the organ) ideally evokes the uneasy calm before the storm.

Ex. 17[4a]

Over an ominous drum-roll the stammering theme (Ex. 15) is heard again, though no longer on the oboe and devoid of its supporting shimmer of the major triad. Clarinet, cor anglais and bassoon begin it in turn, but each time it tails away, either into fragments of the wailing Ex. 17, or into total incoherence. The oboe itself pitches repeated but irregular groups of staccato high D flats into the rarified air with extraordinary effect. There is a strange interjection from a high clarinet like the cry of some bird of prey. A flash of lightning with a distant roll of thunder (piccolo and bass drum) is answered by the descending B flat minor scale of the Symphony's opening. As it sweeps with increasing precipitation down the orchestra it leaves its notes behind—again as in the first bars—filling the previously bare canvas with an opaque mass of sound.

A second and far nearer flash and burst of thunder—yet another, this time almost overhead—and rapid scales rush up in the lower strings, in much the same way as Herod's 'Angel of Death' storm music in *Salome*. Raindrops begin to fall in huge globules (upper woodwind, violin *pizzicati* and harps) and in a very short time the storm is raging all around.

The great storms of music, Beethoven's Pastoral Symphony, Wagner's *Walküre*, Verdi's *Otello*, Britten's *Peter Grimes*, all create more than a mere evocation of the fury of Nature let loose. Whether or not the

---

[4a] cf. yet again the Orestes theme from *Elektra*.

reaction of human beings to the raging elements is to be experienced in
the composer's handling of the scene, thus giving drama or poignance to
the climaxes, the form and harmonic structure is always of paramount
importance in the creation of a fully convincing programmatic movement.

That Strauss's storm would overreach every previous orchestral
tempest in verisimilitude and virtuosity of descriptive technique was a
foregone conclusion. The blinding sheets of drenching rain, the driving
wind, the flashing and thundering, all are portrayed with alarming
reality, as are the occasional lulls followed by renewed bursts of violence
exactly as in real life. Yet, when the tempest has finally spent itself—and
it is a long section—it is hard to escape the feeling that, for all his endless
resourcefulness and unflagging invention, Strauss has not succeeded in
composing more than a clever piece of graphic description.

On the face of it everything seems to be there, including motivic
interest, whilst with engaging skill Strauss couples the storm section with
the Descent, thus not only continuing with his basic programme but also
thereby pursuing the recapitulation of the Symphony. But although
many of the motifs recur one by one, as the sodden mountaineers hastily
retrace their steps through one familiar scene after another, they are
merely superimposed upon the score and except perhaps for the waterfall, the incorporation of which is a masterpiece of ingenuity, cannot be
said to form part of it. The marching theme is heard on the wind-band
in inversion (perhaps rather obviously now that the climbers are descending) followed by the rocky motif, Ex. 5, which also descends although it
keeps its general outline. In due course the glacier is reached and the
appropriate slippery music of the 'Dangerous moments' section passes
across the score. This rapidly gives place to the pastoral, yodelling music
and this in turn to the flowing melody, Ex. 12, giving the impression not
unlike that experienced by H. G. Wells' Time Traveller on his headlong
return journey from the future to the present. The meandering woodland
theme of the lower slopes follows (Ex. 6) after which a tremendous
new onslaught of the storm brings in its train a mighty statement
of the inverted marching tune now in augmentation on tubas and
trombones.

But the storm has almost passed, and the sheet rain gives way once
again to the heavy drops, portrayed as before by pizzicato violins and high
woodwind, though without the harps. One last flash, a final thunderclap,
and the section is over. Solemnly the brass declaim the great Mountain

theme, Ex. 1, the climax chord of which is capped by the full organ,[5] an effect which was used before by Strauss in a similar context during the opening passage of *Also Sprach Zarathustra*. As in the earlier work, the addition of the organ suggests, with considerable power of evocation, the stern beauty of mountains, devoid of life and symbolic of Nature in her severest aspect.

With the re-emerging of the mountain into full view the Symphony's coda has begun, and the remainder of the score has the wistful nostalgia which Strauss knew so well how to conjure up. There are three sections to this closing portion of the work: Sunset, *Ausklang*, and Night. Against the specific depiction of the slowly setting sun (widely spaced out descending phrases of the Sun theme, Ex. 2) a solemn Chorale-like melody is enunciated by the brass and harps, while against this in turn the violins pursue tortuous passages derived partly from the 'Elegy' (Ex. 17) and partly from the marching theme, Ex. 4, which in its subsidiary phrase ⌐ y ⌐ also provides the basis for the chorale. The sunset reaches a glowing climax after which it dies away into the *Ausklang*.

There is no literal translation of this word which suggests finality. The passage is a farewell and constitutes to a large extent a reliving of most of the sheerly beautiful moments experienced during the course of the work. It is marked to be played 'in soft ecstasy' and the value of its spiritual peacefulness should not be underestimated any more than the very real communication in terms of absolute, though possibly somewhat cloying, beauty. The passage corresponds musically with the 'Vision' section of the Symphony's midway point, much of which, declaimed at the time with great sonority, is now recapitulated in soft colours, albeit richly mixed.

The organ continues at first to play a prominent, even soloistic, part, especially during the last glimpses of the setting sun. The full band of woodwind enters gently with the extended Apparition theme exactly as it poured out during the Vision in a flood of ecstatic melodising (Ex. 16). The continuation, with the after-phrase ⌐ x ⌐, and the Bruch-like original Apparition music, Ex. 9 (the horns still soaring over its high phrases), all make their final reappearance. The melodic flood takes other motifs into its sweep such as the Marching tune, Ex. 4, with all its phrases

---

[5] This beautiful touch is also a dangerous one on grounds of intonation, for even if the organ is tuned to exact concert pitch (a curiously rare phenomenon in concert halls) a sustained chord still tends to sound flat against the living timbre of the orchestral wind.

developed separately both directly and in inversion, and the more tortuous winding sections of Ex. 12. Lastly, after what had seemed the final
cadence, the startling Ex. 11 leaps up, spanning as before virtually the
entire woodwind range.

The work is essentially over, but Strauss preferred to leave the mountain as he had first shown it, shrouded in darkness and mystery. He therefore extends the broad flow of melody by means of Exx. 4 and 2 (now
wholly devoid of their original programmatic significance). Gradually,
as the light fades, the music moves away from E flat (in which, like the
opening of the exposition, the *Ausklang* had been firmly established) into
B flat minor, in which gloomy key the Symphony had begun and in
which it is now to end. The texture, therefore, which had contracted to a
single organ chord, opens out again with rising phrases (Ex. 2 inverted)
above a shifting and ever deeper bass, until at last the great unison B flat
is reached, six octaves deep (not seven—the bottom note of the contra-
bassoon is reserved for the last bar). The descending scale is then heard
again, exactly as in the opening of the work with each note sustaining to
form an opaque mass of sound. Against this, the brass, still as in the opening, enunciate the theme of the mountain itself. It is night and the giant
outlines of the noble mass can just be discerned in the gloom. The violins
softly shape a phrase derived from Ex. 4 which rises and swoops down
once more in a glissando to the last note. Much of the Symphony has
glistened and glowed, but its final sounds are of total darkness with a
deep chord of B flat minor picked out against a string conglomerate in
which every note of the scale is present.

6

The full score of the *Alpine Symphony* was ready on 8th February 1915,
and the première was immediately projected for early in the following
season. Strauss had resolved to dedicate the work to Count Seebach, the
Director of the Royal Opera in Dresden, in token of his gratitude to the
house in which the first performances of no less than four of his six operas
had been given. Accordingly, at the Symphony's first performance on
25th October Strauss conducted the orchestra of the Dresden Hof-
kapelle although the event took place in the Philharmonie in Berlin,
where Strauss still occupied a position of some authority. Attenuated
though it had become, Strauss's contact with the opera and Philharmonic

Society in Berlin was not actually severed until 1918. After his sabbatical years for the composition of *Elektra* and *Rosenkavalier*, Strauss had resumed his conducting activities to a fairly considerable extent, including concert tours, festivals devoted to his music in all parts of the world, and opera. Even the outbreak of war did not at first curtail this part of his professional life, which with his enormous prestige he was able to treat in far too cavalier a manner for it to become the drudgery it was to poor idealistic Mahler. The delightful legend has been handed down of performances of *Così fan Tutte* in which Strauss, while conducting from the continuo, as was his invariable custom, amused himself during the recitatives by improvising polyphonic accompaniments containing cross-references to *Figaro* and *Don Giovanni*, as well as to his own operas. Together with Mozart, Wagner was Strauss's favourite operatic composer, of whom he gave a great many performances at this time, particularly of the *Ring* and *Tristan*. The latter he knew so well that he conducted it from memory, and the story is recounted that on one occasion he ran amok during the complicated $\frac{5}{4}$ passage in Act 3. So chagrined was he at having jeopardized the great work at this crucial dramatic moment that as soon as the performance was over he invited the entire company, singers and orchestra alike, to a huge banquet at his own expense. At such moments he revealed the generous personality which lay beneath the increasingly gruff and ungracious exterior. His conducting technique, admirably professional, had early developed into the undemonstrative and unemotional, indeed almost motionless style which made so strong an impression on all who worked with him, or attended his concerts.

In his fascinating autobiography[6] Fritz Busch wrote:

> '[Strauss] conducting shows a strange mixture, peculiar to him, of apathy and masterly directness which is not without an element of suggestion. This style of conducting practically never appears exciting but it *can* arouse excitement in the hearer. Then there seems to be direct contact with genius.
>
> But the real secret of his success is not betrayed, either by the precise movements of his baton, the balanced economy of his gestures or the calm expression on the face of this tall, well-groomed man.'

The first performance of the *Alpine Symphony* caused little stir in the world. In justice it must be recalled that the event took place in the

[6] *Pages from a Musician's Life*. Hogarth Press, London, 1953.

second year of a world war. Had the Symphony been Strauss's greatest masterpiece its impact could scarcely have been felt outside Germany for over three years. In the circumstances, Strauss was not unduly disgruntled. In a tone of almost amused surprise he wrote to Hofmannsthal: 'I do hope we shall see you soon. You must hear the Alpine Symphony on Dec. 5th; it is really quite a good piece!'

And this is possibly a fair assessment. Had it been written for four instead of twenty horns, with the remainder of the orchestra in proportion, the warm beauty of many of its passages, and the intriguing descriptive sections with their virtuosity of orchestral imagination, might well have caused the work to retain a place in the concert repertoire, albeit amongst the lesser works of an acknowledged master. But to mount it is such an occasion that neglect has followed automatically. For when all is said and done, with all its qualities, this last symphonic poem stands at the bottom of the first curve of Strauss's output;[7] thus in the event, performances have rarely been projected, and even more rarely brought to fruition.

Yet it is a naïve view which merely rejects the work out of hand, and there have always been (and still are) commentators of the first rank who appreciate and value its unusual flavour and spirituality. Prejudice and disappointment on account of the qualities it lacks (and especially those qualities which elsewhere form Strauss's strongest artistic contribution) can blind one to the atmosphere of exaltation in the face of Nature's mystery, which is perhaps the most important aspect of the work. It is in some ways Strauss's parallel not only to Bruckner but to Debussy's *La Mer* in that, almost uniquely in his output, he actually describes his elemental subject from an unpeopled, almost detached point of vantage, despite the ingenuous human framework of its avowed programme. Strauss, still in his mood of spiritual preoccupation after the death of Mahler which affected him more deeply than he cared to admit, wrote that he would like to name his *Alpine Symphony* the Antichrist, since it represented 'the ritual of cleansing through one's own powers, freedom through work and the worship of eternal, glorious nature'.

This is all very admirable, but unfortunately the fate which pursued Strauss's invention when he aimed at Eternal and Absolute Truth has already become clear, and much of the writing is disturbingly prophetic of the direction Strauss's work was taking. The music is, in fact, too

[7] See Vol. I, p. 199, for an outline of the interlocking curves which form the pattern of Strauss's work.

comfortable for its subject. In order to reach Strauss's high-minded intentions it is necessary to wade through much that is essentially the half-playful note-spinning of a fluent master. How representative it is of this side of his output is easily seen by comparing it with the other throw-outs of this period. Of these the *Festliches Praeludium*, an inflated trifle, composed for the opening of the Vienna Konzerthaus in 1913, and the *Deutsche Motette*, also an occasional work of unprecedented difficulty and complication for 16-part unaccompanied double chorus of mammoth proportions, will be discussed later.[8] On the other hand, of greater importance, if still only a time-marker, is the ballet *Josephslegende*.

7

By the summer of 1912 the *Ariadne–Bourgeois Gentilhomme* entertainment, with which Hofmannsthal had been keeping the impatient Strauss at bay, was nearing completion without *Die Frau ohne Schatten* having become more than a mere project. Without doubt he needed some further vehicle for Strauss's summer period of composition if the composer was not to be driven to seek his texts elsewhere.

It was precisely at this time that the Russian Ballet was in its hey-day under the inspiring leadership of Serge Diaghilev. It had swept into prominence immediately on its re-formation in Paris in 1909 and within two years not only was its supremacy acknowledged internationally but many of the outstanding composers of the time were producing new and important scores on commission for this brilliant impresario. Stravinsky, Debussy, Ravel, Prokofieff, for the music; Fokine, Nijinsky, Benois, Picasso, for choreography and design; the conductors Gabriel Pierné and Pierre Monteux—these are but a few of the outstanding artists who collaborated over the years with this extraordinary man who had such genius for spotting future masters in every sphere and bringing them together in the service of his great ballet company.

Hofmannsthal, still bearing in mind both his own ballet project of earlier years, *Der Triumph der Zeit*, and Strauss's own incomplete draft *Kythere*, began seriously to consider whether perhaps he could reawaken some interest in the ballet which might lead to a collaboration with the Russians. The fact that Strauss had already rejected outright a similar

[8] See Chapters XIV and XVI respectively.

proposal not three months before in no way discouraged the strong-willed poet.[9] Hofmannsthal was determined that the choice should fall on a biblical subject, and considered for a time the elderly David and the wife of Uriah. After a few discussions with his friend Count Harry Kessler, the German dilettante and quasi-diplomat with whom he had planned the embryo stages of *Der Rosenkavalier*, he decided instead on what seemed an intriguing scenario based on the story of the young Joseph and Potiphar's Wife. Once again, as with Orestes, the central figure of inspiration was that of Nijinsky, upon whom, as the young Joseph, Hofmannsthal and Kessler lavished symbolism upon symbolism in their enthusiastically *tiefsinnig* imaginations. The result they hastily packed off to Diaghilev so that Hofmannsthal could write to Strauss: 'even if you are not keen to set it to music, I cannot withdraw yet another piece from the Russians—Diaghilev and Nijinsky know the sketch!'

Under such pressure the softer-grained Strauss found himself gradually yielding and Hofmannsthal was like a hawk in following up every sign of compliance. For his part Diaghilev was only too pleased to add Strauss to his list of composers and lost no time in getting the negotiations to the contract stage.

By now the summer was upon Strauss and with it his lust for composition. Dutifully he began each morning to fill up his pages of manuscript paper with panoplies of orchestral sound, and the enormously detailed scenario which Kessler quickly provided enabled him to get off to quite a promising start. But by mid-September Strauss reached the first appearance of the title role and was abruptly brought to a halt.

It would be foolish to be misled into attributing the philosophical conception wholly, or even in the greater part, to Count Harry Kessler. In fact, Hofmannsthal himself, though insisting all through in remaining in the background, dictated the basic scheme from first to last, leaving Kessler to do little more than work out the admittedly elaborate details. Certainly nothing in Kessler's career prepares us for a libretto which in high-flown thought and intellectual obscurity bids fair to outstrip even Hofmannsthal's own loftiest and most far-fetched schemes.

Picturing Strauss sitting at his desk in his comfortable villa in the Bavarian Alps, the essentially professional composer-conductor, human, bourgeois, anti-religious and down-to-earth, one is strongly inclined to

[9] i.e. the suggested symphony-ballet on the subject of Orestes and the Furies, see Chapter X, p. 3.

sympathize with him as he found himself confronted by passages such as the following:

FIRST DANCE FIGURE expresses THE INNOCENCE AND NAIVETE OF JOSEPH THE SHEPHERD BOY. The movements show how the devout Shepherd Boy comes into the presence of his God and shows him, one by one, all his body, his head, his breast, his hands, his feet, that they are pure. He seems to say to God: 'Lord, behold, my body and my heart are pure in Thy sight.'

The Movements are slow and a little hesitating, like those of a pious, somewhat timid child full of foreboding.

SECOND DANCE FIGURE, Intermezzo, JOSEPH LEAPS FOUR TIMES IN THE FOUR DIRECTIONS OF THE COMPASS, thus as it were indicating the limits within which the next Dance Figure shall be confined.

THIRD DANCE FIGURE expresses the SEARCHING AND WRESTLING AFTER GOD, mingled with moments of despair.

The Figure consists mainly of high leaps (as those of David before the Ark of the Covenant) as if Joseph were seeking thus to scale the heavens. But he seems bound to earth with heaviness and once or twice he stumbles and falls, as one who has missed his goal. The Character of the rhythm is heavy and irregular, but not in the least hysterical or morbid.

The seeking after God of Joseph is that of a healthy, normal childlike nature.

FOURTH DANCE FIGURE. Joseph has found God. His movements are now glorification of God. They are distinguished from those of the preceding figure by their lightness. Joseph now leaps with 'light feet'. He seems to fly. Without effort he makes high winged leaps, which express sublimest joy. He seems the embodiment of 'Divine Laughter'.

In explanation of the impact of Joseph upon Potiphar's Wife Kessler wrote the following lines during the course of an extended prefatory Argument:

In this moment Joseph becomes a mystical figure. But his mysticism is not that of Parsifal. His mystery is that of growth and being. His sanctity is that of creation and increase, his perfection that of things which have not yet been. He is a god of spring, unapproachable, intangible, impenetrable in his fertility. Nothing mars, nothing dims his joyousness. As a god he knows neither pity nor longing. Filled wholly with the marvel of budding youth, his body shines at the moment when he unveils it as the snow of the high Alps on a starlit night.

These passages are quoted at length in order to emphasize the strange introspective world conjured up by the joint authors and served to Strauss without considering for a moment that his reaction to it might possibly differ from theirs. And when Strauss quickly made it apparent that such was indeed the case Hofmannsthal expressed the utmost surprise. 'Joseph isn't progressing as quickly as I expected', wrote Strauss bluntly, 'The chaste Joseph himself isn't at all up my street, and if a thing bores me I find it difficult to set it to music. The God-seeker Joseph—he's going to be a hell of an effort! Well, maybe there's a pious tune for good boy Joseph lying about in some atavistic recess of my appendix.'

Hofmannsthal's horrified reply to this outburst was entirely in character. 'To me', he wrote '(Joseph) is the best and most successfully conceived character, the only thing in the whole ballet which is genuinely unusual and engaging . . . as I see him, you would have to look for the music . . . in the purest regions of your brain, where the imagination soars to the heights, to the clear air of mountain glaciers. . . .'

If we had not already had evidence of Hofmannsthal's complete self-absorption, to the point where he lost all sympathetic understanding of his composer, it would have seemed hard to explain his totally erroneous picture of how Strauss's mind worked. For him to write further: 'The angel[10] is nothing but the forefinger of this God, who is light and all that is most high—where could you call forth the highest that is in you, if not here?' reveals not merely a serious inability to grasp the very essence of Strauss's greatness as an artist, but (and perhaps more damaging still) a blindness to his weak side as already revealed by the banalities of every attempt to portray the Divine in terms of the C major triad, in work after work since *Tod und Verklärung*.

For nearly a whole year Strauss struggled with little more than the Joseph dance figures. He played over his first drafts to Hofmannsthal one December day with catastrophic results. Strauss had attempted to circumvent his lack of rapport with the mystical world of the pure fool shepherd-boy by music of period artificiality. But Hofmannsthal was not prepared to see his deepest conceptions put into the inverted commas of stylization and actually followed up his remarks with a long letter of

10 An Archangel in golden panoply appears in the closing scene.

rebuke in which he delivered himself of the now famous dictum concerning the whole nature of their collaboration: 'In every task before us the final criterion can only be sensitivity in the matter of style, and of this I must consider myself the guardian and keeper for the two of us.'

Here, if ever, in face of such presumption, such militant autocracy, was Strauss's chance to break free and go his own way. Successful as his courtship of the author of *Elektra* had been in both that great drama and in the contrasting comedy which followed it, *Der Rosenkavalier*, that same author had now not the least intention of allowing Strauss any further say in the subject or manner of his own next stage compositions. The time had come to move on, to discover new worlds and experiences on his own and to seek the stimuli of fresh artistic minds which could inspire him in the ways which came most naturally to him.

Alas for poor Strauss. Had he but known, under cover of these repeated attacks Hofmannsthal was as afraid of him, in actual fact, as he was of Hofmannsthal. But life had become so easy and safe, whether in the luxuries of Garmisch or the unending series of fêted appearances as the foremost composer-conductor of his time. How much simpler it was to bow his good-natured head to the storm and try as best he may to supply what seemed to be expected of him. Once again the discarded sketches of *Kythere* were pressed into service, and six months later, during the early summer of 1913, he wrote to Hofmannsthal that he was doing all he could to get down to the unpalatable task, helped and encouraged by Kessler.

In mid-July the offending dances were completely re-sketched and the 'big and laborious job' (as he described it) moved forward steadily. For better or worse the full score was completed on 2nd February 1914 and was given its première with enormous panache by the Diaghilev company at the Paris Opéra on 14th May the same year, the performance being conducted by Strauss himself.[11]

8

There is little doubt that the action of *Josephslegende* suffered seriously from the complex symbolism with which it was filled, and it is surprising

[11] Despite the elaborate contractual arrangements exacted from Diaghilev by Strauss, the ever-alert business man, his fee of 6,000 gold francs remained unpaid at the outbreak of war and vanished into thin air, together with the substantial resources which he had unwisely left with his good friend Speyer in England.

to find Hofmannsthal fighting against the publication of a *Textbuch* which might have been thought indispensable for just this work in particular.[12] In the event a 'text' was indeed published and, curious document as it is, it does give considerable guidance to the purpose behind the conception.

To begin with, although built around the framework of the Genesis story of Joseph in Egypt, neither place nor time are preserved. Instead the celebrated designer Leon Bakst was persuaded to model his ideas on sixteenth century Venice, with especial reference to the decorative style of Paolo Veronese. Kessler explained this curious decision in a newspaper article at the time of the first performance: 'It is around the deeply tragical contrast between two worlds—the rich, splendid, sensual, cruel world of Potiphar, lashed to fury and destruction in the soul of the woman by the distant, divinely fresh, mysterious world of Joseph—that the interest of the piece centres. And if we have taken the story away from its biblical setting and brought it to Venice it is because we wished to focus the attention entirely on this contrast, with all it might imply poetically, freeing it from all merely historical association.'

Hofmannsthal, also in a newspaper article, though a few years later, took upon himself the responsibility for the decision on the grounds that he 'held, together with Swinburne and Aubrey Beardsley, such anachronisms to be a valuable element of latter-day art. I know too,' he wrote, 'that painters of the late seventeenth century naïvely put their biblical figures into contemporary costume, and that if we did the same, we who are anything but naïve in our stage-craft, it seemed to me endlessly more important and attractive to strive for certain inner conformity in a theatrical work of art than to satisfy the Philistines in the stalls with their historical tableaux.'

Bakst, for his part, gave the reasons for his agreement to the transposition of period to be the sheer luxuriant possibilities of the Venetian setting which appealed particularly to him and which had greater potential variety than a biblical background.[13]

Be all this as it may, the huge marble pillared palace of Bakst's and Kessler's imagining, oozing luxury and opulence at every corner of the

---

[12] A textbook for a wordless ballet might in any case be thought an anomaly but Hofmannsthal had already published one such for *Der Triumph der Zeit*.

[13] Although later Bakst was himself replaced by José-Maria Sert in the preparation of the décor, his ideas and plans were preserved in full. The costumes, moreover, remained his responsibility to the last.

stage, did not this time evoke from Strauss some gorgeous sensual music for the opening bars suggestive of the atmosphere he had conjured up for *Salome*. He decided instead upon a straightforward four-square diatonic theme, announced in direct rather brash colouring by the full orchestra:

Ex. 18

After a few bars in this vein Ex. 18 is repeated as the curtain rises on the flamboyant scene. The harmonies are more adventurous now, as is also the orchestration which features arpeggios on timpani, a rushing figuration on second violins, and rows of rapid turns on D clarinet and third violins, the last-named disposed in the manner of *Elektra*. Hidden in the texture is a rising figure on the tubas which later returns at a key point in the action:

Ex. 19

Strauss now further entertains himself by contriving onomatapoeic references to the stage action such as the downward glissandi for solo violin reminiscent of *Till Eulenspiegel*, which here accompanies the pouring out of gold dust; or the glittering figuration on four harps, celeste, glockenspiel, piano and so forth depicting the heaps of precious stones carried in a giant bowl by one of Potiphar's mulatto slaves. Potiphar's Wife is portrayed by a still chordal theme intended to reflect her brooding weariness but which is not far removed musically from the motif which Strauss had just invented to describe the solemn majesty of the Bavarian Alpine scenery:

Ex. 20

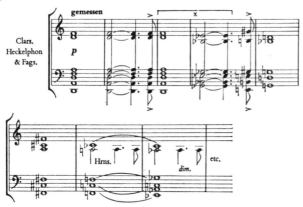

The set dance figures of Scene 2 then follow, consisting first of a procession and three dances for groups of women veiled and unveiled. Kessler described these as Nuptial Dances, 'representing symbolically the unveiling of the bride by the bridegroom on the wedding night'. The procession with which this section begins is interesting as showing Strauss adopting for the first time a conventional ballet style based on the extension and repetition of a single thematic figure with little variation of texture or mood. Moreover, in the dances which follow, we find him adopting what was for him a relatively unusual system of composite metrical patterns based on the alternation of two and three, three and four, or four and six,[14] which are all employed during the dances of the Veiled and Unveiled Women. The climax of this section comes with the Dance of the Sulamith, which although designed as an expression of the most glowing eroticism has, beneath its surging and sweeping gestures, rather the character of a Feuersnot-Rosenkavalier waltz-movement. There is, however, here too a welcome touch of rhythmic variety in the later section of the Dance:

[14] The outstanding example of this in Strauss's previous work is Octavian's first outburst in the opening scene of *Der Rosenkavalier*. The intention there, however, was more to create an effect of restlessness than to emphasize particular irregularities of metre as here.

Ex. 21

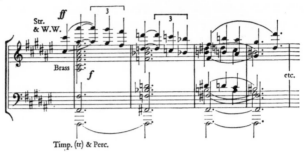

leading to (Ex. 21a):

The entire scene of the women is united motivically by a leaping figure reminiscent of *Aus Italien*, and this now returns in a linking passage after which the procession music returns briefly by way of rounding off the whole episode.

The third scene follows in which the women are replaced by male dancers, centring round the grotesque group of six Turkish boxers. These extraordinary characters indulge in a series of stylized fights which make a suitable contrast with the seductive movements of the women in the previous scene. Their music consists basically of a slinking, stealthy theme rising up in the strings as the combatants prowl round each other ('like beasts of prey' according to the stage directions) and a hammering motif featuring the timpani, descriptive of the formalized yet savage motions of the boxers. The scene is brought to a close by Potiphar's men-at-arms who intervene in the struggle when it becomes apparent that there is a real possibility of the hate-obsessed fighters actually killing one another.

All the previous action has served as introduction to the following scene in which Joseph appears for the first time. He is shown curled up in a golden hammock 'reposing like a flower, and smiling in his sleep'. His themes are announced immediately while the Sheik, whose purpose is to sell him to Potiphar, bows and gives instructions for the hammock to be brought:

Ex. 22

followed immediately by

Ex. 23

and Ex. 23a

Ex. 22 is the first of two themes taken from the discarded ballet *Kythere*, which supplied material for so many of Strauss's works from *Feuersnot* to *Schlagobers*.[15]

A further idea, derived from Ex. 22, but in Strauss's 'divinity' key of C major, depicts Joseph in his purest and most God-like simplicity:

Ex. 24

In due course Joseph rises and executes the dances described in the passage from the libretto quoted above at some length. It was, needless to say, this whole section which caused Strauss so much trouble in finding the right style for the 'chaste Joseph'. One would be fascinated to know

[15] Another stiffly canonic movement from the same source had already come into consideration for the Women's Dances of Scene 2 but had been rejected.

what music Strauss had originally sketched to which Hofmannsthal took so rooted an objection. As it stands today, there is certainly no question of Period pastiche or mannered archaism, although something of the classical dance-measures can be found, parallel in vein to the style Strauss discovered for *Le Bourgeois Gentilhomme*, as in this excerpt from the First Dance Figure:

Ex. 25

Another possibly classical influence, despite the typical false relations, can be felt in the music to the Third Dance Figure in which Joseph is supposed to perform a series of high leaps in his Searching and Wrestling after God. This was an accomplishment in which Nijinsky was unique. Legend has it that he had webbed feet; whatever the truth his levitation was certainly fantastic and he seemed at times indeed almost to fly.

Yet Strauss's essentially profane dance music can scarcely be said to match Hofmannsthal's sacred and idealistic conception.

Ex. 26

Some leaping music follows and a brief return to Ex. 23 leads to a further melody derived from the motif of Joseph's purity (Ex. 24) and thence through developments of Ex. 26 to Joseph's highest leaps of all, as a result of which we are to understand that he has found God. The music is based partly on Ex. 23 and partly on yet another new and broadly melodic idea, the cadence of which becomes significant in the closing pages of the whole work.

Ex. 27

This is the second theme derived from *Kythere* and it is indeed this whole section in which Strauss quoted verbatim and at length from his earlier sketches. At this climax of his dance the passages alluding to Joseph's spiritual purity (Ex. 22) are removed to the highest instrumental colours, descriptive as far as may be of his new-found God-like exaltation.

9

During all this leaping and God-seeking, Potiphar's Wife has been watching with increasing interest until her astonishment and admiration know no bounds. Kessler makes considerable play in the scenario with the extraordinary impression made by Joseph upon the assembled company. One young man, for example, is instructed to 'bury his face in his hands abruptly, sobbing aloud, so that he upsets a bowl of fruit in front of him, the fruit rolling about all over the table.' Strauss wisely ignores these somewhat embarrassing details, concentrating instead on working up the music of the long and elaborate dance to its logical symphonic climax and conclusion. Ultimately only the reaction of Potiphar's Wife is of structural importance and it is to this that Strauss turns when Joseph's dance reaches its appointed end.

A restless shuddering passage based on the chord-sequence ⌐ x ⌐ of her theme, Ex. 20, illustrates the emotions of Potiphar's Wife, as two mulattos take hold of Joseph and guard him while the transaction over his person is conducted between Potiphar and the Sheik (more pouring of gold dust to the slithering glissandi of solo violins, as at the opening of the work). The depth of her feelings is reflected in a complex of new themes which are to be used increasingly in connection with Potiphar's Wife:

Ex. 28

This leads to one of the most tranquil and beautiful passages of the score. It is the first of a series of extended melodisings around the tonic key and in simple affecting harmonies, examples of which recur ever more frequently in Strauss's work. After the intricacy of the preceding sections, its ingenuous polyphony—mostly in two parts of similar character—have a particularly touching quality. Thematically it centres around Ex. 24, although it includes one little ascending phrase for which Strauss found another and more important use in the duet for Barak and the Färberin in Act 3 of *Die Frau ohne Schatten*.[16]

[16] cf. Chapter XII, Ex. 46.

Ex. 29

The section ends with a peaceful statement of the ascending chords, Ex. 28(z).

For some time it has become increasingly clear that Joseph has made a profound effect upon Potiphar's Wife. At first she contemplates his appearance in an attempt to fathom the very essence of his being. She then takes a necklace from the heaped bowl at her side and hangs it round his neck, but in such a way that her hand rests for a moment on his bare flesh. At this Joseph starts up violently, the spell is broken, and all the activity of the palace life is set abruptly in motion once more. At a sign from Potiphar the slaves hastily and clumsily clear the table, the guests form a procession headed by Potiphar and his Wife, ascending by means of an impressive stairway to the rear, through a loggia to the open space beyond. Gradually the stage empties leaving Joseph who remains alone, rigid and proudly upright.

This is the centre-point of the ballet[17] and Strauss, being free from set dances, turns from the more formal movements of the previous sections in favour of an extended symphonic development and reprise. In the course of this, a number of new ideas are introduced, motifs for horns and brass in fanfare style, viz:

Ex. 30

Ex. 31

[17] In the first production *Josephslegende* was presented in two parts with an interval. No allowance is made in the score however for any such hiatus, which in a work lasting no more than an hour would hardly have been thought necessary.

Ex. 32   Ex. 33

The first entry of Ex. 30, which in time is to assume crucial importance, depicts the 'quick, almost harsh movement' with which Potiphar's Wife turns from Joseph, while Ex. 31 is concerned with Potiphar's servants and the peremptory commands which Potiphar issues to them, as to his numerous attendants of all types and descriptions. Ex. 31 also leads to the reappearance of the tuba's theme from the opening of the ballet, Ex. 19, and thence to a triumphant return of Ex. 18 itself (the music of the opening pages), its panoply of orchestral complexity rendered the more elaborate by the addition of numerous more recent motifs.

The undulating triads from the music of Potiphar's Wife, Ex. 28(z), now return though in softer colouring and dominate the music for a considerable period as the darkness of evening falls upon the scene. Joseph is left alone on the stage but the continual weaving of the different themes of Potiphar's Wife in the orchestra makes it clear that her influence still surrounds him like an invisible cloak.

Various forms of Ex. 31 mix with the texture, the ascending fourth being particularly prominent as in Exx. 31 and 33, and also in double augmentation, viz:

Ex. 34

The allusion is, as before, specifically to Potiphar's servants, who have entered on his instructions in order to open up a small underground chamber which, although really a store-cupboard, is to serve as a place where Joseph can spend the night. They lead him there and leave him alone once more, upon which he virtuously says his prayers and is rewarded for his piety, upon falling asleep, with a dream-vision of his Guardian Angel. The music, predominantly soft and sweet, alternates between extended developments of Ex. 34 (though more for musical reasons than for any continued reference to Potiphar) and a descending phrase which becomes associated with Joseph's prayers, and later with their divine response.

Ex. 35

The prayer music contains a particularly beautiful extemporization on and around Ex. 34, the rising interval of which is extended note by note until it reaches a full octave. The meandering effect of the accompanying quaver movement in the violins is very similar to parts of the *Alpensinfonie*, which was of course on the stocks at the time. The dream scene of the Guardian Angel is enacted to a return of the 'finding God' themes from Joseph's long solo scene, the broadly melodic motif drawn from *Kythere*, Ex. 27, and the high-pitched Ex. 23 which appears in pure musical-box colouring of harps, piano and celeste. Beneath the latter the theme of Joseph's purity quietly climbs up from the bottom to the very top of the orchestra and the music thins out into a mere alternation of tonic and dominant chords before coming to rest on the leading note, a high D sharp.

10

At this point Potiphar's Wife enters stealthily. A sinuous melodic strand drawn from various motivic elements in Ex. 28 winds its way upwards in the woodwind. Strauss wanted a softer colour for the first and deepest instrument than the contra-bassoon, to suggest the almost feline figure creeping towards Joseph, and decided to press into service an instrument only rarely encountered hitherto in the symphony orchestra, the double-bass (or pedal-) clarinet.

The peacefully sleeping Joseph is portrayed by a particularly sweet and innocent statement of Ex. 22 on solo violin and viola. As Potiphar's Wife watches him silently she recalls the moment during which she hung a necklace around him and Strauss recapitulates even more softly the earlier tranquil melodisings around Ex. 22 and the ascending phrases of Ex. 29.

Various themes of Joseph and of Potiphar's Wife are now alternated as Joseph wakes to find her enacting the Mary Magdalene at his feet. This phase passes, however, and before long she is making passionate love to him. The complex of themes, Ex. 28, forms the basis of the music against

which the striking triplet motif, Ex. 23a, registers Joseph's repeated gestures of protest. As Potiphar's Wife becomes ever more abandoned in her
eroticism she merges into the figure of the Unveiled Sulamith whose
music, Ex. 21, is accordingly awarded a substantial recapitulation.

Needless to say Joseph rejects her, though the disdainful way in which
he does so may be thought less than politic. Surprisingly for a simple
shepherd-boy, he assumes a pose of dignified hauteur.

Ex. 36

Ex. 36 alternates with the seductive rising phrase from the music of
Potiphar's Wife as, enacting the role of a repentant sinner, she now
kneels before him pleading, uselessly, for forgiveness. In his simplicity
he is offended to his innermost being and Joseph knows nothing of
courteous behaviour or a kind refusal. His sensibilities have been outraged and he reacts with no thoughts but of stern indignation. As a result
her passion turns to bitter hatred.

Suddenly two servants enter hastily and, on the instructions of Potiphar's Wife, seize Joseph who seems to fall into an ecstatic trance. An
utterly grotesque scene ensues in which more servants appear and, mis-
construing the situation, make elaborate gestures of distress. This so-
called 'mourning' section is laid out formally in the textbook as at the
opening of the work, that is to say, with First and Second Dance Figures
and a coda-like dance, which in this instance is described as an Oriental
Witches' Dance. Strauss however, decided to use a different, more continuous technique in which only a single change of texture and tempo
occurs during the hurly-burly of busy, violent and non-thematic
orchestral effects.

The dervish-like frenzy of the dreadful servant-women reaches its
height as the music breaks off abruptly. After a brief silence Potiphar
himself enters, calm and dignified, to a new and stately theme:

Ex. 37

He is quickly put into the picture by the hysterical servants and orders his armed men to seize the literally entranced Joseph, who remains motionless although he is loaded with heavy chains.

The action now focuses once more on Potiphar's Wife as she is revived by a young slave and led over to her Lord and Master. Joseph's cloak is thrust into her hands and she at first has tender memories (various love themes from Ex. 28) but she takes a firm grip over her feelings and hypocritically makes up to Potiphar. Her chordal motif sounds out harshly (Ex. 20) and thereafter, although the wheedling music resumes, Ex. 30 appears ever more threateningly in alternation with Potiphar's theme, Ex. 37, which also increases in sternness. Ex. 30 had made its first appearance at the moment when Potiphar's Wife conceived her insidious plot to denounce Joseph should he reject her advances. The vicious climax of this motif is therefore to some extent the climax of the ballet, for it accompanies the gesture with which Potiphar's Wife, foiled in her lustful scheme, carries out her revengeful incrimination.

Until now there had been little but the *mise en scène* which differs to any substantial degree from the main outlines of the biblical story. Admittedly the lapse of time, from Joseph's arrival in the Potiphar household until the seduction scene, is swallowed up entirely, time during which the historical Joseph was able to ingratiate himself with his powerful master and acquire a position of some eminence in Potiphar's affairs. As a result Joseph's fall, being no longer from distinction to disgrace, is considerably weakened and his quality of goodness becomes insipid. Moreover Potiphar himself had become a wholly unknown and undistinctive figure-head. Yet the main scheme of the action is drawn from legend and could reasonably be said to justify the title of the work.

The denouement in Genesis was, however, altogether too tame for Hofmannsthal and Kessler. Joseph could not be robbed of his privileges for he no longer had any, and prison was not nearly dramatic enough a punishment for the scenes of barbaric splendour the enthusiastic authors were busy conjuring up. Further still, although evil could not be allowed to triumph over good, Joseph's eventual restoration to favour at the hands of Pharaoh remained far beyond the scope of the work.

Nothing therefore could serve as an adequate culmination to the already gaudy scenario but a spectacle of torture by fire, from which Joseph would have to be rescued supernaturally by an Archangel. A glowing furnace of red-hot coals is brought in, and tongs heated within it as Joseph is pinned by the slaves, his head turned towards Potiphar. The sinuous melody, to which Potiphar's Wife entered in order to seduce Joseph, rears itself triumphantly. She is beside herself with sadistic passion and hate, the libretto stressing the significance of the flames of the gigantic brazier.

Strauss accordingly develops the music of her lust (Ex. 28) at some length, building up a stupendous climax from which the music gradually descends as attention is drawn to Joseph, whose face is increasingly lit by a pure white beam. At the height of the climax Potiphar's theme, Ex. 37, is thundered out, after which the music merges into the material of Joseph's prayer (Exx. 34 and 35). As the light grows on Joseph's upturned face, the glow of the brazier fades and eventually is miraculously extinguished altogether.

The ascending phrase from Joseph's 'Finding God' theme returns and leads to a new *Naturthema* recalling the parallel motifs from *Guntram* or *Zarathustra*.

Ex. 38

This is the motif of the Archangel who, as the white light reaches a blinding peak of intensity, has appeared suddenly as if he has swiftly travelled along it and by means of it. During this transformation from the flames of the infernal instrument of torture to the shining radiance of celestial intervention Potiphar and his household have become increasingly still, until at the appearance of the Archangel they are entirely motionless and the focus is upon Joseph and his divine visitant.

The music during which Potiphar's Wife revealed her passion for Joseph returns briefly; then as she watches the supernatural turn of events the expression on her face changes to one of horror and contrition. The Archangel glides forward until he is able to touch Joseph with his forefinger, upon which—the music again building to a climax— Joseph's chains fall from him with a clatter. The heroic trumpet theme, Ex. 36, now peals forth in full splendour coupled with the cadence from Joseph's dance (Ex. 27(x)) and the constantly rising motif of the Archangel. So the vast elaborate structure moves towards the end with the inclusion of some chordal passage-work similar in character to the music of the closing Ariadne/Bacchus scene.

Ex. 39

Such themes are of course the essence of Strauss, and the fanfare figure ⌈ x ⌉ continues to combine easily with the flowing textures of the last few pages of score which are almost exclusively concerned with the abduction of Joseph by the Archangel. There is a brief distraction as Potiphar's Wife in total despair throttles herself with her own string of pearls. The music breaks out savagely; the love theme, Ex. 28(y), surges up violently and as quickly subsides. The young slave throws herself on the body and the oldest and ugliest of all the servants with a diabolical gesture covers the face with a black veil. The subsequent lamentations of the servant-women and Potiphar's horror-struck retreat find no echo in the music, which passes immediately to a repeat of the musical-box version of Joseph's theme of innocence, Ex. 23, now introduced to depict a Christmas card vision of angels playing musical instruments as they sit on the rosy clouds of morning. There is to be no doubt in anyone's mind over the divine origin of Joseph's innocence. He disappears with the Archangel through the rear of the loggia as the curtain falls to the ascending fourths, Ex. 36(x), thundered out, now in the bass, by the assembled percussion and brass of Strauss's mammoth orchestra. The closing pages may be banal but they lack nothing in complexity and fertility of orchestral invention.

II

Richard Specht, in his largely eulogistic treatise on Strauss's work, follows the general consensus of opinion that '*Josephslegende* ought never to have been composed', but adds somewhat naïvely that 'one should not take it tragically'. This is a moot point for it is the first wholly unsuccessful work Strauss wrote as a direct result of the mental lethargy which was for many years to reduce his stature.

In one respect Specht was undoubtedly right—Strauss ought not to have allowed himself to be bludgeoned a second time into composing a work in which he had no interest; with which, moreover, he had frankly avowed himself out of sympathy. It was, however, the tragedy of his weakening purpose that he could so readily take the easiest line of resistance, and the fact that parts of *Bourgeois Gentilhomme* and *Ariadne* had turned out so well musically was a dangerously misleading precedent for him to rely upon in the future.

On the other hand, in his defence, Strauss had certainly been strongly disposed to grapple once more with the problems of writing for the ballet, even though this was a medium which did not particularly suit his natural style. Of course, so enterprising and accomplished a company as Diaghilev's must have constituted a considerable enticement in itself. What is of particular interest is that in the sketches for *Kythere* he had envisaged a score divided into entirely separate musical numbers, yet when embarking on his first definite assignment in this sphere he abandoned this classical *modus operandi* after only two or three set dances near the beginning in favour of his natural symphonic mode of expression. It was no doubt this factor in the music which led most ballet specialists to write the work off as a wordless opera in mime, and it is noteworthy that in his second ballet, *Schlagobers*, for which he wrote the scenario himself, he reverted to a more orthodox lay-out of the music in set pieces.

In his choice of a large orchestra Strauss was on this occasion doing no more than following the example of many of his colleagues who were writing scores for Diaghilev. *Daphnis and Chloe*, *Ala and Lolly*, *Le Sacre du Printemps*, were all written for mammoth orchestras and Strauss was not wrong in believing that the lavish nature of the décor and production fully justified the similarly extravagant orchestral forces he was accustomed to. The use once more of a threefold division of the violins is noteworthy though it is handled with less imagination than in *Elektra*. It is as if the novelty had worn off, and it is perhaps significant that Strauss never again divided his strings in this way.

In the woodwind department the outstanding novelty is the double-bass clarinet. This beautiful instrument fills one of the most important needs of the modern orchestra, a full-bodied, yet soft-toned fundamental.

Nevertheless Strauss seems to have hesitated, for, having decided to introduce this new colour into his already outsize orchestra, he restricted its use to the single passage in which Potiphar's Wife steals in upon the sleeping Joseph, and even this he cued in for contra-bassoon with the result that it is more often played by the latter instrument. His reticence was surprising since both D'Indy and Schönberg had already called upon the double-bass clarinet; the former in his opera *Fervaal* which appeared already in 1897, the latter for the first of his Five Orchestral Pieces op. 16, composed only four years before *Josephslegende*.

A more general feature of the score is the elaborate use of percussion together with the harps and keyboard group. The presence of no less than four harps with piano, organ, celeste and glockenspiel suggests an exoticism of instrumental colouring unusual even for Strauss, while the percussion department specifies small cymbals (Cymbeln) as well as the conventional pair (Becken), *Holz und Strohinstrumente* as well as Xylophone (the difference between the two being largely academic), and four pairs of castanets—all this apart from the usual array amongst which the wind-machine makes an engaging reappearance. The timpani are used thematically, especially during the scene of the boxers, in a manner strongly reminiscent of *Salome*, although the invention of this style of writing dates back to the early Burleske for Piano and Orchestra of 1885.

Yet so much is lacking. However opulent the orchestration, Strauss had generally made a feature of refining his style at some points in each work, treating sections of the orchestra as chamber music, while even the thickly or noisily orchestrated sections had a vivacity and brilliance which prevented the texture from becoming turgid. This is no longer sufficiently the case in *Josephslegende* and the comments of Rolland, who was at the first performance as Strauss's guest, strike a sinister note: '. . . for the rest the music seemed to me of a mediocre quality, docile and rather flat, if always amusing. . . . Strauss considerably aged, thickened, heavier and red-faced. . . .'

Violent and fantastic as much of the score is, beautiful as some sections are, the music too has aged, thickened and put on weight. Even as loyal a friend as Beecham wrote of it as:

> . . . the least attractive and original *Legend of Joseph*. The German master revealed no talent for this sort of thing: in spite of a few vivid and picturesque moments the piece went with a heavy and plodding gait which all the resource and ingenuity of the troupe could not relieve or accelerate. . . .'

In addition to the intrinsic lack of inspiration in the music there were, however, other causes for the failure of *Josephslegende* to survive. In the first place there was the shock, to Strauss and librettists alike, of Nijinsky's withdrawal from the entire project. The importance of this cannot be overestimated, nor its influence upon the very character of the completed work. Not only had the title role been planned for him from the outset, such dances as the leaping movement in Joseph's 'Searching for God' being designed expressly for Nijinsky, for whom there could be no real substitute, but he was to have been wholly responsible for both production and choreography. With this purpose in mind Nijinsky had visited Strauss together with Diaghilev and Kessler during all the early negotiations, and Hofmannsthal had repeatedly stressed the importance of Nijinsky having priority of judgement in the exercise of his imagination. No one, however, could possibly have foreseen Nijinsky's abrupt decision to get married, and the obviously quite insurmountable rift this would cause in his relationship with Diaghilev. There could be no question of his continuing in the company and a substitute had quickly to be found.

The production was undertaken by the incomparable Fokine, at that time the principal choreographer of the company, but although he had tried to stop the gaps in the repertoire as far as possible by himself dancing Nijinsky's roles, he was no longer young enough to undertake the characterization of the 'flower-like' boy Joseph. It was in the search for the right dancer for this role that Diaghilev discovered the young Leonide Massine who, making his début on this occasion, himself subsequently enjoyed a career of the highest calibre.

The part of Potiphar's Wife was taken by Mme Kusnetzova, a Russian opera singer who had also been trained as a dancer, and this choice—not altogether a success it must be acknowledged—gives perhaps a pointer to the nature of the whole work which has sometimes been denied its full status as a Ballet. Strauss did to some extent court such a rejection by committing himself in the popular Viennese press to reforming the whole art of ballet, developing it into Music-Drama without words. Finding that such an intention had proved, not unnaturally, unacceptable to either dancers or musicians, he tried in later years retrospectively to advance yet further ideas of his purpose in composing *Josephslegende*:

> I wanted in *Josephslegende* to put new blood into the Dance.
> . . . The Dance as expression of the dramatic, though not

exclusively. That modern perversion of the Dance in which
it serves as no more than paraphrased or rhythmic action unfortunately leads us often all too far away from that real
kernel of true, pure inspiration—movemnet and the absolute
beauty of consecrated dance: the ballet. It is this that I wanted
to rejuvenate. My Joseph contains both elements: the dance
as drama, and the dance as . . . Dance.

This faintly forlorn attempt at explaining in words a composer's purpose is not a little reminiscent of Stravinsky's dictum concerning his *Duo
Concertante*, for Violin and Piano, in which he applied himself to 'solving
the acoustic problem of associating the sound of strings struck on the
piano with that of strings set in motion by the bow of the violin'.

But Cyril Beaumont put the matter in a nutshell when he wrote:

> *La Legende de Joseph* was not so much a ballet as a wordless
> play in the manner of Sumurun.[18] It contained many dances,
> but these are more in the manner of embroidery than a
> necessary adjunct to the plot.

This is to some extent borne out by the very title of the work 'Action in
one Act'. Even in the literature of Ballet and of Diaghilev, *Josephslegende*
is rarely mentioned except in relationship to Massine's debut.

Lydia Sokolova wrote very entertainingly about both this début and
the ballet as a whole:

> In *La Legende de Joseph* Massine was given the part of the
> young Joseph who, after resisting the advances of Potiphar's
> Wife and being denounced by her to her husband, is rescued
> from the cauldron of boiling oil [*sic*!] by a convenient angel.
> There was very little acting in the part, it was strictly a
> dancing one, but as Massine was not then a very powerful
> dancer Fokine cut down his movements to a minimum and
> the part of Joseph was much reduced. Massine wore a dimi-
> nutive white tunic, which amounted to almost nothing at all,
> and he looked rather touching.
>
> As a spectacle *Joseph* was staggering. A large rostrum ran
> across the whole back of the stage, and on this there was a
> long table round which the big groups and spectacular effects
> took place. The costumes were magnificent, particularly
> those of Potiphar's Wife. She moved about on high gilded
> clogs, attended by servants, two of whom had a couple of

---

[18] *Sumurun* was a Pantomime by Friedrich Freksa and Victor Hollaender, produced in Berlin and Vienna by Max Reinhardt in 1910.

honey-coloured wolfhounds on white leads. Nearly everything in the ballet was some shade of gold, except for Massine's white tunic. I was one of the six slaves in a dance for
three tall girls and three short ones. The ballet on the whole
was not exciting, and it was not given for long.[19]

Amongst other causes for the failure of *Josephslegende* must be counted
the unsuitability of Kessler, who cannot possibly lay claim to literary
stature. This curious enigmatic figure occupied a strange and doubtful
position in pre-war Europe. The son of a German-Swiss father and Irish
mother with Persian blood, he was educated in England (at Ascot, with
Churchill) and Hamburg. An only child of rich parents, he was greatly
pampered and turned into an effeminate dilettante, dabbling in literature,
diplomacy and the printing trade. He owned a private press at Weimar
which later produced a number of quite remarkable editions. Meantime
Kessler had attached himself to the Stefan George literary circle, though
more as onlooker than participant. Here he had met Hofmannsthal.

He was an ardent pacifist and a strong believer in a United States of
Europe. He was even, for a short time, the first German Minister in the
newly created Poland of 1919, and it is clear that, for all his apparent
amateurishness, he had acquired some importance in influential quarters.

12

Whether *Josephslegende* would have remained long in the repertoire of
Diaghilev's company had not the war brought all such ambitious projects to an end, seems doubtful in view of contemporary reports. At all
events they never revived it, and although the work has occasionally
been brought back onto the stage by other companies (notably in Germany during 1921–2), such occasions have been few and far between.

In 1947, two years before his death, Strauss looked back ruefully for a
last time at this black sheep and prepared from it, for a slightly reduced
orchestra, a *Symphonic Fragment*. But all was in vain, for this too has
scarcely ever been heard since its first performance in Cincinnati in
March 1949. Not that Strauss exerted himself unduly over it, for it consists of little more than a cut version of the original score with patchwork
where necessary to link together the sections chosen for inclusion.

The Fragment begins with the opening bars, as far as the gloomy
chordal motif of Potiphar's Wife (Ex. 20), after which it jumps with no

[19] *Dancing with Diaghilev*. John Murray, London, 1960.

Strauss and Hofmannsthal. One of the rare meetings

more than a change of modulation straight into the Dance of the Sulamith which is given intact though with some alterations of instrumental
texture.

The procession music of the servant-women is then omitted together
with the entire scene of the boxers, and the Fragment proceeds to the
appearance of Joseph (Exx. 22 and 23) and without preamble, by means
of a further cut, to his first dance (Ex. 25). This and the second dance are
given complete, but the third (Ex. 26) is severely curtailed and shorn of its
leaping figures as well as the extended symphonic build-up.

The fourth dance is again intact, but the music then passes straight to
the tranquil melodisings which describe the profound effect Joseph has
made on Potiphar's Wife.

After a substantial cut we are at the scene during which Potiphar's
Wife, having disturbed the sleeping Joseph, is playing alternately the
violent seducer and the penitent Magdalene. There are a series of excisions in the passage which follows and the music builds quickly to the
return of the Sulamith's music and Joseph's haughty motif, Ex. 36. A
few more bars devoted to the posturings of Potiphar's Wife then lead to
the second major excision, as the result of which we are, without further
ado, at the arrival of the Archangel. The discovery of the servant-
women, their dervish-like dances of distress, the entrance of Potiphar,
the denunciation, the fiery furnace, all have disappeared. Even the edify-
ing portrayal of Potiphar's Wife strangling herself with her own pearls is
removed by dint of one last cut in favour of the angelic orchestra on its
rosy clouds, from which point the Fragment proceeds without interruption to the end of the ballet.

It is unfortunate that the most stimulating sections of the score are
those which have in general been sacrificed and that what remain are by
and large the pages in which Strauss tried to match the more high-
minded and pretentious conceptions of his librettists. Yet if the Fragment
(the title is possibly a misnomer) were to have any homogeneity or form,
if it were not indeed to disintegrate into a suite of fragments, there was
perhaps little else to be done.

By his choice of excerpts Strauss has concentrated on one facet of the
score at the expense of its exotic character. The flamboyant opening
theme now only occurs once, while the remaining passages are mostly
chosen for their lyrical quality such as the dance of the Sulamith and the
extended dances of Joseph. These are then developed and recapitulated
in the later sections of the Fragment. Hence some opportunities are lost,

especially in the two major excisions, and the inclusion of so much of the pompous ending is unjustified without the dramatic pages which led to it. In particular one might regret the loss of the music which accompanies the stirrings of passion in the heart of Potiphar's Wife (Ex. 28), without which the references included in the latter half of the Fragment are meaningless. The beautiful prayer music (Exx. 34 and 35) is another passage one might have welcomed. There has been all too little attempt at making a new symphonic work out of the best material. Strauss merely cut the whole down to a more manageable length for possible concert performance, and the result is just as much a Fantasia, and contains the same faults as the companion piece actually so-called, taken from *Die Frau ohne Schatten*, as we shall see at the end of the next chapter.

The Fragment has done little or nothing to keep before the world the ill-fated music to a misguided work, despite some agreeable pages of vintage Strauss orchestration. The truth has to be faced that *Josephslegende* is moribund and will never be more than a curiosity. Its chief value was always as Hofmannsthal once described it to Strauss—a *Zwischenarbeit*, a task between tasks. It kept Strauss's imagination working and his pen flowing in preparation for the next huge project which Hofmannsthal was already planning for him—*Die Frau ohne Schatten*.

CHAPTER XII

DIE FRAU OHNE SCHATTEN

I

THROUGHOUT his career Hofmannsthal was attracted to legend and the fairy-tale. In his earlier works for the theatre he drew from Greek mythology not only for his adaptation of Sophocles' *Elektra* but in a pair of similar modern re-dramatizations of the Oedipus saga, while the mass of papers found after his death proved to contain sketches for yet further pieces based on classical mythology (Leda and the Swan, Jupiter and Semele, and so on), all drafted at this early period.

The scheme for a libretto based on the Semiramis legend, which had germinated in Hofmannsthal's mind even before his collaboration with Strauss over *Elektra*, was based on an idea which he found in the works of the seventeenth-century Spanish author Calderón de la Barca. Although Calderón continued to occupy his attention for some time to come, Semiramis did not, much to Strauss's disappointment, and Hofmannsthal now turned his mind towards the purely theatrical reworking of old-time dramatic ideas derived either from the Spaniard or from medieval legend.

In particular Calderón's conception of the 'World Theatre' remained in the foreground of his imagination. On it he had already based his own *Kleine Welttheater* written in 1897, and now, in 1911, with *Rosenkavalier* behind him, he used it again in the preparation of a new version of the ancient morality play *Everyman*, this too being essentially derived in origin from old folk-saga.[1]

[1] The *Grosse Salzburger Welttheater* was also to follow some twenty years after as the central pivot, together with *Jedermann*, around which Reinhardt invited Hofmannsthal to collaborate with him in the creation of the Salzburg Festival.

However, none of these ideas seemed suitable for musical purposes and Hofmannsthal tried a different point of departure with an idea taken from Hauff's fairy-tale *Das Kalte Herz*, a truly old-German story of giants and dwarfs with a stern moral not far removed from some of the more famous tales of the brothers Grimm. Briefly the story tells of a young charcoal-burner in the black forest who, tired of unceasing endeavour in deepest poverty, seeks power and wealth at the hands of one of the two ruling spirits of the forest. He achieves his desire but at the sacrifice of his heart which is replaced by a stone. In the years which follow, he experiences and spreads around him such misery and cruelty that at the end of the story he begs the forest fairy to take back his gifts in exchange for his true heart and the ability to enjoy human warmth and happiness.

Strauss's reaction was infectiously boyish: 'Cheers for *Das Steinerne Herz*! Plenty of nature atmosphere, please: German forest. Thunderstorms as Holländer-Michel fells his trees; this is how the whole thing might start. . . .' Unfortunately such enthusiasm evoked a most discouraging response from Homannsthal who had never at any time intended to adapt this story as it stands. He planned, rather, to use it more as a starting point for some legendary scheme *à la Freischütz* or *Feuersnot*. 'A whole world of houses and narrow lanes, churches and banquets, a scene of conflagration, a cemetery of the dead, human voices and the voices of spirits, organ and cloister, death and the devil.'

Hofmannsthal's preoccupation with such a world of legend was by no means confined to European saga, but was supplemented by Bachofen's encyclopaedic *Myths of the Occident and the Orient*. It carried with it, moreover, a strong predilection for symbolism, for obscurity even, and by 1911 he was ripe for some great work of synthesis. Accordingly, instead of allowing Strauss to pursue paths similar to those of their recent past together, he determined to embroil him in new realms of fantasy, magic and symbolic moralizing. Strauss himself, without having any real idea of what he was letting himself in for, gave Hofmannsthal his head while offering from time to time cautious words of encouragement. Matters had already reached the point where he was no longer sure how best to behave, since it only required him to make too excited a show of enthusiasm for the poet immediately to lose all interest. Hofmannsthal himself acknowledged this in a letter to Strauss in which he wrote:

'So bizarre is my constitution in such matters that, having once spoken to you of a certain possibility ... your repeated allusions to this idea, your taking it up, your acquaintance with it, make the whole thing distasteful to me and have driven it out of my thoughts and dreams, perhaps for good.'

Here then was one of the main causes of the loss to Strauss of both the extremely promising *Semiramis* and the intriguing *Das Steinerne Herz*, although Hauff's stone-hearted theme started Hofmannsthal on a new operatic project involving nothing short of the complete petrification of one of the principal characters.

The origins of this fresh scheme can be traced back some eleven years, to an elaborate poetic drama, which dated from 1900. Entitled *Bergwerk zu Falun*, it is strongly suggestive of the actual matter from which sprang *Die Frau ohne Schatten* (as the new work was called from the beginning).

2

Hofmannsthal originally intended *Die Frau ohne Schatten* to be the immediate successor to *Der Rosenkavalier*. He was even sanguine enough at one time to promise Strauss the first act for setting during the summer of 1912. In this, however, he underestimated hopelessly the enormous complexities of his self-imposed task and thus found it necessary to keep Strauss occupied with other smaller projects. These, the Divertissement and the Ballet, which were simultaneously forming in his ever fertile imagination, have already been discussed in the two preceding chapters.

In addition, however, there was a further consideration which held Hofmannsthal back from rushing too quickly into what he felt was to be their major task of collaboration. He had already come to consider a new line of development to be necessary for Strauss himself, that is to say, away from Wagner and towards classicism. With this in mind he planned to design his own verses in such a way as to tend wherever possible towards set pieces separated by recitative. It was to a considerable extent in order to familiarize himself and Strauss with such a *modus operandi* that he conjured up the *Bourgeois Gentilhomme/Ariadne* scheme as a 'slight interim work' which, he said, would make it clearer 'how to construct a dramatic piece as a whole so that the *set numbers* (Hofmannsthal's emphasis) regain more and more their paramount importance'. Here perhaps, was also the motive behind Hofmannsthal's eagerness for

Strauss to fill in the time by working on a classical ballet (whether on *Orestes and the Furies, Josephslegende*, or whatever) in which, more than in any other form, set pieces were the normal method of construction. In the event, this attempt at influencing Strauss's manner as a composer proved abortive. Try as he could, Strauss was unable to organize *Josephslegende* into separate numbers, apart from a few isolated dances near the beginning, and when at last he came to *Die Frau ohne Schatten* he actually fell back on the most Wagnerian style that he had used since *Guntram*. Hofmannsthal had mistaken form for content as the chief influence in lightening Strauss's mental outlook. On the contrary, Strauss came nearer to Hofmannsthal's ideals when tossing off the gay *Schlagobers* and *Intermezzo* to his own libretti than in the heavy-weight *Josephslegende*, *Frau ohne Schatten* and *Aegyptische Helena* with which Hofmannsthal assiduously fed him.

3

During the greater part of 1912 Hofmannsthal made little or no progress with the mighty master-project. The widely-spaced references to it in his letters blow alternately hot and cold. The early months of the year were to a large extent occupied with the *Bourgeois/Ariadne* project, and the bad summer was at least partially responsible for slowing up the creative flow. Hence it was not until the autumn that any significant advance was made, and even then largely with the overall plan rather than with the text of the first act. At each step forward he aroused Strauss's expectations with ever more exciting accounts concerning the quality of the forthcoming *oeuvre*: it would turn out a *very, very* beautiful thing—a happy profound subject which he regarded with passionate and sanguine affection—which was, moreover, bound to establish him, Hofmannsthal, once for all Strauss's *Leib-, Hof- und Hausdichter*.[2] He began to have visions of becoming Goethe's successor, while the work itself would be the opera Goethe had always hoped to write.

In the late autumn, with *Ariadne* launched, and, as he misguidedly supposed at the time, safely behind him, Hofmannsthal was able at last to devote his full attention to *Die Frau ohne Schatten*, and by January was writing with still undaunted enthusiasm that the elaborate scheme was falling into place. It was indeed a vast new world of symbolic mythology

---

[2] 'Family-hearth-and home-poet', might give the nearest English equivalent to this colloquial expression.

which he was engaged on hammering into sufficient shape to fit some mould practicable for the theatre. The three acts, wrote Hofmannsthal, were to be divided into eight scenes, the seven transitions from one to another sphere of existence providing outstanding opportunities for music to fill out what must perforce be left blank by the librettist. Within the eight scenes there were to be no less than 'eleven significant, almost pantomimically incisive situations, but it is their combination— in which two worlds, two pairs of beings, enhance each other and eventually find their equilibrium—which gives unity to the whole work'.

It is in no way surprising that these abstruse references to the action of the new drama stimulated Strauss's curiosity, and at his pressing invitation one of those rare extended meetings of the two men occurred at the end of March, taking the form of a joint excursion through Italy.[3] This was a success and gave Strauss at last a more detailed idea of the new project, so that he even began to visualize Hofmannsthal's different 'spheres of existence' in terms of contrasted orchestration, the 'Ariadne' ensemble perhaps being suitable for the upper spiritual world, the full orchestra being held in reserve for the 'denser, more colourful atmosphere on earth', as Hofmannsthal put it. In a similar way it became Hofmannsthal's intention to aim at a certain variety of style in his own verses between the contrasting sections. He soon became acutely dissatisfied with the scenes in the spirit world which he had already drafted, and set to work to rewrite them again and again. Accordingly by the following September he was once more apologizing to Strauss for having made so little progress. By this time, however, Strauss was immersed in the heavy waters of *Josephslegende* which he reckoned would keep him occupied at least until Easter.

An additional retarding factor had now to be taken into account. During the autumn of 1913 Hofmannsthal had become so engrossed by the symbolism and magic of the opera's subject matter that he found the limitations of the scenario he was preparing for Strauss too restricted for the potential contained within it. The more he pondered over it, the more ideas crowded into his mind, many of which were frankly impossible in terms of the stage. As a result, while completing the first half of the opera's Act 1 as he had promised, he gave way to the temptation of beginning work on a prose version of the story which he visualized as growing side by side with the opera itself.

[3] Unfortunately no accounts survive of the trip. They must have been a splendid sight in their vintage car.

Here again, after a flying start the poet discovered that he had been over-optimistic. Nevertheless, the first pages of the opera libretto reached Strauss as a New Year's present and the remainder of Act 1 followed in April.

4

But world events were fast overtaking them and although the second act was in Strauss's hands by July, work was inevitably delayed by the outbreak of war. Well might Strauss in later years refer to the opera as a 'child of sorrow'. Hofmannsthal himself was called up, and although before many months had passed he managed to be transferred to a diplomatic branch of the forces and was withdrawn from any area of actual danger, the unsettling effect on a man of his nervous sensibility was undoubtedly acute. Strauss, too, experienced considerable anxiety; not on account of himself, for he was ten years Hofmannsthal's senior and by now a man of fifty, but for his son, Franz, who was coming to the age for military service. Fortunately, however, the call-up was repeatedly delayed until the summer of 1917, and even then the matter dragged on for the better part of a further year. At last a medical board declared Franz once and for all exempt from active service abroad, on the grounds that the now twenty-one-year-old boy had outgrown his strength.

Nevertheless, wartime conditions claimed their inevitable toll. Act 2 was actually composed at lightning speed by October and orchestrated by the following May, but it was only two years later that Strauss was able to write saying that the entire piece was complete. The third act had given poet and musician endless troubles and heart-searchings. Hofmannsthal even agreed to redraft completely some portions after receiving a long letter of detailed critical points. A meeting in Vienna followed, at the house of the conductor Franz Schalk, where Hofmannsthal heard much of the music for the first time and was enormously impressed. Yet while Strauss could criticize constructively from the theatrical point of view it would be idle to pretend that he really understood Hofmannsthal's conception, and in the end he had to confess that after all the effort and confusion he could no longer tell good from bad in what he had done.

He had not even been single-minded in this formidable task. He had, in the intervals of waiting, completed his *Alpine Symphony* after which, there being nothing more interesting on the horizon, he had eventually succumbed to Hofmannsthal's persistent proposals for a redrafted

Ariadne. It was in fact in the early autumn of 1916, at almost exactly the same time as the première of the revised *Ariadne* with its entirely new Vorspiel, that Strauss at long last completed the composition of *Die Frau ohne Schatten*, though the orchestration of the third act occupied him for a further nine months.

It was doubly unfortunate that this third act suffered such delays and interruptions since it was by its very nature the most complicated, the most psychologically abstruse, and thus needing the greatest continuity of creative effort and self-criticism on the part of both librettist and composer. In the event, even Hofmannsthal had later to concede that all was not well with the final result and that it had undoubtedly suffered through too heavy-handed an approach from both of them.

5

Throughout this time the prose version of the opera continued, if laboriously, to take shape. Hofmannsthal described it as an *Erzählung* (narration) although it turned out to be little less than a short novel, and before he eventually completed it in 1919 he found himself admitting that it had proved to be one of the hardest tasks he had ever undertaken. Into it he poured the innumerable fantasies which he had been forced to discard when working on the opera, and while, therefore, the *Erzählung* runs roughly parallel with the main course of the opera's action, there are certain important differences between the two versions. In certain instances indeed the *Erzählung* contains whole episodes omitted entirely from the opera. In order to present as nearly as possible Hofmannsthal's conception as a whole, the succeeding account of the work will follow its course as it unfolds in opera and *Erzählung* side by side.

Hofmannsthal's sources for his new symbolic myth-drama were unusually diverse and served as mere starting points for his own peculiarly tortuous mind. They possess, however, a strongly unifying factor in their derivation from the history or mythology of the *Thousand Nights and a Night*. His precedent in this, a precedent of which he was profoundly conscious, lay in the references to Egypt and Persia in *Die Zauberflöte*. For the semi-divine priest-figure of Sarastro, who owes his origin to the historical Zoroaster, Hofmannsthal substituted the spirit-king Kaikobad. This mysterious character is derived from the real-life ruler Kaikobad the Great referred to in *Omar Khayyam* and who reigned over the Turkish Selyuks during the early thirteenth century.

A further debt to Mozart and Schikaneder also emerged in the conception of two contrasted couples who only reach the path of virtue and wisdom after severely testing trials and ordeals. The chief difference here lay in Hofmannsthal's evolutionary process with the comic Papageno pair, so to speak. In the same way as in *Ariadne*, Hofmannsthal's notebooks show that his mind was running on the Commedia dell'Arte figures, though this time re-enacted in Viennese costume.

> 'Fantastic opera. The one pair: Smeraldine, Harlequin. She wishes to remain beautiful always. He awkward and good-natured. She gives away her child to a wicked fairy dressed as a fishmonger's wife (the shadow thrown in as supplement)—the Kaiserin, a fairy's daughter, has lost her child. She is provided with the strange child. In the end she gives it back to its real mother ... Solomon's judgement (1911)'

Here then, we find the origin of the Färber (dyer or colour-master)[4] and Färberin. He, his character like his name, Barak—coming from Baraka, the term for saintliness amongst (this time) the Berber people— is good, gentle and tolerant.[5] She, on the other hand, came to Hofmannsthal after a meeting with Pauline Strauss de Ahna; 'Your wife', he wrote to Strauss, 'might well, in all discretion, be taken as a model ... she (the Färberin) is a bizarre woman with a very beautiful soul, *au fond*, strange, moody, domineering and yet at the same time likeable.' All the remainder of the personages in the new scheme, as it grew in Hofmannsthal's mind, are in the nature of nameless type-castings—the Kaiser and Kaiserin (Emperor, Empress) the Nurse, the Messenger, and so on.

The underlying theme of the drama can be found in Hofmannsthal's autobiographical sketches *Ad me ipsum*. Based on his favourite concept of the *allomatisches* (a word taken from the Greek and signifying 'transformation through the influence of another') it is shown as a crossing of two philosophies; the question of whether to comprehend and accept one's fate or flee from it, on the one hand, and the ideal of self-purifying

---

[4] The choice of colour-master as the human representative's professional calling was by no means made at random. Throughout the *Erzählung*, and especially in the fantastic final chapter, Hofmannsthal makes great play with colours to symbolize spiritual condition and influences.

[5] Both Barak and Kaikobad also appear in the very first scene of Gozzi's *Turandot* in Schiller's version, a play undoubtedly known by Hofmannsthal. Barak in particular is the name given to one of the characters in the drama, Calaf's one-time Major-domo.

through transformation on the other. The two pairs of characters, Kaiser and Kaiserin, Barak and his wife, epitomize these motifs and are also brought into conjunction by a third philosophy which was very dear to Hofmannsthal: redemption through the unborn. He summed up the essence of the work in a quotation from Goethe's *Die Geheimnisse:*

'Von der Gewalt, die alle Wesen bindet
Befreit der Mensch sich, der sich überwindet' [6]

It is apparent that we are dealing with no light matters. As Hammelmann, sympathetic commentator as he is, well expresses it: [7]

'Perhaps even those who are able to follow the thread through mythology and allegory, through mysticism and philosophy, in a setting now realistic, now supernatural, may find [the poet's] ultimate intention, though undoubtedly high-minded, somewhat disappointing in proportion to the immense effort required'.

Hofmannsthal postulates three planes of existence: the spiritual world, ruled by Kaikobad; the materialistic and sordid world of man; and in between these a kind of floating stage of life, with implications from and reactions upon each of the other two. The shadowless woman herself is depicted as the actual daughter of Kaikobad who inhabits this third, Purgatorio-like world, the country of the Seven Moon Mountains. She is watched over jealously but unsuccessfully by a malevolent Amme (Nurse) who too is condemned, though bitterly against her will, to frequent this middle plane. This spirit daughter, who becomes the Kaiserin, has since early childhood been entrusted by her father Kaikobad with a talisman which enables her to change her shape at will into any other living creature: bird, gazelle, fish and so on. [8] Such freedom of the elements does not make the Amme's task of supervision any easier, and in due course the spirit maiden is captured and wooed by a mortal, whom Hofmannsthal describes merely as the Kaiser, the Emperor of the South Eastern Islands.

Such a union is fraught with danger for spirits and mortals alike: if she conceives, the maiden is lost to the spirit world for ever; if she does not

[6] 'From that power which binds all beings, the man sets himself free who overcomes himself.'

[7] *Hofmannsthal.* Bowes & Bowes, Cambridge, 1957.

[8] According to Specht, the talisman with its power of transmutation came to the maiden from her mother, but there seems to be no corroboration for this. From her mother, on the other hand, she certainly derived a close affinity with the human race. Since the entire plot hinges on this it is accordingly the more tantalizing that we never learn any more about the mother-figure.

within a year—specifically twelve moons—she brings disaster to the
Kaiser, for according to oriental tradition he who marries a peri must
win a child by her within that time or be turned to stone as punishment
for his presumption. 'The curse is upon him, not her', commented Hofmannsthal, 'for he, through his jealous, sensual love is guilty.'

The concern with child-bearing is crucial and is symbolized by the
throwing of a shadow. Kaikobad's daughter has hitherto cast no shadow
—'so little indeed' says the Amme, 'that the light passes through her body
as if it were of mountain crystal'. Should she bear the Kaiser's child,
however, this would cease to be so and the spirit world is in constant
dread of such an eventuality, for with the fact of conception she would
cease to be a spirit, and become a mortal.[9] As a first step towards the
world of humans, she has already temporarily forfeited her talisman of
transmutation at the moment of her union with the Kaiser, a loss as
deeply mourned by the Amme as by the Kaiserin herself though for
different reasons. Whereas for the Amme the talisman might have been
the means of escape from what she can only see as the despised clutches of
the mortal Kaiser, to the Kaiserin it is bound up with the radiant circumstances of her capture and courtship, through which a new meaning of
life has been opened up to her, a meaning the Amme can never understand.

The loss of the talisman also has the effect of giving it new intrinsic
value to the Kaiserin and when it is later returned by the Kaiser's falcon
she reads for the first time, and with growing enlightenment, the letters
carved upon it. Through them she learns that she herself must cause the
downfall of her new-found lover unless she can earn a shadow. Her determined search for that shadow is the subject of opera and *Erzählung* alike.

6

At the beginning of the action the Kaiser and Kaiserin are living in a Blue
Palace far removed from the world of mankind, though connected with
it as well as with the spiritual world. Each day the Kaiser roams the
woods of his South Eastern Islands indulging his favourite sports of hunt-

[9] There is, as will be seen, a confusion during the whole work as to whether the
possession of a shadow denotes actual pregnancy or merely potential motherhood.
At this early juncture there is no doubt that Hofmannsthal intends to signify the
very presence of the child in the womb: 'She throws no shadow, and she knows that
she is not with child; these are one and the same, symbol and reality'. Before long
however, inconsistencies will arise in this connexion.

ing and falconry[10]. Scenes of continual and unabating passion occur every night between the Kaiser and his newly abducted Kaiserin. At the expiration of each month the enraged Kaikobad sends to the palace a different messenger whose duty it is to enquire after the shadow of the Kaiserin, that is to say, whether she be with child or no. In each case the question is asked of the Amme, who crouches at the threshold of the palace, brooding and discontent. Twelve such messengers have come at each new moon, and have received the same triumphantly negative reply. Now three days only remain;[11] the twelfth messenger has come and treats the Amme with the utmost contempt as he warns her of dire consequences not only to herself but to the entire spirit world should she fail to prevent the Kaiserin from conceiving. She for her part complains bitterly of the unfair circumstances of her hopeless assignment.

Both scenario and *Erzählung* open with this sinister interview between the Amme and the Twelfth Messenger, but the *Erzählung* introduces the concept that everything has been predestined in order to initiate a series of trials, as in *Die Zauberflöte*, which lie ahead. Even the loss of the talisman is bound up with the need for the Kaiserin to undergo such an ordeal, for which purpose no circumstance can be made 'easier, no danger minimized. In the course of these testings, says the Messenger, or Bote, there is an awesome danger that the Kaiserin might encounter the Golden Water of Life ('with its secret gifts', adds the Amme).

Although it is not clear to what extent Kaikobad is omnipotent, he does, like Sarastro to some extent, represent the ultimate Deity. From his mighty will spring the events of the drama, and Strauss accordingly begins his musical setting with no more prelude than the direct evocation of his name in the orchestra, just as he had done in the opening of *Elektra* with the name of Agamemnon.

[10] Hunting and falconry were, apart from war, the principal occupations of eastern nobles. Parallels can be found in many places in oriental mythology but it is noteworthy that the whole incident of the gazelle, the manner of the falcon beating its wings into the eyes, and the Kaiser's anger with, and loss of, his favourite falcon can all be clearly found in the 'Tale of King Sindibad and his falcon' from the *Thousand Nights and a Night*, Burton's translation, Vol. 1, pp. 51ff.

[11] It is never explained how these three days of grace come about between the coming of the last messenger and the expiration of the allotted year. Some reference to the intercalary days of the Hebrew calendar is probably at the root. Moreover, in the opera we only become acquainted with the last of the twelve messengers. In the *Erzählung* others are shown to be figures of importance, notably the first, an impressive old man clothed in white, and the seventh, who is identified significantly as 'The Fisherman' (see p. 199 below).

Ex. 1

There is, moreover, a strong analogy with Agamemnon since exactly as in *Elektra* the spirit of the dominant figure-head, in this case Kaikobad, hovers over the entire drama without ever actually appearing.

Behind the heavy declamations of Ex. 1 in the brass and percussion, the clarinets (five, including E♭, basset-horn and bass clarinet) can be heard softly holding a sustained unison, three octaves deep, which in due course moves into an eerie and serpentine motif characterizing the Amme.

Ex. 2 [12]

There is an upward sweep and abruptly the action has begun. With a rushing of flutes, harps and no less than two celestes the appearance of the Bote is heralded. His theme, or, as it becomes, that of the spirits he represents, is picked out of the careering scale passages in various forms with long or short note values:

Ex. 3 [13]

[12] Note Strauss's continuing habit, dating back from earliest years, of accenting all the short notes of a phrase.

[13] It is of interest to compare this motif with the opening theme of Tchaikovsky's *Manfred*, remembering that Manfred himself was a persistent dabbler in the world of spirits.

The Bote's flight is vividly depicted in the orchestration until with a violent statement of Kaikobad's motif he stands before the Amme. Such a wind-swept arrival does not wholly conform with Hofmannsthal's description, in which the Spirit Messenger's progress appears as the flitting of a bright light across 'the ebony blackness of the mountain lake'.

His stern cross-examination with respect to the shadowless state of the Kaiserin introduces two closely connected motifs. The first refers directly to the shadow itself:

Ex. 4

while the second obviously related theme (sweetly announced by a small group of solo strings accompanied by the two celestes) depicts the Kaiserin and provides an ideally translucent setting for the Amme's description of her crystal-like body.

Ex. 5

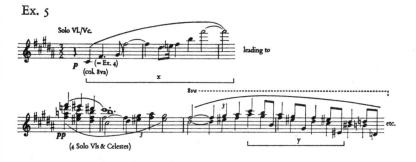

The latter section of this extended theme refers specifically to the spirit-maiden's ability to assume any shape at will.

As the Amme tries to exculpate herself from the Bote's accusations of careless guardianship she refers in turn to the Kaiserin's parental inheritances: her affinity with mankind from her mother (Exx. 6 and 7) and her power of transmutation from her father (Ex. 5(y)).

Ex. 6

Ex. 7

(Vc. Ob.&W.W.)

f

The second of these two themes, Ex. 7, with its starkly accented rising intervals, represents mankind, and is one of the chief motifs of the opera. It derives from the shadow theme, Ex. 4, its perfect fourths distorted, and at times refers also to the Kaiserin's leaning towards humanity and hence her eventual determination to become a shadowed mortal. Ex. 6 gives the first hint of the sinister motif connected with the Kaiserin's involuntary influence upon the fate of those humans with whom she consorts (see Ex. 9 below).

The Amme next describes the regular and passionate nights the lovers have spent during the past twelve months and this initiates the entry of the Kaiser's love theme. It is sung by a solo violin in a soft duet with solo viola, the latter playing the Kaiserin's melody, Ex. 5:

Ex. 8

p espr.

and later:

He is, says the Amme scornfully, 'nothing but a hunter and a lover. His nights are her day, his days her night.'[14]

The Bote then tells the Amme of the three remaining days at the expiration of which the Kaiserin must return to Kaikobad, a prospect greeted by the Amme with overwhelming joy since she herself would also be liberated from an uncongenial assignment, and return with her

[14] This curious but surely figurative statement has been interpreted to imply that the roles of night and day are reversed in the transitory existence of which the Blue Palace forms a part. I find it difficult, however, to reconcile such an idea with the passage of time as it is portrayed during the opening scenes of the drama.

Strauss *en famille*

charge to the spirit world. The Kaiser, on the other hand will be turned to stone.

Ex. 9

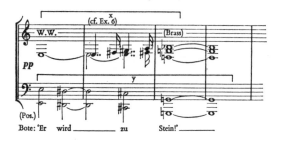

Bote: 'Er wird _____ zu Stein!' _____

7

At this moment the Kaiser himself appears on the threshold and the Amme, turning abruptly, finds that the Bote has vanished. In the *Erzählung* not a single word is exchanged between the Amme and the Kaiser, as he rides off for his daytime hunting. He treats her contemptuously, 'as no more than a strip of carpet beneath his feet'.

One of the most curious facets of Hofmannsthal's concept is this degraded yet responsible position of the Amme, who is despised and hated by every character in the drama including those of the spirit world. Hofmannsthal himself referred to her as Mephistophelian; moreover, 'she harbours', he wrote, 'a smouldering hatred for humanity and the Emperor', while 'she knows the world with a sharp and loveless knowledge'. In the opera, as she answers a stern greeting from the Kaiser, she likens herself to the bitches which lie across the threshold, a role startlingly similar to that of Elektra in the opening scene of Hofmannsthal's earlier drama.

In order to make the action clear on the stage the state of affairs has now to be explained. So the Kaiser, instead of preserving the haughty silence of the *Erzählung*, bursts into an effusive aria in which he reveals his character and philosophy of existence. He first announces his intention to direct his horse and hounds towards the moon-mountains and the dark lake where he first encountered the Kaiserin. He goes on to relate the details of that first meeting: the chase of the shadowless white gazelle and her transformation into a woman, after she has been captured through the intervention of the Red Falcon.

At the mention of the Falcon, high woodwind instruments hint at that bird's characteristic motif which, although only presented in full later, may be quoted already now:

Ex. 10

Falkenstimme: 'Wie soll ich denn nicht wei - - -nen'

The music which has been largely connected with the Kaiser's Ex. 8 and the transmutation motif, Ex. 5(y), now introduces two further themes of the Kaiser.

Ex. 11

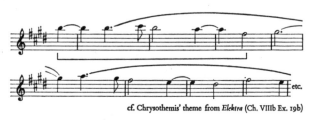

cf. Chrysothemis' theme from *Elektra* (Ch. VIIIb Ex. 19b)

and Ex. 12

If Ex. 8 characterized him as the Lover, these motifs depict the Kaiser as Huntsman, Ex. 12 often referring specifically to his prey even when that prey is his wife. It is indicative of the psychological background Strauss tried to give his score that, whereas these last two themes remain unchanged to the end of the opera, Ex. 8 undergoes considerable development during the closing scene. This motif has the additional function of referring to the unfulfilled nature of the Kaiser's desires, since his jealous love has failed to bear fruit within the Kaiserin's womb.

The Kaiser tells of his unjust anger against the Falcon as the result of which he wounded the bird with his spear 'in the drunkenness of that first hour':

Ex. 13

Since then the Red Falcon has deserted his royal master, who now bitterly regrets his hasty action and mourns the loss of his favourite bird. Were he to find it again, he says, he would pour honour upon it. Meantime he dedicates his hunting to his captured Lady (Ex. 12) whom he commends to the Amme's care, for he may be away for three days.

The Kaiser offers no reason for his decision to remain away for precisely the three last fatal days of grace before the expiration of his allotted time with the Kaiserin. There is no suggestion that he has any knowledge of the imminent danger in which he is placed and it is made clear that so long a period of absence is unprecedented. In the *Erzählung* it is the Amme who with her second-sight later tells the Kaiserin that this time her lover will be away for these three vital days, a remark which passes with no further comment other than that he will know no rest until he has found the Falcon, were it to take thirty days and nights.

The Kaiser flings out with a declaration of passionate devotion which is continued in a brief orchestral tutti. This passage consists of a broad elaboration of all the Kaiser's themes in a form and with a new continuation which become of particular importance in the second and third acts.

Ex. 14

Ex 9

8

The last dramatic chord of the Petrification theme, Ex. 9, melts into a
new and delicate orchestral tone-picture. Dawn is breaking and the
birds can be heard singing, much as in the opening of *Der Rosenkavalier*,
though the meandering of the Amme's Ex. 2 gives a dark undertone.
Strauss's aviary may be less authentic and exotic than Messiaen's but it is
hardly less varied and numerous during the course of the many operas.
Amongst the new specimens can be heard the cry of the Falcon (Ex. 10)
who is hovering overhead, though as yet unperceived. Another sinister
touch is the ominous inverted entry of the Kaiser's Ex. 8 on the trumpet,
which heralds the approaching Kaiserin. This inverted form of Ex. 8
refers to the loss of her powers of transmutation as the direct result of her
union with the mortal Kaiser, whose love theme it inverts. Yet it also
denotes the first stage in her own gradual progress towards becoming
human herself and in a later form in diminution it accompanies
her flight to the world of men (see Ex. 20 below). Meantime she is still

partly spirit and hence shadowless, even while she possesses, and can enjoy, the body and love emotions of a beautiful woman.

The Amme summarily dismisses a group of servants who had accompanied their master as he left for the hunt.[15] They must not be seen by the Kaiserin, she says, and noiselessly they disappear, leaving behind them a faintly eerie atmosphere of indefinable mystery, emanating perhaps from their hateful quality of humanity against which the Amme still strives desperately to protect the spirit princess even though she has been seduced by a mortal.

The Kaiserin now emerges from the royal bed-chamber, fretful both at having been disturbed from sleep so early and at the departure of her beloved whom she cannot follow owing to the loss of her miraculous talisman. Yet if she can no longer assume the physical form of beast or bird she still preserves many of their characteristics despite her deceptively human appearance. The first impression she gives is decidedly bird-like, with phrases like the following in voice and wind alike.

Ex. 15

She tells how she has been dreaming herself back into the form of a bird or gazelle,[16] and her music, scored for chamber orchestra with harps and celeste, reveals her true nature as a volitant creature of the spirit world. Motivically her entrance is largely based on her own theme, Ex. 5, but leading again and again to that of her lover (Ex. 8) heard repeatedly in inversion.

She bewails the loss of her talisman and as she, like the Kaiser in the previous scene, speaks of the 'drunkenness of that first hour' the alternating chords of Ex. 13 return. This curious, rather haunting motif is repeated exactly as it occurred previously, but with the development of the

[15] The scene was originally extended here with references to the Falconer's Lodge which plays so salient a part in Act 2. At Strauss's request, however, the text was curtailed to make a more effective exit for the Kaiser.

[16] There is considerable divergence here from the *Erzählung*, which tells how the Kaiserin during the moments before awakening has dreamt of the race of men, with their wild and hateful faces, so different—she says wistfully—from those of animals.

dramatic situation it is itself later developed in a way which gradually
reveals its psychological significance.

The next episode is given in so much greater detail in the *Erzählung*
that it will be clearer if this version is described first. Here Hofmannsthal
tells how, as dawn breaks (the dawn which will once again reveal to the
Amme that the Kaiserin has still preserved her shadowless condition) a
bird can be seen circling in the sky directly overhead. As it circles progres-
sively lower both the Amme and Kaiserin recognize the Kaiser's Red
Falcon. They see, moreover, that it is hovering near them with intent, and
that it holds in its talons a glittering object which the Kaiserin perceives
with a cry of joy to be the fateful talisman. The Amme spreads out a
silken bejewelled mantle, calling to the Falcon in tones of praise and
adulation, upon which the bird swoops down and drops the talisman into
the centre of the silken gown before flying away.

The *Erzählung* goes on to describe how the Kaiserin seizes the jewel
and, before the Amme can prevent her, reads and instantly grasps the
meaning of the enigmatic inscription upon it:

> 'The Curse of death upon the mortal who loosens this girdle,
> to stone the hand which performs the deed in so far as it buys
> not back its fate from the earth with the shadow, to stone the
> body to which the hand belongs, to stone the eye which lit
> the deed for that body—may the spirit remain living within,
> that it may taste eternal death with the tongue of life. The
> term is established after the time-span of the stars.'

All is now made clear to the Kaiserin as she hangs the talisman once
more 'between her breasts'. She realizes that it is her shadow which has
to be purchased from the earth, and that only thus can her lover be saved
from his fate. She turns on the Amme who, she realizes, possesses both
the knowledge and the power to aid her in her desperate need.

The narrative is of far greater length and complexity than could
conveniently be represented on the stage. Hofmannsthal accordingly
simplified the action in the libretto by throwing upon the Falcon itself
the onus of enlightening the Kaiserin. The role of the Falcon is thus considerably widened and it becomes identified with the spirit world although
it has allied itself with the mortal Kaiser in the pursuit and capture of the
spirit princess. Now its purpose is to assist the lovers in whose union it
has played so vital a part. 'It approaches', wrote Hofmannsthal, 'as with
a high mission; it grips in its claws the talisman as token of authority'.
Musically Strauss gives the bird a new theme which is directly related

to that of the talisman and the delirious hour in which, unnoticed, the Falcon itself robbed the maiden of her jewel of destiny. As the Kaiserin looks up and recognizes the beloved bird there is an upward sweep of orchestral colour:

Ex. 16

This motif alternates with a static and deeper brass chord in the exact manner of the talisman theme, Ex. 13, and by this means Strauss connects the Falcon with the theft of the talisman and with the subsequent fate of the lovers.

The Falcon's 'threatening and mournful cry', continues Hofmannsthal, 'is as intelligible to the Kaiserin's ear as a human voice'. This is a perfectly plausible statement, for spirit can comprehend spirit. Moreover, the Kaiserin not only sees tears in the eyes of the Falcon but blood dropping from its wing, a symptom which, nearly a full year after the bird received the wound, seems far-fetched. It is interesting that Hofmannsthal decided to reverse this in the *Erzählung*, where the Kaiserin specifically comments that the Falcon's wound is healed.

To return to the opera, the bird itself now utters in basic terms the curse of the talisman.

> 'How should I not weep
> The woman throws no shadow
> The Kaiser must turn to stone.' (Ex. 10)

The talisman theme, Ex. 13, is repeated once more in its original form, the Kaiserin ruminating upon the curse, an edict once known in her deep subconscious but barely realized. Hofmannsthal reckoned this question of the Kaiserin's pre-knowledge of her destiny to be of importance, for he elaborates on its origin in the *Erzählung*; her father, Kaikobad, whispered it into her ear while she slept. Extensive philosophical treatises have been written on the connexion between her specifically unconscious possession of this knowledge and her power of transformation into birds and beasts. For she does not reacquire this power after she is made aware of the curse through the return of the talisman.

Certainly some elucidation seems necessary, considering the overwhelming impact the rereading or hearing of the curse has upon her. It is not too much to say that in a flash her entire outlook is revolutionized. Nothing matters now to her but the acquisition of a shadow. Impetuously the Kaiserin demands that the Amme instruct her in the way in which this may be sought, and a violent § movement begins.

9

From this point Act 1 Scene 1 builds up steadily to its climax. At first the Amme is adamant. She insists that in his presumption the Kaiser has accepted the stipulated term within which he must make the Kaiserin human like himself or suffer the consequences. The shadow theme, Ex. 4(x), surges up again and again in the orchestra, ending with gruff entries of Kaikobad's motif. The Amme's serpentine theme, Ex. 2, alternates with these violent outbursts as the Amme reminds the Kaiserin with evil satisfaction that her lover has failed and must pay the penalty (Ex. 9(y)). But the Kaiserin cannot be dissuaded; she has derived inner strength from the very adversities laid upon her by her father, and with this fortitude has come an unshakeable resolution. In fact, did she but know it, she has already taken the first step on the road towards becoming a human being (repetitions of Ex. 20). An extended melody belonging to the Kaiserin but based entirely on themes related to the Kaiser bursts out on the orchestra:

Ex. 17

In the face of such single-minded determination the Amme is forced to reveal her knowledge of the way by which a shadow can be obtained.[17]

[17] In the *Erzählung* the Kaiserin reveals to the Amme that she is aware of her basic malevolence, but despite the psychological importance of this Hofmannsthal omitted it from the libretto.

It might be thought that this could only be accomplished through conception, but it seems there are other means. 'The Amme knows that there can be dilemmas from which a deluded mortal, be it man or woman, can only free himself at the price of his shadow. In these circumstances a shadow might be purchased.'

A new collection of motifs is now presented, still within the prevailing $\frac{6}{8}$ rhythm in which this extended closing section of the scene presses forward.

Whereas Ex. 18 refers also to the Amme's duplicity in the forthcoming events, all these thematic fragments are concerned to a greater or lesser extent with the human race and that deepest plane of existence, the world they inhabit. It is particularly the horrific aspect of mankind as viewed by the malevolent Amme which these motifs, above all Ex. 19, describe, and Hofmannsthal arranges that our own first view of the world of men will also be vile and pandemoniac.

The motifs just quoted are combined with the all-important Ex. 7 (the theme of ascending fourths also connected through the Kaiserin with mankind),[18] Exx. 1 and 2 (the motifs of Kaikobad and of the Amme), and with yet other versions of the Petrification motif:

[18] I am aware that I am at odds here with William Mann who regards this theme as the motif of Magic and the interval of the fourth specifically reserved by Strauss for the Spirit World.

Ex. 24

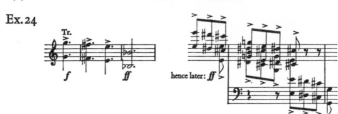

With all this material Strauss builds up a splendid symphonic movement as the Amme tries to frighten the Kaiserin from her purpose (repetitions of Ex. 7). The crux of her argument is that to earn the shadow she and the Kaiserin must not only live amongst men and women but must actually be as servants to them. In the course of drawing the lurid picture of what they will have to suffer, she reveals interesting facts about her own past, spent to some extent amongst just these creatures she so despises, performing malicious pranks upon them whilst ostensibly playing the role of Nurse and even, so she says, of Mother—unlikely as this may seem.

The Kaiserin has heard none of this tirade, however. She has been watching the sunrise, and with it grows her strength and her resolution to continue (Ex. 17). Against the ceaseless warnings of the Amme she repeats in strident tones the Falcon's annunciation of her own curse (Ex. 10). The Amme sees that all dissuasions are in vain and, as the curtain falls, the two spirits embark in the now bright red sky upon the flight which will take them down to earth, a journey described impetuously by the orchestra in an interlude which is the climax of the entire first scene.

At first the orchestra vehemently takes up the material of the preceding duet beginning with the broad lines of Ex. 17. Then gradually sterner elements intrude. The menacing tones of Kaikobad's Ex. 1 thunder out on five tubas and timpani, and the group of Mankind themes (Exx. 18–23) add increasingly discordant undertones. Against the background of a new phrase derived from Ex. 21, symptomatic of the two women's prospective role of servants in a human household, the tubas take up the Falcon's cry, giving it a weird brutality as the music grows wilder and ever more turbulent. Strings and woodwind rush up and down (Ex. 23 with its inversion) and the savage undulating thirds of Ex. 19 are hammered on two large chinese gongs. Whip, castanets, xylophone and other percussion effects join in creating the general furore, in which Ex. 23 becomes strongly featured to exemplify human strife. A new figure in the bass emerges:

Ex. 25

This is shortly to reveal its identification with the grotesque characters of the next scene.

When the curtain rises, the scene disclosed to represent the world of mankind is certainly a dreadful one. In the single-roomed house of Barak the dyer, a hovel of indescribable squalor, his three deformed brothers are fighting, shouting and screaming. One is hunchbacked, the second one-eyed and the third has only one arm. At the height of the turmoil Barak's Wife throws a bucket of water over them and shrieks insults at the top of her voice, upon which they all turn on her. Their fight forgotten, they each revile her for her treatment of them and of their brother, her husband. Very briefly they establish the situation: despite their abject poverty Barak has always made kindness and welcome a feature of the house. The coming of a wife, however, has brought nothing but hard words and blows; her beauty serves for nothing but to slake Barak's appetite.

The reference to her womanly relationship with Barak strikes deep at the root of the Färberin's shrewishness. Like the union of the Kaiser and Kaiserin, her marriage is barren and this has created within her a devouring discontent. She gives a gesture of impetuous ill-humour and Strauss illustrates this with a composite theme which for much of the opera is the only musical portrait she is allowed.

Ex. 26

But if she, with her hard embittered nature, is musically somewhat unsympathetic, Barak, who now enters is certainly not. His themes immediately reflect not only the patient geniality, but also the essential goodness of the man.

Ex. 27

The beginning of the first of his motifs (Ex. 27) shows him, like his wife, utterly human (Ex. 19 again in the bass), with a strong similarity to his deformed brothers (cf. Ex. 25 in the lines of the upper part), yet with all trace of the brutality of these motifs replaced by a comfortable air of good nature not far removed from Strauss's self-portrait in *Sinfonia Domestica*.[19]

After sending the three brothers off to soak skins for dyeing, Barak turns to answer the querulous complaints of his wife, with quiet yet firm rebuke. The melody to which he sings here is one of his most endearing themes, reflecting the tenderness with which he cares for those who are most dependent upon him.

Ex. 28

The Färberin scornfully reviles Barak, shaking him off when he tries to touch her (Ex. 26(x) repeated many times with vehemence), but he sings with great gentleness of her uncouth strangeness from which, curiously, he derives joy. 'And if you are strange and other than is wont, I prize that strangeness', he sings, 'and bow my head to the ground before the transformation. O good fortune upon me, and expectation, and joy in my heart!'

This outburst is in itself the very essence of Barak's good nature and Strauss elected to insert an orchestral interlude in which he attempted to portray Goodness pure and simple. He had recently done something of

[19] Strauss admitted to Hofmannsthal that the musical characterization of the Färberin gave him much difficulty, whereas that of Barak suited him down to the ground. Considering that the Färberin was acknowledged to have been at least partially modelled on Strauss's own wife Pauline, who had been already characterized so successfully in *Heldenleben* and *Sinfonia Domestica*, Hofmannsthal's surprise at such an admission is easy to understand.

the same kind in *Josephslegende*, where he indulged in an extended passage melodising around the tonic key in simple affecting harmony.[20] The section in the ballet was intended to describe the inherent goodness of the simple shepherd Joseph and the influence of that goodness upon Potiphar's Wife. Hence both the intention and the basic effect are similar in this new instance. Here, as there, the purpose is higher than Strauss could ever intentionally achieve, and, remarkably beautiful as the result undoubtedly is, it falls short of the profound sublimity a Beethoven or Wagner might have given it, and which indeed certain commentators have actually claimed for it. It consists of a single arch rising and falling with repetitions of the following phrase:

Ex. 29

Nothing whatever happens on the stage during this interlude, a fact which, like the aria 'Marter aller Arten' from Mozart's *Entführung*, has caused embarrassment to producers and singers in the past. However, when tackled by Lotte Lehmann (the first Färberin) Strauss exploded. 'What should you do?' he retorted, 'Nothing, absolutely nothing at all. Why must you be doing something? After all, in real life people don't keep running back and forth all the time, do they? Just stand there quietly and think yourself into the meaning of the role. I'm sure you'll find the right sort of expression.'

Sullenly the Färberin reminds Barak that in their two and a half years together[21] he has failed to bring her to motherhood. Patiently he replies: she is blessed with the power of recantation and he will wait with gladness of heart for future joys. Two new and important themes appear during this warm song of Barak's. The first of these, a dual theme, belongs once again to Barak himself. This time it is his longing for children of his own which is portrayed, though it is in his nature patiently to endure disappointment and to await what the future may bring:

[20] See above, p. 136.
[21] German *Dritthalb Jahr*, as in medieval English 'thridde half', i.e. a half-unit less than the corresponding cardinal number (*O.E.D.*). There has been some confusion about this.

Ex. 30

Ex. 30a is no new theme for Strauss himself, new as it is to the present work, and especially to the very changed role it now has to play. Its first appearance was in the great Klytemnestra scene in *Elektra* where it described the nightmares of the haunted queen, and subsequently we have seen it portray poor Baron Ochs' *Congestion* during the supper scene in the third act of *Der Rosenkavalier*. With all the luscious harmonic colouring it carries at this its first appearance in *Die Frau ohne Schatten*, it later acquires the more dramatic, even nightmare quality naturally indigenous to it and for which reason no doubt it sprang into Strauss's mind once again.

The second new theme is one of the basic motifs of the opera: that of the Unborn Children. I quote it in the full version in which the Unborn Children themselves later sing it:

Ex. 31

Both the undulating seconds, which are related to Ex. 30b (the children Barak longs to have) and the descending seventh (the reason he cannot have them, as will be shown in due course) are psychologically significant in the formation of this theme.

A further orchestral passage combines these many motifs as Barak loads himself with skins preparatory to taking them to market, and he leaves the stage singing a little ditty:

Ex. 32

[22] 'If I carry my wares to market myself, I save on the donkey who would drag them for me.'

Meantime, in their search for a shadow, the Amme and the Kaiserin have reached the world of men; the Amme has chosen this hovel as a suitable place where so passionate a discontent may be found that the purchase may be welcomed.

No sooner has Barak gone than the two spirits appear amidst shimmering and lightning flashes. The orchestra paints their arrival with a resumption of the music of their flight, the Amme's Ex. 2 and Ex. 20 being particularly in evidence. The choice of Ex. 20 is significant on account of its associations with the Kaiserin and her gropings towards humanity.

The astounded Färberin springs to her feet (Ex. 26(x)) and, without questioning the unusual manner of her visitors' entrance into her home, peremptorily asks them what they want. Strauss vehemently provides the true answer to her question with a rapid allusion in the orchestra to the motif of that answer (see Ex. 35 below). But the moment has not yet come for plain speaking, and instead the Amme humbles herself before the Färberin with fawning adulation and praise of her beauty. She slyly insinuates that Barak, whom she has just seen leaving, his back laden with a heavy pack, can surely only be a servant in her ladyship's household.

The Färberin unashamedly replies with the simple truth, but is smitten with self-pity when the Amme piercingly bewails the fate of so ravishing a creature who must waste her beauty in bearing children for such a lout. (The muttered references to Kaikobad, Ex. 1 in the bassoons, at the mention of Fate throws an interesting light on the functions of the deity.) The Kaiserin plays no part in this monstrous seduction and at once reveals both her single-minded purpose and her instinctive sympathy for the Färberin by crying out that she wants to kiss her shadow (the Shadow theme, Ex. 4, rises up on strings and harps while the motif of the Kaiser's petrification, Ex. 9b, shows clearly her trend of thought). The Färberin becomes increasingly distressed at the Amme's sly allusions to the Secret of the Purchase and of the Price, of which she naturally can understand nothing, and, when the Amme pretends to depart with the Kaiserin in high dudgeon, is reduced to begging with tears of sheer despair for some explanation.

Throughout this section the Shadow theme (Ex. 4) becomes increasingly present in the background, together with a number of varied melodic strands which have the uniform characteristic of beginning with a wide interval, generally the sixth, whether rising or falling, viz:

Ex. 33 a

or b

or c   and so on.

These can collectively be regarded as 'Temptation' motifs, while the Secret of the Purchase and of the Price (i.e. of a shadow) is underlined by a motif featuring the descending interval of a seventh:

Ex. 34   and later: Ex. 34a

This wide chromatic interval which has already appeared in the motif of the Unborn Children (Ex. 31) will shortly prove to be all-important.

The Amme at last reveals that it is the Färberin's shadow which is to be purchased and answers the poor woman's bewildered incredulity by setting upon it the kind of price to which she believes the Färberin will most readily succumb—jewels, slaves, luxury of every kind and, above all, lovers. By way of illustration that her promises are not idle, the Amme conjures from the air a hair-band of pearls and precious stones, and when it is immediately clear that the Färberin is being swayed by the offer of beauty such as she has never dreamed of possessing, the Amme goes on to transform the entire hovel in which they are standing into a gorgeous pavilion, in which brightly-dressed slave-girls attend to the Färberin as to a princess.

Such a scene was a well-designed opportunity for colouristic musical treatment, and Strauss supplied an appropriately glittering orchestral and vocal fabric. Against trills and rapid figuration of strings and upper woodwind, and the sparkle of harps, celestes and the lighter percussion group, the slave girls carol and twitter like so many Flower Maidens from Klingsor's Magic Garden. The Kaiserin adds her persuasion in a broad phrase with many rising sixths (the interval of temptation), and her voice is succeeded by another—that of a young man, seductive and inviting.

The Färberin cannot contain herself and pours out her wonder in an ecstatic phrase. But alas, with her first words the pavilion begins to fade and, lamenting, the slave-girls also disappear into thin air; the dyer's hovel has reappeared, exactly as before the miraculous transformation. In utter distress the Färberin protests that even if she wanted to barter her shadow she would not know how to set about it. This is the moment the Amme has been waiting for and quickly she exchanges glances with the Kaiserin while the orchestra thunders out the motif of Renunciation:

Ex. 35

Here then is the fulfilment of the forceful descending seventh in the theme which refers to the abnegation of motherhood through the sale of the shadow and which constitutes the most fearful threat to the unborn. Ex. 35 is followed by equally powerful statements of the theme of undulating seconds (Ex. 30b) which concerns the children the Färberin has failed to bear Barak. The Amme eagerly presses the Färberin over any regrets she might have on account of the little ones who will not be able to use her body as a highway between non-life and life, but the Färberin sullenly admits that even before she has experienced mother-hood she is already sated with it.

The Amme proclaims the abnegation to Ex. 35 in hieratical tones, as if, indeed, with the pronouncement of the words the deed is already done.[23] But this is by no means so and the matter is a great deal more complicated: three days must pass during which she and the Kaiserin will remain in the Färberin's house and act as her most lowly servants, except for a brief leave of absence each midnight. In return, the Färberin undertakes to surrender her shadow for a reward of untold luxuries and riches.[24]

II

At this moment the Färberin becomes abruptly aware of Barak's impending return home and she frets over his meal not yet prepared and the conjugal bed which is henceforth to be denied him. These trivial matters present no problem to the Amme, who forthwith sets magic in operation to accomplish both tasks. The bed makes itself in two halves, the Färberin's portion curtained off in the rear, while Barak's half establishes itself in the foreground. Meantime, at the command of the Amme, and to a background of Kaikobad's theme, five little fishes[25] fly into the room in a gust of wind and land in the frying-pan on the fire, the flames of which rise up to meet them. Amme and Kaiserin then both vanish, leaving the Färberin in terrified amazement at the extraordinary events and their weird sequel. As the fishes cook in the oil, the sound is heard of little children singing pitifully. It is Barak's unborn children pleading with their hard-hearted mother to be allowed entrance into life out of the darkness and fear which surrounds them in their present state of Pre-existence.[26] They sing the full form of Ex. 31 which now appears as quoted earlier[27] and continues to include references to Exx. 28 and 30b, the themes of Barak's love and longing for children. Their weakening

[23] Hofmannsthal visualized this passage sung to a kind of *Hänsel und Gretel* Witch's dance but Strauss wisely postponed this unavoidably comic effect in favour of the present rather eerie solemnity until after the 'prophecy' proper. He then accompanied the latter part of the Amme's excited pronouncement with music recalling Elektra's Maenad-like dance music.

[24] The nightly departure of the Färberin's two new servants to take their rest elsewhere finds no place in the *Erzählung* but is essential to the opera, as will become clear during Act 2.

[25] In Hofmannsthal's own synopsis of the action, as in the *Erzählung*, he specifies seven little fishes. In the *Erzählung*, moreover, these seven fishes become additionally part of a fantastic hocus-pocus described by the Amme to the Färberin as part of the ceremony of Shedding the Shadow, as it were.

[26] The whole philosophy of the *Praeexistenz* is recurrent in Hofmannsthal's output and was clearly one which occupied his mind a great deal.

[27] See p. 178.

cries strike the Färberin to the heart but she watches helplessly as the fire gradually dies and the voices emanating from the fishes in the pan fade away altogether.[28]

Thereupon the Färberin in a torment sinks to the ground, while the orchestra betrays her thoughts and her regrets in an impassioned symphonic interlude based entirely on Ex. 28, the theme of the kind father whom the children have also just been exhorting. The orchestra itself then dies away to reveal the voice of Barak singing his donkey-saving ditty (Ex. 32). The Färberin gives him no greeting but heaves herself to her own rear portion of the bed and without saying a word draws the curtain. The music now returns to the song of the Unborn Children and their plaintive cries to their beloved father (Exx. 31 and 28), with Kaikobad's theme (Ex. 1) reiterated in the lower instruments.

Against this eerie background Barak naïvely comments 'What a splendid smell of fish and oil', a passage which caused the authors a good deal of trouble. Strauss felt, with considerable justification, that there was an uncomfortable suggestion that Barak was about to sit down to a dinner consisting of his own unborn children. But Hofmannsthal, immersed in the mystic symbolism of his concept, failed altogether to understand the objection; 'After all', he wrote, 'the fishes are not really the children; they are merely the vehicles of magic. I cannot imagine anyone objecting to the passage; it is invariably like that in fairytales.'

Strauss persisted, however, and the unsatisfactory compromise was reached in which the Färberin spitefully answers 'Hier ist *kein* Essen' ('There is *nothing* to eat here'—Hofmannsthal's italics) and Barak takes a crust of bread from his pocket and gnaws at that.[29] Brusquely the

[28] Here we have another outstanding instance of Hofmannsthal's indebtedness to the *Thousand Nights and a Night*, although the actual treatment of the situation is in this case somewhat altered. In the 'Tale of the Fisherman and the Jinni' four fish, each of a different colour, are set in a frying-pan over the fire. The wall parts and a damsel enters holding a wand which she thrusts into the pan. She challenges the fish to their constancy and they reply in a short verse. She then upsets the pan and vanishes, leaving the fish charred black. It later transpires that the fish are the spirits of humans, representatives of the four religious faiths in some far distant township which has been laid under a spell.

[29] Yet oddly enough the full score reverts to 'Hier ist *dein* Essen' ('Here is *your* food') making nonsense of Barak's subsequent play with the bread in place of the tempting supper upon which he had just commented. In the *Erzählung* Hofmannsthal showed that he had not been in any way convinced by Strauss's arguments, for Barak not only eats the fish but puts out a portion for his hunchback brothers to share.

Färberin explains the division of the bed and prepares him for the intrusion of the two beings into their household who will act as servants. This time even Barak becomes despondent and takes hard his unwelcome home-coming. He will not enjoy his food, he says, and considering its nature this is scarcely surprising.

At this point Hofmannsthal inserted an episode not to be found in the *Erzählung* at all and which rounds off the first act of the opera in a most beautiful and moving way. The voices can be heard off-stage of three Night-watchmen patrolling the streets in medieval fashion. But what they sing is very different from the charming old-time conventional phrases enunciated by the watchman in Wagner's *Meistersinger*. Hofmannsthal's watchmen sing in a solemn hymn-like incantation directly to the married couples lying in each other's arms throughout the town, and symbolize them and their work of love as the bridge over which the dead pass across the chasm in their return to life. Barak tries to draw his own wife's attention to the song, and when he fails sighs deeply, and with a resigned 'So be it then' settles down to sleep by himself as the orchestra plays gently with his various motifs culminating, in tones of some sublimity, with that of his goodness, Ex. 29.

The quiet end to this turbulent act is in fact very touching and, for that matter, the whole act itself is well designed and proportioned. It is full of contrasts and variety of colour, while the material is throughout on a high level of inspiration. Only certain specific sections, such as the interlude of Barak's Goodness or the episode of the Magical Transformation of Barak's hovel into the pavilion of a Princess, sound contrived rather than spontaneous, especially when compared with what the Strauss of twenty years previously had done in, for example, *Don Quixote*.

12

'Act II; the trials begin, for all four must be purified; the Dyer and his wife, the Emperor and the Fairy-child; the one pair too dull and earthly, the other too proud and remote from the earth.' So wrote Hofmannsthal in his own synopsis, and it is as well that he did so, because the matter is very far from obvious.[30] The basic idea of these trials is linked, however, with Hofmannsthal's *exposé* in the early pages of the *Erzählung* in which

[30] Indeed this synopsis is an integral part of the whole work and as such utterly indispensable (containing explanatory information not to be found anywhere else). No performance should ever be given without its inclusion in the programme.

the Bote already establishes this concept during his initial dialogue with the Amme (see above, p. 161).

This complicated act is in five scenes, every alternate one of which takes place in Barak's house. As the curtain rises Barak is loading himself for his trudge to the market. The music starts impetuously with the Färberin's motif, Ex. 26(x), though becoming gentler, more insidious, as the Amme bows Barak out of his house with smooth hypocritical words. She then turns eagerly to the Färberin and presses her to reveal the lover of her most secret dreams. The scene is accompanied with sinuously seductive music full of the temptation motifs with their sixths, falling or, especially, rising (Ex. 33), but also introducing three new melodic ideas of increasing significance.

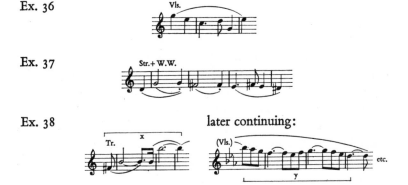

Ex. 36

Ex. 37

Ex. 38   later continuing:

At first the Färberin denies that she knows of any man other than her husband,[31] but gradually the importunate suggestions of the Amme make their mark upon her and at last she murmurs of how she once passed a young man, nearly a boy still, on the bridge in the town, who did not even notice her.[32] In a flash the Amme calls to the broomstick

[31] There is a most curious allusion here to Kunrad's theme from *Feuersnot*. Bearing in mind that Kunrad was an allegorical picture of Strauss himself and that the character of the Färberin is to some extent suggested by Strauss's own wife, this may have been an intentional shaft of sly humour.

[32] This incident, seemingly satisfactory as it stands, appears not to have expressed adequately what lay in Hofmannsthal's mind, for in the *Erzählung* he replaces the vision of the Färberin's dream-boy with an Ifrit, beautiful still but exuding evil with all his being. Moreover, so far from standing passively, a vehicle for the Färberin's admiration, he takes an active part in the seduction, filling the Färberin's soul with terror and the Kaiserin with abhorrence. (An Ifrit, it should be observed, is a variety of Jinn—or Genie—'generally a malignant being, hostile and injurious to mankind' (Koran, XXVII, 39.)

and kettle to aid her in her magic, throws some straw over the Färberin, and claps her hands.

The Kaiserin is intensely distressed and bewails that all this must happen before her very eyes. Although the course of events have been set in motion for no one's benefit but hers, these events have the effect of inspiring a feeling of self-guilt in respect of the human being in whose affairs and sufferings she is now involved. Strauss portrays this with a new poignant motif.

Ex. 39

She is at the same time deeply shocked at what she takes to be the fickle-ness of mankind and watches with repugnance as, summoned by the Amme's magic, the boy of the Färberin's dreams appears in a flash of light. His arrival is heralded by Ex. 38(x) which during Act 2 is specifically identified with the idea of a phantom lover. At first he stands as if inani-mate, but gradually life flows into him and, despite her fear, the Färberin cannot resist stretching out her hands towards him. The Amme presses her to hurry and her words are echoed by an invisible chorus of women's voices.

But already there is no time left. With a scream of anguish punctu-ated by a hammered statement of Kaikobad's fate-like Ex. 1 on the orchestra, the Kaiserin reveals her consciousness of Barak's rapid approach. She sees in her mind's eye a terrible encounter between the magic boy who has no reality and thus no heart, and Barak the quality of whose heart she has already begun to appreciate. The vital motif of the Kaiserin's affinity with Mankind (Ex. 7) rears up in sinister guise on muted brass but gives way to Barak's genial music as the colour-master himself enters in high spirits, surrounded not only by his brothers but by a hoard of children. In a split second, during which the light in the room is momentarily eclipsed, the Amme has caused the boy to vanish, restored the broomstick and kettle to their normal functions, and cast aside the bale of straw. As the humans enter the room there is nothing abnormal to be seen, except perhaps the appalling condition to which the Färberin has been reduced.

13

In the brief time since we saw him last, Barak has had an enormously successful day at the market. Now he is jubilant, and in a hilarious ensemble he, his brothers, and the local children all rejoice over the wonderful things to eat he has bought with the proceeds. His motifs and that of his brothers are combined in this hymn of joy and even the donkey-saving tune can be heard winding its way gaily upwards through the texture.

The Färberin takes no part in these celebrations. At first she turns her back on Barak but later is provoked into snapping at the boorish husband whose ill-timed return banished, untasted, the most wonderful moment she ever thought to experience. She works herself up into a paroxysm of weeping and draws herself away into a corner, head in hands, sobbing bitterly.

Barak does not reply to her directly but, telling his brothers to begin their meal, launches into another of his great shows of big-heartedness. As the violins softly begin a long, wide-spanned statement of Ex. 30a with its leaping intervals, he repeats his philosophy that, however sharp her tongue, her speech is blessed with the power of revocation on account of her fundamental virtue and purity of heart. (It is hard to suppress a feeling of sympathy for the Färberin; Barak must have been a maddening husband to live with.)

He sends the Kaiserin over to her with some sweets, as to a naughty child now forgiven, but naturally, her thoughts being still on her dream lover (Ex. 38 poignantly starts up on flute and oboe), she recoils with a vulgar comment, adding that she wants nothing but bitterness in her mouth. The musical phrase to which she sings this is transformed in a later scene to a striking new motif (see Ex. 40 below).

The three brothers decide that her tantrums are not worth fussing over and pick up the threads of their hilarious singing, even as they eat. The scene ends with a full recapitulation of the jovial ensemble, undisturbed by the addition of the despairing voice of the Färberin singing wildly of her hopeless misery.

A curtain falls for the first scene-change (there are no less than four in this act alone) and the cheerful working out of Barak's motifs gradually fades away to be replaced by the most contrasted music possible, sounds that we have not heard since early in the entire opera—the cry of the Kaiser's Falcon, Ex. 10. The time, long delayed, has at last come to pursue the fate of the Kaiser himself, who had set out on a three-day hunting bout, partially with the object of searching out his favourite Red Falcon.

He has since received and read a letter from the Kaiserin. Much is made in the *Erzählung* of the writing of this letter—the characters painted in oriental fashion upon swanskin (!)—in the moments before her descent amongst mankind. In it she tells of her enforced departure from the Blue Palace during the three days of the Kaiser's own absence. Now we are to learn that she has also written of how she will be living for all of this time in the royal falconer's pavilion in the woods, attended only by the Amme, safe from mankind and the world.

The Red Falcon has, however, unexpectedly returned to its master and has, as part of the overall ordained scheme of the Trials, deliberately led him to that very pavilion. Before the curtain rises, the themes of the Falcon are heard (Exx. 10 and 16) together with two motifs of the Kaiser, the hunting motif, Ex. 12, and his love theme, Ex. 8. In addition, the fluttering theme of the Falcon, Ex. 16, is continually used with the alternation of two chords recalling the motif of the Drunkenness of the First Hour experienced by the royal lovers (Ex. 13); for all that is now to take place is directly consequential upon the actions of that reckless delirium.

There is a long and extremely beautiful passage for a completely unaccompanied solo cello, after which the more lyrical theme of the Kaiser as huntsman, Ex. 11, enters *cantabile* in all the cellos supported by two harps. The mood is one of deepest melancholy. The curtain has risen and the Kaiser can be seen quietly dismounting from his horse and hiding behind a tree near to the darkened falcon-house. He observes it narrowly, seeing that the door is shut and that it appears unoccupied. From time to time the solo cello resumes its gentle meanderings, while the Falcon can be heard repeating its mournful cry (Ex. 10).

At last the Kaiser addresses the bird, begging again and again for the meaning of his journey, of the deserted house now standing before him.[33]

Then, just as he is coming to the conclusion that he has been brought to no purpose, he glimpses the Kaiserin and the Amme flitting through the trees. The Amme swiftly opens the house, the two enter and light it up from within. Now the Kaiser is seriously disturbed: is this the prey (Ex. 12) to which the bird has led him? He can detect the atmosphere, the very breath of mankind hanging around his wife, though how he, himself a man, has developed such fine perception, is a little obscure. How-

---

[33] Unlike the Kaiserin, the Kaiser, being mortal cannot understand the Falcon's cry which accordingly throughout this scene is heard only in the orchestra.

ever, he knows that he has been deceived, and as the music rises to a pitch of agonized intensity he bewails that there is no choice but she must now die.

Having come to this decision, made without a moment's thought as to what may have been the purpose behind his wife's strange behaviour, he now considers by what means her death should be brought about. He apostrophizes in turn his arrow, his sword and his bare hands, but rejects each for the part they played in his courtship.

The scene which has built up to a magnificent extended aria now gathers all the Kaiser's themes symphonically on similar lines to the parallel passage in Act 1 illustrated in Ex. 14, though more extensively and tragically handled. The Stone theme (Ex. 9) in particular thunders out at intervals, each time more menacingly, and also returns one final time blazing in the full brass *fff* after the demented Kaiser, in total bewilderment, has leapt onto his horse and cried out to the Falcon to lead him far away to a rocky gorge where his lament can go unheard by man or beast. So it is decreed that he shall fulfil his unavoidable destiny, as presaged by the inexorable repetitions of the Stone motif.

14

A quick scene-change takes us back again to the affairs of Barak and his Wife. We are to understand that a night has passed and we are now in the second of the three fateful days. The Amme has been watching eagerly for signs that Barak will again leave the house to go to market, so that she can summon back the beautiful young man and continue with the seduction of the Färberin. The Färberin herself is no less impatient, as she has never found peace of mind since that tantalizing vision was snatched from her. She is now unable to be near Barak without uttering sneers or vitriolic comments even though in her heart of hearts she feels her fate to be bound up irrevocably with his.

Meantime Barak has been vigorously pursuing his vocation as dyer, and in the *Erzählung* we read of him working on the flat roof of his house with great strength and energy, aided in his tasks by the sympathetic Kaiserin. This account of his back-breaking work with skins and colours is both interesting and valuable to the complete picture of the Barak ménage. Now at last, even his ox-like strength is spent and as the curtain rises he is relaxing his efforts.

Strauss, perceiving a dangerous similarity likely to arise between this
scene and the first scene of the act, accompanies the Färberin's grumbles
with a highly characteristic theme which is developed at some length
and thus imbues the section with a musical character of its own.

Ex. 40

This, though transformed through diminution, is in fact the phrase in
which during the first scene of this act the Färberin sang of her desire for
nothing but bitterness. In its new guise a likeness can be seen with Barak's
donkey tune, Ex. 32, which to some extent it now caricatures. Ex. 32
itself also appears in the texture during the early part of the scene, but in
a lazy, easy-going manner. Barak is tired and hot after his hard work, and
he asks his wife to fetch him something to drink; but to his surprise she
roughly refuses.

At this brief but significant altercation one of the most important
motifs of the opera makes its unobtrusive entrance simultaneously with
Barak's genial Ex. 28 from which, indeed, it is partially derived.

Ex. 41

Although seemingly so innocent here, the violin's counterpoint to the
cello melody later transpires to be the great majestic motif of the Trials,
a motif which becomes nothing short of momentous and with which
ultimately the whole opera is to end.

The Amme takes the opportunity afforded by the Färberin's dis-
obliging rebuff to offer Barak a drink into which she has put a sleeping
draught strong enough, says the *Erzählung*, to put an elephant to sleep
for ten hours. The drink is carried to Barak in all innocence by the
Kaiserin (Ex. 20 scurrying on solo violin) and without hesitation he
drinks it.

The Amme then draws the Färberin on one side and reveals how she has taken it upon herself to drug Barak; with him safely unconscious many wonderful hours may lie ahead. The Färberin, however, now turns on her with vituperation and pours out all her resentment that the Amme should presume to know and pander to her secret desires. Bending anxiously over Barak's prostrate body, she rails against the evil Amme who has failed to understand her heart.

But as the Färberin's tone softens in speaking of her dream lover, the Amme seizes the opportunity and in a flash has summoned back the vision of the enchanted boy.[34] It is nevertheless in vain; the Färberin reviles the Amme, refusing to have anything to do with her or the creatures she can summon. The whole scene is a tremendous struggle within the soul of the Färberin, and Strauss tries to follow this in his choice of motifs in the construction of the musical fabric. The temptation themes Ex. 33, the Amme's serpentine motif, Ex. 2, and the rising phrase of the Phantom Lover, Ex. 38, are all worked in together with Barak's Ex. 28 (reflecting her deep-seated attachment to the husband she wishes to reject but cannot), and its derivative Ex. 41, the motif of the Trial she is unconsciously undergoing.

Now with the reappearance of the Youth the screw is turned once more and the colourful orchestration emphasizes and develops material from the earlier temptation scene including, in particular, Ex. 37, which is given insidious seductive overtones. The elusiveness of the beautiful lover, as indeed the unreality of the whole situation, is brought out by the curious device of having the boy played by a dancer (even a danseuse) facing upstage, that is to say, back to the audience, while his voice is projected by a singer placed in the prompter's box, doubled for the greater part by an off-stage trumpet.

The Amme blows into the fire, intensifying the magic, and the Youth falls unconscious and unresisting at the Färberin's feet. The Amme then quickly tries to slip out of the room with the Kaiserin, leaving the Färberin faced with this supreme erotic temptation. But she has overplayed her hand and with a shriek the Färberin breaks the spell, calls them back and goes to extravagant lengths to awaken Barak, shouting in his ear, shaking him and sprinkling water over him.

[34] This reappearance is sacrificed in the *Erzählung* as a result of the change by which the Phantom Lover has become a malignant Ifrit. In the appropriate chapter the Färberin refuses to countenance any such intrusion while Barak lies unconscious from the sleeping draught. The whole passage is worthy of attention, for in place of this colourful episode Hofmannsthal substitutes a remarkable psychological study of the different characters of the drama.

Considering the strength of the drug administered to him it is incredible that Barak responds even to this treatment; but wake him she
does, deriding him for keeping such poor watch over the house and herself. Meantime the Amme has thrown her cloak over the Youth with
hurried and somewhat ludicrous apologies.

Hearing his wife speak of a man in the house, of robbers and thieves,
Barak heaves himself to his feet, looks around him wildly, swinging his
hammer and shouting for his brothers. But the Färberin wrests the
hammer from him and rebukes him for his loutish behaviour. Her tone
of voice and manner are still sharp, even scornful, but the music which
punctuates her remarks is no longer based on her spiteful phrase but on
his more genial motifs, and from words that she lets fall Barak is able to
perceive the genuine concern for him which lies behind her rough
manner and he is touched to the heart.

Yet if the Amme, being anti-human, has failed to comprehend the
Färberin's soul, Barak fails equally for the opposite reason. To her basic
dissatisfaction and restlessness he can only offer deep humanity, and
such toleration mixed with kindness only irritates her afresh. Her
bitterness theme, Ex. 40, which had dropped out during the return of the
Phantom Youth, creeps back into the texture as her exasperation builds
up once more. Barak becomes increasingly perplexed; things are happening that he cannot understand, this sleep, the unexplained breakage
of his best mortar (a highly obscure and possibly supernatural manifestation), the strange behaviour of his wife; 'he feels that something is
threatening him', writes Hofmannsthal, 'it is as though something were
calling to him for help. Is it—unknown to him—the voices of his unborn children?'

As Barak's music becomes more and more that of the artisan (Ex.
27(y) receives special development here) so that of his wife acquires
additional and sinister motifs. Beginning with the threat of the mysterious lover (Ex. 37) her taunts gradually imply losses more serious to
him than a mere mortar. The Renunciation theme (Ex. 35) creeps into
her vocal line and is echoed by the bass instruments of the orchestra as
she hints darkly of the serious consequences of his utter lack of compre-
hension. She compares him with a mule (which is just as barren, she adds
in the *Erzählung*) walking across an abyss 'untroubled by the depths'
(Kaikobad's Ex. 1) 'and the secret' (the motif of the Secret of the Purchase, Ex. 34).

None of this makes any sense to Barak who replies quite simply of his concern lest he become incapable of caring for his dependants. As he speaks the Kaiserin moves sympathetically towards him and the theme of her realizations of self-guilt, Ex. 39, pours down expressively in the violins.[35] The Färberin answers with yet another tirade, giving Strauss the cue for a symphonic coda to the scene based on her Ex. 40 and a melodic extension of the lover motif, Ex. 38. During the course of this excellent stretch of symphonic writing the Amme and Färberin sweep out, leaving Barak sitting dejectedly in the middle of the room surrounded by his tools which are scattered everywhere. Suddenly he becomes aware that he is not alone. The Kaiserin, who is deeply stirred by all she has witnessed, has remained and is gathering together his effects. The wide-spanned theme, Ex. 30a, surges out on the orchestra and Barak looks up in bewilderment to ask who is there. The curtain falls as, accompanied by her own motif and that of her guilt, the Kaiserin answers him in tones of infinite gentleness and humility.

The orchestral interlude which follows continues this line of thought, being entirely concerned with the Kaiserin's increasing pity for Barak and her awareness that she herself is guilty of his misfortunes. But this is by no means the total extent of her guilt for, as we know, it is through her that the Kaiser is at this moment turning to stone.

A detailed account of this formidable event is given in the fourth and central chapter of the *Erzählung*, in which an extraordinary scene is recounted in the course of which the Kaiser is entertained to a banquet by his own unborn children in an underground grotto beneath the mountains. The whole episode is weird in the extreme and full of symbolic cross-references which can find no place in the opera, since the whole concept is far out of reach of theatrical representation. The children, in particular, are portrayed as an active force, built out of their strong but sympathetic personalities which are in striking contrast to the pitiful voices that were heard crying from the frying-pan in the first act. In his synopsis, Hofmannsthal states that it is on them that the whole play centres, but it is only here that this is made plain. For the first time they are shown to be fully conscious of every step of the drama, the progress of which they even influence from time to time. The vault in which they receive the Kaiser is in the realm of Kaikobad, with whom they seem to

[35] The *Erzählung* elaborates this growth of human sympathy within the breast of the Kaiserin. When the Färberin is trying to stir Barak out of his unnatural sleep the Amme discovers to her speechless amazement that the Kaiserin's eyes are swimming with tears 'just like a mortal woman'.

be in league, or under whose jurisdiction they are enabled to act. As the Kaiser petrifies they gradually leave him, and in the end a statue remains in the darkness of the vault, silent and alone.

For purposes of the opera Hofmannsthal recreates this focal scene so that it all takes place in the mind of the Kaiserin as she lies sleeping in the Falconer's pavilion. The music surges up and down, descriptive of her dreams which are at first of Barak. Even as she sleeps she describes his essential goodness to the Amme, although she too lies asleep on a couch at the foot of the bed. Barak's theme, Ex. 28, here acquires increasingly the new twist as shown in Ex. 41, indicating the Trial the Kaiserin is now undergoing. She cries out for the first time in direct self-accusation and the music pauses for a terse dramatic moment before plunging into a further section of passionate orchestral development which prepares the way for the next episode in this visionary scene.

Hofmannsthal's recasting of the action was certainly well planned to give ample scope for music, and Strauss built upon it a huge symphonic synthesis of all the main material, in which the Kaiserin's ejaculatory remarks emerge as intensifications of the melodic and dramatic schemes taking place primarily in the orchestra. Although the chosen motifs follow the line of her dreaming thoughts (her own theme, Ex. 5, her guilt, Ex. 39, the Amme, Ex. 2, the Kaiser's love, Ex. 8, his turning to stone, Ex. 9, and so on), the main theme of the whole section—during the scenes and surrounding interludes alike—is the leaping theme of Barak and the unborn children, Ex. 30a, which now reacquires much of the nightmare chromaticism it had in the earlier operas in which it appeared.

The Kaiserin has plunged into still deeper sleep, in which she has a vision. By an ingenious device of stagecraft, the audience is shown the Kaiser's arrival at the scene of his doom and his entrance into the fatal vault. The wall of the Kaiserin's chamber becomes transparent and through it can be seen a rocky gorge with the mouth of the vaulted cavern in which the Kaiser's ordeal is to take place, dimly picked out by shadowy lamps. The Kaiser himself approaches, led by the Falcon. He knocks on the heavy bronze doors which open and, in the midst of sinister sounds of rushing water and roaring voices, swallow him.

Here Strauss could give full rein to his imagination in the creation of a symphonic poem on the lines of Zarathustra and the Alpine Symphony. Against the persistent cry of the wretched Falcon the Kaikobad theme, Ex. 1, alternates with the Kaiser's themes, Exx. 8, 11 and 12 (the lover

and huntsman alike are undergoing trial). The motif of the Bargain,
Ex. 34, is now used as the bass for a row of granite-like chromatically
rising brass chords which begin majestically as in Ex. 34a but are later
thundered in savage diminution. The woodwinds trill and the strings
rush about in a manner descriptive of the most awesome mountain
scenery, while off-stage men's voices call threateningly about the Water
of Life, the Threshold of Death, 'Nearing, Daring, Daunting and
Woe'.[36] The Falcon's cry appears again through the medium of a
woman's voice singing the original curse, and the motif of the great
Trials appears at last, highly impressive in its complete form as a fanfare.

Ex. 42   and Ex. 42a

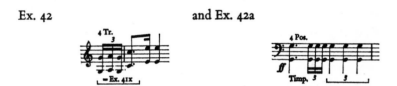

The vision fades and the wall of the Kaiserin's bed-chamber becomes
opaque once more, as during the last section of this complicated scene
the Kaiserin fully awakens from her dream and in utter despair pours out
her agonized conviction that it is she who should incur the punishment of
being turned to stone.

The curtain falls for the last of the interludes in which the nightmarish
Ex. 30a leaps repeatedly in higher and lower registers of the orchestra
against a middle background of extremely interesting harmonies giving,
as in *Elektra*, a quasi-atonal effect. Gradually the music sinks from passionate wildness to mysterious gloom with the appearance in the deepest
instruments of Kaikobad's Ex. 1. When the curtain rises again we are
back for the last time in Barak's dwelling in preparation for the decisive
scene in the transaction of the Shadow.

15

The *Erzählung* now inserts a curious episode in which the Färberin, hotly
pursued by the Amme with the Kaiserin in tow, pays an impulsive visit
to her mother's grave. After praying there for a while she rises and begins
the return journey. But a storm is brewing and the midday sky darkens

---

[36] The resemblance of this passage to the central climax of Busoni's monumental Piano Concerto is too striking to be ignored.

as if night were approaching prematurely. It is the third of the allotted days. Suddenly, troubled by the persistent soft voice of her dead mother in her ear, the Färberin staggers and falls, but the Amme revives her with a drink taken from a child who appears and disappears magically. With this drink her original resolve is restored and she returns home in order to confront Barak and complete the bargain. She finds Barak in apparent conversation with a group of invisible children to whom he is explaining the details of his métier as colour-master. He is surrounded by his crippled brothers who are convinced that he has taken leave of his senses.

It is at this point that the opera's final scene of Act 2 begins. The increasing darkness, despite the time of day, perplexes the brothers and adds to the Färberin's restlessness. The Amme whispers to the Kaiserin of higher powers playing with their destinies but she promises the fulfilment of their scheme. An elaborate ensemble follows and builds up to the moment the Amme has been waiting for, in which the Färberin addresses Barak with the formula which will seal the pact.

The rising theme of distorted fourths, Ex. 7, rears up on the trombones to inaugurate this great turning-point in the lives of the two beings, the one veering towards, the other away from, humanity. The Färberin taunts Barak with the appearance during his absence of her dream lover, abnegates his marital rights to enjoy her beauty and tells of the pact in which she has agreed to participate, decisively banishing from her body the unborn children and her own fertility (Ex. 35, the Renunciation theme, and that of the children, Ex. 31, strongly in evidence).

Barak, in the greatest consternation, calls to his brothers to make up the fire that he may see her face. The words are shouted, not sung, over a curious effect in which four trombones hold a loud sustained chord by fluttertonguing. There is a tremendous upward surge and the brothers call out in horror that 'she throws no shadow', following the pronouncement with a hectic ensemble based on the Mankind theme, Ex. 19.

Barak's patience and kindness are at last exhausted. He calls out for a sack of heavy stones with which to drown his wife and is with difficulty restrained by his brothers from laying hands upon her there and then. Their urgent pleas to him not to taint his hands with blood are voiced to a new and vigorous passage:

Ex. 43

The Amme urgently presses the Kaiserin to seize the now ownerless shadow for herself, but this is for the Kaiserin no longer possible. In her new-found sympathy for mankind through Barak's saintliness she perceives that the shadow is tainted with blood and she refuses it.

The Amme, hearing Barak's cries for the means to destroy his wife, comments in the midst of the raging ensemble that all he needs is a sword and this she can soon provide, in order the more quickly to gain possession of the shadow. Immediately a flashing sword appears from thin air and leaps into Barak's hand;[37] the brothers have scarcely the strength to prevent execution from being carried out on the spot. A new motif symbolizing the Long Arm of Retribution is declaimed by the brass:

Ex. 44

But this is Barak as the Färberin has never seen him before and with eyes bright with admiration she sings a ringing aria in which she claims that she has not in fact clinched the bargain; her tongue has run away with her, has betrayed her, and therefore she surely need not die over what has not actually happened. She caps this outrageous piece of sharp practice by calling on 'mighty Barak, stern judge and great husband' with the plea that if she must die let it be quick. For all its bogus sentiments the Färberin's aria provides a fine piece of heroic sustained singing in the manner of Sieglinde in what has otherwise become a scene of unmitigated frenzy.

Ex. 43 bursts in again and the brothers renew their pleas to Barak not to fulfil the slaughter, but the matter is put beyond question by the sudden disappearance of the sword,[38] amidst the raging of a violent storm echoed appropriately in Strauss's orchestra. The ground opens and Barak and the Färberin vanish from sight. The brothers rush out

[37] Hofmannsthal, in his synopsis, obscures what seems a plain case of the Amme's malevolent magic at work by writing as follows: 'have the Unborn Ones thrown down the executioner's sword to arm their father's hand against the evil mother who will lock life's door before them?'

[38] There is nowhere any authentically suggested explanation for this phenomenon, but the ingenious solution is put forward by William Mann that 'punishment is not for Barak to execute'.

howling into the street as the river overflows its banks and pours over the ruins of the hovel. The Amme calls out, as at the beginning of the scene, that higher powers are having sport with them. Quickly grasping the Kaiserin she puts her in a little boat which has appeared magically in the midst of the chaos, and the two spirits escape in it as off-stage fanfares reiterate the Trials motif, Ex. 42, in menacing tones. The curtain falls upon a cataclysmic orchestral furore in descending chromatic passage-work, with a gigantic double statement of Kaikobad's Ex. 1 in heavy augmentation. The Almighty One has manifested himself through the elements.

16

Theatrically effective *à la Grand Guignol* as the operatic version obviously is, it leaves too many loose ends to be acceptable as a full exposition of Hofmannsthal's vision, and for this we must turn once again to the *Erzählung* in hopes of clarification before passing on to Act 3.

To return first to the Bargain, the *Erzählung* makes it plain that a good deal more hocus-pocus with the fishes must take place before the compact can be completed, and this the Amme sets in motion as the Färberin begins to address Barak. Hence it would not have been enough merely to pronounce the words of renunciation as in the opera. But in the event, faced with the fishes (which have been conjured up again by the Amme), Barak's fury, and the whispering in her ear of her dead mother, she cannot even complete the formula, let alone throw the miserable little creatures over her left shoulder into the fire as required by the ritual: words and actions are, however, performed on her behalf by the Amme.

The Färberin rushes out of the house followed by the others and the remainder of the scene takes place in the full fury of the tempest. It is perhaps disappointing to find that the miraculous sword does not appear at all in this context. Flaming brands are collected from the fire at Barak's command by the three brothers. Barak himself stands, gigantic and terrible, the Kaiserin lying prostrate in deep humility at his feet, face to face with the radiant, motionless, staring figure of the Färberin, each seeing the other as if for the first time. And only now does the shadow 'taking heed of the banishment and in obedience to the spoken words and the burnt fishes', tear itself from the Färberin's back regardless of the fact that the pact was completed in intention only and fulfilled by proxy.

The Amme tries to seize it on behalf of the reluctant Kaiserin, but is frustrated by the appearance of none other than the Bote, Kaikobad's last representative, who has come to whisk off Barak and his wife to complete their Trials elsewhere. He vanishes as abruptly as he came, carrying the disembodied shadow over his arm, leaving the Amme to follow with the Kaiserin as best she may, in pursuit of the shadow she claims to be theirs, rightly and hardly earned. The magic boat does not appear at the Färberhaus as in the opera, ready to convey the two women on their journey. Instead they travel in the Amme's mantle which, wrapped round them, flies them directly back to the Spirit Kingdom. It then transforms itself miraculously into the little boat in order to negotiate the river which winds through the mountain crags and gorges of Kaikobad's abode. Thither the Kaiser, in the form of a statue, Barak and the Färberin have all preceded them, and the third act of the opera, like the last chapter of the *Erzählung*, is concerned with the final stage of their Trials which takes place under Kaikobad's direct supervision.

When they too arrive in the Spirit Kingdom, Barak and the Färberin are, in the *Erzählung*, tended and guided, the one by an old man clothed entirely in white, the other by the silent Fisherman[39] and his inquisitive wife.

In the opera, on the other hand, they are at first condemned to languish in solitary confinement in subterranean caverns, near to one another and yet unconscious of each other's proximity. The third act begins with an ominous statement of the Bargain motif, fully clothed in its granite-like rising chromatic chords, Ex. 34a, as it always will be from now on. This is succeeded by a deep pedal note sustained by the basses and bass drum over which a lonely bassoon lugubriously winds its way round motifs of the Färberin and her unfortunate husband. As the curtain rises the upper wind enter and, supported by celeste and two harps, play reminiscences of the music of the Unborn Children, Ex. 31. We are to understand that this represents the voices of the children themselves resounding in the ears of the distracted Färberin who can just be discerned in the gloom rocking to and fro in her misery.[40]

[39] It was demonstrably part of Hofmannsthal's intention that this strange figure (who does not appear in the opera at all) should arouse associations in the reader's mind with the Fisher King, and hence, via Amfortas, with Christ.

[40] It was in fact Strauss who pressed that the Unborn Children should not actually sing again until towards the end of the opera for the sake of greater clarity. This is the first of a series of fairly considerable alterations which Strauss prevailed upon Hofmannsthal to make to his first draft of this immensely complicated act.

At last the Färberin's mental anguish becomes unendurable and she cries out begging the voices to cease and protesting still that the deed of abnegation was never fulfilled. The sounds collapse into vehement statements of the Färberin's Ex. 26 (the theme with which the bassoon had originally begun) and, in a passage which owes much to the opening of *Lohengrin* Act 2, the cellos are left growling by themselves in their lowest register.[41]

In the course of their wanderings the cellos outline a new theme suggestive of Barak's forgiveness.

Ex. 45

(In moments of great rhetoric this rising seventh is often widened to the octave.)

To a background of Ex. 45 and various of Barak's previous motifs the Färberin now apostrophizes him. Her song is full of regrets at losing him, the husband whom she never learnt to know, and during the more poignant climaxes she takes over from the Kaiserin the motif of Guilt, with which she has at last been stricken (Ex. 39 passionately declaimed in voice and upper instruments). But she also initiates a melody which is to be the subject of a broadly lyrical duet which Strauss insisted on inserting at this point:

Ex. 46

followed shortly by:

Barak, unaware of her presence, her song of remorse and the retribution which hangs over her (Ex. 44 softly on a single horn), now begins

[41] In fact they are below their compass much of the time, for Strauss, in what was now becoming his customary disregard for practical details, writes for them, as for the basses, down to low B flat.

to sing to himself of his own sadness at having failed the wife who needed him and who should have been able to depend on him utterly. She, equally ignorant of his presence in the adjacent cavern, joins him in the duet, which swells to a climax in rich glowing colours.

This in turn gives way to a quiet section where, in combination with Barak's earlier themes of Goodness (Exx. 28 and 29), his forgiveness theme, Ex. 45, enters repeatedly in different instruments. The Färberin is now silent and Barak, left musing on his own, laments that he cannot see his wife once more in order to allay her fears.

With these sentiments he has passed the first stage of his Trials, and a heavenly voice accompanied by Ex. 42a on solemn trumpets tells him that he is free to leave his dungeon:

Ex. 47

'Auf, geh nach o - - - - ben, Mann,   der Weg___ ist frei' [42]

A beam of light illuminates a flight of stone steps and slowly he ascends them and disappears from view.

There are renewed surgings of Ex. 45 and against the Trials and Retribution themes (Exx. 42 and 44) the Färberin calls out to Barak acknowledging her change of heart. This in turn is reckoned sufficient for the first Trial and the heavenly voice with its accompanying beam of light summons her too (Ex. 47 repeated). As she rushes up the steps from her cavern heavy clouds cover the scene which fades from view. A passionate orchestral interlude recapitulates the vehement developments of the leaping theme, Ex. 30a, though now combined with the lyrical Ex. 46. It builds to a peak of intensity in which Barak's Ex. 28 and its derivative Ex. 41(x), symbolic of the Trials, repeat themselves as in an ostinato.

There is a split second of silence and the leaping theme crashes in again on the full tumultuous orchestra, but this time combined with the Kaiserin's rising motif, Ex. 5, and the broad phrase of the Kaiser, Ex. 11. The clouds have parted and now a different part of the Spirit World is revealed. It is, in fact, the scene of which we have already had a brief vision during the Kaiserin's nightmare in Act 2: a rocky gorge with stone steps leading up to a central massive door set into the sheer face of the cliff. Hofmannsthal describes it as resembling the entrance to a

---

[42] 'Up, go towards the upper region, Man, the way is free.'

temple, and the analogy with *Zauberflöte* and Sarastro, with the concomitant Trials and Ordeals, reasserts itself.

The Bote, with attendant spirits on either side,[43] stands waiting at the steps leading down to the river which, as we have already learnt from the *Erzählung*, winds through Kaikobad's kingdom.

As the music softens, the themes change to those of the Dream Lover, Ex. 38, and of Guilt, Ex. 39, although the leaping Ex. 30a is perpetually in evidence. Suddenly the Kaiser's love-theme appears in the form in which it had been given in Ex. 17, and this heralds the arrival of the little boat which floats, self-directed, to the foot of the steps; the Kaiserin is asleep with the Amme kneeling beside her. The boat comes to rest and an ominous section begins based on Kaikobad's Ex. 1 and the Purchase theme, Ex. 34, to which the heavy brass add in very soft tones the motif of the Trials, Ex. 42. The attendant spirits comment on the arrival of the two women, but the Bote dismisses them and himself retreats through the great bronze door, which closes behind him.

17

A curious scene now takes place between the Kaiserin and the Amme. Bearing in mind the Amme's eagerness to return to Kaikobad's domain, as evinced in the very first scene of the opera, one might have expected her to be overjoyed now that the moment has arrived and she is actually there. And so indeed she is, in the *Erzählung*, and confident moreover that she has behaved correctly, even in a praiseworthy manner, from first to last. Her only anxiety is that she may be separated from the Kaiserin, and this fear is, in the event, substantiated.

Such sentiments are wholly logical and credible, but the opera shows things quite otherwise. The Amme inconsistently describes the Spirit Kingdom as a fearful place of horror, and the boat as being fashioned from evil wood, bringing them thither of its own volition. She can think of nothing but flight and tries to entice the Kaiserin to flee with her without delay, repeating her phrase that higher powers are having sport with them. Kaikobad's menacing motif (Ex. 1) is strongly in evidence and is, together with the fanfare-like theme of the Trials (Ex. 42),

---

[43] This again was an idea which owed its origin to Strauss, who persuaded Hofmannsthal to change his original plan of entrusting the intervention of Kaikobad and his minions entirely to unseen voices. Such a device, he insisted, would be absolutely fatal because voices of this kind are invariably impossible to understand.

very much in the foreground during much of what follows. Ex. 1 is extended into a fanfare played by six trombones off-stage, in addition to its ominous use as a motif in the bowels of the orchestra.

But the Kaiserin has no intention of leaving. The boat has brought them with clear purpose to a place she recognizes. She also interprets the fanfares as the call to a judgement to which she wishes to submit herself. She speaks of Kaikobad rather touchingly, the father she has not seen for so long, and tells of his sitting upon his throne like King Solomon of old. Hofmannsthal's analogy with the biblical legend of Solomon's Judgement, which had been at the back of his mind from the very earliest sketches, had now caught Strauss's fancy in connexion with the Trials scene.

> 'I can't get the Judgement of Solomon out of my head;' he wrote, 'wouldn't its dramatic climax—i.e. the outburst of the real mother and her renunciation at the moment when the child is to be killed and halved—be applicable also to our piece and its climax in the scene of the Empress before the statue of the Emperor?'

Nevertheless Hofmannsthal did not see the way clear and the moment passes, not to return.

The Kaiserin's song outlines the notes of Ex. 3 which makes a long delayed reappearance. This is the motif associated in Act 1 with the Bote, the sharply characteristic phrase being reiterated everywhere in the orchestra as well, making Strauss's point clear that the Bote should represent nothing less than the *alter ego* of Kaikobad himself.

The six off-stage trombones blare out the Judgement motif and the Amme looks around her feverishly like a fox run to earth (Ex. 2 in hectic diminution). The Kaiserin on the other hand is radiant in her anxiety to suffer in return for the misery she has caused.

Ex. 48

'was er lei - det, will ich leiden   ich bin in ihm,   er ist   in mir!' [44]

---

[44] 'What he suffers I too will suffer; I am in him and he in me'. Strauss spoke of this phase as being in the manner of a heroic, ecstatic resolution.

A frenzied $\frac{6}{8}$ section follows during which the despairing Amme promises the Kaiserin the impossible if she will only flee with her forthwith. She will remain a spirit and yet acquire a shadow (continual references to Amme and Shadow motifs, Exx. 2 and 4). But the Kaiserin is not deceived by such duplicity. Meaningfully she asks the Amme what lies behind the mighty bronze door, and when with shudders the Amme replies that it is the Water of Life, she corrects her vehemently in a phrase which in its immense span rivals Kundry in *Parsifal* or Die Frau in Schönberg's *Erwartung*:

Ex. 49

'Zur   Schwelle   des To-------des!'[45]

The text here is quoted from the off-stage voices heard during the Kaiserin's dream. She remembers the words but does not understand their meaning, although she associates them with her journey to mankind and the bargain which was there enacted on her behalf (Exx. 20 and 34, with the Amme's Ex. 2 lurking in the background). The love theme, Ex. 8, enters transfigured on pianissimo trumpets and is linked to the Summons to the Trials, Ex. 47. The Kaiserin feels herself illuminated and ready for her ordeal. The rapid $\frac{6}{8}$ movement is resumed, though this time developing the Guilt and Kaiser's Prey motifs (Exx. 39 and 12) as, to the Amme's dismay, she now invokes the Water of Life.

The music returns with which the Amme had once sought to warn the Kaiserin against the human race (Ex. 18), and she sings with horror of the magic fountain which, like the Bote and the invisible voices, symbolizes Kaikobad's actual presence and intervention. She even tries as a last resort to paint Kaikobad himself as a fearful god of vengeance, much as the Queen of the Night blackens Sarastro's character, and it must be admitted that the change of viewpoint which is so confusing a feature of *Die Zauberflöte* finds its echo here. The Kaikobad of Act I, a wrathful spirit bent on retribution, here appears as a wise if stern, fatherly figure.

[45] 'To the threshold of Death!'

The Amme stresses how angry Kaikobad will be at the Kaiserin's mixing with the accursed race of man (Exx. 7 and 43) and inculpates the Kaiserin's mother, this mysterious figure of whom we have heard nothing since the very beginning of the opera, but who seems to be responsible for the Kaiserin's leaning towards humanity (the long-delayed reprise of Ex. 5(y) makes its appearance here).

At this the Kaiserin reaches a tremendous decision. The Amme's outlook and sympathies have become too narrow for her and from this moment she separates herself from her guidance for ever. In a glowing passage full of motivic references she announces the parting of the ways and mounts the central steps. The bronze doors open of themselves and close behind her. The Amme is left alone.

18

The fate of the Amme, as indeed her very identity, is one of the more bewildering mysteries in an already over-complex situation. It is apparent in the *Erzählung* that Hofmannsthal was himself none too clear on the subject for, having arranged for her to be abducted by the Christ-like Fisherman and set down in a different part of the spirit kingdom, the poet exposes her to the threat of transmutation into one of the Lower Animals, 'like all malignant beings', from which she flees only to lose her way on the rugged mountain slopes. There he leaves her, face down on the barren, cold stone, and this is the last we hear of her.

Whatever Hofmannsthal's original intention for the opera might have been, Strauss was positively determined on a dramatic exit after a supreme aria of evil ('in the manner of Ortrud' as he put it, *Lohengrin* still being strongly in his thoughts). Although Hofmannsthal was unhappy about the Amme's music in general he complied willingly enough with this suggestion with the result that the scene which follows is one of the most vivid in the opera.

The $\frac{6}{8}$ movement resumes yet again, this time based on the Amme's motifs (Exx. 2 and 18) mixed with many of the Mankind, Barak, Forgiveness and other themes. The whole complex is held together by a rhythmic figure strongly reminiscent of Schumann's Adagio and Allegro for horn and piano which Strauss must have known well.

Ex. 50

The Amme's ragings against humanity, which have been accompanied by a particularly striking development of Ex. 7, are interrupted by the voices of Barak and the Färberin calling to each other from distant caverns. At last, in their searches, each appears separately on the scene in turn, only to be deliberately misdirected by the enraged Amme. Both rush off in opposite directions to continue their hopeless search and the Amme, her anxieties at fever-heat, imagines the Kaiserin confronted with the Water of Life. Strauss, now thoroughly enjoying himself, contrives a section in multiple tonality almost worthy of *Wozzeck*:

Ex. 51

The Amme shrieks out to Kaikobad and a ghostly sixfold echo throws back her cry. Suddenly the Bote stands there before her, cold and himself brazen in appearance like the door through which he has emerged. The Amme pleads her case: as far as she can see, she has done all that can be expected of her; now she demands to see Kaikobad in order to beg for a hearing in person. The Bote is adamant, however; Kaikobad's own daughter is before him, and the Amme, unwanted anywhere or by any-one, may go where she will. A violent storm breaks out and the voices of Barak and the Färberin from the surrounding caverns combine with those of the Bote and the Amme in another frenzied ensemble.

The music stops abruptly and the Bote scornfully announces a new and highly appropriate fate for the Amme. She is to live out her life on earth amongst the humanity she so hates and despises. The continuing despairing voices of Barak and the Färberin reveal the Amme's failure and hence the reason for such a punishment. She must endure a fate corresponding to the wretchedness she has caused through her lack of human feeling. The little boat is once more pressed into service; the Bote hurls the Amme into it where she collapses still shrieking, and, at a final word of command from the Bote, it drifts away down river, earthwards, with her despairing form.

There is a fearful outburst of the storm which is depicted graphically in the orchestra as the heavy clouds return once more. This time there is a formidable cataclysm with wind machine, thunder machine, and every kind of heavy percussion contributing to a passage in which many of the outstanding motifs are combined, the strings rushing up and down as in the Act I interlude, the whole dominated by the blaring stage fan-fares. As the weight of the storm begins to subside, the voices of Barak and the Färberin can still be heard in the total darkness crying out hope-lessly. The three dominating motifs of Mankind (Ex. 7), Kaikobad (Ex. 1) and Retribution (Ex. 44), give way at last to that of the Bargain (Ex. 34a) presented repeatedly in soft tones with majestic interludes from the strings. To the distant voices of the colour-master and his wife are added those of attendant spirits making helpful comments such as 'Have reverence', or 'Courage, fulfil your destiny!'

The scene has changed to the interior of the Temple, which the Kaiserin has just entered as if from below. A niche in the centre of the precincts is mysteriously curtained off with hanging draperies. The attendant spirits have come to meet their royal mistress with flaming torches, and then they vanish. The orchestral brass softly declaim the solemn summons, Ex. 47, and then it too falls silent. Now the Kaiserin is alone, on Trial before her invisible judge and spiritual father.[46] A solo

---

[46] The *Erzählung* includes a fascinating scene preceding the Kaiserin's trial in which she meets the Unborn face to face. They are identified clearly as the same Beings who entertained the Kaiser to dinner prior to his petrification, but they now also include among their number divine personifications of Barak's crippled brothers without their deformities.

violin soars against an infinitely soft string background, outlining the
relevant motifs as it follows her thoughts from consciousness of her
identity as Kaikobad's daughter (Ex. 5), to Barak's distress (Ex. 30), to her
own guilt (Ex. 39) and her resolution to suffer (Ex. 48). Then she addresses her father directly, humbly acknowledging her failure to acquire
a shadow although she feels that she has learnt to sacrifice herself, and
begging for guidance. As she does so, her Suffering motif, Ex. 48, is
outlined on the horn, merging gradually into a new variant of the love
theme (Ex. 8) which blossoms out in warm lyrical colouring:

Ex. 52

In answer to the Kaiserin's pleas, the Golden Water of Life springs up like
a fountain from the floor. Two harps, two celestes, glockenspiel, even
glass-harmonica, all ripple and tinkle in description of this divine manifestation, which the Kaiserin welcomes in an ecstatic though restrained
song of appreciation coupled with self-denial. She is filled with love and
therefore needs no fortifying by even so wonderful a draught. Nevertheless a Spiritual Being becomes visible at the side of the fountain urging
her by drinking to acquire the Färberin's shadow, and thus also her
coveted quality of humanity.

Hofmannsthal intended that the Voice should, like the Water, convey
an impression of divinity, though by no means benevolent. Nor was
he sure how many such beings were to appear. At first he wrote of two
tempters emerging, one on either side of the stage, mysterious satanic
shapes whom he described as 'Guardians of the Threshold'. But a few
months later he was writing of the *three* Guardians as: 'deceitful sor-
cerers or demons, tempters, [for whom] I imagine highly peculiar
voices, male or female, alluring and at the same time repellant, as if a
serpent were to sing. Perhaps it is possible to use a very high pitched
male voice (falsetto) or a female one of exceptional depth, or something
far more beautiful than I can think of.'

Strauss, unable to conceive of anything specifically serpentine, and
clearly perplexed by the intricacies of Hofmannsthal's vision, merely
repeated the poet's suggestions in the score verbatim, though reducing

the number of these alluring demons to a single shadowy Guardian who becomes alternately visible and invisible as the Water of Life springs upwards from the floor or falls away.

The Heavenly Summons, Ex. 47, is heard gently on the trumpet and the Kaiserin asks anxiously what will become of the Färberin if she, the Kaiserin, accepts her shadow. As if in answer, the voices of Barak and the Färberin are heard again calling to each other in despair and bewilderment while the theme of the Färberin's own temptation (Ex. 38) meanders in the background against the melody of the duet, Ex. 46.[47]

The Kaiserin's remorse and conscience are evoked by the motifs of Anxiety (Ex. 30a) and Guilt (Ex. 39) which surge across the orchestral texture. She proclaims her guilt afresh and refuses the drink which will give her a stolen shadow at another being's cost. The fountain of magic water sinks and subsides altogether. The Kaiserin has passed the first test satisfactorily but the more severe ordeal is still to come. She calls resolutely to Kaikobad to reveal himself and a light grows from behind the central drapery, increasing steadily until the interior of the alcove is at last revealed.

But instead of Kaikobad, it is the enthroned stone figure of the Kaiser which is disclosed before the horrified eyes of the Kaiserin, and two chinese gongs reiterate the menacing threat of Humanity's undulating thirds, Ex. 19, leading to the fateful petrification motif, Ex. 9b, on the strings of the orchestra reinforced by, amongst others, ten trombones. The mortal Kaiser has paid the ultimate penalty. The talisman's curse is fulfilled.

The Kaiserin is now in such desperate case that she is beyond song, expressing herself exclusively through the spoken voice.[48] Her tortured

[47] The complexity of the instrumental colour in the sections of the 'Guardian of the Threshold' is such that twenty years later, on 8th September 1939, Clemens Krauss wrote to Strauss begging him to revise the passages. Although unwilling to undertake any drastic recomposition, Strauss agreed to thin out the orchestration and shortly afterwards sent Krauss some pages of manuscript with suggested alterations. These have, however, never been incorporated into the printed score. One of the pages appears reproduced in facsimile in Joseph Gregor's biography of Clemens Krauss (Walter Krieg: Vienna, 1953) and shows an almost distressingly watered-down version of what is in the original a most beautifully imaginative web of sound. The page is headed by a quotation: 'Prima le parole, doppo [sic] la musica', a now well-known reference to the opera *Capriccio* in which Krauss was to collaborate with the composer as librettist (see Vol. III).

[48] This was Strauss's idea, and one on which he was determined. Unfortunately performers of this role tend to find these passages so embarrassing to speak that the section is invariably cut to a minimum.

utterances are wrung from her innermost being. They are punctuated by
motifs such as Ex. 48 (the theme of her desire to suffer), which is interspersed phrase by phrase as she bewails the Kaiser's failure to 'loose the
knot of her soul'. When she speaks of the fate which has overtaken him
as the result of her guilt, Ex. 43 unexpectedly rushes upwards in rapid
diminution on upper strings. The Petrification and Trial motifs are
repeatedly in evidence, while a deep threatening F sharp rumbles per-
sistently in the basses, organ, double bassoon and the off-stage trombones,
reinforced by four tam-tams.

In her extremity the Kaiserin approaches the Statue, demanding that
she be allowed to die too, and this supreme act of self-sacrifice is declaimed between phrases of a new melody:

Ex. 53

To her terror the eyes of the stone figure follow her movements, expressing stern judgement. Underground voices repeat the curse of the talisman to the tones of the Falcon's motif, Ex. 10(x), and the Water of Life
springs up anew, in shimmering gold. The Guardian of the Threshold
reappears and once again repeats the words of insidious seduction. This
time, however, the promise is additionally made that if the Kaiserin
merely says the words 'I will', not only will the Färberin's shadow belong
to her but the Kaiser will return to life and be able to depart with her.
She appears indeed to have nothing to lose and everything to gain by
complying, but still she holds back, the hopeless voices of Barak and the
Färberin ringing in her ears to the end. Kaikobad's motif hammers out
and she cries again to him begging to be granted death rather than have
to submit to such an ordeal.

She has collapsed, but gradually raises herself as the Motif of Renunciation of the Unborn (Ex. 35), and that of the Amme's indoctrinations
(Ex. 18) build to a climax of almost unendurable intensity. The music
then breaks off abruptly and the Kaiserin chokes out the words 'I will
not'. The Water of Life sinks abruptly and amid total darkness there is a
long silence.

A string tremolo can just be heard, infinitely high up; a solo violin out-lines the Kaiserin's theme, Ex. 5, and other solo strings begin to trace the fourths and seconds of the shadow motif, Ex. 4, though now in a series of *descending* trellis-like passages, a glass-harmonica picking out the salient notes in augmentation. A beam of light begins to grow, piercing the darkness from above, and in its dazzling brightness there can be seen a sharply-defined shadow. It is attached to the feet of the Kaiserin who has once again drawn herself up to her full height.

The Kaiser rises from his throne and descends the steps towards her. As he does so he declaims a dictum, 'a prophecy', says Hofmannsthal, 'which the spirits sang to him at the moment of petrification'. It is, of course, hard for the Kaiser to communicate the inverted commas in which this prophecy is intended to be delivered. Hofmannsthal wanted it to sound 'most unearthly, a wondrous message of one only just returned to life.' Strauss tried his hardest to oblige but, despite some delicate pages of orchestration with strings divided and subdivided into many parts, the Kaiser's and Kaiserin's motifs mingling with those of Kaikobad and the Unborn children, the prophecy remains obscure: 'when the Crystal Heart shatters in a Cry, the Unborn come hurrying, shining like stars,' and so on. Strauss could not derive inspiration from such a text and the musical content behind the glittering sounds remains uncomfortably banal.

For this is in some ways the most unacceptable moment of all, occurring as it does at the very climax, just where one's sympathies need to be most aroused. In fact, for all the camouflage of the high-flown language, Hofmannsthal seems not to have solved the problems inherent within his own concept, which had indeed overreached itself in its very complexity.

The Kaiser proceeds to praise his wife's victory over herself while the voices of the Unborn can be heard joining in the general hymn of rejoicing. The Kaiser's themes all reach their ultimate stage of development, and in particular the derivative of his love theme, Ex. 52, now finds its true context. Their love need no longer be unfruitful, nor guilt-ridden (Ex. 39 receives due prominence), and the music of the Children, Ex. 31, is all-pervading.

It is apparent that we are now in the finale of the opera, but the affairs of Barak and the Färberin still await resolution and the curtain falls for the last scene-change, mercifully hiding the ecstatic forms of the Kaiser and the Kaiserin who have fallen on their knees, their faces hidden in their hands, before the cherubic voices of their own 'not-yet-born' children. Introduced by the Celestial Summons (Ex. 47) on the trumpets, the last transformation music combines the motifs of the reunited Kaiser and Kaiserin, the one in broad flowing lines, the other in rapid intertwining passage-work, while the broad hymn-like phrases of Ex. 53, the theme of the Kaiserin's final self-sacrifice, binds the whole together. In due course Barak's themes are introduced together with the Trial fanfare. The Färberin is also represented, though significantly no longer by her irritable Ex. 26. It is the leaping theme originally associated with her phantom lover Ex. 38 which, with its flowing extension, has been increasingly used to portray the figure of the Färberin herself, purified as she now is through suffering. Moreover the love theme, Ex. 8, and its new lyrical version, Ex. 52, are introduced with an altogether more general application than hitherto.

The curtain has risen to reveal a beautiful landscape in Kaikobad's kingdom. The Golden Water of Life now flows in a cascade between the rocky heights. Above the waterfall the Kaiser and Kaiserin can be seen descending from the higher regions; at a lower level, on a narrow footpath, Barak and the Färberin appear in order to play out the last phase of their drama.

Hofmannsthal has once more been forced to curtail his scheme for stage purposes; in order to find the explanation of where the two couples now find themselves, and how they got there, one must turn again to the *Erzählung*. Here all is accounted for in dramatic detail: the Kaiser and Kaiserin have been swept by the Golden Water of Life out of the temple and on to the soft grassy banks of the river of which we have heard earlier. In due course Barak and the Färberin are escorted to this same spot by the mysterious beings who have tended them since their arrival in the spirit world: the Fisherman and his wife bring the Färberin along one bank of the river, while the old man in white brings Barak on the other. The Red Falcon and the Twelfth Messenger, the Bote, also join this scene of general reunion, the latter bringing with him the fateful shadow which, quickly seeking out its true owner, rushes to the Färberin's feet, to which it attaches itself without her being aware of what is happening. Barak, who is on the far bank of the river, ignores the boat which in the *Erzählung* has been retained for his specific purposes, and impetuously wades across the river to her. She attempts to flee, believing herself still shadowless and guilty in his eyes; but he, instead of coming in judgement, now bows in all humility before his wife who has come to a standstill in bewilderment, having caught sight of the shadow which flows, like that of the Kaiserin, between her and the husband with whom she is at last reunited.

Despite the simplified circumstances of representation in the theatre, it is this scene of reunion between Barak and the Färberin which is enacted in the opening bars of the opera's final scene. Her initial fear of Barak, and expectations of judgement at his hands, are depicted with reiterations of the Retribution motif, Ex. 44, while Barak calls to her over music reflecting Guilt and Love (Exx. 39 and 52). Then abruptly the shadow becomes visible and their reconciliation is quickly effected. It is significant to discover that the Färberin's shadow is no longer characterized by the motif in fourths, Ex. 4, but by a series of descending figurations built from the Schumannesque Ex. 50 and from Barak's Ex. 28. In body and shadow alike, the Färberin has found her true identity in the person of her husband, and their Unborn Children sing joyfully from behind the scene. The shadow is now transformed into a golden arch symbolic of the bridge referred to by the Night-watchmen at the end of Act 1, the bridge of parenthood by means of which the dead return to life. The orchestra builds up a huge climax and breaks off for Barak's Great C Major Song of Jubilation:

Ex. 54

Nun＿＿ will ich ju - - beln wie kei ＿＿ner ge - ju ＿＿ belt

The Kaiser joins in, the Kaiserin and Färberin sing a duet, the Unborn chortle away in the background, actual children's voices are added to the score, and six further solo sopranos contribute from the orchestra pit to an extended finale which has more than a little in common with the 'closing scene from Faust' movement of Mahler's Eighth Symphony, both in setting and conception. The final tableau shows the two pairs, the Kaiser and the Kaiserin wending their way towards the spiritual heights beyond the rocky chasm, Barak and the Färberin in each other's arms on the rainbow-like bridge, while the last extended symphonic argument in the orchestra and chorus comes finally to rest in C major after a huge arch of development with the principal motifs, Barak's theme being featured in its transmuted form symbolizing the Trials of Purification through which both couples have passed, Ex. 42(x).

15

The *Erzählung* adds just one further enchanting incident. Barak and the Färberin have naturally no further purpose in the Spirit Kingdom and they are therefore allowed to return to the world of men. They are conveyed there by the little boat which has been laden with food and flowers of every kind, providing bountifully for the needs and comforts of the happy colour-man and his wife, and the boat itself glowing with every colour of the rainbow. Finally the Red Falcon hovers like a benign spirit over the whole radiant scene. The tremendous phantasmagoria is over.

20

In later life Strauss was fond of referring to *Die Frau ohne Schatten*[49] as his greatest opera, and during recent years there have arisen champions of the work who take extremely seriously this wistful verdict of its progenitor. Yet Strauss was by no means unique in cherishing his less successful brain-children at the expense of the popular masterpieces on which his reputation most firmly stands, and it is possibly a little ingenuous to mistake this affection for a considered artistic judgement, still less a *prima facie* evidence of the work's stature.

To arrive at Strauss's true and honest opinion one should at least be ready to take into account his misgivings during the composition of the last act:

> 'To change the style in *Frau ohne Schatten*, a style that pleases you and at which we both must aim—that's quite impossible. This isn't a case of a little more or less music or text; the trouble is the subject itself with its romanticism and its symbols. Characters like the Emperor and Empress, and also the Nurse, can't be filled with red corpuscles in the same way as a Marschallin, an Octavian, or an Ochs. No matter how I rack my brain—and I'm toiling really hard, sifting and sifting— my heart's only half in it, and once the head has to do the major part of the work you get a breath of academic chill (what my wife very rightly calls 'note-spinning') which no bellows can ever kindle into a real fire. Well, I have now sketched out the whole end of the opera (the quartet and the choruses) and it's got verve and upward sweep—but my wife finds it cold and misses the heart-touching flame-kindling

[49] He nicknamed it 'Frosch' (frog); actually, of course, the initials Fr.o.Sch.

melodic texture of the *Rosenkavalier* trio. I'm willing to
believe her, and I keep probing and searching—but believe
me:

> Schatten zu werfen
> beide erwählt etc.

does not go to music like

> Hab mir's gelobt
> ihn lieb zu haben.

I shall make every effort to shape Act 3 in line with your
intentions, but let's make up our minds that *Frau ohne
Schatten* shall be the last romantic opera.'

The fact has to be faced that as in all Strauss's most pretentious and
high-minded works, the often fine music contains much that is striking
and memorable, something even that is touching, but also a considerable
amount that is merely bombastic and, especially in the all-important
moments of Transfiguration, distressingly banal. How else could it be
when he became bogged down by the spurious symbolism and endless
insoluble intricacies of the extraordinary text? Not since *Zarathustra* had
Strauss encountered a subject the philosophies of which he understood
less, and *Zarathustra* had at least been his own choice for music treatment.
It is ironic that Hofmannsthal should have planned such a work just when
he had mapped out for Strauss a future modelled on Mozart and Offenbach.

The effect, so far from inspiring him to lighten his style, was on the
contrary to pitchfork him into the creation of a music drama more
heavily overladen with Wagnerian motifs and psychological cross-
references than ever before.

It is apparent, of course, that Hofmannsthal could not possibly perceive how he was to blame in the situation. Far from this, he actually
recriminated Strauss with having ruined his libretto by creating the
wrong sort of music, not only for much of the third act but in the whole
of the music for the Amme. This was not the first time he had taken such
a view; he had made similar complaints to Strauss over the music for
Zerbinetta and at several places in *Der Rosenkavalier*.

For all his avowed admiration of the past accomplishments of his
great collaborator, Hofmannsthal seems to have formed too clear a picture of the kind of music he wanted Strauss to write now and in the
future. But such demands upon a creative mind can be crippling, and to

confront Strauss with the accusation that he was at cross-purposes with Hofmannsthal over the characterization of the Amme, arguably the most obscure personage in the drama, was to leave him hopelessly confused.

Yet for all the difficulties one must also remember that at the time of the composition, at least of the first two acts, Strauss was only just past the second major peak of his life work, and there are many pages in this vast score which are built on musical material of a very high standard and a positive flavour of its own. Moreover, the unfailing ingenuity and resourcefulness of the vast orchestral and vocal setting is still wonderfully imaginative, though it is a little disappointing that Strauss abandoned his intention of contrasting the Ariadne orchestra with the main body as he had proposed to Hofmannsthal. One feels that something very original might have come from such a scheme, and the spirit world sections which were to have been allocated the chamber-orchestral accompaniment must surely have benefited from the resultant lightness of touch, especially in the third act. The fact that Hofmannsthal himself recognized the deficiency of this very quality in the completed work is significant in itself, and certainly it is here that one of the principal causes may be found of the work's comparatively few productions over the years.

First performed in Vienna on 10th October 1919 under Franz Schalk, the work made slow progress everywhere except in German opera houses, though even in these its success was moderate. The première had been deliberately delayed until a reasonable time had elapsed after the armistice, but Strauss continued to blame the too recent impact of the war for the opera's unenthusiastic send-off. Despite the fine cast with Jeritza as the Kaiserin, Lotte Lehmann as the Färberin, and Richard Mayr a highly sympathetic Barak, it seems to have been a somewhat lukewarm occasion. The staging in particular lacked imagination; Alfred Roller, previously a man in whom Strauss and Hofmannsthal had the greatest confidence, had no sympathy with trick supernatural stage effects, which he accordingly either suppressed outright or minimized.

In Italy the work had to linger until 1938 for its première, in America until still another ten years had elapsed—even then it was in Texas that it was first performed; it still awaits a presentation at the Metropolitan, New York, as also at the Paris Opéra and Covent Garden.[50] Such a

[50] Since this was written both the Metropolitan and Covent Garden premières have at last taken place.

reversal of fortune for the authors of *Elektra* and *Der Rosenkavalier* cannot be lightly dismissed as the shallow response of an untrustworthy public. Rolland, perceptive as ever, wrote in his Journal:

> 'The poem of Hofmannsthal affirms the scenic incapacity of the writer. His obscurity of thought trails an icy shadow behind it. It weighs heavily upon any passion. Strauss suffers from this collaboration.'

As with *Josephslegende* Strauss was loath to let so much hard work fade altogether into limbo, and during the last five years of his life spent a few of his working mornings contriving a Fantasia for orchestra based on some of the passages for which he had particular affection. This was first heard in Germany in the summer of 1947 and, in the following October, I gave the British première in Strauss's presence at Drury Lane under the auspices of Sir Thomas Beecham. In preparing the score for performance I noticed with some surprise that Strauss had omitted all reference to the music of the Kaiser, music which had been included in an earlier Fantasia of a similar nature, though based on different material, compiled by Strauss's friend and publisher, Dr Ernest Roth. At my request, Sir Thomas obtained Strauss's acquiescence in the addition of part of this earlier piece to his own score, and I accordingly made the insertion between the opening statement of Exx. 1 and 2 (Kaikobad and the Amme's motifs) and the Goodness of Barak section (Ex. 29) to which Strauss's Fantasia jumps so abruptly.

There is a short linking passage based on the Färberin's motif of ill-humour (Ex. 26(x)) and the Fantasia continues with the music of the magical transformation scene. Inevitably much is lost through the absence of the twittering slave-girls, although Strauss cued some of the voice parts into the orchestra. The Kaiserin's line is given to the trumpet, that of the young man to the horn. The motif of Motherhood Abnegation (Ex. 35) then enters as in the opera but leads directly to the orchestral development of the Färberin's grumbles from the second act (Ex. 40). This automatically introduces the Phantom Lover theme in its extended form (Ex. 38) and other themes from Act 2 are incorporated in a coda which Strauss added to round off a passage which in the opera passes directly to a new and different section.

Next comes the Barak/Färberin duet 'Mir anvertraut' from the first scene of Act 3. Barak's voice is taken by a solo trombone, an effect with which Strauss expressed himself dissatisfied during my rehearsals at Drury Lane, though without proposing any alternative. A reworking of

Barak's touching passage of resignation during the closing bars of Act 1 leads to his summons to higher regions as in Act 3 scene 1 (Ex. 47 on trombones), while the Färberin's similar summons is preceded by the section towards the end of Act 2 in which she protests that her tongue has betrayed her and that she has not yet sold her shadow. The music then plunges into the violent $\frac{6}{8}$ movement (once again from Act 3) in which the Amme desperately pleads her cause with the invisible Kaikobad against the frantic off-stage cries of Barak and the Färberin.

The Fantasia then passes without interruption to the closing scene of the opera with the two couples reunited above and below the rainbow bridge. From this point the music continues to the end of the opera with only minor compressions and reorchestration. The final effect is perhaps a little more representative of its original than its sister *Fantasie*, the *Josephslegende* Fragment, but hardly more satisfactory as a serious symphonic composition by the master-mind which created the great tone poems. Nor does its undoubted authenticity make it in any way superior to the bogus so-called Suite from *Der Rosenkavalier*. Accordingly its subsequent total neglect cannot be regarded as a tragedy, nor does it reflect on the quality of the opera itself. If the latter comes to occupy a place amongst the enduring works of Strauss it will be on account of its own undoubtedly unique atmosphere and its impressiveness in the theatre. If it should fail, a possibility to which Strauss had to resign himself, it would be through its heavy-handedness and lack of spontaneity which, in their more clear-sighted moments, both he and Hofmannsthal ultimately recognized.

CHAPTER XIII

WORKING ALONE

I

THE end of the war found Strauss in a curious and unsettled frame of mind. He had inevitably suffered some financial losses as, for example, his securities in England. He wrote bitterly in his Memoirs: 'the British confiscated my capital deposited in London with Edgar Speyer— the savings of thirty years. For a week I was very depressed, then I . . . started again from the beginning to earn money by the sweat of my brow just when I had entertained hopes of devoting myself exclusively to composition from my fiftieth year onward.'

Nevertheless it would be unwise to be misled by this into inferring that the shrewd composer had been left in anything approaching penury. In truth he had emerged relatively unharmed by the terrible cataclysm which had ravaged Europe. On the other hand it was impossible not to be affected by the profound changes of political system and world psychology which such an upheaval carried in its train. The principal artistic centres of the German-speaking countries, the courts of the many Princedoms in which Strauss's career had blossomed, were a thing of the past; the Empire of the Hapsburgs, the great Austro-Hungarian state with its centre in Vienna, was shattered, the aged emperor Franz Josef, who was its very personification, was dead. In place of the more or less benevolent autocracies (musically speaking at least) of the Fürsten and Kaiser, of the Royal Operas, the Court orchestras and theatres, the fate of German and Austrian musicians now lay in the hands of the State Theatres, the Town or City Operas and managements with their intrigues and political manoeuvres. It is not to be imagined that such a change-over could be effected without local frictions of every kind whether each individual instance reflected a change for the better or worse.

In such a restless climate the 55-year-old Strauss, the acknowledged figure-head of German composers, saw no purpose in returning to an active life of regular conducting after the four-year semi-retirement of the war period. He felt himself out of sympathy with the new world of music which was springing up out of the ashes of the old which he had loved, however much he had in his youth reacted against its conservatism. The abrupt acceleration which the war had given to advanced techniques of composition also repelled him and he was driven into an isolationism from which only the public duties of his position could drag him back.

His administrative post at the head of the Berlin Hofoper, the final surviving link of a liaison which had lasted since he took the artistic reins from Weingartner in 1898, came to a close in 1918 after a series of quarrels with the Intendant Georg von Hülsen and with Hülsen's successor Droescher. Nevertheless he temporarily assumed directorship of the new Berlin State Opera for a further year and conducted the concerts of the Kapelle (formerly the Court orchestra) until 1920, when he relinquished these too, in favour of Furtwängler.

Similarly when, despite considerable opposition in some quarters, he was invited to see the newly-formed Vienna State Opera through its teething troubles, he stipulated that he would provide no more than an interregnum; and a troublesome interregnum it certainly turned out to be. Hence it was not without some feeling of relief that in 1924 he handed the reins altogether to his colleague Franz Schalk, with whom he had in practice shared the Directorship, and with whom he had by now also quarrelled to the point where collaboration had become unfeasible.

One of the chief bones of contention was over the production of new and contemporary works in respect of which Strauss struck an unexpected and somewhat disturbing attitude. In contrast to his earlier policies in Weimar and Berlin, he strove, on assuming office in Vienna, to limit severely the performances of works by composers of his own or younger generations in favour of extending and re-establishing the classical repertoire. The arguments he proffered in a published manifesto to support this policy are ethically most problematical, bearing in mind the exalted standing as well as the conservative traditions of the Vienna

Opera. But they came especially ill from the composer, however eminent he might be, who had in the past benefited so greatly from a more progressive policy, and was at this very time enjoying the opportunities of his position to launch two of his more ambitious enterprises, lulling himself with the comforting thought that he was bestowing a favour—nay, an honour.

It is with equal distaste that one reads the cynical and facetious 'Ten Golden Rules for the album of a Young Conductor' which Strauss also jotted down at this time (1922). Despite an occasional note of practical wisdom they might even be said to lack integrity: here, as in the field of composition, the lost opportunity for exerting a powerful and objective influence in the energetic encouragement of the post-war musical scene is disappointing, even allowing for Strauss's lack of sympathy with the new stylistic movements. Indeed this whole period of Strauss's life presents an uncomfortable picture.

In this connexion it is fascinating to find Hofmannsthal revealing himself as a shrewd judge of his famous colleague. To some extent Hofmannsthal acted as intermediary during the negotiations between Strauss and the Vienna Opera though he had serious misgivings at the time, as he could already foresee that Strauss could no longer be trusted to make his policies and decisions in a wholly disinterested manner. In writing to Strauss of his anxiety he appears a wiser man and truer friend than at any time during their collaboration:

> 'Forgive me if I use very harsh and unduly strong language in order to explain to you my attitude. What I am concerned with are the merits of the case, and it is on the merits of the case, in this case, that I have no confidence in you.
>
> I believe that about fifteen years ago you would have been the ideal person to bring about the urgently needed renaissance of the Vienna Opera, but I cannot think that you still are today. I believe—and what has given me this impression is the manner in which you yourself with hundreds of little brush strokes, have painted the picture of your activity in Berlin—that today you would put your own personal convenience, and above all the egoism of the creative musician, before the uphill struggle for the ultimate higher welfare of that institution. I believe that, though you are still eminently *capable* of throwing yourself whole-heartedly into the task of building up the repertoire, into a Mozart or Wagner cycle, into protracted serious rehearsals (the ever-renewed youthfulness of your mind is the finest aspect of your

personality and the most obvious assurance that you are a
man of superior qualities), you would no longer be willing
to do so. I believe, when it came to engaging artists, making
friends, enemies, etc., etc., in short in handling the whole
policy of the theatre, the advantage to your own works
would be uppermost in your mind and not the advantage
to the institution. . . .

I am very fond of the good and fine aspects of your
personality where I meet them in the artist or, by sudden
flashes, in the man as well. . . . The great danger of your life,
to which you surrender and from which you try to escape in
almost periodic cycles, is a neglect of all the higher standards
of intellectual existence. Any attempt to place oneself above
ideas and institutions is an utter negation of what matters to
civilised human beings and, in so far as your works themselves form part of what matters in intellectual life, it is they,
however much you mean to foster them, which will have
to pay the eventual penalty. But I do not think that you have
yet reached the point at which you can understand the connexion.

I wish you well, better than most people have done in
your life. You have not looked for many friends, and have
not had many.'

However, Strauss at least found the association with Vienna by no
means unfruitful, and it was here that *Die Frau ohne Schatten* was given its
première conducted by Schalk, as also Strauss's next work which he conducted himself at its first performance five years later. This was a
second ballet composed on a subject and to a scenario planned and carried
out entirely by Strauss himself.[1] He seems to have turned to the *Casse-
Noisette* story by way of reaction after his years of struggle with psychological symbolism which had infected even his first ballet. Strauss unquestionably still felt the smart of the *Josephslegende* failure, and hoped
that left to his own devices he might achieve a triumph comparable with
that of *Till Eulenspiegel*, itself a light relief after more serious endeavours.

Bearing in mind his success with the Viennese idiom in *Der Rosenkavalier* and his present association with that city, he decided to capitalize
these assets and concoct some gay confection which would prove both to
Hofmannsthal and to himself that the Eulenspiegel within him was by
no means played out. It was after all specifically this flair for lightness and
caricature which had in the first place raised him head and shoulders

---

[1] There was in addition an intermediary work in pastiche which Strauss also
produced himself in Vienna. See Chapter XIV, p. 274 below.

above his contemporaries. The question was whether he could summon back into service a quality more characteristic of the impish youth of thirty years ago than of the country squire of the Bavarian Alps. Be this as it may, Strauss defiantly set to work on his gay Viennese ballet which he entitled *Schlagobers*, the word used and loved by all Austrians for their peculiarly luscious form of whipped cream.

2

The scenario of the two-act ballet *Schlagobers* is so similar in content, and even at times detail, to that of Tchaikovsky's *Casse-Noisette* that it seems inconceivable that Strauss did not have it at the back of his mind when planning the work. Yet the framework of the action is even slenderer than that most fragile of ballets. In order to emphasize the Viennese character of the work Strauss used as a basis the custom, peculiar to Vienna, of treating youthful candidates for Confirmation (known as *Firmlinge*) to a ride in an old-fashioned horse-drawn fiacre. These excursions traditionally ended at one of the sumptuous confectioners (*Konditorei*) where for once in their young lives they were allowed to stuff themselves, unrestrained by adult authority, with chocolate and sticky cakes liberally garnished with whipped cream—Schlagobers.

The opening movements of the ballet accompany precisely this scene: the music is placid and easy-going—Strauss at his most *gemütlich*.

Ex. 1

Ex. 2

Ex. 1 represents the Firmlinge themselves, Ex. 2 the Konditorei and its delectable wares. When the young guzzlers have gorged to their satisfaction (one boy has plainly overreached himself and has to be removed before it is too late), they get up from their little tables and dance a gentle Ländler. Again the music is comfortable and amiable in style, recalling much of the early *Bourgeois Gentilhomme* idiom, though lacking the distinction of that admirable score. At the climax the motifs of the Firmlinge and the Konditorei are combined with the Ländler in the manner of Bubi's Scherzo from the *Sinfonia Domestica*:

Ex. 3

The children finish their dance and, together with their doting godparents (who have been watching over them with benevolent forbearance) leave the chocolate-shop as the scene darkens. When the lights come up once more we are in the confectioner's kitchen itself, and surrounded by gigantic boxes all marked ostentatiously with tantalizing labels. A grotesque movement starts up, very much in the character of a marionette's march, with appropriate emphasis on the bassoon department as various members of the Sweetmeat family come to life:

Ex. 4

Puppets of marzipan, plum-cake, Lebkuchen and so on enter in march formation and, to the stiff caricature of military music, execute a mock war. The movement rises to a glittering climax and then gradually dies away. It is already apparent that Strauss is deliberately working much more towards a succession of set pieces in the classical ballet tradition than he was able to achieve in *Josephslegende*.

Next, in direct imitation of Tchaikovsky, follow three dances devoted in turn to the representatives of the three beverages—tea, coffee and cocoa, though the music itself could scarcely be more different from the parallel *Casse-Noisette* movements. The Dance of the Tea-leaves is a graceful and colourfully orchestrated $\frac{5}{8}$ movement with virtuoso solos for flute and violin. Strauss's tea, like Tchaikovsky's, comes from China, but whereas the coffee movement in *Casse-Noisette* is a Danse Arabe, Strauss composes a March 'in the style of a Brazilian Matschitsch'. A curious effect is created by a wailing theme for muted trombone which, out of rhythm with the remainder of the orchestra, cuts dolefully across the texture:

Ex. 5

At this point Strauss, feeling the need for a moment of romantic lyricism, inserts an effusive *Träumerei* which he describes as a Notturno for Prince Coffee with his *Trabanten* (myrmidons). In the first production, however, the cast list included a 'vision' who danced this scene as a solo.

Ex. 6

Here Strauss is once again in his element and, for all its extravagant lushness, the interpolation makes an attractive interlude in an idyllic manner for which Strauss was to find a more sincere purpose in his next opera, *Intermezzo*. With the lack of appropriate relevance in the scenario of the present ballet Strauss may even have been aware of the need to force more interest into the piece than he truly felt, for some of the harmonic chromaticisms seem a little strained, almost as if he had lost patience, relying on the prevailing homogeneity of his natural idiom to smooth over any unconvincing part-writing. In the end it all works tolerably well, though it cannot be compared with the imaginative finesse and exquisite workmanship of Strauss's sometime genius.

There is a curiously gawky violin cadenza, a passionate climax and a long languishing cadence, after which the *Träumerei* comes to a clearly-defined end, giving way to a brief return to the Brazilian March which rounds off the Dance of Prince Coffee.

If the Coffee movement has been long and discursive, the succeeding Dance, in which Prince Cocoa rolls about the floor like a human cannon ball, is disconcertingly short. Don Sugar appears in Spanish costume and to the music of the three beverages makes advances to each in turn. The theme to which he enters alternates with theirs, though it dominates the music as Don Sugar dances round with all three.

The act ends with a Waltz entitled, appropriately enough, *Schlagobers-walzer*—the Whipped Cream Waltz. A monstrous automatic chef appears at the rear of the stage whipping in a vast bowl great masses of the glutinous mixture, which overflows downstage metamorphosed into the corps de ballet, frothily costumed to create the required illusion. The Waltz itself, if not Strauss's best, and somewhat vulgarly over-scored, nevertheless has infectious panache and vitality. It is based on a little figure which, to those acquainted with the works of Strauss's Indian Summer, is affectionately enjoyed in a very different context:

Ex. 7

Ex. 7a

leading to:

(cf. ⌐x⌐ with Oboe Concerto)

The impression left by this early display of unrestrained flamboyance is one of bewilderment coupled with an element of distaste. Not only has there been no development of the plot, but there has been a total lack of motivation in even such action as we have witnessed in the course of the Introduction and six dances which constitute this first part. In previous ballets of the kind, whether *Boutique Fantasque*, *Casse-Noisette*, or

Petrouchka, the appearance of life in inanimate objects—toys or sweet-meats—is always delicately handled, and above all purposefully: midnight strikes in the one, in another a magician appears, in some way the moment has arrived when the toys reveal their hidden talents and lovable personalities through which they control the course of events. Curiously for a man with his understanding and feeling for the stage, Strauss overlooked the necessity for the atmosphere of magic, of child-like wonder, and as a result his work lacks sensitivity, let alone the fastidious taste of the Russian masters. His foods, rich and indigestible, spring unsummoned to life and indulge in war manœuvres or dances in praise of each other and of overeating. When the stage is filled with marzipan, Lebkuchen, pralines, tea, coffee and cocoa, all inundated with whipped cream, the curtain falls.

3

It is abundantly fitting that when the curtain rises on Act 2 we find the doctor has been summoned. An uncomfortable shifting harmonization of Ex. 1 describes the plight of the gluttonous Firmling, while repeated references to Ex. 7a emphasize the cause of his fever, that is to say, over-indulgence in Schlagobers.

The doctor enters the sick room to an impressive motif worthy of Potiphar and addresses himself to his young patient, taking his pulse and administering medicine from an enormous flask. Smilingly he shakes his head in mock disapproval and takes his departure, leaving the Firmling to sleep off his indisposition.

The boy's theme in its original form (Ex. 1) alternates with that of the doctor in a coda-like passage as the stage darkens and the scene changes to the court of the Princess Pralinée. Inevitably comparison is again invited with the parallel opening of the second act of *Casse-Noisette* in which the action is transplanted to the royal domain of the Fée Dragée—the Sugar Plum Fairy. But there is no similar link with the previous act in the manner of Clair's arrival with Casse-Noisette himself and the recital of his debt of gratitude to her for saving his life. No such heroics can be looked for in the Firmling, who indeed has no further active function in the work whatever.

The ceremonious entrance of the Princess Pralinée is accompanied by a number of new themes which, although closely integrated at this first appearance, later acquire independent importance.

Ex. 8

Picc. & Celesta

Ex. 9

cf Ex. 9a

(Mozart K 550)

Ex. 10

Ex. 8 represents the delicate trippings of the Princess, Ex. 9 the more boisterous prancings of the little Pralines, while Ex. 10 forms part of the rumbustious Galop to which the members of the Court cavort about the stage. Ex. 9 is quoted here in the form in which it appears later, although for the time being it is compressed into the texture, so as to lose its characteristic rhythmic variation. Strauss describes it as an old Peasant's Dance from the Oberfalz region, but it bears a quite remarkable resemblance (albeit in the major key) to the Minuet from Mozart's G minor Symphony (Ex. 9a), a fact which gives rise to interesting speculations over the origins of Mozart's melodic vernacular.[2]

The Princess Pralinée descends from her ceremonial carriage and dances a Waltz on a graceful, if rather trite, little theme:

Ex. 11

Solo Vl.

[2] The discovery of the similarity of Haydn's themes to Croatian folkmusic enhances the pertinence of such conjectures.

16

(though Strauss does his best to give it piquancy with endless false relations and harmonic side-slips), after which the little Pralines dance to
Ex. 9, now announced clearly in its a-rhythmic form. This is followed
by a leaping dance for the *Knallbonbons*, a sweet scarcely known in Britain but apparently enjoyed in America under the name of 'Snappers'.
The leaps are pointed in the orchestra by strong accents on the last weak
beats of each half-bar, while against the prevailing $\frac{6}{8}$ rhythm a strong
$\frac{3}{4}$ theme in Strauss's *Feuersnot*-idiom pursues a relentless path. The confused mêlée of sound gradually dies away and subsides into a galop
which, beginning quietly though comically, soon develops into a furore
as one by one the themes of the preceding movements are added to it. The
climax comes with Ex. 9 declaimed exultantly in the brass leading to a
sudden hiatus in which all the themes stop dead, leaving only the percussion pounding away grotesquely by itself. The strings then burst in
with Ex. 10 as the Princess mounts her carriage once again and is
drawn away to the rear of the stage. The trumpets carry the $\frac{3}{4}$ theme
of the bon-bons up to the heights and with the last crashing chord the
theatre is plunged abruptly into total darkness.

4

In his scenario Strauss directs that the black-out should allow the audience
to become momentarily aware of the Firmling's sick-room, though it
should be no more than a mere suggestion. Certainly the music of the
entr'acte which follows has a nightmare quality about it. Against a background of chromatic harmonies drawn at first from the music which
accompanied the opening of Act 2 (the sickroom scene), disturbed
memories of the preceding dances are heard mingled with fragments of
the Schlagobers Waltz.

   Gradually the Princess Pralinée dance-theme, Ex. 11, comes to the
forefront of consciousness and as the trills and chromaticisms slowly
dissolve the curtain rises to reveal the same show-case from which
(though we now learn this for the first time)[3] the princess previously
emerged. A graceful minuet on the lines of the *Bourgeois Gentilhomme*
begins, at first featuring Ex. 11 which, however, fades from the texture
as it becomes apparent that the show-case now shelters an entirely

---

[3] The occasional divergences between the stage directions in the libretto and the
score suggest that Strauss changed his mind at certain points during production.

different group of characters. These unlikely candidates for a small boy's nightmare take the form of monstrous bottles of liqueur.

The following rather peculiar and unnecessary scene concerns the rivalry of Vodka and Slivovitz for the hand of the beautiful Chartreuse. Their names seem to have given Strauss some cause for doubt, and Slivovitz in particular was changed from Michel to Ladislaw at so late a stage that little printed slips appear stuck on piano scores and full scores alike every time he appears. It has been suggested that Strauss intended to symbolize some political reconciliations in this scene, after the bitterness of the world war, but it is hard to find the logic in such a theory.

The episode is, at all events, clear and self-contained. Marianne Chartreuse dances her Minuet:

Ex. 12

admiring herself the while in an elegant hand-mirror, until her coquettish behaviour attracts the dashing Ladislaw Slivovitz, who rushes in and proceeds to pay court to her. She is at first frightened and embarrassed, but when the half-drunk Boris Wutki staggers in and also tries to woo her, she realizes that her first suitor had much to commend him. Accordingly she dances a Pas de Deux with Ladislaw (not unlike the Chrysothemis music from *Elektra*) and ends by giving him her hand. Wutki is momentarily disappointed, but quickly resigns himself to the success of his rival and submissively holds the train of Marianne's long dress as the three disappear into the gathering darkness.

The shifting chords of the unfortunate Firmling's sick-room are briefly heard for the last time in yet another rapid scene-change, and lead to an extended Passacaglia entitled 'Chaos (Variations on one and the same theme)'. The 'same theme' in question is clearly still that of gastronomic indisposition, and musically the ground bass consists of two adjacent statements of the Konditorei theme, Ex. 2(x), though the second is chromatically altered.

Ex. 13

The scene represents an armed revolt of the comestibles in what may be regarded as an elaborate allegory on the disturbance in the Firmling's stomach. The little fanfare motif, Ex. 12(x), lingers on in the texture as the darkness gradually lifts to reveal a street scene. Starting from the gaily decorated suburbs, rows of popular candy figures march in military formation towards the centre of the city, the famous Kärntnerstrasse. This is the Viennese street in which are housed the principal Konditorei, and towards the confectioner of their origin the candy-men resolutely advance. Oddly enough, Marianne, Ladislaw and Boris also join forces with them, waving flags (which the score describes as yellow, but the libretto emphasizes as being white). The flags are of varying size, Wutki's being so large that he constantly becomes entangled with it. Their music mixes with the Passacaglia as the Variations gradually work up to a climax and, at the appearance of the battalions of Marzipans, Lebkuchen and the like, the theme of their military operations from Act 1 is heard (Ex. 4). There is a dramatic pause as oriental magicians with tall hats and long beards appear and shower the crowd with propaganda leaflets.

A 'Rebellion Polka' then begins, descriptive of the general uproar, with various themes (Exx. 12 and 13, Marianne's minuet, etc.) rushing about in diminution. The Polka is additionally built on two galumphing themes, the one in the minor key, the other—which is to some extent derived from the first and from Ex. 2—in the major:

Ex. 14

Ex. 15

At the moment when the candy-men reach the Konditorei and their threatening behaviour is at its height, a huge tea-urn which has appeared in the background tips forward and pours its contents over the crowd, followed in quick succession by similar giant urns of coffee and cocoa. Suggestions of the appropriate themes which appeared with these beverages in Act 1 are heard in the accompanying orchestral convulsions and these are followed by an even greater inundation. To a fanfare of herald trumpets on the stage two gigantic tankards of German beer sluice the precious liquid in torrents over the still milling throngs of rebellious candy.

The mêlée on the stage, with its street scene full of drenched people, naturally put Strauss in mind of the finale to the second act of Wagner's *Meistersinger*. Accordingly the orchestral cataclysm which accompanies this last and most effective deluge is built on the Beckmesser theme of consecutive fourths which Wagner employs in the similar circumstances.

The much loved draughts of 'Hofbrau Vollbier' (such as Uncle Georg Pschorr's brewery produced) at last achieve the pacification of the rebels, who dance a cheerful round to the second Polka-theme, Ex. 15, now transformed into a swinging Ländler. This change from rebellion to hilarity is the signal for the Princess Pralinée to make her triumphal re-entry. The background of the stage is now fully illumined and the Prin-cess emerges once more from the show-case together with her full retinue, and preceded by a bodyguard of quince sausages dressed up appropriately as Frankfurters.

Musically Strauss marks her appearance with an unexpected return of the *Träumerei* from the Dance of Prince Coffee (Ex. 6) which combines ecstatically with the transformed Polka theme in a long outpouring of broad melody. In her glass palace, which has appeared at the rear, the Princess welcomes to her court the three liqueurs (Marianne, Ladislaw and Boris) and instructs her Negro Pralinée-attendants to distribute chocolate money to the fully pacified crowd.

The *Träumerei* now alternates with the theme of the Princess's Waltz, Ex. 11, and leads to a conventional Ballet Finale. This General Dance is a rapid Tarantella whose main theme comes once again from that source of so many ideas, the earlier ballet sketch, *Kythere*, in which it was projected for the Finale of Act 2.

Ex. 16

Ex. 16 pursues its bustling course with the principal themes of the previous scene combining with it until ultimately it merges into a last full-
scale restatement of the Princess's Waltz, Ex. 11, passing in turn to an
even more rhetorical outburst of the *Träumerei*. The glass palace has been
metamorphosed into a tiered wedding cake around which a Tableau
forms with the Princess in the centre. When the universal homage and
acclamation reach their zenith the Firmlinge appear on either side of the
stage foreground and contemplate the fantastic scene with bewildered
enthusiasm. The herald trumpets renew their fanfares on the stage, the
Schlagobers Waltz (Ex. 7a) bursts out in the strings with the Konditorei
motif (Ex. 2) on the woodwind and horns, and the ballet reaches its
uproarious final curtain amid general jubilation.

5

The first performance of *Schlagobers* took place in the Vienna State
Opera on 9th May 1924 as part of a Strauss Festival held in honour of the
composer's 60th birthday. Strauss himself conducted and all the auguries
seemed set for a resounding success. To Strauss's chagrin the work was
not well received, nor has it since found much favour with ballet companies. It was perhaps tactless to stage a work on so opulent a subject
amidst the austerity of post-war Austria, and this, together with the
disastrous inflation, lay behind the none too friendly nickname given to
the work—'Milliardenballett'.

Twenty years later there was a proposal to make a film from it, but
this scheme Strauss sourly opposed. A shortened Suite of detachable
movements was arranged by cutting down scores and orchestral parts for
the purpose, but was never officially published. At least some of the
better movements have been more widely played and even recorded as
a result, but the ballet as a whole remains one of Strauss's least known
stage works.

It was not to be expected that Strauss would sympathize with adverse criticism, but his defensive reasoning is hardly convincing:

> 'I am always expected to produce new ideas, grandiose conceptions. Surely I have the right to compose whatever music I like. I have no patience with the contemporary mood for tragedy, I want to give pleasure, and need it myself. . . .'

No one has ever wanted anything from a composer but good music, whether tragic or gay, light or serious. The misfortune of *Schlagobers* is that so much of it is weak and tasteless, and as so often happens, the poor material tending to outweigh the good, none of it is played.

Even the Suite includes both good and bad, although it omits little worth preserving. It contains from Act 1 the military manœuvres, Ex. 4, (an excellent movement), the Tea and Coffee Dances, the latter together with its beautiful Nocturne (or Dance of the Vision), and the Schlagobers Waltz; while from Act 2 it selects the Entrance and Dance of the Princess Pralinée, the Dance of the little Pralines, the Pas de Trois of the liqueurs, and the closing General Dance.

It is significant that left briefly to his own devices, after being for so long under Hofmannsthal's spell, Strauss no longer resorted eagerly to his natural bent of exotic character-study or of caricature, in both of which he had once so greatly excelled. It was as if, having been forced to cudgel his brains too hard in pursuit of deep psychological concepts, he now wanted to avoid the profound and concentrate on the merest entertainment until such time as Hofmannsthal was ready to set his nose back to the grindstone. That *Schlagobers* was no isolated instance, but part of a whole change in his psychological approach, is shown by the other major stage work which he composed at this same time, the opera *Intermezzo*.

6

The roots of *Intermezzo* date back to the spring of 1916, when *Die Frau ohne Schatten* was near completion and Strauss was half way through the Vorspiel to *Ariadne II*. As always at this time of year he found himself looking ahead, wondering if there was going to be enough to occupy him for the summer months. During his work on the Vorspiel he had aimed deliberately at a new and lighter vein of recitative which he felt to have been a great success. Indeed, so pleased was he that he had begun to have visions of himself as a kind of latter-day Offenbach, even going so far as to promise rashly that he 'had now definitely stripped off the Wagnerian musical armour'. One idea leading naturally to another, his head was full of schemes for satirical comedies which he outlined enthusiastically to Hofmannsthal. There were to be beautiful spies, ambassador's wives turning traitor for love, all amidst a world of politics and intrigue. Perhaps it was all rather ingenuous: in his letter Strauss nervously wrote, 'you'll probably say Kitsch. But we musicians are known for our bad taste in aesthetic matters.'

Sure enough Hofmannsthal replied that the idea had seemed so ghastly to him that he had burst out laughing. 'The things you propose to me are to my taste really dreadful and might put one off becoming a librettist for the rest of one's life.' Strauss ill-advisedly pressed the matter, labouring the Offenbach angle, and this time nearly provoked a veritable onslaught. In a letter which was at the last minute withheld from the post (though carefully preserved), Hofmannsthal went so far as to reveal how his whole intention already in the planning of *Rosenkavalier* had been precisely to guide Strauss away from his previous manner towards the path of operetta. Unfortunately, as he now acknowledged in retrospect, he had been disappointed by Strauss's failure to match his own burlesque style with just such an Offenbach-like idiom as Strauss was planning to affect for his future works. The footmen at the end of Act 1 (of *Rosenkavalier*), the Faninal servants at the end of Act 2, the exit of the Baron in Act 3, all had been ruined by this 'smothering with heavy music'— passages which had been designed as operetta pastiche.

Yet paradoxically Hofmannsthal no longer wanted to follow up their joint successes of the past, as Strauss 'already had too many devotees' and was already 'all too obviously the hero of the day, all too universally accepted'. How much better for his character would it be to 'reach new and unexplored regions ... that element which was sure to bewilder people and provoke a certain amount of antagonism'.

There was therefore a conflict in Hofmannsthal's mind, and although in principle a successor to *Der Rosenkavalier* was a congenial idea ('I could imagine that I might draw ... the inspiration for a future libretto, a deli-cate comedy with a great deal of love; I am glad you are mentioning this just now'), the moment he reflected on it seriously he recoiled and suggested instead that if Strauss wanted to pursue such a course he should invite assistance from the Austrian dramatist Hermann Bahr, with whom Hofmannsthal was in close contact at the time.

Bahr occupied a faintly discomfortable position in respect of his dual relationship of colleague and professional critic. After being a full-time journalist in Vienna for some twenty years, Bahr had in 1907 additionally become the manager of the Deutsches Theater in Berlin. His connexion is thus self-evident, not only with Max Reinhardt, who was at the time doing some of his most famous work at that theatre, but with Strauss and Hofmannsthal, whose *Elektra* emanated from this very source. Bahr's wife, Kammersängerin Anna Mildenburg, was also a prominent opera singer and was particularly celebrated for her interpretation of the role of Klytemnestra. The appearance in the local newspapers of Bahr's reviews, containing opinions which Strauss and Hofmannsthal could hardly be expected always to share, was not conducive to the most sympathetic friendship. But whereas Strauss considered Bahr's knowledge of music primitive Hofmannsthal, for whom at one time no words were too ill with which to speak of Bahr, nevertheless preserved enough respect for his standing as an author in his own right to maintain a cordial understanding as between two eminent men of letters.

Bahr's most successful play was *Das Konzert*, which he wrote in 1910 and which concerned the matrimonial difficulties of a musician and his wife. It so happened that Strauss himself had experienced just such difficulties in his own private life a few years before and the idea occurred to him to base an opera on this very subject. The story of the incident was afterwards told in a magazine article.[4]

> 'One day—he was away on tour—a letter was delivered to his home, 17 Joachimsthalerstrasse, Berlin, and was opened by his wife. To her alarm it read as follows: "Darling love! Do get me the tickets. Your faithful Mitze. P.S. My address is: Mitze Mücke, 5 Lüneburgerstrasse." This Mücke woman provoked a mammoth incident, half tragic, half comic. Frau Strauss immediately took it that her husband was unfaithful and, as Ludwig Karpath[5] once described it most amusingly, set all heaven and hell in motion. She was determined to get to the bottom of this shady secret. She instigated divorce proceedings and left unopened all letters from her husband. In the end Richard came home and went through such a scene as he had never even witnessed on the stage. His protestations were simply derided, his conjectures as to the possible explanation laughed at (for example there

---

[4] 'Die fatale Mücke'. Ernst Decsey, *Bohemia*, 26th October 1924.

[5] Karpath, a mutual friend, was the Ministry of Education adviser for the Austrian State Theatre.

was a conductor by the name of Edmund von Strauss who was with him in the Berlin Opera). It was useless for him to swear black and blue that he did not know this Mücke, had not even the least idea who she was—and it was only after long investigations that strand by strand the rope of the affair was disentangled and his innocence re-established.

This is how it all came about: an Italian company was at that time appearing for a guest season at the Kroll Theatre in Berlin. The performances were conducted alternately by Vigna and by the Prague Kapellmeister Josef Stransky, who had appeared with them during their previous visit to his city. The star artist of the season was a tenor named de Marchi, whose manager was the American Edgar Strakosch.

One night after the show the three—de Marchi, Strakosch and Stransky—repaired to the Bar of the Bristol Hotel and were sitting there with great enjoyment and not the least misgivings, when suddenly a female came and sat next to them. Hearing de Marchi and Strakosch talking Italian, this creature—a real Berlin tart—at once jumped to it that they came from the opera and without the slightest embarassment asked for a ticket for the next performance. At this, de Marchi in his German-Italian double-dutch, remarked, "Oh, Herr Strausky will look after that. . . ." He always said "Strausky" for "Stransky" and the latter never thought any more about it, of doing anything for this female, least of all laying on a ticket. He sent her nothing.

Brazen as she was, she looked him up in the Directory, and there she found a "Kapellmeister Strauss, Joachimsthaler-strasse Nr 17" and took it for granted that the conductor she had seen in the Bristol Bar, the "ky" in whose name she either forgot or overlooked, must be the "Joachimsthaler-strasse" one.

And that was how the disaster snowballed; it needed endless diplomatic intervention on the part of Rösch, one of Richard Strauss's most intimate friends, to put the affair to rights—and not before Richard had endured some agonizing moments. . . .'

7

On the surface it seems a most unlikely tale, and yet it is not really incon-sistent with the tenor of Strauss's family life. Frau Pauline had never for-given him that she, the General's daughter, a de Ahna, had married socially so far beneath her. All his success, his position in the artistic world, the villa he had bought her in the most idyllic surroundings, could not altogether mitigate the fact that he was *au fond* no more than a *petit bourgeois* with lower-class taste, outlook and manners. Even his music she saw as plebeian, vulgar stuff, entirely derivative and undistinguished. If peace was to be preserved Strauss had to tread a very straight and narrow path. Not that he found this difficult where his sex life was concerned. There was never at any time a breath of scandal surrounding Strauss, although in Germany the conductor has always been regarded as such a romantic figure as normally to be especially subject to amorous escapades. For all the emotionalism of his music, and the eroticism of so many of his subjects, Strauss himself was a strict member of the Bavarian bourgeoisie in his private life. He seems indeed to have been oddly indifferent to women, and even to a large extent to have escaped from the over-frequent company of his wife, to whom he gave, nevertheless, not the slightest cause for jealousy or suspicion. Had it been otherwise, indeed, *Intermezzo* could never have come to be written.

In more harmless matters, however, he must have found it hard to avoid trouble, being subjected to endless humiliations, especially in front of visitors. Incredible tales are told of curious tappings which came from a screen in the corner of the room during interviews with some female visitor or artiste, Pauline emerging from her hiding place only as the guest was leaving. Moreover, in addition to petty disciplines about the house, such as being sent like a small boy to remove his shoes for fear of dirtying the carpet, he suffered even severer rebuffs in his professional life. After the première of *Die Frau ohne Schatten*, for example, Pauline loudly proclaimed that it was the most stupid rubbish he had ever written and that she would not be seen walking home with him. She then marched back to the hotel leaving him to trail along behind.

Strauss's dictum that such treatment was 'just what he needed' is as revealing as his faithfulness to the librettist who had assumed the superior role in their relationship. He once wrote to Hofmannsthal: 'nothing does me so much good, nothing stimulates and fructifies my ambition and creative energy so much as adverse criticism from one to whose judgement I attach some importance.' Nevertheless the truth is less clear-cut; deflation was not altogether what he needed, but in some curious masochistic way was what he liked.

Over the years it even contributed to his general loss of initiative. His very life-work of composition was threatening to degenerate into a hum-drum routine, alternating daily with a regular game of cards which had fast become as much a part of him as his musical life. He was as proud of his prowess at Skat as of his world-wide reputation as a composer, and it would be unwise to hazard which, during the latter part of his life, he enjoyed more.

Nor did he confine his Skat to his free afternoons at home. He would race through performances of his works in order that there should be plenty of time for a good session immediately afterwards. The story filled him with glee that when he asked the Intendant, Heinz Tietjen, at the première of his new ballet, 'Are we playing this evening?' and Tietjen answered, 'Yes, indeed, Herr Doktor, we are performing your *Schlagobers*', Strauss was able to answer, 'Good Heavens, who is talking about that? I meant, are we playing Skat later on?'

There is a clear affectation here, a pose of good-humoured boredom with his life of luxury as a famous man; it seems as if something within him needed to exhibit to the world this image of himself, together with his curious home life in which he also had a conscious pride. There is ample evidence that his wife's shrewish behaviour afforded him infinite gratification. He had already publicly paraded it in two major works. Hofmannsthal's proposal of Hermann Bahr as his librettist for some social comedy reminded him of the subject of Bahr's *Das Konzert* and this in turn of the parallel situations within his own life. It was perhaps time for another autobiographical piece. After one more abortive attempt to cajole Hofmannsthal, Strauss made up his mind to put his ideas in front of Bahr.

8

Inevitably some months passed in making the preliminary approaches, and when at last, after some initial hesitation on Bahr's part, his goodwill had been secured, the summer of 1916 had passed. It was thus late September before the two men met in Salzburg to compare first thoughts. Bahr naturally had views of his own, and was a little doubtful whether he could direct his mind away from the 'fantastic and sharply satirical piece' which he was at present engaged upon, and towards the 'delicate Rococo-affair' which Hofmannsthal had told him Strauss was looking for. It thus stands much to his credit that he applied himself so willingly and courteously to the surely unexpected subject of Strauss's own private life, supplying the draft sketch of an appropriate marital comedy within a few days. It was, however, already apparent that Strauss would have to be exceedingly tactful if the collaboration was to reach a successful conclusion, for almost every line of Bahr's accompanying letter betrayed his qualms. Strauss did his utmost to mingle praise and encouragement with his censures, but inevitably some of these were radical. After all, this new plot concerned real people whom Bahr, the skilled dramatist, was bound to caricature, while Strauss wanted as near a true-to-life representation as possible. Further meetings were held in Munich and Berlin during the autumn and winter in which these problems were thrashed out. The character representing Strauss himself presented relatively few problems. At first his name was to be wholly different—Kranich was one suggestion—then gradually it came closer to reality via Albert Storch. Pauline became Christine, and, to begin with at least, she was no major stumbling block. Oddly, or so it seemed to Strauss, it was the third figure in the comedy who was causing Bahr the most trouble.

This character, a young aristocrat with whom his social snob of a wife amuses herself during her husband's absence, was also based on a living person. Strauss was amusingly tolerant when describing to Bahr this Baron with whom at one time Frau Pauline had had some sort of mild flirtation, though without divulging his name: 'the original was a shy young man of few words, whose character as an adventurer came out only when he half-shamefacedly tried to get money from my wife; until then he had been extremely modest and . . . had aroused her sympathy. . . .' But when it came to modelling his character for representation on the stage, Strauss described this impecunious Baron less generously: 'a young person lazy and without talent, who would really like to pursue his studies but prefers sports; who himself does not realize that he is turning into a trickster; who while he has no money does not seriously consider how he should go about getting any; who first comes to sponge on the Wife through her surprising sympathy for him. . . .'

An important issue upon which Strauss now began to lay increasing emphasis was the extent to which the task of characterization should be left largely to the music—the dialogue was to be drawn up with the lightest possible touch. At this point Bahr took fright. In the first place Strauss was so precise in the very details of how he wanted the characters handled that he allowed for the minimum of personal initiative or imagination on the part of his librettist. Secondly it was becoming clear that the Baron's individuality was only to emerge as an offshoot of Pauline Strauss's own character, the delineation of which was itself no enviable task. Lastly, to rework on behalf of someone else a subject which Bahr had himself brought to a successful outcome on his own account must have seemed inconceivable. For six months Strauss heard not a word from his colleague, and when with the arrival of June and the summer upon him he sent a nudging letter, he received almost by return of post a long and apologetic explanation why the best solution would really be for Strauss to write the text himself.

Instead of discouraging the composer, Bahr's letter had the precisely opposite effect. In a matter of hours Strauss had sketched out the dialogue of the two opening scenes and these he sent to Bahr, together with the draft scenario of the whole (dating from the previous autumn) and a pleading letter. He now not only urged Bahr to reconsider his decision of the moment, but to join with him in the production of a further piece based on Frau Strauss when this one was complete. Indeed, he envisaged five—ten—a whole cycle of little comic operas with small orchestra, 'analysing her poetically' from every angle.

Bahr remained firm however; complimenting Strauss on his skill, and assuring him of a great popular success, he bowed himself gracefully out of this embarrassing situation so cleverly that Strauss set to work, persuaded and stimulated, to complete the opera entirely by himself. The following May (1918) he returned Bahr's sketches and the matter was closed.

During all this time, Strauss had been embroiled with the final *Bourgeois Gentilhomme* version, but a brief stay in hospital enabled him to make such excellent headway with the text of his new work that in a very short time he made up his mind to send a complete draft libretto to Hofmannsthal for his approval and comments. This gesture was greeted with a somewhat cool reception, but Strauss pressed on and by the middle of 1918 he wrote a postscript in a letter to Hofmannsthal saying how well the composition was going: '... the whole thing is well planned, and its structure and music will no doubt make up for what the piece lacks in poetic power'. For a long time, however, Hofmannsthal remained unreconciled to the piece, considering it—not perhaps without some justification—to be 'uncultured'.

Nevertheless, despite Strauss's enthusiasm for his 'realistic comedy' there were many interruptions in its composition of the kind which suggest that, like the *Alpensinfonie*, he worked on it when and because he had nothing better to do. Apart from other works which interrupted the composition—important groups of songs such as the great Brentano Lieder, the ballet *Schlagobers* and his renewed collaboration with Hofmannsthal in preparing a new version of Beethoven's *Ruins of Athens*—there were certainly many and varied calls upon his time during this unsettled period. His administrative work in the Berlin and Vienna opera houses attendant upon the end of the war, the long-delayed production of *Die Frau ohne Schatten,* and the tours abroad which once more were opened up to him, all cut severely into his progress with the new opera. He visited the United States again after a gap of some eighteen years, and twice toured South America. In was during the second of these tours that *Intermezzo*—as his little Marriage-comedy was now called—was finished, on 21st August 1923, and it was first performed on 4th November 1924, the date coinciding with his resignation from the Intendantship of the Vienna Opera.

9

In the early draft scenario the situation of the drama had been introduced gradually, the Wife giving a kind of half-apologetic self-analysis to a friend at a Munich masked ball. Strauss was right in considering such psychological explanations to be weak and laboured, but his alternative —in which the Wife abruptly reveals herself by her real-life talk and behaviour—is exactly as if we had called uninvited at Strauss's villa and remained watching a private family scene in all its uproar instead of politely withdrawing to make our visit on some more auspicious occasion.

There is no Prelude, and as the curtain rises in the first bar we at once hear the Wife's shrill bickering at her maid in the utmost ill-humour. Hofkapellmeister Robert Storch is frenziedly packing for his next conducting tour more or less assisted by his wife Christine. His name, it will be seen, has approached still nearer to reality, the change from Albert to Robert now preserving Strauss's own initials. So keen was Strauss that his own identity should be unmistakable that the singer of the first performance wore a mask in order to make himself look as much like the composer as possible. This is a striking *volte-face* after Strauss's anxieties over the young Composer in the Vorspiel to *Ariadne II* not so many years before.

In the course of this bad-tempered and quarrelsome first scene Storch flings out of the room to enjoy a hasty breakfast in peace next door while his wife vents her spleen on Anna the maid. In due course he comes back and there are more arguments, Christine alternating between savage recriminations and abrupt bouts of solicitous sentiment for her husband's well being. At last the latter rushes off to catch his train and, left alone, Christine bemoans her fate to the long-suffering Anna.

Suddenly the telephone rings: finding it is one of her friends inviting her to go tobogganing, her mood changes in a flash and in high excitement she searches her wardrobe for suitable clothes. The curtain falls to her renewed shouts for Anna and the orchestra surges into the first of the Symphonic Interludes which, stressed in the very title of the work, constitute its chief musical substance.

The altercations between the various characters are exchanged in pure everyday conversation, and the incidents dug up during the furious repartee are, throughout, of the most prosaic nature possible: Christine's inability to obtain or, least of all, to keep, servants; her vicious reproaches over unimportant trifles and triumphant self-righteousness when she makes a point in the argument; she is shown screaming down the telephone, ranting at the cook; we hear her complaints of overwork and disdain for her husband's métier, above all how poorly he compares with other men, and how she despises his low class of origin. She is scornful of his being a celebrity, which she regards as being undeserved. Nevertheless, she is not averse to playing the social advantage of his prestige for its snob value.

For his part Storch is shown to be good-natured and tolerant. He argues as best he may with Christine, talking sensibly though ineffectually. When stung to the quick by her most iniquitous gibes he tries to persuade himself and her that she does not really mean what she says, and goes away to let her get over her tantrums.

The maid, Anna, clearly one of a series of such domestics, tries amidst the turmoil to be respectful and to pour such oil as she can on the troubled waters. Pathetically she persuades her mistress that everything is all right and puts in every possible good word for the master.

Musically the scene is played to a rapid recitative style, accompanied and punctuated by light orchestral passage-work through which Strauss introduces the many themes and motifs which he afterwards develops in the interludes. The first of these, which opens the opera, is a composite theme of two motifs which portray the basic unity of Robert and Christine (Strauss labels them *Die Frau* and *Der Mann* somewhat in the manner of the type figures of *Die Frau ohne Schatten*) amidst the virtually ceaseless turbulence of their life together.

At Skat

Ex. 17

The descending figure ⌈ x ⌉ returns at various points during the
opera to represent Storch himself and the tiresomeness of his ways as
seen through Christine's eyes. Her own character is gradually sketched in
by a string of short, essentially simple motifs consisting largely of scale or
arpeggio fragments—her shouts for the maid:

Ex. 18

her liveliness and flashes of gaiety:

Ex. 19   Ex. 20

Her impetuousness:

Ex. 21

her ill humour:

Ex. 22   and Ex. 23

Ex. 21 also appears in an augmented form which enjoys an independent,
more amiable existence:

17

Ex. 24

Other themes which show a less vitriolic side to Christine's character include:

Ex. 25   or Ex. 25a

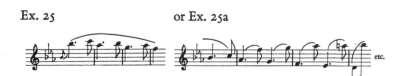

note the ever widening intervals of the later version)

and Ex. 26

with its inverted form:

Ex. 26a

There also occur a number of themes which seem to have specific application at their first appearance but are used in a more general way as the opera progresses. The first and most important of these is used initially to accompany a discussion on work, be it housework or the more intellectual kind which Robert naturally puts at a higher ethical level, much to Christine's disgust.

Ex. 27

Ex. 27 later proves, however, to be more directly connected with Robert himself as a person, his good-humoured approach to life, the enjoyment he derives from his creative occupation.

The other three themes are concerned with Christine's reactions to Robert's journey away from home—relief at having peace and quiet, though not without some feelings of loneliness (Ex. 28); then boredom, followed by excitement at his return (Ex. 29); and lastly her moods of self-pity, with especial reference to her home and child (Ex. 30).

Ex. 28

(This theme is first heard as the bass to an elaboration of Ex. 17.)

Ex. 29   Ex. 30

These motifs, together with a number of little characteristic cadential figures, make up the wealth of thematic material on which the scene is built, and which also reappear at suitable moments throughout the work. In addition Strauss amused himself by inserting quotations into the texture, such as themes from Gounod's *Faust* or Schumann's 1st Symphony. It must be admitted that the lines of thought which prompted their choice is not always self-evident, emanating as they did from private family jokes.[6]

10

The curtain has fallen during the first interlude, which now builds to an almost hysterical climax. At the peak violins are left holding an exceedingly high major third which then slithers down into the depths. Other similar slithers follow and as the curtain rises it becomes apparent that these are onomatopoeic. The stage represents a sleigh run and a succession of toboggans hurtle across and vanish into the wings.

[6] The appearance of the Schumann theme at Christine's unjust implication that Storch is Jewish is particularly curious. I am disinclined however, to concur with William Mann's suggestion that Strauss, the profoundly *routiné* conductor, confused it with a work by Mendelssohn. More probably Pauline was prone to make just such a blunder in her over-use of a favourite taunt.

Spectacular as it undoubtedly is, the scene is a short one and serves purely to bring into the picture the young Baron, who enters on skis accompanied in the orchestra by his motifs:

Ex. 31   and Ex. 32

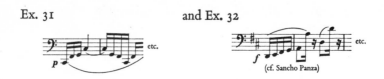

(cf. Sancho Panza)

He is no sooner fully on stage than Christine's toboggan cascades down and they collide in a confused flurry of snow, skis, sleigh and bodies. Although the accident is palpably Christine's fault she hurls invective at him until he introduces himself as Baron Lummer. On hearing his rank she allows her overriding snobbery to get the better of her annoyance. With sugary friendliness she claims acquaintance with his parents and parades her husband's position as Court Musician to reinforce the social right already hers through her own parents. The curtain falls again as she urges the Baron to call on her, and the orchestra continues the interrupted Interlude.

This time the mood becomes calmer and more light-hearted until imperceptibly it merges into one of the most extended and successful of Strauss's symphonic waltzes, on an entirely different level of spontaneity from those composed for *Schlagobers*. It is built on a further collection of themes and melodies which crowd in one after another, headed by Ex. 33 which acts as symphonic first subject:

Ex. 33   leading to

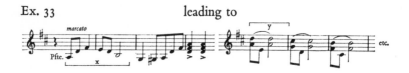

There is a trumpet fanfare and the curtain rises for the third scene, which is even shorter and more sketch-like than the last. It simply shows Christine and the Baron out dancing at Grundlsee, a well-known lake-side restaurant. The acquaintance has clearly flourished in a very short space of time and Christine is enjoying herself enormously. When this fact has been established the curtain quickly falls again and the orchestra continues the waltz by way of further interlude.

With the appearance of Christine and the Baron on the stage, yet further as it were second-subject themes have been brought into the flow of the music:

Ex. 34

Ex. 35

and an important derivative of the Baron's Ex. 31:

Ex. 36

(note the motivic reappearances of the Baron's fourths in Exx. 33(y), 34 and 36.)

The dance surges onwards with mounting excitement, other themes joining in including Christine's Ex. 20 and even suggestions of a motif from *Die Fledermaus*, by that namesake whose success in this idiom Strauss so dearly longed to challenge.

When at last the frenzy has spent itself the waltz-interlude gradually fades away. Little by little the tempo, oddly, quickens until wisps of themes are heard fragmentarily on isolated instruments as if in the extreme distance. The violas are reduced one at a time to a single player until suddenly the piano interrupts with some brusque chords.

The curtain is up again and we are watching Christine prattling away to her friend, the wife of the family lawyer. Christine, accompanied by Therese, another of her maids, is in fact viewing a furnished room in the Notary's house which she is proposing to rent at her own expense for her new protégé. She pours out the young Baron's troubles and ailments, his difficulties at working, unsympathetic family, congenital headaches, his need for fresh air and exercise and so on, to the justifiably incredulous Notarin, and fusses absurdly over the position of the desk or the proximity of the bed to the window.

Against the almost ceaseless chatter, the snatches of orchestral accompaniment are mainly built out of the various Christine themes, (Exx. 19, 20 and 25) and those of the Baron, Exx. 31 and 32, the latter sounding ever more like the Sancho Panza theme from *Don Quixote*. These motifs of the Baron also form the basis of the next short but pretty Interlude which follows, though an interesting little figure also gradually enters the texture:

Ex. 37

The centre-point of the Interlude is a dazzling transition to an unexpected new tonality in which Ex. 29 sweeps in with Christine's Ex. 19 in its train. The implication is perfectly clear that Christine's enjoyment of the Baron's company is no more than a stop-gap in her boredom during Robert's absence.

In scene 5 we are back in the Storch villa, this time in the dining-room watching Christine read over a letter to her husband. She tells him of her new liaison, establishes her freedom to follow her whims and enjoy life as she pleases while pledging Robert's influential assistance in furthering the young Baron's affairs. A brief reference in her soliloquy to Robert's more hostile critics evokes the appropriate quotation from *Heldenleben* in the orchestra.

Christine next has a brief contretemps with her cook, after which Baron Lummer is announced. She immediately recruits his aid in doing her household accounts after which, bearing in mind the disparity of age and interests between Christine and the Baron (we have learnt in the previous scene that he is just 22), it is hardly surprising that conversation soon flags. Christine proceeds to read the newspaper, leaving the Baron to sit there only periodically regaled with a few choice tit-bits which she reads out to him.

During the isolated snatches of conversation with which Christine punctuates this inhospitable pursuance of her regular evening routine she unexpectedly, and to her irritation, discovers some of Baron Lummer's less agreeable qualities: his laziness, his lack of tenacity, his moodiness, above all his suspicious reluctance to meet Christine's husband who, after all, is to be pressed to use his influence on Lummer's behalf. If

Robert can be made a little jealous that might also, she thinks, not be a bad thing. Altogether she puts Lummer into an unsatisfactory position which begins to damp his growing ardour. The more Christine extols Robert's virtues the more Lummer recoils, while at the same time hinting at some mysterious favour which he wishes, though seems to find it difficult, to request of her.

At last, sensing that he is attempting to become over-familiar, she interrupts him, emphasizing the platonic nature of their relationship, fixes a rendezvous for the following day at Grundlsee and bustles him out, the exact nature of his request remaining undisclosed.

All in all, this scene shows Christine in the most favourable light we have yet seen, and Strauss matches this with some most attractive music in which he recaptures momentarily some of the actual timbre and magic of *Rosenkavalier*. This is especially true of the passage in which she describes her turbulent but devoted relationship with her famous husband and her half puzzled, half admiring view of his dedication to his work and his good-natured readiness to lend a helping hand to others.

Left to herself by the fireside, she now lapses into a reverie as the orchestra begins a rhapsodic development of the themes which symbolize her sentimental flirtation with the Baron, Exx. 35 and 36.[7] She reflects on the attraction of the young aristocrat, her loneliness, her husband's loyalty, until, as melancholy overcomes her, the curtain falls leaving the orchestra to complete the symphonic treatment of the themes in this most beautiful of the Interludes.

The new counterpoint on first the clarinet and then solo violin must be quoted for the metamorphoses it undergoes in Act 2:

Ex. 38

At the climax, Ex. 17, the theme of Robert and Christine's marriage breaks out poignantly and leads to a long and affecting cadence. The whole passage once again reflects a relatively high level of inspiration,

[7] The origin of this fine piece can be found in the beautiful cello solo from *Die Frau ohne Schatten* Act 2.

especially when contrasted with the similar movement from *Schlagobers*, the *Träumerei* in the Dance of Prince Coffee.

The next scene gives us a closer view of the Baron whose irresponsibility and insincerity is laid bare. He is shown flirting with a young woman (her name, confusingly enough, is Therese—Resi for short—though she is unlikely to be the same Therese as Christine's maid.) The motifs of Lummer's Waltz-scene with Christine are vulgarized into snatches of flippancy, the fourths of the Baron's Ex. 31 being exploited in a number of ways through chords and *arpeggiando* figures against which he whistles and hums a comic love-song to his 'Theresulein'. He calls to the landlady for his trunk and is clearly planning a little gallivant with Resi, who now puts her head round the door and appears in full sporting outfit.

But he is not quite ready for her; his head is full of Christine and her boring ways, her propensity for lecturing him. He speaks scathingly of her kindness, especially her belief in what turn out to be his fictitious headaches. He has never had the least intention of applying himself seriously to work. All he wants is to have a good time and for this the escapade can still serve some useful purpose. While Resi goes on ahead he begins a letter to Christine in which he will at last put forward his mysterious request. The curtain falls as he writes, and when it rises again we see an outraged Christine reading the letter. All is at last made plain: he has asked to borrow 1,000 marks. To a dismal memory of Ex. 35 on the bass clarinet Christine hints at the better things she had hoped from him. Abruptly he arrives to present himself in person, only, like Strauss's own experience of such treatment, to be sent back outside to wipe his shoes before being invited to enter.

His pleas are useless: Christine is adamant. She had looked forward to such a nice friendship and this has spoilt everything. The ensuing argument is interrupted by the arrival of another letter. It is, of course, the famous note from Mitze Meier (alias Mücke, in real life). Suddenly the roles are reversed: so far, however harmlessly, Christine has been the guilty party. She had even intended, by provoking jealousy in Robert's breast, to make clear to him that she regards it as her right to enjoy herself as she pleases in his absence. Now, when it seems that he has done the same, everything looks quite different. Not that it is any surprise: she has been expecting it all along. Words can scarcely do justice to her fury. She peremptorily dismisses the Baron, saying she will call for him if she needs him, scribbles a vicious telegram to Robert, and calls to Anna to pack for immediate and permanent departure as the curtain falls amidst a veritable tornado.

A precipitous rush of violins leads to the next passionate Interlude which develops at some length the theme of self-pity so far heard only briefly in the opening scene of the opera (Ex. 30) and which, together with the motif of Christine's anger, also dominates the closing scene of the long first act.

Ex. 39

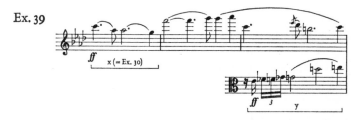

In this embarrassing scene we see Christine at Bubi's bedside trying tearfully to persuade the child to see his father in the role of villain, whereas Bubi keeps interspersing contradictory comments that it is she who is horrid. The curtain falls as she proclaims herself and Bubi to be 'abandoned' and kneels in prayer at the foot of the bed.

II

If Act I has been largely centred on Christine, her actions, and in particular her point of view, the second act begins by focusing correspondingly on Robert. The first scene introduces us to Strauss's favourite game of Skat. Skat is a card-game peculiar to Germany and Austria, where it is played to an enormous extent. It is a typical man's game of considerable skill and amongst regular players sizeable sums of money change hands. It is played by three people, but a fourth, or even a fifth player can take part and then cut out in turn.

Although the players need all their wits, it is an excellent game for relaxation. Moreover, as the hands are quick to play it can be begun in a few odd minutes and resumed later; it is thus quite normal for the score to be carried over from session to session and the account settled after a month or more. It is ideal for the musical profession, where in German-speaking countries it is habitually played by the singers, orchestral musicians, soloists, conductors and administrative officers alike during rehearsals and even performances.

In character it has this much in common with bridge or whist, that it uses trumps and involves the calling of a contract which has then to be fulfilled. At the same time it is closer to poker in the sheer speed with which decisions are taken and in the bluff—intimidation even—which marks the interplay between personalities. It is a common sight for a player to slam his cards down upon the table and look his opponents belligerently in the eye.

Strauss's passion for the game was universally known and his pre-eminence, in view of his position, conceded: it would, for example, be a rash Konzertmeister (leader of the orchestra) who would win money from Strauss at Skat. Nor was Strauss averse to allowing this worldly prestige to work to his advantage: the story goes that on one occasion a trumpeter blundered badly during a performance of *Rosenkavalier* and went round afterwards to apologise. Strauss waved aside his abject remarks but insisted on his joining him for a session at Skat, where he fleeced him of some 300 marks.

Although anyone from even the humblest member of the chorus or orchestra might at any time have found himself in a Skat school with Strauss, he might just as easily be playing against the Intendant, the second Kapellmeister (or assistant conductor) and one or more of the star opera singers.

The group we see presented on the stage is in fact a mixed one. One of Strauss's closest friends and Skat partners was Willy Levin, an eminent man of affairs, and as a matter of course Strauss includes him in his cast under the thin disguise of the general appellation *Ein Kommerzienrat*, literally 'Councillor of Commerce', a title which used to be given to dis-tinguished financiers and business men. Another non-musical friend is included, a man of law described as *Ein Justizrat* (literally 'Councillor of Justice'), and the party is completed by the junior Kapellmeister, whose name is given as Stroh (so that a confusion with Storch becomes credible), and a Kammersänger who is known to have been drawn from the real-life figure of Paul Knüpfer, the resident bass of the Berlin State Opera.

The session, which has clearly been progressing all evening, is taking place at the Kommerzienrat's house and the stage represents a comfort-ably appointed sitting-room. Only Storch himself is missing; he has had *Tristan* rehearsals which reluctantly he has found it impossible to curtail. As they play, the four friends are discussing Storch and his impossible wife. They are so unequivocal in their remarks that it is with an effort one recalls that the words have been put into their mouths by Strauss himself. It is clear that he had no illusions over the prevailing view the outside world held of Pauline, but it is amusing to note how well he makes his friends and colleagues speak of himself.

At last Storch hurriedly arrives and takes his place at the card-table. In much the same way as in Act 1 we heard how Frau Storch speaks of her husband, so now we hear Storch's account of his life with Christine and his affection for her despite all her faults. Indeed it is her very sharpness of character which stimulates him—it is all, he says, a matter of training. He has had her letter and he talks with amused toleration of the new companionship she has found in his absence.

As he chats and plays, a telegram is delivered to him; it is Christine's, and he is dumbfounded. He passes it to Stroh who reads it out to his friends. They are all solicitous with the exception of Stroh himself who makes some caustic remarks, inadvertently indicating that Mitze Meier is no stranger to him and that he well understands how awkward it can be when the little wife finds out. Offended, Storch breaks up the party with curt apologies and rushes off. The others exchange a few comments of incredulity; Storch was the last man they would have suspected of such a liaison. The Kammersänger appropriately makes his contribution in operatic quotations (from *Parsifal* Act 2 and the finale of *Der Freischütz* respectively, though the former is quoted inexactly), and as the players resume their interrupted game the curtain falls.

It is an amusing and enjoyable scene, while the music is amongst the most original in the opera. With the exception of the brief outburst when the enraged Storch dashes out with his telegram (the orchestration of which is suddenly worthy of Salome with the head of Jochaanan), the treatment of the instruments takes a step further the conversational style of chamber orchestral writing which Strauss had first exploited in the new Vorspiel to the revised *Ariadne*. The chatty card-players are depicted by this easy-going music:

Ex. 40

The shuffling of the cards is brought to life by a most amusing passage for
piano and loud pizzicato strings, followed by a rising phrase and tiny fanfare suggestive of the dealing and stacking of the cards. Robert's entry is
accompanied by an important derivative of Ex. 17(x):

Ex. 41

His intense anxiety at the contents of the telegram is marked by a new
motif:

Ex. 42

Lastly the amiable adaptation of Ex. 38 which accompanies the resumption of the game by the remaining four after Robert's frenzied exit
could, without being too unfair to Storch's friends, be taken to illustrate
the wisdom behind La Rochefoucauld's famous maxim that 'in the misfortune of our best friends, we find something which is not displeasing
to us.'

Ex. 43

12

In scene 2 we are back with Christine as she visits the Notary in order to put divorce proceedings in motion. But she has failed to take two things into account: the first that the Notary himself (we never learn his name or that of his wife) is a personal friend of Robert whom he greatly esteems; and secondly that with Baron Lummer lodging in his own house at Christine's expense, the Notary is far more willing to put the cause of Christine's action down to her own affair with the Baron (Ex. 33(y) and much play with the characteristic fourths) than to that of her husband, of whose guilt he needs proof before he will consider the matter seriously.

Christine is outraged: she is beyond question in the right and will therefore keep the house and child (Ex. 30). When the Notary demurs she marches out to seek another lawyer as the curtain falls.

The next Interlude is violent and stormy. It describes the emotions of Robert who, in the next scene, is shown pacing to and fro in the Prater, the famous Viennese park. He is in a feverish bewilderment at the sudden inexplicable collapse of his private life. To lend colour to his feelings an actual tempest is raging, and Strauss portrays the scene orchestrally with gusto; the marriage theme (Ex. 17(x)) mingles with Christine's Ex. 20, with the theme of her anger (Ex. 39(y)) and that of Robert's despair (Ex. 42), while the motif of Robert's character as a sensitive artist (Ex. 27) now comes into its own, broadly declaimed by the horns.

Robert ruminates in exasperation on the useless letters and telegrams he has sent, all returned unopened, when Stroh comes running up. Dismally, hesitantly, he explains how, unwittingly, he is to blame and how, with the similarity of their names, the fatal letter had been intended for him. Storch naturally rages at him and insists that he go at once to Christine and take full responsibility for putting the whole affair to rights. The tables are now turned, and the genial self-satisfied Ex. 43 becomes the urgent theme with which Stroh, desperately concerned for his own career after such a débâcle, eagerly accepts his assignment.

Ex. 44

Stroh: 'Mit tausend Freuden, ich tue alles'[8]

---

[8] Literally, 'with a thousand joys I will do all.'

At the fall of the curtain the orchestra resumes its stormy progress in a symphonic development of Storch's Ex. 27 which, together with Ex. 43, builds to a climax worthy of the more cataclysmic moments of *Die Frau ohne Schatten*, even the mighty C major fanfares making an appearance.

In the closing cadence the widening intervals of Ex. 25a lead to a declamatory statement of the Marriage theme's second phrase, Ex. 17(y), and abruptly the music changes in character for scene 4. We are back again with Christine who is frenziedly packing up all her belongings preparatory to leaving. The place is in the wildest disorder and Christine herself hardly *compos mentis*. At every moment she thinks of things she should do or should not have done. In particular she has pangs about her Baron, whom she has sent to Vienna to confront Mitze Meier. The maids Anna and Therese rush to and fro, while Christine shrieks at them. They look madly for objects, linen, rings, which she herself has put away and finds again in due course. She is convinced that they are all taking sides against her and it speaks much for Anna's patience and sagacity when, already under notice (which is later revoked), she mildly suggests that it might have been wise for Baron Lummer to have taken a photograph of Robert to Mitze in order to establish positive identification.

Although Christine calls Lummer a cretin for not having thought of this himself, she for the first time allows the possibility of a mistake to enter her mind. The way is thus paved for Anna and when a further telegram arrives she begs Frau Storch not to send also this one back unopened. Reluctantly Christine allows herself to be persuaded and Anna reads it out to her.

It is from Robert, explaining the confusion with Stroh and announcing his immediate return home. Seizing the telegram, Christine dissects it in her mind, word by word, considering the possibility of it being either the truth or some monstrous plot, with Stroh a voluntary scapegoat. Suddenly Stroh is announced in person.

We are mercifully spared the appalling interview which presumably follows, and the jubilant $\frac{6}{8}$ Interlude which bursts in with the curtain drop describes Christine and Robert's excitement at coming together once more. This is in fact the last of the Interludes and combines an immense number of the work's motifs in a movement with a strong finale character.

Since Christine's grass widowhood is soon to end, the dominating theme is appropriately Ex. 29, with Ex. 28 whimsically added with an emphasis hitherto denied to this striking motif. As the Interlude

approaches its close the cadences are marked by a drum figure which
we are to see again in an almost identical context in the Pot-pourri to
Die Schweigsame Frau.

Ex. 45

(Timp.)

13

With the finale of the Interludes we have also reached the closing scene
of the opera. Not that all is quite plain sailing yet for poor Storch. Just as
he rushes in and she is going to greet him she checks herself, and coldly
gives him no more than her hand lest he should think her too easily won
over. This inevitably changes the reconciliation to mutual recriminations, she claiming that he takes her sufferings too lightly, can even joke,
that what she feared might in actual fact easily have happened; he then
reproaches her for mistrusting him, believing him capable of such conduct to the point to sueing for divorce without even troubling to verify
the facts.

From this it transpires that the Notary has communicated direct with
Robert, a breach, she insists, of professional conduct: she is fed up with
men, he has never appreciated her, she will continue with the divorce
proceedings after all. He, convinced that it should be she who should be
apologizing for his own sufferings, now slams out of the room in a towering rage.

At this point the Baron returns, his mission hardly a triumphant success. In the absence of a photograph he seems to have established Robert's
guilt even further. The fact that he could have obtained a picture of so
famous a man in any book-shop has wholly escaped him, as Christine
wastes no time in pointing out. Drily she reveals that Robert has also
returned and that the whole misunderstanding has been cleared up. She
spares him nothing in underlining the patent incompetence with which
he has carried out his assignment and, abjectly, he leaves.

At this moment, Robert re-enters the room and is highly amused to
learn whom he has just missed. Gently, and with infinite good humour,
he tries to show how her little affair was beginning to appear in the eyes

of the world; of this too, he has learnt from the Notary, and it was indeed the chief reason for his rapid return home. Even now she is unable to see the two incidents, his and hers, in perspective, and reiterates her claim that she would have retained both house and child. She makes light of the Baron, though acknowledging that he had attracted her up to the moment when he tried to borrow money.

When shamefacedly she reveals the dismal end of the story, he cannot help laughing outright. Instead of evoking further furies from Christine, this leads to a recapitulation of the *Träumerei* from Act I in which she recalls what she had hoped for now that it is all over. Robert is touched and sympathetic, especially when it transpires that what she most missed in Lummer was the quarrelling, which after all is only worth while with one's husband. The unusual experience of seeing Robert in a rage had quite revived Christine's love for him; theirs is, she says ecstatically, a truly happy marriage.

As the work descends into deeper and deeper sentimentality the final curtain falls on a love duet which welds together his motif (Ex. 27), one of the more important of hers (Ex. 20), and the marriage theme (Ex. 17), while hints of the *Träumerei* (Ex. 38) show with psychological insight that the incurably romantic nature which lies beneath Christine's shrewish exterior is essentially only dormant, and is indeed one of the qualities for which Strauss was, to the end of his life, in love with his Pauline.

14

The opera as a whole leaves one with mixed feelings. Strauss certainly recaptured at times the lighter style of composition, as he did that of caricature which was once his strength. The melodic interest is also more distinguished than much that he had been writing in recent years. The orchestral treatment, if not as refined as that of *Ariadne*, is once more for a small ensemble with only three horns, two trombones and a limited string body often used soloistically.

This is part of the deliberate policy which Strauss set out to elaborate at length in a *Vorwort* after the manner of Gluck's Preface to *Alceste*. In it he describes with disarming candour his artistic intentions in composing a contemporary comedy about middle-class family life, set to a variety of vocal techniques ranging from pure spoken dialogue to *bel canto*. Much of it makes very interesting reading, especially his views on

Strauss, 1919

the various forms of recitative as handled by Mozart, Weber and Wagner; while his claim to have blazed a trail in the presentation of everyday life on the operatic stage was to find its justification in, for example, Hindemith's *Neues vom Tage* and Schönberg's *Von Heute auf Morgen*, both composed some four years later in 1928–9.

Unfortunately, when the score came to be published Strauss felt unhappy about his Preface and entirely rewrote it.[9] The revised *Vorwort*, as printed in the score today, is far drier and less conversational in tone. Strauss's now somewhat caustic references to his performers lack the charm of the original and tend at times to overstate the case. Speaking, for example, of the primary consideration being perfect audibility of every word, he claims that this is an accomplished fact in ideal performances of *Salome* and *Elektra*, whereas at the time of composition, some twenty years previously, he would have spoken quite differently.

Again one might doubt the literal sincerity of his expressed desire that in all but a few *bel canto* passages in the finales to the two acts the singers should perform in a *mezza voce*. As a result, he says drily, the words must prevail against even the most insensitive conducting.

Yet although one misses so many fascinating paragraphs from the original *Vorwort* much that is valuable remains. His methods of obtaining vocal clarity when pitted against orchestras of various sizes reflect his immense professionalism, while of outstanding value is the account of his intentional modifications of style from *Ariadne I*, via *Frau ohne Schatten*, to *Intermezzo*. 'It was in the first act of *Ariadne*', he writes, referring to the Vorspiel to *Ariadne II*, 'that I first used with full assurance, in the alternation between ordinary prose, *recitativo secco*, and *recitativo accompagnato*, the vocal style which I have now, in *Intermezzo*, carried to its logical conclusion.' This is a subject about which there will be more to say when we come to *Capriccio*.

15

The most disturbing factor in *Intermezzo* is inevitably Strauss's treatment of his family life. Apologists for the opera have worked hard to show that this was the greatest compliment Strauss could have paid to Pauline, that what he revealed was the strength of his devotion. The fact remains that to the unbiased observer he painted her unflatteringly exactly as she

9 The original *Vorwort* was published posthumously in the expanded volume of *Betrachtungen und Erinnerungen*. Atlantis Verlag, Zurich, 1957.

appeared. Even Lotte Lehmann, dear sweet person and the soul of generosity, tells how after the première she herself tried to express her hope and belief that

> 'this was Strauss's confession and testament, proof that he was happy at the side of the often misunderstood Pauline, he alone understanding her true self. . . . "This opera", she said to Pauline, "is really a marvellous present to you from your husband, isn't it?" Tensely, everyone waited for her answer. She looked round, cast a quick glance at her husband, then said in a loud, clear voice: "I don't give a damn." Embarrassed silence. Strauss smiled.'[10]

The charge of tastelessness is hard to answer, for all the many witty handlings of the situations and *ben trovato* shafts of dialogue. Strauss showed the libretto to Reinhardt who was sufficiently amused to say carelessly that it was 'so good that he could produce it as a play without altering a line', a casual remark inconceivable to be taken literally, but of which Strauss remained proud to the end of his life.

Nor are the strictures only applicable to the text. Gay and lightly handled in Strauss's best manner as much of the music is, some passages reflect the same miscalculation in the adjustment of scale to subject which had been so worrying a feature of *Sinfonia Domestica*. The violent Interlude in Act 2 with the C major fanfares (see p. 258 above) is a clear example, thrilling though the orchestral writing undoubtedly is.

The sentimentality of other sections is a further stumbling block; even the conductor of the first performance, Fritz Busch, found their unashamed exhibitionism unpalatable, and the closing duet particularly embarrassing. And Busch considered the 60-year-old composer himself, whom he naturally came to know in this connexion, nothing short of baffling.

> 'Even his appearance and bearing, simple as they seemed, were ambiguous. If one recalls to memory his head, which so often fascinated the caricaturists, with its bullet forehead and almost expressionless watery blue eyes, on top of a tall, lanky, slightly stooping body, he appears sometimes . . . to be simple, almost insignificant. But he could adopt a majestic bearing and . . . display the superior simplicity of genius.'

Strauss's unreliability as an artist of taste worried Busch particularly:

> 'The lack of genuinely warm feeling which Strauss's music often shows was recognized by the composer himself; he

[10] *Singing with Strauss*. Hamish Hamilton, London, 1964.

knew exactly the places where his music became sentimental and trashy. Nothing annoyed him more than when conductors... wallowed in his lyrical outpourings and thus unpleasantly brought his sins before his eyes. He himself, the older he grew, passed ever more indifferently and unemphatically over such passages when conducting, as if he were ashamed at having composed them. His inconsistency showed itself in his continuing to write such things.... The puzzle of Strauss, who in spite of his marvellous talents is not really penetrated and possessed by them like other great artists but, in fact, simply wears them like a suit of clothes which can be taken off at will—this puzzle neither I nor anyone else has yet succeeded in solving.'

16

While *Intermezzo* has never held a secure place in the standard repertoire of even German opera houses, it contains too much good music to be allowed to fade altogether from view. Since most of the more inspired pages lie in the Symphonic Interludes, Strauss showed perspicacity in detaching four of these and arranging them for the concert platform. They make a highly successful Suite and it is surprising that they are not more regularly performed. The four movements are entitled:

No. 1 Travel Fever and Waltz-scene
  2 *Träumerei* by the Fireside
  3 At the Card-table
  4 Happy Ending.

The first excerpt is actually misnamed, since after the opera's opening bars consisting of Ex. 17, the marriage theme, and Christine's shouts for Anna, it cuts to the excited Interlude describing Christine's preparations for a toboggan expedition. The music is then taken to the high climax and first glissando sleigh run, upon which it cuts again to the following scene, the Ball at Grundlsee. This is given virtually intact, only a few minor excisions of isolated bars having been made during Christine's brief and breathless conversation with the Baron between waltzes.[11]

The *Träumerei* appears exactly as in the opera, where it has the same self-contained ending (the few overlapping phrases for Christine are

[11] Oddly enough these bars are restored in an edition of this Waltz-scene published separately, and which also contains a loud closing chord not added in the Suite.

jettisoned without musical loss). 'At the card-table' is naturally concerned with the music to the first scene of Act 2, giving the opening bars
of the act—including two shuffles and deals. It then cuts to the end of the
scene at the point where, with the exit of Robert, the four friends resume
their game (Ex. 43). The succeeding entr'acte is also given complete and
comes to the full close as in the opera score.

The last title, 'Happy Ending', refers to the final entr'acte and is perhaps
a little premature in its application. Its finale-like ebullience admirably
suits its position in the concert suite, and all that was necessary was to fill
out the orchestration of the opening bars. A decisive concert ending is
also provided after the climactic appearance of Ex. 45 by cutting it short
with two sharp cadential chords.

Thus, although both products of Strauss's period of working alone
for the stage, Schlagobers and Intermezzo, must remain minor works, each
containing, though for different reasons, serious elements of poor taste,
each also offers concert excerpts of original and attractive music well
worth restoring to the repertory. This is particularly important in
Strauss's case since the number of such works, especially those for a small
or normal-sized orchestra, are unexpectedly few, as will emerge during
the course of the next chapter.

CHAPTER XIV

ORCHESTRAL MISCELLANEA

I

D URING the early 1920s Strauss's collaboration with Hofmannsthal was at a low ebb. Since the production of *Die Frau ohne
Schatten* in 1919 there had been a hiatus, and although their work
together was eventually resumed this was at first on a small scale and only
gradually led back to more rewarding enterprises.

Strauss had never lost the need for regular subject-matter on which to
concentrate his creative bouts in the summer months, and now there was
the possibility that he might have to bear these in mind as a source of
reliable income. Lucky he had certainly been, and continued to be, in
these times of depression; thanks to his business acumen in the drafting
of royalty contracts for pre-war successes such as *Salome* and *Rosenkavalier*, the Strauss family had not so far needed to fear any positive threat
to their way of life. But at the collapse of the Mark, with businesses
bankrupt and homes ruined all around him, Strauss must have had
twinges of uneasiness which the mediocre reception of *Schlagobers* and
Intermezzo can have done little to allay. Indicative indeed are such tales
as his buttonholing a rich young amateur cellist at a party, and within a
matter of minutes offering to write a concerto—immediate delivery—
for a thousand dollars.

If the composition of concert works, overtures, suites, concertos and
the like had been a regular part of Strauss's output, the undertaking of
commissions for distinguished soloists amongst his acquaintances might
not have seemed an unlikely proposition. Curiously, however, for such a
master of the orchestra this had long ceased to be the case, and the few

instrumental pieces which Strauss produced during the years up to and including the 1920s, other than the great series of symphonic poems, form an odd collection which it might at this point be opportune to outline and discuss.

Looking back as far as 1884, the first orchestral work to follow the C Minor Overture[1] was a curiosity in the form of a Polonaise for flute, bassoon and orchestra entitled *Der Zweikampf*. This amusing little trifle, which has only recently come to light, is lightly scored for strings, horns and brass, leaving the canvas clear for the two woodwind soloists with their characteristically wide-spanned themes. The great leaps are the most Straussian feature of the score which is otherwise more typical of the young composer of the *Festmarsch* op. 1.

There are indeed two more *Festmarsche*, dating respectively from 1884 and 1889. Of the first, in D, Strauss thought highly enough to make a revised version four years later, while the other, in C major—composed in the year of *Tod und Verklärung*—was dedicated to his father's amateur orchestral society, *Wilde Gungl'*, on the occasion of its 25th Anniversary.

On 8th October 1892, during Strauss's term of office in Weimar, the Grand Duke and Duchess Karl Alexander and Sofie of Saxe-Weimar-Eisenach of the Royal House of Oranien (Orange) celebrated their golden wedding. The festivities included the performance of a series of eight *Lebende Bilder* (Living Tableaux) which were represented on the stage of the Court Theatre.

The accompanying music was provided not only by Strauss but by his colleague Edward Lassen and the Weimar Intendant, Hans von Bronsart; for the Finale a composition of Liszt was used, based on a Weimar folk-song. Strauss's contribution (Nos. 3, 4, 6 and 7) consisted of four pieces of varying length and elaboration, descriptive of various historical incidents surrounding the Thirty Years War.[2] No. 3 is a melodrama in which William the Silent, of the House of Orange (the contemporary of Egmont) sacrifices his treasures for the cause of the fatherland. The tableau, dated 1573, was based on a painting by the nineteenth-century French painter Claudius Jacquand, and Strauss incorporated into his score the old Netherlandic *Wilhelmslied*, which is to this day the Dutch National Anthem.

---

[1] See Vol. I, p. 14.
[2] Steinitzer changes the order of the pieces, giving first the battle of Lützen (No. 6).

The next tableau (1609) showed Prince Moritz von Oranien negotiating a peace treaty with Spinola, the Italian general who led Spanish troops into the Netherlands, making his name with the capture of Breda in 1625, the subject of the famous Velasquez picture. Strauss accompanied this peace-meeting between the great generals with an impressive and stately movement which was, incidentally, resurrected three years later for the unveiling of the Bismarck memorial in Munich. Strauss's third piece is a violent movement depicting the Grand Duke's illustrious forebear, Duke Bernhardt of Saxe-Weimar, at the Battle of Lützen in 1632. It was due to the initiative of this fiery soldier that the Swedish advantage was lost, and in this battle King Gustavus Adolphus was killed.

Strauss's music is full of heroic gestures, starting fortissimo in the thick of the fighting and leading to a statement of the 'March of the Finnish Cavalry from the 30-Years War' (Finland being at that time part of Sweden).

Ex. 1

Duke Bernhardt challenges this formidable and confident opposing army with a gallant charge:

Ex. 2

There is a fierce affray; Ex. 1 is treated in imitation rather in the same way as *Funiculi, funiculà* in the last movement of *Aus Italien*, and with Ex. 2 thrusting upwards through the ranks until, as the music gravitates to C major, Ex. 2 peals out in triumphant tones in a full orchestral statement similar in mood once again to the various *Festmarsche* of earlier years.

Lastly Strauss composed a dramatic scene described as the Reconciliation of the Admirals De Ruyter and Tromp (1672) through the intervention of William III, Prince of Orange, later King of England.

Although this piece is dismissed by Steinitzer as short and unimportant, it runs to 141 bars and incorporates the *Niederländische Prinzenlied*.[3]

Although none of these pieces can be regarded as anything but occasional in character, Strauss seems to have retained an affection for them. The three purely orchestral movements were performed at a concert in April 1897 by the Munich Orchestral Society, together with a tone poem by Schillings and the Bruckner Second Symphony. Strauss took his pieces through at the *Generalprobe*, conducting—according to a contemporary account—with great gusto.

Nearly thirty years later when in need of battle music to accompany the Feldmarschall's activities in the *Rosenkavalier* film, Strauss again turned to his *Weimar Festmusik* and extracted the Battle of Lützen, and having been thus reminded of it, he used this movement yet again on 2nd March 1931 at the Eighth Vienna Philharmonic Ball. On this new occasion he gave it the title of *Kampf und Sieg* and under this title it was simultaneously published with a short explanatory preface by Strauss.[4] The other movements of the Suite are still unpublished.

2

In 1904 when Strauss, the great tone-poems behind him, was the musical director of the Berlin Opera, the Crown Prince attended a performance of *Sinfonia Domestica* and attracted the attention of his father, the Kaiser, to this most eminent musician of his Court. An account has already been given of the Kaiser's ensuing visit to a performance of *Der Freischütz* under Strauss. The interview which followed led not only to a formal if qualified sanction of future performances of *Salome*,[5] but to a summons by the Kaiser for Strauss to go to the palace and listen to old German military marches. For an hour and a half in the presence of his monarch Strauss obediently did so and then went home and, as it were, did likewise. The fruits of this expedition emerged over the next two years: the two *Military Marches*, op. 57, an arrangement of a *Präsentiermarsch*—entitled *Der Brandenburgsche Mars*, two *Parademarsche*, and the mighty

---

[3] There is some confusion over this item, as the official programme gives Lassen as the composer. Whether Lassen also composed a movement or whether he stood down in favour of Strauss for this one number is impossible to determine.

[4] It was in this preface that Strauss mistook the date of composition (see Vol. I, p. 415).

[5] See Vol. I, pp. 280–1.

Königsmarsch which all received their first performances one after another at a Court Concert on 6th March 1907. The Kaiser then graciously accepted the dedication of these really rather awful tub-thumpers and rewarded Strauss with the Order of the Crown, 3rd Class.

Nonetheless the Kaiser never became reconciled to the modernity of Strauss's music and used to refer to him as a viper he had cherished to his bosom, from which arose the nickname often quoted in Strauss's biographies of 'Hofbusenschlange'—(Head-Court-bosom-viper).

Of the above mentioned compositions, the two *Parademarsche,* together with *Der Brandenburgsche Mars*[6] which he used twenty years later for the *Rosenkavalier* film, are best quickly forgotten. On the other hand the op. 57 pair of marches, and the *Königsmarsch* (the latter also incorporated into the Rosenkavalier film) are not entirely devoid of interest. The first of the op. 57 marches—actually the second in order of composition by eleven days—has a delicate and imaginative opening:

Ex. 3

The *Königsmarsch* is on an altogether bigger scale and is scored for mammoth forces. Eight horns, four each of trumpets and trombones, the percussion department also augmented by twelve off-stage drummers, all contribute to a mighty Teutonic demonstration. Yet the thematic material, differently handled, might not have been so far removed from the Marches of Mozart, and Ex. 5 suggests a melodic invention which Strauss himself put to tasteful use in the works of his last period.

---

[6] See Vol. I, pp. 415–6. This particular March is not an original composition, but is arranged from two marches (one a slow march, the other for cavalry) which Strauss found in the collection of Royal Prussian Army Marches.

Ex. 4

Ex. 5

This piece of pageantry consists of an arresting Introduction, March, and Trio, the reprise of the March in full panoply leading to a grandiose Hymn:

Ex. 6

The March then concludes with a coda characterized by fanfares and drumrolls. It seems likely that the *Königsmarsch* formed the peroration of this Gala Court Concert in which Strauss discharged his duty by the Royal Command in one fell swoop.

Yet whereas displays of military pomp and circumstance amused Strauss sufficiently for him to scribble off suitable works for the purpose, they had no war-like significance for him. His approach to his inevitable responsibilities as a leading musician was in this respect not materially different from the way he tackled the ceremonial pieces which he was invited to supply for civil occasions. The first of these, which he composed in 1909, was a Fanfare for the Solemn Procession of the Knights of the Order of St. John.

This most noble and ancient Society was founded in Jerusalem during the First Crusade. Over the centuries it naturally suffered many vicissitudes as a result of which the Order divided into various branches, some of which survive into the twentieth century. The Sovereign Order of the Knights of Malta is perhaps the best known of these, but two Orders of Protestant origin also pursued their dignified career: the English and the Prussian. Members of the Prussian Order had to be of noble birth and belong to the Evangelical Church. As in England, where the

St John's Ambulance Brigade serves with such distinction, the German Order has been especially noted for its valuable work in the establishment and maintenance of hospitals.

Strauss wrote his *Feierlicher Einzug* originally for brass and timpani, once again making use of herald trumpets. He called for no less than fifteen trumpets, three of these being called solo-trumpets, four each of horns and trombones and two tubas. There are two main elements in the composition, the one built up out of a number of rising fanfare-like motifs:

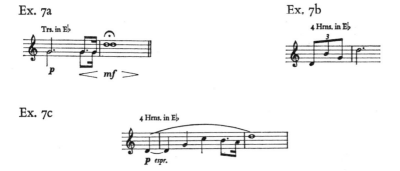

Ex. 7a

Ex. 7b

Ex. 7c

the other element being a long majestic chorale, the procession itself, which recalls the March of the Priests from Mozart's *Zauberflöte*. Although not, one might have thought, of any very great musical consequence, Strauss thought well enough of the piece to rescore it for full symphony orchestra with an *ad libitum* organ part.

The next important event which called for a special composition from Strauss was the consecration on 19th October 1913 of the Konzerthaus in Vienna. This brings to mind a parallel commission for which Beethoven composed an *Ouvertüre zur Weihe des Hauses*, one of the most stimulating and accomplished of his shorter orchestral works, built in the form of a March, Fanfare, Interlude and monumental double fugue in C major. The occasion for which Beethoven made so magnificent a contribution was the consecration in 1822 of the Josephstädter Theater. Now, nearly a hundred years later, the Viennese decided to mark the inauguration of the new Konzerthaus with a series of concerts for which Strauss was invited to provide a new work to open the very first concert, preceding a performance of Beethoven's Choral Symphony, the concert to be conducted by Ferdinand Löwe.

Like the existing Musikverein, the new building was built on a lavish scale, containing three main halls—the Mozart Hall, the Schubert Hall and the Great Hall, the latter planned for an audience of 4,000. It was here that the Festival Concerts took place.

After a few days of indecision Strauss agreed, and planned a Festival Prelude orchestrated to match the scale of the beautiful new hall. All instruments of delicate or subtle colouring, harp, celeste and so on, he decided to exclude, concentrating on massive effects with simple contrasts of colour. A string group of nearly a hundred players, huge wind and brass resources on the scale of *Elektra* though with the addition of six stage trumpets (or twelve, he added hopefully), and the full, overwhelming power of the new organ, which competes in single alternation with the huge orchestra; these were his ingredients.

In the event, it seems that even at the splendid occasion for which it was composed some of Strauss's fantastic demands were not met in full, and certainly the work has been extremely rarely performed since. To a large extent this must however, be attributed to the wholly occasional character of the work which leaves the hearer unmoved after the overwhelming volume of sound has finally died away. If Beethoven's overture contains echoes, however fleeting, of the *Missa Solemnis* and the Ninth Symphony, on which he had been working at the time, Strauss's *Festlisches Praeludium* has more in common with his *Königsmarsch* than it has with *Rosenkavalier* or *Ariadne*.

The comparison is perhaps unfair, the analogy inexact, but it may serve towards explaining Strauss's failure to produce even an interesting, let alone a great work of art for such an exciting event. Strauss only found himself as a composer when his imagination was stimulated by literary or other external influences, and it is arguable that had he not, through the encouragement of some Alexander Ritter, found emancipation away from the classical forms of Absolute Music in which he had grown up, he might never have blossomed into an outstanding genius at all. He himself later acknowledged this: 'I have long recognized' he wrote, 'that when composing I am unable to set anything down without a programme to guide me.'

The fact is, therefore, that face to face with the necessity of working with thematic material purely for its own sake Strauss found himself wretchedly at a loss. Even more than in the days of the F minor Symphony or the Piano Quartet did he find it hard to drag up symphonic themes out of his imagination, and least of all did he know what to do with them when he had found some which might serve his purpose. Not all the skill and vivacity of invention which had so recently flooded into his mind when at work on *Salome* or *Elektra* could come to his aid, now that he had nothing but the opening of a new concert hall to think about.

So we find that for all his early training, even the form of the *Praeludium* is curiously unsatisfactory. If Liszt's symphonic style consists, in Tovey's words, of a series of Introductions to Introductions, Strauss's is here little more than a series of Perorations leading to further and greater Perorations. The opening organ solo, which returns at significant points during the piece, is itself a climax rather than a beginning:

Ex. 8

while the brass fanfares which instantly greet it might well cap a symphonic structure of some forty-five minutes' duration.

Ex. 9

Moreover when this has all subsided and the ninety-six string players launch the C major allegro subject, this proves to be diffuse and characterless for all its initial emulation of the manner of Brahms's finale to the First Symphony;

Ex. 10

and its continuation with reminiscences of Weber's *Euryanthe*.

Ex. 11

An *arpeggiando* theme in swinging triplets and a wide-spanned melody very much like the *Alpensinfonie* (which was just turning over in his mind at the time) completes the material. There is an all too brief excursion into a distant key, but with the return of Ex. 10 we are back to C major for the remainder of the work. Imposing themes thunder out, the triplets swing to and fro in the woodwind; at one of the many climaxes the organ solo, Ex. 8, peals forth; long new climaxes are built up incorporating Ex. 10 now metamorphosed into the prevailing triple metre, in which guise the six (twelve ?) herald trumpets, placed above or on either side of the orchestra, take it up jubilantly. The fanfares, Ex. 9, resound with increasing pomp and with a final reference to the cadence of Ex. 8, played by the full gargantuan forces, the last colossal chord of C major is reached.

3

It is clear both from the nature and the character of the preceding works that Strauss's heart was not in such endeavours, and where his heart failed him his talents failed him also. Yet during the bleak post-war years he did make further efforts to add to his output for the concert platform. The first occupation to which he turned in this respect arose out of his recent work on 'the distilled mustiness' of 'old Lully' which, despite himself and the débâcle of the redrafted *Bourgeois Gentilhomme*, he had actually enjoyed. Now the thought occurred to him to concoct a Suite by orchestrating some of the clavecin *Pièces* of the French eighteenth-century master François Couperin. At first he had planned a purely concert work, but as he started to make his selection so many were dances of one sort or another that he decided to write specifically a Dance Suite. Then, taking the opportunity of his position on the establishment of the Vienna State Opera, he arranged for the first performance to be given by this company as a simple classical ballet.

The occasion which was described as a *Ballett-Soirée* took place as part of the Vienna *Fasching* (Carnival) festivities on 17th February 1923 in the Redoutensaal of the Wiener Hofburg. For this special purpose the work was given the following elaborate title: *François Couperin: Gesellschaft und Theatertänze im Stile Ludwig XV bearbeitet von Richard Strauss.* The first concert performance of the *Tanzsuite* took place in Dresden under the direction of Fritz Busch on 21st December of the same year.

It so happened that a young conductor by the name of Clemens Krauss had been recently called to Vienna through the intervention of Franz Schalk. Krauss has himself described his early devotion to Strauss's work:

> 'Even in my young days, when I was going the round of the theatres, I kept crossing Richard Strauss's path. When I was at the Conservatorium in 1910 I was once able to listen to him rehearsing with the Vienna Philharmonic Orchestra, thanks to the complicity of one of the hall attendants who smuggled me into the organ loft in the Musikverein. During his time as Director of the Vienna Opera I conducted there in February 1922, after which he confirmed my appointment as Kapellmeister at this great theatre . . . which meant that . . . I was much closer to him, both as a person and as an artist. I saw and listened to him conducting all his own works, and was all ears for the various little particular nuances he . . . brought to performances of his music.'

During the course of the next fifteen years Krauss was to become especially celebrated for his Strauss performances, giving a number of important premières (*Arabella, Friedenstag,* etc.) and finally collaborating with the then ageing composer in the gestation of one or two new compositions.

The first of these arose out of Krauss's memory of that 1923 *Ballett-Soirée* and his suggestion that this could be repeated, perhaps even on a bigger scale than before. With the advent of the Second World War Strauss was to find himself once again in his long life cut off from active music-making in the opera house, with his most recently completed opera *Die Liebe der Danae* still unperformed and likely to remain so for immeasurable years to come. Accordingly, Krauss's request that he orchestrate a further group of Couperin *Pièces* came just when time was threatening to weigh heavily on his hands. So, during the latter months of 1940, he applied himself to the task and produced a further six movements. These were then added to the original *Tanzsuite* and performed for the first time on 5th April 1941 in the Munich Nationaltheater by the State Opera Ballet, under the conductorship of Clemens Krauss.

On this occasion there was an even greater attempt to emulate an atmosphere of bygone days. Not only was the music drawn from the early eighteenth century but the dancing itself was based on the choreographic style of Le Feuillet, a ballet master who flourished in Paris around the year 1700. A new title was also found for the ballet: *Verklungene Feste*: that is to say, 'Bygone Festivities the sounds of which have faded away'.

The title proved all too apt and this revival also faded away, leaving little trace behind other than the new arrangements. Strauss grouped these together once again for concert purposes adding yet two more movements to complete a Divertimento which was published in 1942 and received its first performance on 31st January 1943 by the Vienna Philharmonic Orchestra, once again under the direction of Clemens Krauss to whose initiative it owed its existence.

4

The twenty-seven *Ordres* of clavecin *Pièces* composed by François Couperin le grand (he was in fact known as 'le grand' already during his lifetime) appeared in four *Livres* between 1713 and 1730, although the five *Ordres* of *Livre Premier* containing the first seventy-one *Pièces* had been compiling over close on fifteen years. There are in all well over three hundred, which are as extraordinary in their variety of mood and character as the comparable collection of harpsichord sonatas by his younger contemporary Domenico Scarlatti, from which they differ predominantly in Couperin's reliance for the greater part on the classical dance measures of his day.

Couperin made a feature of giving many of his *Pièces* a title; sometimes this would indicate the character, though often enough linked with some personage or extra-musical idea ('La Milordine'—'L'Auguste', etc.), sometimes it would show the *Pièce* to be itself a character sketch ('Les Matelots Provençales'—'Soeur Monique'—'La Petite Pince-sans-rire', etc.); while sometimes the title actually reveals an early example of programme music: ('Les Petits Moulins à vent'—'Les Tricoteuses'). There is often considerable humour, as when 'Les Vieux Seigneurs' is followed by 'Les Jeunes Seigneurs, cy-devant Les Petits Maîtres', or when 'Les Tricoteuses' drop a stitch, which is not only graphically described in the music but is carefully written into the copy lest the conservative performer be too outraged or perplexed by so daring and unconventional a coda.

Strauss's *Tanzsuite* consists of eight movements each based on two or more of Couperin's *Pièces* except for the closing March which consists of only one, viz:

I: Einzug und feierlicher Reigen (Pavane)

'Les Graces Incomparables, ou la Conti'	16ème	Ordre	No.	1
'La Superbe, ou la Forqueray'	17ème	,,	,,	1

II: Courante

'Première Courante'	1ère	,,	,,	2
'Seconde Courante'				
'Les Nonètes' (1) 'Les Blondes'	1ère	,,	,,	12
(2) 'Les Brunes'				

III: Carillon

'Le Carillon de Cithère'[7]	14ème	,,	,,	6
'L'Evaporée'	15ème	,,	,,	3

IV: Sarabande

'Sarabande: La Majesteuse'	1ère	,,	,,	3
'Sarabande: Les Sentiments'	1ère	,,	,,	10

V: Gavotte

'La Fileuse'	12ème	,,	,,	6
'Gavote'	26ème	,,	,,	2
'Les Satires Chévre-pieds (seconde partie)'	23ème	,,	,,	5
'La Bourbonnoise, Gavote'	1ère	,,	,,	13
'La Princesse Marie'	20ème	,,	,,	1

VI: Wirbeltanz

'Le Turbulent'	18ème	,,	,,	4
'Les Petits Moulins à vent'	17ème	,,	,,	2
'Les Tricoteuses'	23ème	,,	,,	2

VII: Allemande

'Allemande à Deux Clavecins'[8]	9ème	,,	,,	1
'Les Charmes'	9ème	,,	,,	3

VIII: Marsch

'Les Matelots Provençales'	3ème	,,	,,	10

Generally speaking Strauss adheres fairly closely to the original texts, though omitting repeats and occasionally adding new inner parts. He holds himself free, on the other hand, to use only part of a *Pièce*, or more

---

[7] No doubt in selecting this *Pièce* Strauss's mind cast back to his earlier sketches for a ballet on the subject of *Kythere*.

[8] The only piece for two harpsichords in Couperin's entire output.

than one at a time in the construction of his own somewhat larger-scale designs. In No. 1 for example, 'La Superbe' is used as a contrasting middle section to 'Les Graces incomparables' the second section of which is curtailed at first hearing, though the original coda is used to round off the movement. 'La Superbe' is itself also abridged, a substantial cut being made in its own second section.

The 'Courantes' stand very much as in Couperin's original, despite the omission once more of repeats, and a brief cut at the end of Courante II. It is disappointing though, to see Strauss suppressing the original alternation between $\frac{6}{4}$ and $\frac{3}{2}$, that is to say duple and triple rhythm within the bar, a variation of pulse characteristic of the classical Courante. The graceful 'Les Nonètes', descriptive in turn of blondes and brunettes, are added as a simple appendage.

As in the first movement, 'L'Evaporée' is used as a trio section to the Carillon which is then repeated in full. (It is surprising to come upon the one bar cut just before the end in an arrangement which is otherwise particularly faithful to the original). After the *da capo*, however, Strauss for the first time allows his imagination freer rein and the Carillon ends with a new and stimulating coda.

The Sarabande is another simple scheme, Strauss's arrangement concentrating on a new background of flowing triplets to 'Les Sentiments' which again provides a central section to 'La Majesteuse'.

It is with the Gavotte and the Wirbeltanz that Strauss's ingenuity is shown in its true colours. These movements incorporated between them no less than eight *Pièces* chosen from across the whole of Couperin's output for their similarity of character and organized cumulatively to build bustling climaxes. In the Gavotte the vigorous section characterizing the rumbustious dance of the 'goat-footed satyrs', of which Strauss shrewdly extracted the later more memorable portion, is admirably suited for the second of his two Trios, while the lengthy coda sweeps in with two further *Pièces* before combining several of them in an exhilarating fortissimo passage. The Gavotte then dissolves quietly and elegantly in a manner strongly reminiscent of Strauss's best *Bourgeois Gentilhomme* style; but the Wirbeltanz, on the other hand, is a veritable whirlwind. Again the discovery of three so closely associated *Pièces* was happy, even though Couperin had intended them to depict subjects as widely divergent as windmills and women knitting. The gentle $\frac{3}{8}$ Allegretto shortly after the beginning is the only interruption to the general frenzy, and is introduced as a contrasting section in the same way as in Couperin's original, 'Le Turbulent'. The exciting coda owes more to Couperin than might at first be thought, and derives from the highly entertaining passage already referred to in which the unfortunate knitters begin to drop stitches. Incidentally, it was this movement which Strauss afterwards borrowed from the Suite for the purposes of the *Rosenkavalier* film.

Lastly comes the March which Couperin had actually intended to be descriptive of the gait and manner of Provençal sailors. It is elegant and jaunty, and played more or less as in the original text, though with a long coda dying away in place of Couperin's last four bars which had previously led to a 'seconde partie' in $\frac{6}{8}$ rhythm. Strauss's conclusion is a happy and tasteful one while the orchestral colouring is also fine-grained and transparent, leaving behind an agreeable memory of a Suite which has much to commend it for all its periodic longueurs.

It is, naturally enough, accomplished and even well fashioned, though the excessive similarity of some of the movements accentuates its stylistic misconception. To see this in its true perspective one should compare it with its opposite number in the output of Stravinsky, the ballet and suite *Pulcinella*. This entirely successful and ever-popular work was composed no more than four years before, in 1919, and similarly based on classical sources, in this case sonatas attributed to the early eighteenth-century Italian composer, Pergolesi.[9]

Despite Strauss's use for the first time of the classical cembalo, or harpsichord, his orchestra of thirty musicians never succeeds in reflecting the classical manner in the way which Stravinsky could do with such consummate ease with his orchestra of thirty-three. Moreover, although the liberties taken with the Pergolesi texts are at first innocuous and only gradually become more eccentric as the work progresses, every bar of *Pulcinella* is vintage Stravinsky. This could hardly be said of Strauss, although his procedure in the Couperin Suite is similar. Even when he has found his feet, and is indulging his imagination to the full, few moments are really typical: perhaps specific places in the codas to the 3rd, 5th and 6th movements could be conceded or the orchestration of parts of the Gavotte (No. 5), which certainly recalls vividly the Dance of the Tailors from the *Bourgeois Gentilhomme* music.

When, eighteen years later, Strauss published his second Couperin Suite, this time under the title of Divertimento, he refrained from giving

[9] Yet another admirable work in this genre, Casella's *Scarlattiana*, was composed in 1925.

the new movements similar generic character headings of his own, listing instead Couperin's own titles. Thus when, as in the *Tanzsuite*, he incorporates into a single movement several *Pièces*, each is headed by its original title (and repetitions of the name François Couperin) as it arises. This naturally presupposes a stricter and less elaborately organized combination of the *Pièces* than in such movements of the *Tanzsuite* as the Gavotte and Wirbeltanz.

Here, in the same manner as before, is the scheme of the Divertimento with its sources:[10]

I: 'La Visionaire'[11]	25ème Ordre No.		1
II: 'Muséte de Choisi'	15ème ,,	,,	4
'La Fine Madelon et la Douce Janneton'	20ème ,,	,,	5–6
'Le Sezile', (Pièce croisée sur le grand Clavier)	20ème ,,	,,	7
'Muséte de Taverni'·	15ème ,,	,,	5
III: 'Le Tic-toc-choc, ou les Maillotins'	18ème ,,	,,	6
'La Lutine'	3ème ,,	,,	12
IV: 'Les Fauvétes Plaintives'	14ème ,,	,,	3
V: 'Le Trophée'	22ème ,,	,,	1
'L'Anguille'	22ème ,,	,,	4
'Les Jeunes Seigneurs. Cy-devant les Petits Maitres'	24ème ,,	,,	2
'La Linote Éfarouchée'	14ème ,,	,,	2
VI: 'Les Tours de Passe-passe'	22ème ,,	,,	7
VII: 'Les Ombres Errantes'	25ème ,,	,,	5
VIII: 'Les Brinborions'[12]	24ème ,,	,,	5
'La Badine'	5ème ,,	,,	6

[10] The titles are quoted here according to Couperin's original. In Strauss's score the spellings are modernized and sometimes abbreviated.

[11] Eight bars of the 'Sarabande la Majesteuse' from the fourth movement of the *Tanzsuite* are interpolated into this movement in a setting for solo violin and cembalo alone. This was, however, purely for choreographic reasons and a note in the score instructs that it be left out of concert performances.

[12] A mystery attaches to the movements interpolated after the stage production of *Verklungene Feste*. The score is prefaced with a brief note by Strauss giving the circumstances in which the Divertimento was composed, and stating that Nos. III and VIII of the above were the added movements. From internal evidence, however, it seems possible that a misreading has occurred.

The juxtapositions, additions and reworkings to be found in the Divertimento are a little nearer in flavour to the original Couperin than the *Tanzsuite*, and bring to mind Strauss's handling of fragments from the Fitzwilliam Virginal Book in the opera *Die Schweigsame Frau* which Strauss composed between the *Tanzsuite* and the Divertimento, in 1934.

Nevertheless Strauss's procedure in making his adaptations of the Couperin works is not markedly different. Apart from generally filling in the textures with new and often elaborate counterpoints, the emphasis is still on abridging the original simple binary pieces by the omission of repeats or by lopping off the closing bars in favour of newly devised and extended codas.

The first movement, devoted exclusively to an orchestration of 'La Visionaire', is simple and straightforward in its adaptation, apart from the curious interpolation referred to in the footnote on p. 280. The contrasted section which follows is not, as one might expect, a different *Pièce* selected by Strauss for the purpose, but an original *alternative* used in just this way by Couperin himself. Strauss does not bring the first section back in the *da capo*, however, and the first movement of the Divertimento ends, perhaps a little inconclusively, with this quicker middle section.

With the second movement, the stringing together of a number of short *Pièces* begins. The three central charming feminine character-studies stand adjacent in Couperin's *Ordres* just as Strauss presents them, while the two outer Musettes were also originally placed side by side though in an earlier *Ordre* and in a different key.

For No. III Strauss curtails both 'Le Tic-toc-choc' and 'La Lutine', which he alternates with it, but contrives an elaborate coda containing a combination of the two *Pièces*, the return of 'Le Tic-toc-choc' being most colourfully orchestrated.

No. IV is again devoted to a single *Pièce* and is a short, simple movement though the additional figurations given by Strauss are unusually interesting, the pizzicato accompaniment strongly recalling the manner of Bruckner.

In No. V on the other hand, four *Pièces* are assembled and linked together into a more or less continuous scheme although, unlike the Gavotte and the Wirbeltanz from the *Tanzsuite*, the constituent *Pièces* of this movement have not been selected for their similarity in order to produce a cumulative effect. On the contrary, 'L'Anguille' and 'Les Jeunes

Seigneurs', two graceful *Pièces* delicately scored, are treated as a middle contrasting section to the robust 'Le Trophée'. This latter is then repeated in full before leading in its turn to 'La Linote Éfarouchée' which, despite its title and Couperin's intention by way of nature study, Strauss transforms into a full-blooded finale, adding an extended and brilliant coda marking the original conclusion to the ballet *Verklungene Feste*.

The last three movements of the Divertimento run consecutively and it is difficult to understand why they are listed as three separate movements. In No. VI Couperin's amusing evocation of the juggler's art receives some additional tricks of dexterity at Strauss's hands, although Couperin's melodic line is also materially altered—not, it might be hazarded, for the better. 'Les Ombres Errantes' which follows after the briefest of links, is appropriately orchestrated in veiled shadowy colours with meandering trills and running figures in clarinet and violins. Again a short connecting phrase leads to the final movement, itself consisting of two similarly linked *Pièces*. The first of these, 'Les Brinborions' (which Strauss spells with an 'm') is a light-hearted scherzo, while 'La Badine', to which it leads without a break, is one of Couperin's most typical *Rondeau* movements. Strauss preserves the two central *Couplets* while varying the returns of the *Rondeau* theme itself, the last of which merges into a coda increasing in velocity until it brings the Divertimento to an end with appropriate panache.

5

So great a revolution has occurred during the last twenty years in the performance of seventeenth- and eighteenth-century music that a valid assessment of the merits of Strauss's two Couperin Suites have become obscured by the very ethics of the case. The following present-day criticism puts the position clear, if in a highly coloured and subjective light:

> 'There are two ways of interpreting old music. The easy one, favoured by virtuoso conductors, is to bring it up to date. This means re-orchestrating the composer's score, ignoring his performance conventions and choosing tempi which give a superficial brilliance to quick movements and a Romantic glamour to slow ones. The other way

is much harder to follow but the results are vastly more rewarding.[13]

Within the terms of the current inflexible insistence on purity of scholastic idiom Strauss's treatment of Couperin's *Pièces* become indeed virtually unendurable and their failure to gain any foothold in the repertoire is thus not hard to understand. The inescapable memory of thick, smooth, overladen textures appears to us particularly unsuited to the delicate clarity and wit of the eighteenth-century French harpsichordist.

Yet even so, their neglect cannot be wholly ascribed to mere fashion. Even when taken on their own terms both Suites suffer from being too inconsistent in fixing the attention, although their best movements are very attractive and amusing. It is perhaps noteworthy that in the Divertimento Strauss could not restrain himself from enlarging, albeit to a limited extent, both the string and the percussion sections of his ensemble, while the cloying background of an organ or harmonium is also added to some of the earlier movements. Modest as are these extra requirements, the implication is clear, particularly with regard to Strauss's once conventional approach to the modern presentation of classical music. It is his misfortune that such solutions to this ever fascinating problem are in themselves no longer acceptable, and, if not without some regrets, these two works can only rank amongst Strauss's achievements as curiosities of variable quality and interest.

6

In 1924 both Munich and Vienna gave Strauss the Freedom of the City in celebration of his 60th birthday. Vienna was particularly generous in further supplementing their gesture with the donation of a valuable site on which he built himself a second villa. Here he was to live on and off for the next twenty years, despite the temporary bad feeling connected with his departure from the administration of the State Opera.

This year saw the wedding of Strauss's now 27-year-old son Franz, still known as Bubi in the circle of family and close friends. On 15th January 1924 Bubi married his father's charming secretary, Alice Grab, and Strauss marked the occasion by writing a little *Hochzeitspräludium* set for the unusual combination of two harmoniums. Whilst scarcely

[13] Basil Lam, *Radio Times*. 14th December, 1965.

a composition of any consequence, it is an agreeable enough hotch-potch centred entirely in or around its home key of B flat. Over a series of deep pedal-points, themes from *Sinfonia Domestica* come and go, with the trio from *Rosenkavalier* and the broad melody from *Guntram* worked in for good measure.[14]

Two fanfares were also composed during 1924 for important Viennese functions; the first was for the Vienna Philharmonic Orchestra, to open its first Carnival Ball on Shrove Tuesday which fell on 19th February, the other opened the Festival week of music held by the city the following September. Both fanfares are for identical brass bands with eight horns, six trumpets and trombones, and two tubas supplemented by timpani. They differ however in character, the *Musik Woche* fanfare being predominantly quiet and stately for much of its length, while the *Faschingsdienstag Ball* naturally called for a more flamboyant affair.

When in 1919 Strauss took up his appointment with the Vienna Opera he had made a temporary home for himself in the Mozartplatz. Previously, for his more isolated visits to the great musical capital, he had been accustomed to stay with friends, prominent amongst whom were the Wittgensteins, a high-born Viennese family whose connexion with music dated back to Brahms and Joachim, the latter having lived with the family when a boy, and been sent to Mendelssohn for tuition on their advice.

The present head of the family, Paul, had actually embarked on a professional career as a concert pianist but had the extreme misfortune to lose his right arm when in action on the Eastern Front during the First World War. With remarkable courage and determination he rebuilt his life by training himself anew as a one-handed pianist, and in the course of time contributed greatly to music not only on account of his accomplishments as performer but by commissioning works from the great modern composers of the day, including Prokofieff, Ravel and Britten. Strauss was amongst the first to be approached in this way when, profiting by his presence as a guest in his house, Wittgenstein asked him for a concerto, a genre which Strauss had abandoned after the *Burleske* nearly forty years before.

Little as the idea of such a work in an abstract idiom interested Strauss, he was encouraged some years later to accede to Wittgenstein's request

[14] The themes used are, in order of appearance, as follows: Chapter VI, Exx. 26, 31 and 35; Chapter IX, Ex. 63; Chapter IV, Ex. 2.

by a domestic circumstance which had for a time caused him some considerable anxiety. Only a couple of months after his marriage, Bubi had been through a serious illness, and it seemed to Strauss a happy idea to celebrate his recovery by fulfilling Wittgenstein's commission with a concerto centring round this very subject, which would supply just the programmatic stimulus he needed.

Towards the end of January 1925 the task was complete; not a conventional concerto, as it turned out, but a very substantial piece all the same, and Wittgenstein gave the first performance the following October in Dresden under Fritz Busch.

Strauss gave it the strange title of *Parergon zur Sinfonia Domestica*. In its true sense, a Parergon is a companion-piece, an offshoot, and this concerto is only partially that since neither in subject nor mood can it be said to partner the earlier tone-poem with its happy evocation of family life, flamboyantly exploited by a vast orchestra. But it does take one of the principal themes and develop it extensively in an entirely new way; this is, of course, Bubi's theme: (cf. Chapter VI, Ex. 37 in Vol. I).

Ex. 12

Strauss had to be careful over the matter of quotation from the 22-year-old *Sinfonia*, if he was not to run into difficulties over copyright. The publishers of this work happened to be Bote und Bock, with whom Strauss had recently quarrelled in connexion with some song-cycles,[15] and they were scarcely in the mood to make concessions. They could not, however, maintain that an illegal infringement of copyright existed over the three bars which Strauss now presents in strange shifting harmonic colours, perpetually tormented by a persistent C sharp. Like an *idée fixe*, this note returns incessantly throughout the work in much the same way as the threatening rhythm in *Tod und Verklärung*.

It is with this C sharp stabbed out by muted horns and trumpets that the work begins. Its first function is to lead into a statement of Bubi's theme in F sharp minor, a restless feverish version accompanied by disturbing chromatic scales and gloomy harmonies. Further entries

[15] The complicated story of *Krämerspiegel* and the *Lieder des Unmuts* will be dealt with in the chapters on Strauss's Lieder in Vol. III, but see also p. 299 below.

of Bubi's theme appear below or within the confused textures, often beginning outside the prevailing tonal centre, though the last note always turns out, however unexpectedly, to harmonize with it.

Ex. 13

The music descends to still deeper gloom and the piano enters with a free rhapsodic series of flourishes which contain references to two of the important themes which are new to the work.

Ex. 14   and Ex. 15

Even here, however, there are backward glances, for Ex. 15 is at least partially descended from Ex. 12 while Ex. 14 bears some relationship to the Child theme from the opera *Intermezzo* (see Chapter XIII, Ex. 30), a resemblance too apt to be merely fortuitous. [15a]

Even in the long solo recitatives the ominous C sharp continues to threaten and, during the subsequent stormy dialogue between piano and orchestra, becomes impassioned in its insistence. At last, as the violins and flutes take it up in a high register, the music wins through to a brilliant and jubilant passage built out of Ex. 15.

But the air of triumph is short-lived; Ex. 14 appears in the lower instruments and the sky clouds over once more. Not all the air of buoyancy is lost, however, and as the music progresses new and hopeful motivic figures appear:

Ex. 16

leading to:

Ex. 17

The figure ⌐ x ⌐ which is common to both Exx. 16 and 17 plays an important part in the build-up which follows, while the undulating motif ⌐ y ⌐ is also a prominent if less reassuring factor. Nevertheless, all appears to be going well, the patient seems to be recovering, Bubi's theme from the *Domestica* (Ex. 12) rears itself joyfully, when suddenly there is a fearful relapse. The music plunges down and the gloomy tones resume; even the sinister C sharp is omnipresent once more, though in new tonal surroundings in which it is often enharmonically rewritten as D flat. Bubi's natural resilience tries to assert itself (Ex. 15) but is repeatedly swept under the cascades of chromatic chords, while the Domestica theme becomes a restless ostinato. The struggle rages in ever fluctuating key centres until at last the music subsides exhausted into more feeble demonstrations of protest.

[15a] Strauss was soon to find a more enduring home for this affecting phrase as the Forgiveness motif in *Arabella* Act 3 (cf. Ch. XVII, Ex. 31).

Ex. 18

With a fragmentary cadenza, still haunted by the C sharp, the sufferer floats upwards into a health-giving sleep. The bassoon takes the threatening note and leads it gently into F major, a key which is also to acquire programmatic significance. A simple nursery melody is now chanted by the full wind group.[16]

Ex. 19

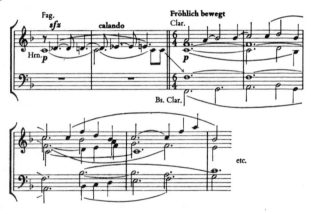

Abruptly Bubi is awake, refreshed and invigorated by his brief but happy dream of childhood (Ex. 15 on solo piano echoed by the orchestra), and the work passes quickly into its final section.

This is based on *scherzando* variants of Ex. 19 and of the Domestica theme against which a new and soaring melody is introduced.

[16] Wittgenstein, who for many years possessed not only the rights but the only available material of the work, interpolated at this point—ostensibly with Strauss's authority—an extended section containing both a more elaborate cadenza and a first statement of Ex. 19 given to the solo piano.

Ex. 20

The long symphonic development which follows incorporates all the
previous material, including the dreaded C sharp, though this has lost
much of its sting and can more readily be overcome, after a few moments
of hesitation, by beginning the finale once again, recapitulating the
opening *scherzando* bars and Ex. 20 almost exactly as at first. An enthusiastic version of Ex. 16 bursts in and leads to a brief altercation over key,
in which the *Domestica* theme plays a salient and most interesting role.
A complete restatement of the nursery-song, Ex. 19, follows, in which it
is combined with an extended melodic version of Ex. 14, all raised up to
the tonality of F sharp.

But the invalid is in an advanced state of convalescence and can leave
the artificial atmosphere of the sick-room for the healthier air of the
world outside. Accordingly the final cadence of the Song suddenly slips
down into F major, the home key of the parent work (*Sinfonia Domestica*). It has emerged that, for this very reason, F major is to be taken to
represent normality and good health in the Strauss family. Ebulliently
the coda leaps forward with fragments of Ex. 15. Again most of the
motifs of the work are incorporated, and again the C sharps appear,
though now they are handled in a manner making it clear that Bubi's
strength and well-being are beyond all fear of further relapse.

This section is of particular importance, for it contains in microcosm
the essential musical, as divorced from programmatical, scheme of the
work with its intrinsic conflict of two tonalities, F and F sharp, linked by
the varying functions of a pivot note (as indicated by the arrows in
Ex. 21).

Ex. 21

The work ends, firmly and unshakeably in F major, with Ex. 20 broadly intoned on the four horns.

7

Characteristically Strauss makes no concessions either to his handicapped soloist's limited weight of tone or to his endurance. Apart from the introductory bars, the announcement by the wind of the Nursery tune, and one or two brief respites in the finale, the piano is not only playing ceaselessly, but much of the time battling bravely against the thick and elaborate orchestration with florid *arpeggiando* passage-work or floods of consecutive octaves. Nevertheless there are more grateful sections, especially the recitative passages and the delicate opening of the finale, which coming twice gives the soloist each time happy altercations with the orchestra. It is from every point of view a truly virtuoso solo part, though much of it must inevitably be lost or submerged in the concert hall.

Yet clearly both Wittgenstein and Strauss enjoyed the experience, since a further commission was immediately put in hand, the second work being completed just over two years later, in February 1927, receiving its first performance with the Vienna Philharmonic Orchestra under Franz Schalk in March 1928.

This new concerto proved to be as unconventional as the first. It consists of a continuous series of variations on a ground bass with an introduction and finale. Strauss described the work as 'Symphonic Studies in the form of a Passacaglia' and gave it the fanciful title of *Panathenäenzug*.

The Panathenaea was the great annual festival of ancient Athens, every fourth year of which worked up to the climax of a brilliant procession. The occasion being the supposed birthday of the goddess Athena, not only youths, maidens, sacrificial animals, chariots and cavalry took part in the procession, but an elaborately embroidered robe for her personal use—known as a peplos—was hoisted to a ship on wheels and trundled through the city. The embroidery on this long, flowing peplos was narrative in character, somewhat in the manner of the Bayeux tapestry, and depicted the popular mythological scenes of battle between the gods and giants. The whole magnificent affair is the subject of a frieze on the Parthenon.

Strauss's attention had been drawn to the Panathenaean procession and its peplos some three years before when working on the *Ruins of Athens* in which an attempt was made to reproduce it on the stage. His whimsical and perhaps far-fetched idea for the new concert work lay in illustrating the multifarious events of this Ancient Greek festival procession by means of an extensive series of short, highly-coloured variations. With this in mind, the Passacaglia, being built upon a constantly repeated ground bass, became a natural choice of form. The *Panathenäenzug* falls into four main sections, with introduction, two interludes and coda, thus also emulating the Lisztian one-movement sonata which Strauss had already followed in so many of his previous symphonic works. The introduction opens with a brass fanfare which sets at once a festive atmosphere.

Ex. 22[17]

Tr. & Pos.

f

[17] The origin of this example can be found in Act 2 of *Die Aegyptische Helena* (see Chapter XVII, p. 331.)

A cadenza follows for the soloist, based partly on Ex. 22 and partly on the passacaglia theme into which it leads with a brilliant ascending flourish:

Ex. 23[18]

A continuous sequence of eighteen variations is next superimposed on this ground bass while the solo piano indulges in a ceaseless variety of figures and arabesques. At first the orchestral colours are predominantly sombre, with elaborate use of bassoons and bass clarinet, but gradually the higher-toned instruments make their appearance. The texture also becomes increasingly busy in character as the end of this initial series of variations approaches together with the work's first climax, marked by a broad and extended chorale-like variation.

The harp now enters for the first time, joining the piano in two linking variations which superimpose a new broadly melodic idea.

Ex. 24

Below Ex. 24 the ground bass still continues, though used with a little more freedom than before. In the second of the link variations the strings take up the melody and help to lead the music into the next main section.

This, which may be regarded as the scherzo of the symphonic scheme, changes the rhythm into triple metre, in which dancing character Variations 22 and 23 carry the work forward with considerable *élan*. Brass fanfares, woodwind trills and string *saltato* figures all contribute to the

[18] This theme shows Strauss's characteristic disregard for the limitations of his instruments, both cellos and basses being expected to tune down to the low B flat (an unpopular exercise). By way of acknowledgement, as it were, the basses are in the score additionally designated by the old name of *Violone*, which largest member of the viol family possessed the distinction of going considerably lower than its descendant, the modern double-bass. (Hence the very low notes to be found in, for example, Bach's bass parts.)

invigorating but still consistently thick quality of sound against which the soloist's ceaselessly occupied single hand struggles to make itself heard. As this scherzo section progresses, the original fanfare, Ex. 22, is more and more clearly in evidence, and the climax comes in an extended linking passage after Variation 32, in which it is proclaimed by trumpets and trombone.

The music then collapses into Strauss's most seductive key of F sharp as the slow movement follows, comprising Variations 33 to 39. The still continuously-flowing patterns of the soloist here become a rippling background to soft cascades of orchestral colours on the lines of the magic transformation scene from the first act of *Die Frau ohne Schatten*. To the harp and piano Strauss adds the liquid, bell-like tones of the lyra, a species of glockenspiel shaped like a lyre and still used in German military bands. This is later replaced by the celeste which takes over the running passage-work from the piano, leaving the latter free to improvise new melodic variants of the linking tune Ex. 24.

The slow-moving $\frac{6}{8}$ of this section grows steadily in intensity and textural complication, lyra, celeste, harp, piano, all mingling their glittering colours to add to the kaleidoscopic nocturne. Then suddenly the brass enters and the character changes from rippling coolness to violence and leaping flames. The tempo quickly increases until at the raging climax, in which both piano and orchestra are hammering away, the clamour abruptly fades into a soft and impressive return of the fanfare, Ex. 22. The next turning-point of the work has been reached, the long second interlude which Strauss also employs as the main cadenza and bridge passage leading to the finale.

The piano ruminates on the three principal subjects quoted above, while after a long silence the orchestra creeps in with soft string chords and with some meditative entries of the fanfare on bassoon and horn. A further climax is built up which resolves into a return of the majestic opening of the whole work. There is an upward rush and the March-Finale begins.

The eleven variations which this contains (numbers 41 to 51, Strauss having slipped one complete variation into the passage-work of the previous accompanied section of the cadenza) are very varied both in length and in the freedom with which they treat the ground bass. Variation 48, for example, plays the two halves of the theme simultaneously and is only two bars in length, while Variation 51 declaims the theme in the widest augmentation against soaring violins and upper woodwind. It

20

leads directly into the coda, a rapid but powerful $\frac{3}{4}$ movement, itself contributing no less than four further variations, similar in substance to the earliers cherzo section, before rounding off the complete work with a last jubilant statement of Ex. 22.

8

It is a curious, even perplexing work. In its proportions, its duration of nearly the half hour, its fantastic demands on the one-armed soloist who, as in the *Parergon*, rarely has a single bar's respite from his Herculean labours, it should rate as a major accomplishment in any composer's output. In the event, however, for all its fluent ingenuity *Panathenäenzug* savours strongly of note-spinning, and is now very rarely played.

The same is true of the last work to be considered in this chapter, the *Festival Music* which Strauss composed in 1940 to celebrate the 2600th anniversary of the Japanese Empire. The Mikado's dynasty was supposed to have been founded on 11th February 660 B.C. by Jimmu Tenno—although the date itself is in actual fact pure invention, as is also the name of Jimmu, the first sovereign's name having been Kami Yamato Ihare-Biko.

However, the leaders of Japan perpetuated the legend in order to preserve widespread belief in the antiquity of the imperial lineage, and, in addition to Strauss, composers in France, Italy, Hungary and Britain were approached for works to be included as part of the magnificent festivities in honour of this great date of Japanese history. (The British composer was Benjamin Britten, who submitted the deeply Christian *Sinfonia da Requiem*, with results which need not, perhaps, be entered into here.)[19]

Strauss quickly completed his score during a stay in the Italian Tyrol and it was first performed in Tokyo on 7th December 1940. He had hesitated before accepting the commission in just the same way as he had done twenty-eight years earlier with the *Festliches Praeludium*, and it is this work of which one is strongly reminded when confronted with the *Japanische Festmusik*. As before, it is a single-movement work in which a vast orchestra piles one towering climax upon another. Again within the one continuous symphonic flow there are a number of subsections, but

[19] For more details see Eric Walter White, *Benjamin Britten, a sketch of his life and works*, pp. 16–17. Boosey & Hawkes, 1948.

with the difference that this time Strauss had originally conceived titles for them, although these do not appear in the score:

1. Seascape
2. Cherry-blossom Festival
3. Volcanic Eruption
4. Attack of the Samurai
5. ·Hymn of the Emperor

A further obvious difference from the earlier Festival piece lies in Strauss's use in his score of local colour in the form of Japanese-tuned temple gongs, to which he entrusts the opening subject.

Ex. 25

The violins then lead the strings in with suitably undulating wave-music against which woodwind and harps intone an impressive chorale-like theme:

Ex. 26

As the watery undulations sink to the lower strings, the violins introduce the third melody on which the work is based.

Ex. 27

This builds to a climax at which point the second section begins with the leaping gong motif now given to trumpets and trombones, answered by a new figure in the violins which is used sequentially to produce running passages of considerable brilliance.

Ex. 28

A broadly melodic development of all the above material follows, in the course of which the little three-note figure ⌐ x ⌐ from Ex. 26 becomes especially prominent as the woodwind introduces little turns and trills suitable for the Cherry Blossom theme of this section. Harps and glockenspiel also add colouristic effects to a syncopated, spasmodic passage which breaks up to advantage the otherwise uninterrupted stream of thick orchestral polyphony.

At last the music subsides and a drum-roll leads to the third section, the one purely illustrative part of the work. There are five eruptions to Strauss's Fujiyama, based on swelling organ chords and with a hard core of Ex. 25 on the trombones beneath the fiery cascades of lava depicted in Strauss's best Picture Postcard manner by the remainder of his immense orchestra.

The last eruption brings two minor upheavals in its train and we pass at once to the 'Attack of the Samurai', a violent fugue based on a variant of Ex. 26.

Ex. 29

The *Samurai* are the hereditary soldiers of Japan, a race of men bound by one of the strictest codes of ethics and behaviour ever known. It was therefore apt for Strauss to choose the fugue, one of the strictest musical forms, by which to depict them. But as so often with orchestral fugue, it is not long before the strict part-writing merges into a polyphonic development of a more general character, and this gradually incorporates the other themes of the work in a symphonic build-up, the climax of which is the last section, the 'Hymn of the Emperor'. The gongs re-enter, extra brass instruments are pressed into service[20] and the work ends with an accumulation of pæans and fanfares.

[20] These seem at first to have been intended as alternative to the organ, but once they were there Strauss could hardly restrain himself from using them.

It cannot be pretended that the *Japanische Festmusik* is a work of any stature, and this chapter has shown the same to be true of all Strauss's works written to special commission, regardless of whether they belong to one of the periods when his genius was at its height or not. The affairs of the world around him were rarely a matter of interest or concern to Strauss, and it was therefore more than could be expected that his imagination could be stimulated at will for specific occasions not of his own choosing. It is disappointing nevertheless to find in the minor works of so great a composer little more than an uneasy swing to and fro between the equally disconcerting pitfalls of bombast and notespinning.

CHAPTER XV

THE COLLABORATION RESUMED

I

DESPITE the hiatus in Strauss's collaboration with Hofmannsthal after the completion of *Die Frau ohne Schatten* in 1917, it would be misleading to suggest that negotiations or, above all, correspondence flagged between the two men during the six years before their next important undertaking, *Die Aegyptische Helena*, was begun in earnest. Nor was this period entirely barren, certainly not of individual enterprise; yet there was also some joint accomplishment, if on a small scale, while even the plans which failed to reach fulfilment are of considerable interest. It will thus be clearest to take this mixed category of activity in chronological sequence.

The first project to occupy Strauss and Hofmannsthal at this discouraging time was the unsuccessful reorganization of the *Bourgeois Gentilhomme*, which has already been discussed exhaustively in Chapter X. By April 1918 this was a thing of the past and the question lay before each what he should do next. Relations were undoubtedly somewhat strained while, in the closing months of the war and in the immediate period of its aftermath, Strauss found himself heavily embroiled in the political affairs of both the Berlin and Vienna opera houses. Hofmannsthal had also been led towards politics through his wartime occupation in the diplomatic service and was composing addresses to Scandinavia, Austria and Switzerland containing elaborate schemes for a new Europe.

Nevertheless Hofmannsthal found time to finish the *Erzählung* version of *Die Frau ohne Schatten*, to help in the eventual preparations for mounting the opera, and to consider the various schemes which Strauss kept putting before him: Plautus' *Miles Gloriosus*, a satire on military character; the decline of Sparta presented as a Singspiel; comedies with music *à la Bourgeois*; political satires centred about the second-century Greek dramatist Lucian—Strauss's imagination teemed with ideas for their future work together. Meantime he bridged the threatening gap with plans for the opera *Intermezzo* and the composition of some more Lieder, including the great Brentano settings.

A quarrel with music publishers over the exorbitant contractual terms forced upon German composers threw Strauss into a brief collaboration with Alfred Kerr, the critic of the *Berliner Tageblatt* who wrote for him the amusing if scurrilous song cycle *Krämerspiegel*. Kerr also began sketching out a libretto for a comic opera on the subject of Pereigrinus Proteus, the Mysian cynic who, according to Lucian, committed suicide in A.D. 165 by throwing himself on the flames at the Olympic Games. Kerr saw him as 'a philosophizing world-improver . . . tormented by his craving to achieve something startling . . . the idiot blundering in a tragic drama'. 'The combination of biting humour and death', he added, 'seem to me to make an excellent scheme.' It came to nothing, however, and the libretto was never finished.

Hofmannsthal, for his part, came across with an idea for a 'rustic bucolic opera' setting down in his notebook: 'Festival of flowers, almost pagan-mythical, as the centrepiece, or a peasant wedding . . . the whole a ceremony; mysterious and comic figures.' It requires no great stretch of imagination to see in this idea, stillborn in 1918, the germ from which sprang the one-act opera *Daphne*, which Joseph Gregor recreated for Strauss in 1935.

Much of 1919 was taken up with the October première of *Die Frau ohne Schatten*, after which Strauss turned—between extensive conducting tours—to *Intermezzo* and the ballet *Schlagobers*. Hofmannsthal was also deeply involved in his own personal career and not only launched an important novel, *Andreas*, a Calderón translation and two comedies, but took a leading role in the creation of the Salzburg Festival, for which he had written major theatrical works.[1]

Even so, Hofmannsthal did his best to keep the liaison with Strauss alive, trying this time to meet the composer's desire for a light piece based on ancient Greek mythology, especially bearing in mind the Greek dramatist Lucian and his *Satiric Dialogues*. In addition, noticing

[1] See p. 151, footnote 1.

that Strauss was renewing his interest in ballet, Hofmannsthal drafted a plan for a half hour Ballet-Divertissement. These approaches date from the early part of 1920 at a time when the composer was being tempted into collaborating on a full-length ballet with a mysterious Herr S, of whom Hofmannsthal took an exceptionally poor view.

The Divertissement sketch is a very stylized piece of work, with gauche flirtations between 'Real' people—a boy and a young married woman, her husband and a girl with an admirer hovering in the background, and preposterous dances by 'Imaginary' figures, including Robinson Crusoe and Man Friday. The whole was closely interrelated to the Commedia dell'Arte and to its function in Schumann's *Carnaval*. In the event, since Strauss understandably took no interest in the scheme, Hofmannsthal followed it to its logical conclusion by reducing it to an actual scenario for Schumann's work, which was performed as a ballet by the Vienna State Company under Franz Schalk in June 1922.

Another idea which Hofmannsthal toyed with briefly at this period was *Die Tochter der Luft*, Calderón's Semiramis drama, which had already been mooted and dropped many times since as long ago as the days of *Elektra*. During nearly a whole year, between December 1917 and August 1918, Hofmannsthal worked intermittently on it, giving it the new title of *Die beiden Götter. Ninyas Semiramis Tragödie*. But eventually he abandoned it yet again.

A Greek comedy on the other hand, which Hofmannsthal had promised to Strauss during the April of 1920 in the same letter enclosing the Divertissement, progressed for a considerable way before it too was discarded. This was a three-act operetta on the subject of *Danae oder Die Vernunftheirat*,[2] for which Hofmannsthal left substantial sketches. These will be examined in detail in a later chapter, for here we have the basis for the third of the operas written for Strauss by Joseph Gregor (the second—actually the first in order of composition—was *Friedenstag* which Gregor built out of an idea by Stefan Zweig).

For the present it suffices to say that Hofmannsthal saw *Danae* as just the necessary light contrasting work that was needed after *Die Frau ohne Schatten*, 'continuing', he wrote 'exactly the line *Rosenkavalier, Ariadne-Vorspiel, Bürger als Edelmann*'. In view of this it is far from clear why the scheme was dropped forthwith and never again arose in discussion between the two men.

---

[2] *Danae*, or the *Mariage de Convenance*.

2

Hofmannsthal's work on Schumann's *Carnaval* led him to another line of thought in the revival of the works of older masters, and Strauss took an active part in stimulating his interest in these tasks; he himself was similarly at work on his Couperin arrangements. In discussing *Carnaval* he drew Hofmannsthal's attention to Beethoven's ballet *Die Geschöpfe des Prometheus*, the scenario of which had long been lost and the action totally forgotten. This new idea led both men to another neglected work of Beethoven's, the Incidental Music to *The Ruins of Athens*.

A curious by-product of the mature Beethoven, *The Ruins of Athens* was the first of two works commissioned from him in 1812 on the occasion of the opening of a new theatre in the Hungarian city of Pesth (Buda and Pesth were not united into a single city until 1872).[3] The text of the celebration *Fest- und Nachspiel*, as it was called, was by the German dramatist August von Kotzebue, who in addition to his prolific output of plays and historical sketches occupied various offices in the Russian public service before being assassinated at Mannheim in 1819.

The action with which Strauss and Hofmannsthal were faced is somewhat fantastic in its contrivance. It presupposes the return to earth after long sleep of Minerva (or Athena as she was also called)[4] and the reappearance of Mercury, come to summon her back to Olympus at her father Zeus' behest. To her dismay Mercury reveals the state of collapse and decay to which her beloved city of Athens has been reduced. Some present-day Greek citizens are heard bemoaning their lot as they go about their arduous daily tasks while in turn a chorus of Mohammedan dervishes and an army of Turks pervade the Acropolis.

Minerva laments the passing of art and drama from the world, upon which Mercury assures her that, on the contrary, it has merely moved its centre, which is now to be found in what were once barbarian lands. The city of Pesth with its new and magnificent theatre is where the two divine beings should be, and they forthwith set out on a pilgrimage to Hungary in search of this great new seat of the arts. The scene changes appropriately to Pesth and the remainder of the work consists of a pæan in praise of so enlightened a city and one so fortunate in its benevolent ruler. A wise old man welcomes the arriving pilgrims who, disclosing their godhead, conjure up the image of the king to occupy the central position

---

[3] The second work was *König Stephan*, which also had a text by Kotzebue.

[4] Minerva was in fact the Italian name of the goddess and is thus doubtfully used by Kotzebue in this context.

before the assembled citizens between Thalia and Melpomene, the muses of Comedy and Tragedy respectively.

To this piece of amiable nonsense Beethoven contributed an Overture and eight numbers. At first an invisible chorus awakens the sleeping Minerva, announcing that the years of vengeance are past and Zeus' anger appeased. No. 2 is the dirge of the two Greek workers (soprano and baritone). No. 3 is the Dervishes' Chorus and No. 4 the famous Turkish March.

With No. 5 the scene has changed and an off-stage wind band plays graceful music; the Hungarian sage declaims the beauty of the peaceful scene as the happy populace forgather in festive clothing. No. 6 is the centrepiece of the work, the great March and Chorus which accompanies the procession to the new Temple of the Arts, during which the scene changes once more, this time to the ceremonial precincts. Over the first bars of the music Mercury explains to Minerva the significance of the occasion.

As the March draws to its conclusion the procession has arrived and a tableau is formed. The high priest then addresses the assemblage honouring the Muses of the Drama, and in No. 7—which follows without a break—the people sing a beautiful chorus in their praise. The high priest now rises and, in an aria featuring the four horns in a manner worthy of the 'Abscheulicher' aria from *Fidelio*, expresses the desire that their noble king take his place amongst his beloved people.

This gives Minerva her cue and a brief prayer to Zeus achieves the miracle with a clap of thunder. The bust of the king appears above a third ceremonial altar sentimentally inscribed 'To our Father', at which the people shout in acclamation and fall on their knees. After Minerva has placed a wreath of olive branches round the head of the king's effigy No. 8 closes the festivities with a chorus of devotion and jubilance.

It is apparent that so palpable a *pièce d'occasion* could never be legitimately revived as it stood. Yet trivial as the commission must have seemed to so profound a creator as Beethoven, his execution of it contains much fine and interesting music. To bring some of this out of its inevitable neglect was certainly a labour of love. 'This is both a difficult and at the same time most attractive task', wrote Hofmannsthal during the Easter of 1922, 'I imagine a kind of ballet pantomime but with choruses, perhaps even with arias. It will have to be something which does not fly in the face of the original intention. To succeed in this would give me immense pleasure.'

Strauss's chief anxiety was that there was not really enough material to make up a new piece. Accordingly Hofmannsthal, remembering the other Beethoven score in which Strauss had interested him, now put his mind to working out some plan which might couple the *Ruins of Athens* with the ballet music to *Prometheus*, since their common connexion with the figures of Greek mythology seemed too fortunate to waste. 'To include the music to the *Geschöpfe des Prometheus*', he wrote, 'seemed possible although it stems from a different period of Beethoven's life, because it shows the same affection for the antique-paradisical.'

Even so, this is not to say that the link was easy to forge. A month later Hofmannsthal wrote again to Strauss:

'After racking my brains for a while, I have, I believe, arrived at a solution how to introduce fittingly and in good taste the *Geschöpfe des Prometheus* into the ballet spectacle *Die Ruinen von Athen* so as to satisfy your wish to lengthen the duration of the whole thing. Taking the Wanderer or Stranger as an idealized German artist of those half-forgotten days and giving him the line: "Das Land der Griechen mit der Seele suchend" as a kind of motto,[5] I present him as he meditates on the ruins of the past in the deserted market place of Athens and is lighted, like Goethe, by a Promethean, productive, creative spark (which he expresses in the aria with the horns). In short I turn him into Prometheus himself, surrounded by revived figures of the classic age who dance to the rhythm of the ballet music, until at the end we come to the vision of the Panathenaic procession (march and chorus) as the crowning climax. For this I envisage Mme Gutheil[6] as the leader of the procession of the virgin priestesses, with all the other mimers in support. How I have made use of all the remaining beautiful passages from the *Ruinen* the enclosed scenario will show you. I would like to omit the overture, which is not very impressive, and to open instead with the chorus and a suitably modified text.'

Strauss answered by return from Karlsbad where he was taking a rest-cure.

[5] 'His soul yearning for the land of the Greeks', a famous line from Goethe's *Iphigenie*.

[6] Marie Gutheil-Schoder was a famous member of the Vienna Opera, where she performed a number of key Strauss roles both as singer (Salome, Elektra, Octavian, Färberin, etc.) and as dancer (Potiphar's Wife). Strauss himself had an exceptionally high opinion of her. At the end of her career she became a producer. Her husband, Gustav Gutheil, who died in 1914, was a prominent composer and conductor in Weimar and Vienna.

'Many thanks for your fine draft which represents a very happy solution of the idea I've had in mind. I would only ask you to consider: who is to represent the Wanderer-Goethe? An actor—or even—*horribile dictu*—a singer? If an actor— how would it be if an invisible contralto voice, perhaps stationed in the orchestra, were to sing a few Goethe-Beethoven songs while he is lost in his dreams? Do please get Alwyn to play all the Beethoven songs for you. By the way, I once orchestrated *Wonne der Wehmut*.[7] As an Overture, the one from *Prometheus* would be suitable: it could easily be used as music to a milling Greek crowd, with the curtain rising during its last third. Then the opening chorus you have mentioned, which could be positioned in front of the curtain, perhaps invisibly in the orchestra pit as in the *Flying Dutchman*.'

At this juncture Hofmannsthal suddenly decided to wait until he had seen and approved the stage designs with their 'decorative architectural problems' before continuing. Nothing was more natural than once again to call in Alfred Roller who had created the scenery and costumes for *Rosenkavalier* and *Frau ohne Schatten*, and still occupied the position of chief designer at the Vienna Opera. The choreography, also a major consideration, was put in the hands of Heinrich Kröller, Ballet Master of both the Munich and Vienna Operas, who was also the creator of *Schlagobers*. Strauss champed at the delay while Hofmannsthal consulted with both these men before completing his libretto, but in the end the extra months seem to have been well spent. Towards the latter part of September Hofmannsthal replied to Strauss's urgent messages:

'The discussions with Roller . . . proved very necessary . . . if only to find out what was to be the visual stage business of the big final festival (March and Chorus). "Panathenaea", "Eleusinian Mysteries", these after all are nothing but words. The best of the Parthenon frieze; naked humans, horses, bulls are out of the question on the stage. What would remain? An insipid procession of white-shirted figures, carrying humdrum emblems, the whole in the classicism of 1810. That would be intolerable. What is needed therefore is an occasion, festive and meaningful, which demands more than a mere procession. We have found it. The culmination of the Eleusinian Mysteries were "nuptial rites": I am sure an echo of this still lingers in the symbolic nuptials of Faust and Helena. Here is our chance. We mate the Wanderer, our German artist, with the virgin-bride Athene stripped of her

7 This orchestration seems to have disappeared.

armour and of her golden helmet. She is not to be a singer, but a beautiful actress. Two nuptial processions will move towards each other to the strains of this glorious music, cross each other's path, mingle with each other, separate again until finally they lead bride and bridegroom together—who disappear at the very end among jubilant rejoicings in a blaze of celestial light. This is another idea of mine in which I take some pride; the first was the linking up of the two Beethoven works through the figure of the poet as Prometheus/Pygmalion.

Now to the ballet centrepiece which is, as you say, Kröller's real task. Here, in my view and Roller's, everything is already definitely predetermined by the music. The visual content of this music cannot be anything but bucolic; shepherds and a vintner's festival (in the classicist taste of late rococo), with now and then some mocking fauns—quite plain in the music. If there is to be conflict, it must be of roving shepherds breaking in on the vintners as they take their ease with their girls and carrying off the girls or nymphs. . . . This shepherd's play has now become merely an interlude in a serious and solemn work. I cannot see that individuals (Achilles, Pandora) would be much use at this point and with this music; it is, after all, in the whole context an attractive, but to our taste inadequate, vision of the classical age, and one which is anyway being pushed aside afterwards. Not this kind of thing, but something more solemn, more lofty, that's how I see the unity and mounting intensity of the whole piece.'

3

The correspondence over the gestation of this slender enterprise is quoted at length to show Hofmannsthal's high-minded approach to any venture, however fragile, to which he addressed himself. In the end Strauss's contribution remained minimal, almost a mere matter of shuffling together the appropriate pages from the two volumes of Beethoven's scores, with one or two minor additions to the orchestration of the final March. It would indeed have been literally no more, had not Hofmannsthal—after laying the work aside for nearly two years—received a definite commission for its completion and production which caused him to take it up again with a critical eye. It must immediately have been clear to him that there had been a somewhat disproportionate interest in the task between him and Strauss, and it was with diffidence that he approached the composer for an extra number of original music, a request which he incorporated into a most touching letter on the occasion of Strauss's 60th birthday:

> 'Herewith the only trouble to which I for my part will put you in connexion with the commission I have received for *Die Ruinen von Athen*. It is the monologue of the Stranger as he stands, at nightfall, at the foot of the Acropolis and before he begins his song (that aria with the horns). I find it quite unbearable to imagine this monologue unsustained by a single breath of music. It was always the intention to have some musical under-painting, however slight; just a soft touch of strings here and there so that the spoken word should not hang in the air all too barely. Alwin would presumably be quite capable of providing these trifling chords; but since it is important that not even the most fastidious ear should be able to discover a discrepancy between this particle, however minute, and Beethoven's style, I naturally submit it to you.'

Strauss accordingly obliged with a short movement in which he amused himself by quoting themes from the Third and Fifth Symphonies. Even with this insertion Hofmannsthal doubted the wisdom of allowing the score to be published and printed together with his libretto, but in the event the vocal score was engraved though not the full score which simply consists of pages from the Breitkopf & Härtel complete edition of Beethoven's works bound together with the addition of a few sheets of manuscript.

The score begins, as Strauss had proposed, with the Overture to *Prometheus*. Although doubtless the stronger work, such usurping of its sister overture's rightful position cannot remain without some criticism. The whole purpose of the exercise was the rescuing of some of Beethoven's lesser-known music, and although the *Prometheus* ballet-music demonstrably belongs to this category it is by no means true of the Overture. The *Ruins of Athens* Overture, on the other hand, is more rarely heard and is by no means as weak a piece as is so often made out. It contains, moreover, apt quotations from the Duet of the Greeks (No. 2) and the central March (No. 6) before springing into its main section, which is an exhilarating Allegro movement in Beethoven's best 'unbuttoned' mood.

Strauss and Hofmannsthal thought otherwise however, and used the linking horn octave from the original truncated ending of the C major *Prometheus* Overture[8] to bridge the music straight into the E flat opening

---

[8] The familiar spaced out C major chords with which the Overture is normally concluded are actually an extension provided by Beethoven for concert purposes.

chorus of the *Ruins of Athens*. This first number is then retained in full
though with the words partially rewritten in order to meet the altered
purpose of the invisible chorus. Instead of addressing Minerva, who does
not appear until the very end in Hofmannsthal's scenario,[9] it is the ruins
themselves which the voices invoke. The curtain then rises to show the
decay into which Athens has fallen. The chief difference in this first scene
lies in the supplanting of Minerva and Mercury as observers by a single
nameless Stranger, upon whom the downtrodden Greeks comment in
wonder. The duet and the two Turkish numbers then follow though
the order of the Dervishes' Chorus and the Turkish March is reversed,
with a repeat of the second half of the Duet interpolated between them.
The reason for this arises out of the increased role of the Greek people.
Hofmannsthal brings many more individuals into prominence than was
the case in Kotzebue's text—a beautiful fruit vendor, a beggar, and so on.

It is now the Stranger's turn to come forward. His identity remains to
the end in doubt and one cannot escape the feeling that even Hofmannsthal was never really very clear in his mind on the subject: Pygmalion,
Prometheus, Goethe, perhaps Hofmannsthal himself in some degree if
truth be told.[10] He has witnessed with horror the Dervishes' Chorus and
now addresses the ancient goddess of Athens. Twilight falls as he speaks,
and the evening light illumines the picturesque ruins. Strauss's inserted
movement with its naïve quotations from the Beethoven Symphonies
belongs to this episode:

Ex. 1

9 It must be acknowledged that although she is present in the published libretto
in the list of characters under the correct title of Pallas Athene there is no specific
reference to her in the text. Only, in fact, in Hofmannsthal's letter quoted above
does he make plain his intentions where she is concerned. The vocal score is even less
informative, referring to her (again only in the Dramatis Personae) as 'Die Göttin'
('The Goddess').

10 Hofmannsthal had visualized the Austrian baritone Hans Duhan in the role,
but in fact it was created by Alfred Jerger.

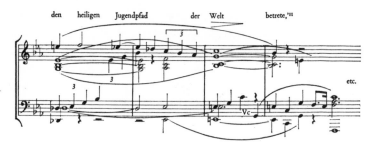

This leads directly into the aria with the horns, originally sung in the Hungarian temple of the arts by the high priest, but now by the Stranger as part of his Invocation to Athene. The stage has become quite dark and at the end of the aria the curtain falls and the orchestra takes up the ballet music to *Prometheus*, starting with the Storm Introduction which comes immediately after the Overture to that work. This in its turn is followed by a number of selected movements from the ballet, viz:

No. 1 (first 78 bars only).
No. 5 (the famous movement with the harp, Beethoven's only use of this instrument in his entire output).
No. 6 (omitting the last 2½ bars).
No. 10 Pastorale.
No. 13 (with a cut of 106 bars and a short introduction added, similar to the introduction of No. 6).
No. 8 (starting from the 113th bar).
No. 16 Finale, omitting the last eight bars and passing instead into the March and Chorus from, once again, the *Ruins of Athens*.[12]

This long interpolation accompanies a set of Greek dances devised by Heinrich Kröller around Hofmannsthal's conception, which was that the curtain rising would reveal a vision of the Acropolis as it had been in the

---

[11] 'For I am a child of evening and at a late hour tread the world's holy path of youth.'

[12] In order to avoid the necessity for a stage orchestra, as in the original score, Strauss adapts for his purpose Beethoven's later version of the same music published under the separate opus number 114. This was a revival called into being for the celebrations at the opening of the Josephstheater in Vienna, for which occasion Beethoven also wrote the Overture *Zur Weihe des Hauses*. In the later score Beethoven incorporated the stage band parts into the main orchestra as well as extending the choral parts to allow for the changed text in the new circumstances. Strauss naturally reverts to the earlier version in this respect.

days of ancient Greece. The dances are at first supposed to be seen as in a dream by the entranced Stranger, but during the Bacchanale which Hofmannsthal set to the well-known 'Eroica' finale to the *Prometheus* ballet-music[13] the Stranger wakes to find his dream turned to reality. He is led by beautiful maidens to take part in the revelry but his mind is on higher things than these dionysiac excesses. As if his thoughts were transparent, priests come forward to lead him away from the dance and toward the majestic procession of the last scene in which he takes part in the Panathenaea (described above, see p. 291) and, at the climax, is united with the goddess Pallas Athene herself.

4

It is hard to persuade oneself that Hofmannsthal succeeded in making the piece either more significant or successful than it was in the first place, while the chopped-up fragments of the *Prometheus* and *Ruins of Athens* music as Strauss presents them are also unsatisfactory. It is scarcely surprising that at the first performance the critics were scathing and spoke of the 'rather feeble Beethoven', much to Strauss's fury. The Vienna State Opera, where the première took place on 20th September 1924 in a double bill with the *Don Juan* ballet by Gluck, was in any case not the right house for so specialised a new offering by the most famous operatic authors of the day. Strauss and Hofmannsthal might have been wiser to have assented to an unexpected and apt request from Munich that the first performance be granted together with a suitable dedication for the inauguration of the new Deutsches Museum in that city, instead of so assiduously striving to preserve it for Vienna which expected greater things. Strauss gave the argument in favour of the new proposal with typical perception: 'As some 5,000 visitors from every country of any importance will attend this opening, the work which has been brought back to life will become instantly known throughout the world.'

Compliance would have entailed nearly a year's delay, however, and Vienna's claim seemed paramount. Unfortunately this was a privilege which it failed to appreciate, and the reconstituted work made little impact, subsequently falling indeed into a neglect even more profound

---

[13] So called because the last of the four totally different works in which Beethoven employed its principal theme was the finale of the *Eroica* Symphony.

21

than that from which Hofmannsthal had rescued the original. The smart of failure was lessened, nevertheless, by the fully revived activity which had by this time led Strauss and Hofmannsthal at long last towards the creation of a new opera, *Die Aegyptische Helena*.

5

The eight-year gap in his role as operatic librettist had been for Hofmannsthal one of considerable heart-searching. Although his reputation as a poet in his own right had never been higher, and indeed this period saw the production of some particularly important works from his pen, he yearned for the inspiration which music had always offered him. The truth of this came vividly before him while chancing upon a reference to himself in a history of German Literature,[14] which actually claimed that collaboration in the field of opera was necessary for him—had indeed been implicit in his earliest dramas.

With his peculiar, even tortuous mentality, he needed now to find the justification both for his resumption of work on libretti for Strauss, and for the very hiatus without which the word 'resumption' would have had no relevance. Not for a moment could he acknowledge, even to himself, that the collaboration was in abeyance. Had he been prepared to consider such a possibility he might have sought the reason for it in the last texts with which he had supplied Strauss. For it can hardly be said that they had been particularly suitable for Strauss's specific genius, even though that genius had sometimes made remarkable capital out of what had struck him at first as unpromising material.

On the contrary, Hofmannsthal persuaded himself that it had been the unshakeable demands of his independent career as dramatist which were predominantly to blame, and that the path back to a joint endeavour must be sought within the development of his own psychology. With this in mind, together with Strauss's continued request for a mythological subject, he tried to find a peg in classical antiquity on which to hang the profound study in logic and dialectics towards which his most recent writings had been leading him.[15] His choice fell on Helen of Troy for precisely the reason that the myths surrounding this proverbially

[14] Joseph Nadler, *Literaturgeschichte der deutschen Stämme und Landschaften*. Regensburg, 1922.
[15] *Der Schwierige*, *Das Salzburger Grosse Welttheater*, and especially *Der Turm*.

most beautiful woman of all time are outstandingly complex and even contradictory.[16]

As early as 1920 he had been pondering on how, after the fall of Troy, Helen and Menelaus had come together again as husband and wife. That Menelaus should willingly, and of his own accord, accept back the woman who had been the cause of such a cataclysm and so many heroic deaths seemed to Hofmannsthal a fascinating enigma worthy of the simplest dramatization through argument. The setting in the Ancient World was no more than the merest back-cloth; any French or American author, he remarked, would probably treat the subject as a simple conversation piece with entirely different characters. He was particularly attracted to what seemed 'the outstanding modernity . . . of treating with a light hand this famous and horrifying subject'.

Yet he was conscious that despite the example of Bernard Shaw, for a drama (let alone an opera) to develop through polemics contained a serious element of risk.[17] 'I don't care for a drama to move on a dialectical level,' he wrote, 'I distrust the use of purpose-bound dialogue as the vehicle of the dramatic. Words frighten me, they rob us of the best.' At the other extreme he envisaged Shakespeare and Aeschylus, whose use of words put the emphasis on expression rather than information. His own task lay in steering the middle course of lyric drama which would allow for the musician's artistic medium. After an intensive study of the different treatments of the myth by Homer, Euripides and Stesichorus, he jotted down an outline scenario postulating the psychological dilemma, and took it round to Strauss's office at the Opera. We cannot of course know exactly how Strauss received it but several years later, at the time of the première, Hofmannsthal expanded his revised scenario into an extended article containing in addition an imaginary résumé of his conversation with Strauss, which was widely published in the press and also utilized in an abridged form for the programme synopsis. In telling Strauss about the article he said: 'I hope, indeed I am sure that I am not making you say anything . . . which you might not, in fact, actually have said.' And Strauss raised no objections on this score, even though the reasoning is sometimes far from clear. For instance, he is made to welcome the scheme as outstandingly suitable opera material for him in

[16] Helen's role as the mystical embodiment of ultimate beauty in the second part of Goethe's *Faust* had already been in Hofmannsthal's mind since working on *Ruinen von Athen*.

[17] There will be more to say on this subject later with respect to Strauss's last opera *Capriccio*.

particular—'but not for others'—without any reason why this should be so. For his part Hofmannsthal shows himself encouraging Strauss's penchant for returning to music drama based on mythology, though with new and intricate philosophical argument:

> '. . . the artistic means of lyric drama . . . seems to me the only one through which the atmosphere of the present day can be expressed. For if this present day is anything it is mythical—I know of no other expression for an existence which takes place in front of such frightful horizons—for this encircle-ment with millenia, for this flooding into our identity (*unser Ich*) from the East and the West, for this fearful inner dis-tance, this raging inner tension, this here and elsewhere which is the hallmark of our life. Let us write mythological operas, it is the truest of all forms, believe me.'

So we are to presume that Strauss had believed him and, at least in principle, welcomed the idea. He was in any case quite happy to resume the collaboration once more in a search for stability after the troubles and unsettled work of the last few years. Moreover, despite all the experience of the past, he still believed Hofmannsthal's talk of a 'little light opera' with wistful visions of *La Belle Helène* in Offenbach's famous treatment floating before his eyes. The fabric was to be 'finely and slenderly woven, with few words', for Hofmannsthal's inveighing against words was now leading him to speak of them as 'the greatest force for destruc-tion, the greatest obstacle to decisive action'.

At first the piece was to have three acts, the third following closely upon the second, and we find Strauss writing from his 1923 South American tour that he hoped to find *Helena* waiting for him on his return in September with 'delightful and entertaining ballet interludes in every act, please.'

But when September came, Hofmannsthal was already inclining towards compressing Acts 2 and 3 into a single unit. 'The second act is good', he wrote, 'at least as good as the first, the third quite short; it leads to complete reconciliation amid a great feast. Yet, let me say at once that I am increasingly drawn towards combining the third act with the second. The third is the natural festive finale to the second act and gives the latter a quickening of tension; the feast, since it is at the same time full of inner meanings for the characters, would give the act an intrinsic goal towards which it gravitates, dynamically and psycho-logically. This would lead to the unusual form of two very rich acts of roughly equal length.'

In fact, although he did not acknowledge it until some time later, he had encountered a serious snag in allowing the end of Act 1 to come to such a point of finality that he had difficulty in finding the dramatic justification for a second, let alone a third, act. Nor did the opera ever recover from this, the second concluding act remaining to the end so much weaker than the first that the whole structure was fatally undermined.

6

Hofmannsthal was for some time undecided about the name and nature of the central character, an enchantress in whose home and through whose machinations the marriage drama of Helena and Menelas[18] was to be played out. At one stage he speaks of her as Sistra, an Egyptian name which he may have encountered during his reworking of the Semiramis legend. But soon he came back to his first idea of Aithra, which name can be found more than once in Greek mythology. Aithra is best known as the mother of Theseus, but some authorities also identify her with Pleione, mother of Pleiades by the giant, Atlas. Hofmannsthal makes her an Egyptian princess, a sorceress and the mistress of Poseidon, mighty god of the sea. Something of both origins of the name appears in his reconstruction since on the one hand Theseus' mother was supposed to have been visited secretly by Poseidon, while in the latter part of the drama Hofmannsthal's Aithra magically transports Helena and Menelas to a desert oasis close by the Atlas mountains.

The allusion to Poseidon is important, although the god never appears in person during the action. One of Hofmannsthal's sources for his new music-drama was a baroque opera entitled *Die Egyptische Olympia*, produced in Vienna in 1665,[19] which contained the parallel situation of Virenus being united with his beautiful Olympia in a similar locality and through the magical intervention of Poseidon. Hofmannsthal, however, was determined not to allow any gods to appear in his drama, and instead

[18] Hofmannsthal took from Goethe the Doric form of the name, and in discussing the opera I shall, as often before, refer to the specific characters exactly as they appear in the score.

[19] The composer's name has disappeared and the title page reads quaintly: 'Die Egyptische Olympia, Oder Der flüchtige Virenus. Ein mit Theatralischen Machinis geziertes Schawspiel Denen Oesterreichischen Halb-Bottinnen Und Holdseeligsten Donaw-Nymphen Zu gnädigem Wolgefallen und unterthänigen Ehren In Wienn den 14 May MDCLXV præsentieret Von den hier anwesenden Comoedianten.' There was a prologue and five acts ending with a 'Nachspiel oder Ballet'.

endowed his sorceress Aithra with an all-knowing mussel or conch—a giant sea-shell which, supposedly the gift of Poseidon, both entertains the lonely girl and provides a link with the outside world, in the affairs of which she is sometimes able to participate, even on her remote Egyptian island.

Strauss became a little worried when he actually saw this preposterous object which appears in full view during the first act perched on a tripod. 'It does look', he wrote, 'a bit like a gramophone'.[20]

On the other hand he did not even comment on Hofmannsthal's fantastic proposals for its quality of voice: '. . . let it sound really gay and marvellous! When I mention "gurgling" I have in mind the noise of water "speaking" in a pipe. It is not absolutely vital that one should understand what it says: it might in fact be amusing if the sea-shell were to sound distorted like a voice on the telephone when one stands beside the receiver—if so the servant girl would have to repeat what it says.'

Indeed, in the correspondence with Hofmannsthal during the gestation period, Strauss showed a remarkable equanimity over the subject matter of this curious and unpromising new piece with its obscure ethos based once more on the researches of Bachofen and the psychological marriage dramas of Strindberg.

Strauss was, however, justifiably enthusiastic over the ease with which the actual text suggested musical setting. Hofmannsthal's virtues as librettist, he said, were making progress all the time, praise which the poet was quick to appreciate. Certainly, whatever his faults, Hofmannsthal always wrote beautifully.

In his hopeful requests to Hofmannsthal, Strauss also asked for a 'few delightful elf or spirit choruses'. It would, after all, be only natural for a German Offenbach to lard his gay arias and ballet movements with some light choral movements in the manner of Mendelssohn's *Midsummer Night's Dream*. Here Hofmannsthal, who had been a little reticent over the ballet idea, was perfectly agreeable. A chorus of elves would fit very nicely as part of the great play of deception and mixed identity which he had discovered in certain obscure versions of the Helen myth, and which he had at once characteristically incorporated into his scheme.

Ancient classical literature is oddly blank over the adventures of Helen and Menelaus between the moment when Menelaus reclaims his

---

[20] An odd impression of the Muschel is to be found depicted on the cover of the libretto and vocal score. Here it is even capped by the three doves which, as the Muschel says in the opening bars of the opera, bring greetings to Aithra from Poseidon.

truant wife over the body of Paris amidst the ruins of burning Troy, and the time so many years later when Telemachus finds them happily re-united as King and Queen of Sparta. The explanation put forward by Stesichorus in his famous Palinode is ingenious if complicated and far fetched. It stipulates no less a theory than that of a mere puppet-Helen who went to Troy and caused all the trouble, the true Helen having been spirited away by the gods to Egypt. Here she was kept on ice, as it were, until Menelaus came to fetch her after the fall of Troy.[20a]

It seems scarcely credible nowadays that such twisting of the legend could have been taken seriously, but to understand the situation one has to allow for the mentality and beliefs of the ancient world. In Sparta Helen was considered to have been divine, and already the legend of her birth had been reshaped in order to give her Zeus for a father (the well-known myth of Leda and the swan). So great was the zeal with which her origin was reconstituted that she was now supposed to have been hatched from an egg. At first Stesichorus had composed a poem adhering to the original and natural account of Helen's life, but this was considered sacrilegious and he was blinded for a punishment. The elaborate revision of the myth which he offered in the Palinode was in effect a recantation dictated by dire necessity. It would be quite unimportant had not Euripides taken it over in his *Helena*, from which in his turn Hofmanns-thal took the comedy of errors he sought for his marriage drama.

The central idea was to be the gradual transformation in the mind of Menelas, from his self-appointed task of slaying Helena in retribution for those who fell in the Trojan Wars on her account, to the moment when he drops the sword at her feet and conducts her back to join him on the throne of Sparta. This transformation was to be effected by means of delusions and counter-delusions in the course of which Menelas loses all track of who is the real Helena and who a mere phantom image. The intricate network of deception is to be weaved by the sorceress Aithra with the agency of magic potions and Strauss's chorus of elves.

The elves were not to be Mendelssohnian in character, however. Hofmannsthal saw them as 'evil creatures, importunate like flies, and aggressive', expressing 'the mocking, scoffing manner of night imps, the sneering hatred of man'. Yet paradoxically he thought that the dia-bolic laughter and vampire aspect of these Ifrits should 'create an atmo-sphere of comedy'.

[20a] Herodotus gives another, and extremely interesting account of how Helen came to be in Egypt.

In view of what the work became, it is important to emphasize Hofmannsthal's light conception during these early stages—attractive as *Rosenkavalier*, lither than *Ariadne*, everything imagined as song: 'The word operetta', he wrote, 'if only one takes it in a pleasing, uncommon, earlier sense, covers it all. For dances and choruses we have plenty of room in the second act—and here I hope with your advice, to build up a strikingly ingenious finale, not massive and artificial as in *Die Frau ohne Schatten*, but light and full of ideas, like fireworks throwing out bunches of flowers'.

Intending to provide the promised opportunities to Strauss, as well as adding variety to a scanty cast list, Hofmannsthal next created two new and highly problematical characters; an Arab Sheikh, Altair, and his son Da-ud.[21] The main function of both was to fall instantly in love with Helena,[22] thus increasing Menelas' perplexity while at the same time incurring his furious wrath.

> '... the juxtaposition of the sexes is built into this whole action as a latent tension. Helena, the woman *par excellence*, is set against the men, against manhood as a whole. Is it not this that makes the situation of Menelas so tragic that he wants to separate himself from this collectivity, from this promiscuity, as an individual, as the husband, as Helenas husband! This is the famous comic situation which had led me across the narrow line of tragedy! As soon as Helena makes her appearance anywhere, though her name be unknown, the male element in the world immediately gather for new conflicts, for another Trojan war. This is symbolized here in father and son who are both at once enamoured with this matchless woman.'

Since, then, one of the principal facets of the drama was Helena's femininity and its effect upon any male with whom she came in contact, Hofmannsthal naturally became extremely agitated on realizing that Strauss was planning to cast Da-ud as a woman *in travesti*. Strauss had always viewed tenors with a certain sour apprehension, but in the end he agreed to give way and risk a 'small-part tenor' for what was, when all is said and done, a minor role.

[21] These names, which have given rise to a certain amount of speculation, are both authentically Arab in origin. Da-ud is simply the Arabian form of David, while Altair ('flying eagle') is the chief star in the constellation Aquila.

[22] Hofmannsthal's synopsis states that each is prepared to kill the other for Helena's sake, but this blood-thirsty refinement did not reach the actual text.

7

When the first act was more or less complete and Strauss was beginning
to turn his mind towards setting it to music, he tried to discipline himself
in the direction of light opera or perhaps Singspiel, by planning the
action in terms of set numbers which he proposed to separate by spoken
dialogue. But although in speaking of his text Hofmannsthal was always
referring to this little song, or that small trio, in practice the language
was not markedly different in style from his earlier libretti and Strauss
found himself obliged to be quite candid: 'passages like the first duet between Helena and Menelas cannot be treated in light character and will
go considerably beyond Singspiel—I'm afraid you'll have to reconcile
yourself to that'.

And Hofmannsthal, after at first reacting quite favourably to the idea
of spoken dialogue, found objections wherever Strauss suggested using
it. He seems to have had a kind of mental image of the music he wanted
Strauss to write. But it was Strauss who actually had to put the notes
on paper, and when it came to the point what actually flowed without
appreciable difficulty was the typical post-Wagnerian *Durchkomponieren*
into which he always fell so readily whenever the subject was over
his head and he could not get to grips with what was required of
him.

A few good leit-motifs would always get the opera off to a fine start:

Ex. 2

Manuscript of the opening of *Die Aegyptische Helena*

This brief orchestral prelude contains a whole cluster of themes which will be referred to and identified in closer detail as they return at the relevant points in the action. For the present it will suffice to say that in the mass they represent Menelas' agonized state of mind through his memories of, in turn, the phantom Helena, the burning ruins of Troy, and his own participation in the role of an avenging whirlwind.

The orchestral cataclysm then collapses and the curtain rises. Strauss, anxious to keep the shape—and his own mind clear—broke down the first act into an Introduction, four Scenes and Finale even though his attempt to separate these numbers by spoken dialogue proved abortive. The Introduction is largely concerned with Aithra[23] whose palace stands on a lonely island close to the Egyptian coast. She is bored with being continually deserted by her lover Poseidon, and rejects the artificial comfort of a 'Draught of Oblivion' with which the god has thoughtfully provided her in anticipation of just such periods. Poseidon is represented musically by an impressive *Naturthema*, a gentle lulling version of which is heard on the harps at the beginning of the scene, but which comes to assume fearsome proportions during the subsequent storm.

Ex. 3

The draught also has its motifs, the first being of particular importance in the musical development of the act:

Ex. 4

The second draught motif is more lyrical in character, bringing memories of Ariadne and the Kaiserin in its train:

[23] Hofmannsthal was very insistent that her name should always be pronounced as three syllables, though Strauss was not infallible in observing this throughout his settings.

Ex. 5

'Ein   hal - bes   Ver - ges - - - sen   wird   sanftes__   Er - - in - - - nern;'[24]

Even the servant-girl who runs to fetch this absinthe of antiquity has her own theme which is reintroduced on each of her many appearances:

Ex. 6

Not so, however, the Alles-wissende Muschel, which has no motif other than the cymbal and tam-tam roll which accompanies its sepulchral utterances. In a footnote in the full score Strauss expresses the pious hope that this percussion sound will give the effect of the soughing of a giant sea-shell, but he was conscious that it was only a half-measure. The contralto taking the role is directed to sing through a speaking tube, the resultant loss of clarity worrying Hofmannsthal despite his previous talk of gurglings and telephone distortions. He later came to revise his ideas radically:

> 'In order to clear the Sea-shell entirely of all trace of obscurity, I have found the following device. The Sea-shell (a trident star of immense size) lies on a stand in an alcove. Whenever the Sea-shell is supposed to sing, a mermaid with green hair and blueish cheeks appears in a veiled and sparsely lit alcove behind, so that this vocal part comes properly and clearly out of a human mouth. The shell after all has to provide the actual exposé [of the drama].

There is certainly need for clarity, for after providing Poseidon with an elaborate alibi the Omniscient Mussel goes on to describe in some detail the activities on board a ship passing near Aithra's island. This ship is conveying Menelas and Helena from the ruins of Troy to their own realm of Sparta. But Menelas, in obedience to a devouring sense of mission and retribution, is on the point of murdering Helena with the very dagger with which Paris has already been slaughtered. The Sea-shell begs Aithra to interfere and save Helena.

[24] 'A half forgetfulness will turn to gentle memories.'

We now have a further set of motifs. Firstly Menelas and Helena:

Ex. 7   and Ex. 8

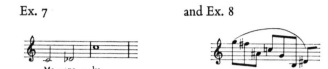

Ex. 8 is, however, only the first of many themes devoted to the different aspects of this most celebrated of women. A dignified melody symbolizes her supreme beauty:

Ex. 9

while her seductive powers are evoked by a series of descending chromatic phrases (e.g. Ex. 2g) which later crystallize into Ex. 10:

Ex. 10

Ex. 11, on the other hand, represents her specific image as Helen of Troy.

Ex. 11

For his part, the heroic Menelas is depicted by Ex. 12 (an important derivative of Ex. 7) while Exx. 13 and 14 are two of the many figures which portray his murderous intentions.

Ex. 12

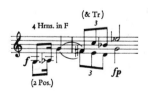

Ex. 13

Ex. 14

Aithra causes a violent storm to arise (manifestations of Ex. 3—Poseidon answers her summons promptly if only in his capacity as god of the sea; Hofmannsthal was from the first adamant that he should not appear in person) and in the ensuing tempest Menelas' ship is wrecked. Only he and Helena are saved, and she is unexpectedly brought safely to shore in his arms; a watery grave formed no part of his gruesome plans for her. The Sea-shell describes his life-saving activities and Aithra bids the storm to cease, its purpose in bringing the celebrated couple to her palace successfully accomplished. The music dies down to total silence, the Introduction is at an end.

8

Scene 1 consists of an extended duet between Helena and Menelas. There is no attempt at suggesting that they have narrowly escaped drowning, the fate presumably suffered by their entire crew, and from the start we are involved in polemics. Menelas is gloomy yet determined. For her infidelity and for the countless deaths she has caused she must die. He refers to their daughter (who appears briefly at the end of Act 2 but whose name, Hermione, is never actually spoken throughout the opera); she must bear no shame from the guilt of her mother. Finally Menelas calls on the gods to support him in his resolve and raises the dagger.

Helena has been in no way abashed by these seemingly incontrovertible arguments, and is shown to be in complete command of the situation from the moment she enters the palace. She refers to her original choice of Menelas from amongst her many suitors, her power over Menelas' affections and his repossession of her through the murder of Paris. Finally she too calls for divine aid but it is to the powers of darkness that she addresses herself. Hofmannsthal explains this in a very moralistic way:

> 'Menelas and Helena appeal . . . to opposing and mutually hostile groups of deities. Helena, who is a demon, invokes the ancient demons of nature; earth and night, moon and sea, so that these wholly amoral forces of nature may lend her their

magic . . . these are the allies of ever-deceitful womanhood, not of a man claiming his rights . . . Menelas the husband on the other hand, calls upon the higher, the Olympian gods as guardians of law and custom . . . the contrast between the daemonic element of Helena and the human-moral one of Menelas is the hinge, so to speak, upon which the whole opera turns. . . .'

Be this as it may, Strauss used the beauty of Hofmannsthal's poetic style as the basis for his natural outpouring of warm symphonic music in which the previous motifs are combined with some new and equally important themes. First and pre-eminent amongst these comes a harmonically shifting phrase which Strauss uses to symbolize the concept of ultimate Reconciliation:

Ex. 15

Ex. 15 first occurs during the extended solo for Helena, 'Dir ist auferlegt' which is one of the better known excerpts from this rarely performed opera. Menelas replies with a theme in which he refers obliquely to Helena's favours as the kiss of death:

Ex. 16

This brings the discussion round to the slaughter of the weak Paris, who is brought to mind beseeching Menelas vainly and feebly for mercy:

Ex. 17

In contrast to so diffuse a musical character-study, the crooked dagger (crooked surely only to make it more sinister) is depicted briefly and harshly:

Ex. 18

The climax of the scene is Helena's and Menelas' invocation to the gods which provides an operatic duet of unwonted conventionality for these sophisticated authors, especially after what had gone before:

Ex. 19

leading to:

9

As Menelas raises his dagger, a miraculous delay is effected by a moonbeam falling suddenly on Helena's face; abruptly Menelas is spellbound by her beauty, and stands motionless. At the same time Aithra, who has been a bewildered onlooker throughout the previous scene and now to

25 'Earth and Night, moon and sea, help what must need be—help the woman.' Hofmannsthal approved the combined use of these words by both voices on the grounds that 'each attaches to them the opposite meaning'.

her alarm sees Menelas prepared to complete the fatal deed, decides to intervene. She conjures up an array of sprites who play an inconceivably complicated trick on Menelas. By simulating the Trojan battle-cries and by transforming themselves into the exact semblance of Paris and Helena they try to lure Menelas away to a mock scene of carnage. As Hofmanns-thal explained to Strauss, 'Menelas' mind is deranged by too much excitement and strain ... so that nothing, however preposterous, is impossible for him to believe'.

If not quite what Strauss originally had in mind, the chorus of elves nevertheless gives the much needed element of contrast at this point. The music is abruptly flashing and kaleidoscopic in character with a number of darting motifs, of which Ex. 20 stands out in its quality of spiteful angularity as specified so emphatically by Hofmannsthal:

Ex. 20

Finding that Menelas remains frozen and undecided, Helena with a gesture of supreme self-sacrifice urges him to strike; a new melody soars up representing Menelas' ultimate fulfilment, which he believes to lie in a murder of retribution:

Ex. 21

After Aithra's summons, giving good opportunities for florid color-atura singing, the elves take up the strains with an intricate chorus evoking the sounds of battle and especially the supernatural return of Paris, whose theme is strongly in evidence in the orchestra (Ex. 17). Suddenly Menelas reacts to the elves' persistent calls of 'Paris' and rushes off, surrounded by will-o'-the-wisps and brandishing his dagger.

At last Aithra is alone with Helena and in scene 3, described by Strauss as 'the rejuvenation of Helena', convinces Helena of her devotion. With the aid of magic she restores Helena's beauty which has, it seems, been impaired by her recent experiences.

22

Aithra's benevolent sorcery is illustrated by a gentle descending figure:

Ex. 22

while Helena's revived loveliness also bears a motif though deriving from earlier material, especially from the theme of her seductive powers, Ex. 10.

Ex. 23

This theme, like Ex. 21 with which it is later repeatedly combined in diminution, is brought into increasing prominence as the climax of the drama is reached.

There is a brief duet for the two women, comparable in its operatic conventionality to the duet at the close of the Helena-Menelas scene, and Aithra prepares to administer to Helen her Draught of Forgetfulness brewed, we learn, from lotus seeds. The relevant themes are accordingly introduced (Exx. 4 and 5) as well as that of the servant-girl (Ex. 6) who, after serving Helena with the potion, conducts her to the bed-chamber when she finds herself becoming increasingly drowsy.

Before she retires, however, she sings to the now distant Menelas a little slumber song (including, as Strauss suddenly realized—not for the first time in his life—a line intended for a stage direction[26]) based on a

---

26

Helena: Hab's ge - hört (schon in hal - ben Schlaf hin - ein)

cf. Vol. I, p. 372, footnote 24 for a similar slip during the composition of *Der Rosenkavalier*. I quote Strauss's own slightly inaccurate quotation when confessing to Hofmannsthal.

variant of Menelas' motif, Ex. 7, and an answering phrase on the oboe
which we shall meet again at the centre-point of the act:

Ex. 24

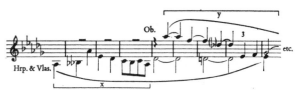

Menelas now returns still surrounded by the diabolical sprites who
have led him to perform all over again the mass slaughter he has recently
committed in real life, though this time including—as he thinks—Helena
herself. The music, wild and frenzied, is based on the motifs of the burning Troy and Menelas' course through its ruins like a flail of heaven:

Ex. 25

The crashing ruins of majestic Troy itself are portrayed by a massive
chordal theme:

Ex. 26

Menelas believes his dagger to be dripping with blood although, as
Hofmannsthal was at pains to point out, the audience must clearly see
that it is in fact spotlessly clean. The whole turmoil has indeed no existence outside Menelas' feverish brain, and under Aithra's soothing influence (Ex. 24(x)) eventually melts away. She calls for the lotus potion
to be brought to him too, while she cautions him against disturbing the
real Helena asleep in the adjacent room, thus leading up to an account of
Stesichorus' version of Helena's history.

Aithra's tale is briefly that the true Helena was abducted by the gods ten years ago,[27] was transported to Egypt in a trance, and left sleeping in the care of Aithra and her two elder sisters, Salome[28] the haughty and Morgana the fair, both sorceresses like herself. The Helena who went to Troy was merely a phantom substitute. As the astonished Menelas imbibes the draught of forgetfulness she reiterates the words a 'phantom image', echoed by her chorus of elves, while the orchestra introduces and repeats the motif of the phantom Helena.

Ex. 27

He receives the extraordinary and unlikely tale with interjections such as: 'Beware woman, lest I punish you,' or 'consider your words before you speak', which Hofmannsthal reckoned, if set to the right music, would 'depict [Menelas'] indignant wrath which remains at the same time always *chivalrous*'.

For a reason which is never explained, the potion does not act on Menelas in the same way as on Helena, but in his fuddled state of mind he finally believes Aithra. As a result, his anger (Ex. 13) changes to excited anticipation when she bids him prepare to see his real and blameless wife brought back, as it seems to him, from the dead (Ex. 16). A huge orchestral peroration heralds the Finale which opens with the comparatively well-known scene of Helena's Awakening.

This is the climax of the act and the music Strauss wrote for so impressive a moment is extremely beautiful. Against a softly undulating background based on the lotus-draught theme, Ex. 4, haunting fragments of melody float up and down in solo wind instruments. They have all appeared before (Exx. 19(x), 24(y) etc.) but they strike the ear as if for the first time, while Helena, radiant from her enchanted sleep—even though it was in truth ten minutes, not the ten years of Aithra's make-believe—is revealed slowly rising from her couch in the inner chamber.

[27] Strauss, finding clumsy Hofmannsthal's 'Three times three and a year', left out the last year, much to the poet's alarm.

[28] Lest there be any confusion with a certain more notorious lady Strauss set the name this time with the accent on the second syllable.

Menelas is overcome with her beauty (Ex. 10) and his desire for her is mixed with a sense of wonder (Ex. 15 pianissimo with shimmering strings). His own theme (Ex. 7) is also transformed in a version linking it with his appeal to the gods (Ex. 19 (x)), giving rise to a haunting phrase:

Ex. 28

The music becomes more agitated and, as Aithra joins the reunited lovers, blossoms into an extended trio which introduces a new and striking variant of Menelas' motif.

Ex. 29

Exx. 21 and 23 are also increasingly in evidence, representing Menelas' happiness and as such the ultimate solution of the drama. They will thus be heard again in the corresponding place at the end of Act 2, the eventual finale of the whole opera. Ex. 23 can now be seen to derive from Ex. 25(x) which is itself the inversion of Ex. 13. By thus transforming the theme of Menelas' anger to that of his joy Strauss tried to match, through his musical construction, the psychological slant of Hofmannsthal's conception. Yet he conferred no individual motif on Menelas' daughter who plays a vital if distant role in this aspect of the drama. During the trio Menelas sings repeatedly of his longing to restore Helena to her as a beautiful mother-cum-sister.

Under cover of the magical situation Helena softly expresses to Aithra her natural anxiety that Menelas' change of heart may not last beyond the effects of the drug. Aithra promises to transport them with her magic cloak[29] to an oasis in the desert where in the shadow of the Atlas mountains they can recreate their happiness in a second honeymoon. A climax is developed, but before it can be resolved the orchestra

---

[29] cf. the Amme's cloak at the end of *Die Frau ohne Schatten*, which has similar volitant properties.

breaks off abruptly. Aithra turns secretly to Helena (Ex. 22) and presses a casket upon her containing the flask of lotus draught which will keep submerged the evils of the past.

Herein lies one somewhat slender device by which the opera, which is already clearly drawing to a premature end, is enabled to derive a new lease of life for a second act. Another such device is the re-introduction of the elves who snigger sardonically at this illusion of a happy end with 'a significant irony which profoundly affects the meaning of the whole action'. They can thus be heard throughout the closing portion of the finale's third section in which a long descent succeeds the magnificent build-up and climax of the trio between Helena, Aithra and Menelas.

The lovers have retired arm in arm to the inner chamber and are hidden from view. Aithra gathers up the magic cloak and the casket with the potions and is just about to make the necessary preparations for her enchantments when she becomes aware of the continued chattering and laughter of the elves (Ex. 20). Furious at their malicious rejection of her all too easy happy ending, she shouts irritably to them to be quiet. The motif of the Phantom Helena (Ex. 27) twice soars ominously on the flutes and the curtain falls with blissful repetitions of Exx. 4 and 21. Menelas' happiness is at this stage built on sand.

10

For all its faults Act 1 is compact and well-shaped; the second act was to prove more troublesome. Hofmannsthal's purpose in adding it was in itself none too comprehensible. He reasoned that Act 1 alone amounted to little more than 'a frivolous little comedy in which a husband was made a fool of by two women after his terrible adventures'; now, however, transplanted into the desert, where the fame of neither Troy nor Helena could possibly have reached, the married couple would be able to resolve their psychological destiny.

Act 2 thus begins with a scene for Helena and Menelas which Hofmannsthal regarded as a kind of Overture. 'It indicates', he wrote, 'the deep-seated principal motivation of the action: how they are *both* compelled from within to loosen with their own hands the knot fastened by deceit. . . .' First, Helena has an extended monologue while Menelas lies at her side still fast asleep, which provided an opportunity for the kind of extended soprano *cantilena* in which Strauss had long been the outstanding specialist. Hofmannsthal remarked that this aria should be 'thoroughly triumphant in expression: the woman, the great mistress, the goddess—a jubilant singing of Leda's daughter!' and Strauss followed these injunctions to the letter. It is by far the most celebrated passage in the opera and ranks amongst Strauss's most ecstatic outpourings for soprano and orchestra.

Menelas wakes up and quickly throws a gloom over the proceedings. He is thoroughly confused; uppermost in his memory is Aithra's palace and the scene of carnage which, under the influence of the elves, he believes he has committed there. The radiant being he now sees standing before him, and with whom he has just spent a night of love, can therefore only be a spirit.

As soon as she grasps Menelas' line of thought, Helena comes to the conclusion that the effect of the potion must be wearing off and decides to administer a fresh dose. Unfortunately, in unpacking the trunk she negligently lets slip to the ground Menelas' crooked dagger, which has inadvertently been put in as well. The sight of this has an electrifying effect on Menelas, corroborating all his doubts and feelings of self-guilt. He rejects the potion which Helena holds out to him and, turning from her, makes as if to plunge headlong and irrevocably into the wilderness. Helena, angry with the lotus brew, returns it to the trunk and brings the scene to an end with an impassioned outburst addressed to the dark powers whom she had already invoked during the duet in Act I.

This scene is to a large extent the counterpart to the earlier duet with which it is closely linked motivically. All the important themes recur as in a symphonic recapitulation; those of Helena—especially during her monologue—Exx. 8, 10 and 11; those of Menelas, Exx. 12 and 28, and others of more general significance such as the Draught motif, Ex. 4, and that of Menelas' self-fulfilment, Ex. 21. Aithra's enchantments are also evoked by Ex. 24(x) at the moment of Menelas' awakening, while the Death theme, Ex. 16, underlines Menelas' anxiety that the Helena who stands before him may have just returned from the Underworld.

In addition, however, when Menelas gazes in bewilderment at his new surroundings a new and vivid figure appears in the orchestra:

Ex. 30

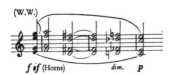

Ex. 30 represents Menelas as he searches his clouded memory for the clear understanding of past events which has been denied him through Aithra's magic draught. A connexion is later established between this phrase and the motif which accompanies the idea of memory restored (see the motif of Recollection, Ex. 37).

Another and more important new theme appears at the moment when the crooked dagger (from this moment on inexplicably referred to as a curved sword) falls to the ground. At first the earlier dagger motif, Ex. 18, bursts forth in the deepest instruments of the orchestra, followed immediately by Ex. 31 on the trombones:

Ex. 31

Both this first statement and many later passages featuring Ex. 31 clearly identify it with Menelas' sword, but there is more to it than that. The opening figure ⌐ x ⌐ is identical with Ex. 19(y), Helena's invocation to the dark powers; towards the end of the present scene, in her despair at Menelas' rejection of herself and her offered draught, Helena has once again turned to the forces of evil, calling for their renewed participation in the unsatisfactory turn of events.[30] The prominent part of Ex. 31 in this new invocation suggests a symbolic connexion between the demoniac force of Helena's will, the powers of darkness, and Menelas' dependence upon the fatal sword which plays so significant a role in the psychological drama.

II

So far, Act 2 has been entirely on a dialectical level. Now it is time for the outward action to begin. Hofmannsthal's intention was that it should be 'brisk and rapid where that of the first act resembled a dream or fairy-tale. The desert wind dominates now instead of the damp moonlit night by

---

[30] A curious extra thematic reference at this point, though in the minor, is to the opening fanfare motif from the Left Hand Piano Concerto *Panathenäenzug* which Strauss was also sketching at this time (see Chapter XIV, Ex. 22).

the seaside'. Unfortunately the approach of a group of Arab warriors on horseback headed by an obscure Sheikh had Strauss completely flummoxed. The idea of contriving some bogus local colour depressed him and for some time the composition ground to a standstill.

Hofmannsthal was very solicitous, reminding Strauss that twice before in their collaboration the entrance of a new character had caused a similar hesitation in the creative flow of music—both Klytemnestra and Bacchus had seemed stumbling blocks for a time, though each was triumphantly surmounted in the end. One thing pleased Hofmannsthal particularly; Strauss had spoken wistfully of reverting to a purely classical style after the manner of, for example, Gluck's *Iphigénie*—of which he had made a complete adaptation for the German stage some thirty-eight years before.[31] To Hofmannsthal, with what he himself acknowledged to be his limited understanding of music, it somehow seemed an ideal solution to hark back to a pastiche of eighteenth-century opera and would, he considered, make for just the unity of style the work most needed. The finale would also be admirable if set to music in the style of Gluck or Handel. As for the rushing on of all the horsemen, eunuchs, slaves, warriors and so on, this could be transformed into a solemn march if Strauss preferred. The one thing to be avoided was any hint of mock-orientalism; if only Strauss kept his mind firmly on Ancient Greece all would come right.

Strauss knew that Hofmannsthal was trying to be encouraging and helpful but all this did not solve his difficulty. Wild and savage hordes of mounted Arabs can scarcely burst on to sounds of a stately march. It was hard enough to adapt his natural style to fit this unlikely situation in the desert with sufficient characterization and yet 'without degenerating into the so-called realism of *Salome* or the eccentricities of today's modernists. . . .' To try to incorporate a stylistic throwback to the music of Gluck and Handel was, for all his dreams of a 'pure, sublimated' idiom, only to aggravate the problem which principally arose out of the grotesque new characters, Altair the Sheikh himself, and Da-ud his son.

In the end, therefore, the music remained obstinately Straussian, with a jerky new rhythm evoking the thunder of horses' hooves, and splashes of orchestral colour trying to conjure up the rapidly approaching cortège. Altair is given the following somewhat enigmatic and sinister motif:

[31] See Chapter XVI.

Ex. 32

while Helena receives him with a new theme full of queenly grace and dignity.

Ex. 33

    During the scene which follows, Altair explains his mission. He has been sent to pay his respects by Aithra and her two sisters, to whom he is bound in allegiance. In their name he offers Helena and Menelas the freedom of the desert. A group of young men, prominent amongst whom is Da-ud, shout their enthusiastic loyalty to Helena and promise to die in her service, 'for she is the most beautiful woman on earth'. Altair is now himself smitten with love for Helena and contrives a scheme to get Menelas conveniently out of the way. He will institute a hunt, and will send Da-ud with Menelas as boon-companion.

    But Menelas has taken one look at Da-ud and has recognized in his young and good-looking features once again the image of Paris. He reaches for his sword while Helena tries to pacify him, but her tender attentions to Menelas whet the appetite of the watching Altair, who contemptuously advances the arrangements which will remove his irksome presence. Slaves give Menelas some hunting clothes and he goes unwillingly into his tent to change. Altair summons Da-ud to stand by in attendance and then he too departs, to await the more propitious moment he has planned.

    Da-ud, finding himself alone with Helena, immediately declares his love but she only laughs at him. He rushes off and Menelas comes out of the tent. To him the situation is ominously reminiscent of the parallel occasion ten years ago when he went off to hunt and returned to find that Helena had eloped. An off-stage fanfare of horns and brass reiterates Ex. 32 in ever more menacing tones, summoning Menelas to the chase, and he storms away leaving Helena to brood over the palpable failure of the potion in its much vaunted 'quick forgetfulness of every ill'. In the last bars of the scene she decides, with magnificent self-contradiction, that Aithra's magic was both 'not strong enough and too strong for Menelas' heart'.

Musically, after an unpromising start and some patchy moments, scene 2[32] had turned out better than Strauss had feared. Altair's Hagen-like Ex. 32 with its gawky intervals enabled him to produce some interesting clashes of harmony which lend vitality to the texture. Menelas' psychological troubles are again graphically described with the aid of all the relevant motifs: Paris and the Phantom Helena (Exx. 17 and 27), his own relentless mission as avenger (Ex. 25), the sword which will yet again accomplish the deed (Ex. 31, which now largely replaces the dagger motif, Ex. 18), and the derivative of Helena's seductive powers (Ex. 23) which constantly floats over and through the music, suggesting that her beauty is weaving its insidious spell over every member of the male sex who comes anywhere near her orbit.

Two new themes are also heard describing Da-ud, whose little love-scene is a vignette within the larger canvas of scene 2. The boy himself, wholly guileless in his youthful beauty (one wonders whether Hofmanns-thal had the chaste Joseph in mind once again) is depicted by Ex. 34:

Ex. 34

whilst the scene is played against an ostinato of this figure:

Ex. 35

Ex. 35 is actually derived from a subsidiary motif of Altair, not quoted.

[32] Although indicated in the piano arrangements, these scene headings are not given in the full orchestral score as in Act 1, possibly because the formal design of the second act is so very much less clearly defined.

This is first introduced as an accompaniment to Ex. 17, the motif of Paris, whose role Da-ud is unconsciously playing to an amused and clear-sighted Helena. Later, however, it is joined by Da-ud's own theme, Ex. 34, as his personality begins to emerge, then by that of Helena's charms, Ex. 23, and by the sword or Dark Powers theme, Ex. 31. Da-ud's impending doom is already foreshadowed.

Fritz Busch, who conducted the first performance, felt strongly that Ex. 34 was banal and had the courage to tell Strauss so to his face when Strauss was playing the score through at Garmisch to his new Kapellmeister. To Busch's amazement Strauss was neither angry nor even taken aback. On the contrary, delighted, he repeated the criticism gleefully to Pauline who had just come into the room. He then turned back to Busch and added, 'That's what's wanted for the servant girls. Believe me, dear Busch, the general public would not go to *Tannhäuser* if it didn't contain "O Star of Eve" or to *Walküre* without "Winterstürme". No, no, that's what they want'. Busch was profoundly shocked.

With Da-ud's exit and Menelas' return the dialectics of the royal couple are carried a stage further, and Strauss follows the argument with a skilful symphonic development of the appropriate material. In addition, however, he introduces a new and passionate melody which symbolizes Helena's knowledge of Menelas' deep-seated love for herself, the true living Helena (as opposed to all the images and phantoms with which he is so hopelessly confused).

Ex. 36

At the end of the scene the violent orchestral tutti, during which Menelas storms away, dies down to an ostinato based on Paris' Ex. 17 accompanying Helena's brief closing monologue 'Er ist dahin. . . .' The manner of both text and music is here overpoweringly Wagnerian recalling, for example, Mime's 'da stürmt er hin' when the hero rages off in *Siegfried* Act 1, or Brünnhilde's monologue after Wotan's similar exit in *Walküre*. There are many such passages in Wagner and their calmer mood of aftermath is dramatically welcome after the preceding climax. They also provide a highly effective link to the contrasting scene which in each case follows, so that Strauss's embracing of the device, if derivative, is perfectly justified.

12

Scene 3 brings the reappearance of Aithra. She is joyfully received by Helena who tries to explain how the lotus brew has failed its purpose, but her expostulations fall on deaf ears. Aithra has followed the royal pair swiftly to their desert retreat together with two of her slaves; she has discovered that when Helena's trunk was packed two potions were put in by mistake. It would be fatal if Helena had taken one for the other and had administered the wrong potion to Menelas. Fortunately the slaves, on ransacking the trunk, discover both phials untouched.

The allusion to all these phials and fatal potions came to fill Strauss with apprehension. It was so dangerously akin to Brangäne and Isolde; this gay, light operetta he had hoped for had become more cumbersome and Wagnerian every minute. He begged Hofmannsthal only a matter of months before the first performance to write an article proving that the potions were of very ancient origin and therefore common property. Hofmannsthal replied in the heaviest indignation:

> '. . . what is all this about *potions*? I am utterly at a loss to understand. After all Wagner did not, for heaven's sake, *invent* these potions! One (in the *Ring*) comes from the *Edda*, the other from the Tristan legend. In sagas and myths these potions are a standing institution, in the Indian sagas *ages before* Homer, in the Celtic ones, the Teutonic, everywhere! Are these people really such Hottentots?! Surely one must presume some sort of education.'

So we now have a second potion, the Draught of Recollection.

Ex. 37

To Aithra's dismay Helena, hearing about this antidote, welcomes it as the solution to her troubles. She must restore Menelas to full normality and face the consequences. If she cannot win Menelas back by the sheer power of her will and her beauty she will gladly face death at his hands. She sets about brewing a draught into which she pours a strong libation of Recollection.

The incantations which accompany the mixing of the potion form a set piece based entirely on Ex. 37 which leads eventually to the return of Altair. His declaration of love follows, together with his announcement of a banquet which he is giving that night in Helena's honour.

Altair's eulogies are interrupted from time to time by Aithra's two servants who, having hidden the pots and ewers in which the new potion was being brewed, now give a running commentary on the hunt which they can see in the distance. The description of the falcon chasing the gazelle recalled *Die Frau ohne Schatten* so vividly that Strauss could not resist a sly reference in the orchestra to the Falke motif (Chapter XII, Ex. 10,).

Aithra herself has still remained on stage half-hidden during Altair's courtship, so Hofmannsthal wrote some lines for a potential trio which, he said, could be cut if Strauss preferred. In the end Strauss used them to form a lyrical centre-piece for the two women, alternating with Altair's wooing, as this enabled him to insert a suavely beautiful development of Ex. 36. Helena rejects Altair in the confident security of her and Menelas' love in which she believes herself protected by the immortal gods. For her part Aithra rejoices in Helena's faith in her destiny which she knows to have been rendered additionally secure through the sublimation of suffering.

Like Da-ud, Altair has a new motif on which the music of his courtship is based, and which dominates this second half of scene 3.

Ex. 38

The similarity of Ex. 38 to the opening figure of Ex. 31 and thence to Ex. 19(y) is not without significance, suggesting the influence once again of dark powers in the ominous course of events. This becomes particularly suggestive during the central trio when it is used as a terse, recurrent fanfare.

At Altair's reference to drums which can be heard heralding the forthcoming feast Strauss felt himself obliged to introduce a further group of offstage musicians, and did in fact fall into the trap of imitating the shrill and agitated wailing of Arabian reed instruments with the typical use of augmented intervals. Six each of oboes and clarinets all in unison, supported by two tambourines, four triangles and timpani, work hard to create the required illusion, but Strauss would have been better advised to heed Hofmannsthal's warning not to attempt any local colour. Already in the Dance of the Seven Veils he had shown his inability to achieve true orientalism, and the new example is very weak.

The servants' excited account of the chase turns to alarm when they become aware that Menelas and Da-ud have started hunting each other, and the scene reaches its climax when Da-ud falls at the hand of Menelas (the Dagger motif, Ex. 18, makes an abrupt and savage reappearance). Altair is unmoved—he has plenty more sons, he says with cold indifference—but all the off-stage instruments thunder and wail until the mighty funeral music announces the approaching cortège of the dead Da-ud.

13

To Hofmannsthal this point marked the beginning of the finale, but what follows is so long and involved that Strauss refused to commit himself and simply headed it 'Scene 4'. To clarify the dénouement had been the problem from the beginning, since so much complex interaction takes place simultaneously. Au fond Hofmannsthal saw the work as a drama of marriage and in this respect its resolution lay in the strength of mind shown by Helena. She insists upon offering the Draught of Recollection to unhappy Menelas, who believes that in Da-ud he has slaughtered Paris for yet a third time. Like Tristan he drinks the potion in the belief that it is a draught of death and, like Isolde, Helena partakes of it as well. In place of death, complete memory of the past comes to both of them and with it realization of their basic indestructible love. As the two embrace the conflict is behind them and Helena and Menelas are ready to return to Sparta and resume their regal offices.

But there are more complicated issues to be accounted for. In the first place, Altair is now strongly on the warpath and cannot be left in the background. Aithra is also too important a figure to be quietly neglected merely because Helena has rejected her intercession and taken control of her own destiny.

But most significant of all, Hofmannsthal had come to realise that something more was needed on stage to make an operatic climax than a resolution in purely dialectical terms. So he decided to draw the loose threads together with an old fashioned *deus ex machina*. Aithra perceives the acute danger behind Altair's ostensible preparations for an elaborate feast and calls for help from her divine protector Poseidon. Hence at the precise moment when Helena and Menelas fall into each other's arms, not only does Altair have Menelas seized and put in chains, but an impressive band of armed men suddenly appears, 'motionless, like a wall', reducing Altair's warriors to powerlessness by their mere presence.

Moreover, miraculously and inexplicably, Hermione, the daughter of Helena and Menelas, of whom we have heard in the first act, now also appears. She is on horseback, radiant and resplendent, and as she is led on she innocently asks for her beautiful mother. Altair becomes aware of Aithra's intercession and in abject despair acknowledges defeat. At the same time Menelas, freed from Altair's bonds, is reunited with his wife and daughter. As the royal couple prepare to mount the horses brought for them, the curtain falls.

Strauss's main task was to create some sense of unified progression, of climactic shape, from these heterogeneous elements. This he tried to accomplish by organizing his musical scheme into sections, each building towards one of the turning points in Hofmannsthal's text.

The first of these sections deals with the effect of Da-ud's death upon Helena and Menelas. It begins with Da-ud's cortège, an extended funeral-march based on Da-ud's themes (Exx. 34 and 35) and those of Menelas' revenge (Exx. 25 and 26). In the mourning scene which follows Ex. 36 is prominently featured as Helena, gently and with the understanding born of devoted love, confronts her perplexed husband with his cruel and unnecessary crime. The music here reflects his confusion with some interesting excursions into polytonality, in which Ex. 31 plays an outstanding part.

Altair's threats and prophecies of disaster (Exx. 32 and 38) at first scarcely interrupt the sequence of ideas as Helena probes Menelas' mind, bringing memories of Paris and the many dead (Exx. 16 and 17) to the surface. At last, with Ex. 36 reaching a climax of intensity, Helena's love pierces Menelas' defences. A glimmer of memory returns (Ex. 37), he becomes overwhelmed with his guilt and vows to follow Da-ud in death. This leads naturally to Helena's determination to administer without delay the Draught of Recollection and hence to the completion of the potion-brewing which was earlier interrupted by Altair's sudden intrusion. Confusion is added by the accelerated preparations for Altair's feast (evoked by the strains of the off-stage Arabian music) and by the renewed warnings of Aithra and her servants. Through all this mêlée Ex. 37 pursues its path in a series of varied ostinati combining with the continuous wailing of the Arab band. The section closes with Helena's jubilant accouncement that her own feast is about to begin. The potion is brewed and ready for serving.

The second of Strauss's subsections takes the drama to the scene in which Helena and Menelas both drink the potion and look into each other's eyes in the immediate expectation of death.[33] This, therefore, completes the drama of marriage, the polemic kernel of the opera. All the more confusing elements are concentrated into the earlier part in which an orchestral tutti, based on the Arab music, is followed by a somewhat dreary chorus of Altair's slaves formally inviting Helena (Ex. 33) to the banquet. This was the only place in which Hofmannsthal could motivate his *coup de théatre* and he therefore incorporated Aithra's cry for help to Poseidon. But Strauss, his eye fixed on less obscure dramatic issues ahead, whisked past this necessary piece of explanation with no more than a pianissimo reference to Poseidon's Ex. 3, all too easily missed amongst the general conglomeration. Even the news of the approaching cohorts (sent instantaneously over the waters to Aithra) delivered in a rapid exchange between Aithra and her servant, and set to a few bars of appropriately aquatic music, fails to make clear this somewhat unrealistic sequence of events.

Aithra's continued warnings are brushed aside by Menelas, who sings with Helena the duet which culminates in the drinking of the potion. In this way Strauss was able to turn the duet into the climax of the opera rather than the obvious theatrical climaxes which follow. Nor was this inconsistent with Hofmannsthal's scheme, for in it he had tried to solve the elaborate riddles and arguments of all the previous duets, and Strauss in his turn aimed at welding together his own thematic material into a musical argument worthy of the occasion. The relationship between Exx. 30 and 37 is firmly established at last, the harmonic distortions posed by Ex. 31 are resolved, and Helena's themes are brought into conjunction with that of her love, Ex. 36, while the Phantom theme, Ex. 27, also hovers about.[34] Helena herself sings her declaration of faith in love to a

---

[33] Despite Hofmannsthal's protests, the analogy with Wagner is devastating; nor is it materially altered by the fact that, whereas Menelas expects death as the result of the potion, Helena awaits it at the point of Menelas' sword.

[34] Hofmannsthal reluctantly arranged with Strauss for a cut in the libretto although it meant 'leaving out Menelas' anxiety that, if Helena be a phantom, all the Greeks have died for a hallucination (. . . an important, profound idea).'

23

recapitulation of her 'Helen of Troy' motif, Ex. 11, and at last, following her example, Menelas puts the goblet to his lips and drinks.

For a moment it seems as if he will slay her, and smiling to Aithra she prepares to die. Ex. 31 thunders out on the trombones followed by the retribution music, Ex. 26, while the Remembrance theme rushes around compressed first into savage triplets and then tearing semiquavers. In desperation Aithra has called out to Helena that she must live, for her child is even now being brought to her.

Suddenly Menelas drops his sword (Ex. 31 disintegrates in the basses), opens his arms and sings a panegyric to Helena. This time Strauss parades his motifs one at a time; Death (Ex. 16), Living, i.e. Awakening (Ex. 28), Helena the woman (Ex. 8), Helen of Troy (Ex. 11), Helena the epitome of sensual attraction (Ex. 10), and at last Helena the supremely beautiful woman of all time (Ex. 9). As Menelas warms to his subject the other relevant themes join in, headed by Ex. 36 and including fragments of Ex. 27, though no longer the whole of that 'Phantom' motif, for this illusion of Aithra's making has also been dispelled. Even poor Da-ud's theme (Ex. 34) returns when Helena sings of Menelas' repentance. In the last few bars Aithra joins the lovers, blessing their reunion which, she says, could never have been achieved without so much past suffering.

Into the third of Strauss's sections fall Hofmannsthal's *Dei ex machina*. Altair's vain attempts at impeding the course of events provide a last and dramatic return of his motifs, Aithra's armed cohorts appear against stern enunciations of Poseidon's Ex. 3, and Hermione (surely one of the most ungrateful roles in all opera) sings her handful of notes against repetitions of the chromatic Ex. 15, for she is the visual embodiment of the Reconciliation symbol.

The remainder is pure coda based on motifs of Helena and Menelas, while the themes of beauty and happiness (Exx. 21, 22 and 23) are also reintroduced and combined as at the end of Act 1. Menelas sings of his daughter's good fortune in having such a mother and, as they mount their horses, joins Helena in a final invocation to the elements which are to waft them safely back to their kingdom.

Strauss worked hard, possibly too hard, piling climax upon climax in his struggle to make the elaborate end convincing, and he must have been profoundly discouraged suddenly to receive a letter from Hofmannsthal containing plans for a whole extra scene of the utmost sentimentality which was to be tagged on. The new appendix had been suggested in principle to Hofmannsthal by his friend Dr Eger, a prominent Austrian theatre manager and at that time director of the Berlin State Theatre. Eger had felt (by no means without reason) that the end was grandiose rather than gay, that Aithra was left out in the cold, and that the absence of any trace of eroticism in a piece about the most beautiful woman in the world would leave the audience blank and dissatisfied. He had expressed these pungent views so tactfully that Hofmannsthal ended up in entire agreement and worked out an extra scene in which, against all his original intentions, Poseidon really was to appear in person:

> 'a *young beautiful silent* Poseidon, a scream of Aithra's, and a sinking on to the bed—enraptured and divine, divine and exalted beyond pain, beyond all the suffering of human kind ... Poseidon, holding the silver trident, raven hair, wholly beautiful (a dancer) ... Aithra flings herself round ... her lips utter an ardent: "Ah!" not a fierce cry, but like a dove, almost as if it were laughter ... Curtain.'

To say that Strauss was dubious would be to put it mildly, and in his reply, together with some highly practical objections, he made some entertaining counter-proposals on *Flying Dutchman* lines:

> 'Wouldn't it be possible to have Poseidon appear with the Men in Armour, standing on a cliff above them, to have Aithra ... throw herself into his embrace, and to have them all, including the Men in Armour, swallowed up by the sea ... or else, instead of the spirits from the sea, have a ship appear in the background. ...'

Hofmannsthal quickly retreated and decided to leave matters as they were, for fear (like Hilaire Belloc) of finding something worse.

14

It was a failure; despite some deceptively good houses during the first year it was unquestionably the worst failure they had yet suffered. Whether the standard of the first performances was responsible to any appreciable extent is debateable. Certainly Hofmannsthal was far from satisfied with the casting and even Strauss had occasional qualms over the way the preparations were being handled.

- A serious bone of contention had always been the role of Helena herself. Hofmannsthal insisted that the opera would fall to the ground unless the Prima Donna really was the most beautiful woman imaginable. But here he was thrown into opposition with Strauss who was above all a professional musician. However much Strauss might pay

lip-service to Hofmannsthal's claims to absolute equality when it came
to performance he always managed to ensure that the musical side had
first priority.

Worse still, when it came to singers Hofmannsthal was not only up
against Strauss but also the strong-willed Pauline, to whom he was
practically allergic. It was to an appreciable extent on her account that
Hofmannsthal resisted Strauss's repeated invitations to Garmisch (preferring to stay in a hotel on his infrequent visits), and her constant interference, her often vitriolic opinions, set his teeth on edge. In the casting
of Helena she had the most decided views to which, since she was herself
a fine and experienced singer, Strauss was highly deferential. While
there was a question of Jeritza[35] singing the title role all went smoothly,
but unfortunately the negotiations broke down and a substitute had to
be found. This was easier said than done, as Jeritza was quite exceptional
in being beautiful, a fine actress and a fabulous singer. After some hesitation Strauss decided on Elisabeth Rethberg, an excellent singer though
with less striking qualifications as actress and beauty. Immediately, he
was subjected to torrents of abuse from Hofmannsthal:

> 'I am utterly struck dumb by your letter. How am I to recon-
> cile all this. You want me to write something new for you,
> and yet at the same time you inflict on me what I consider
> more loathsome than anything else that could happen. It
> looks as if, although we have known each other for so long,
> and mean well by each other, you have not the least idea of
> what it is in our collaboration that gives me pleasure and
> what has the opposite effect. I do not think there is anyone
> who knows me so little. . . . This opera is not a dead certainty,
> I am well aware of that, but it has very real chances of
> genuine success on the stage, provided the histrionic ele-
> ments go hand in hand with the musical ones . . . Mme
> Rethberg may sing like a nightingale, I understand nothing
> about that . . . this will ruin Helena, completely ruin her . . .
> one must not simply be out for what is most easy and con-
> venient . . . how can one give in so easily in so *vital* a matter !
> Just remember what a fight Wagner used to put up for this
> sort of thing, for the *performers*, for the suitability of a singer
> as an actress. Are you really so indifferent to the fate of your
> works on the stage ? . . . I am a poet, but not a man of the
> theatre, you are not primarily a dramatist either (but some-
> where between this and a symphonist) or else you would

[35] Strauss had first seen Jeritza in a Munich production of none other than
Offenbach's *La Belle Helène*.

have redeemed *my* blunders on occasion and would not
have written yourself a libretto like that for *Intermezzo*
which consists of static tableaux rather than compelling if
commonplace *action*. . . .'

Strauss was stung to a sharp reply:

'Why do you always turn so poisonous the moment artistic
questions have to be discussed in a business-like manner and
you don't share my opinion? To accuse me immediately of
not understanding you is neither polite nor just. If I may say
so, I think I have understood you a good deal sooner than
many other people; otherwise I wouldn't have put your
books to music against the advice of the most "competent"
people—among whom theatre managers and critics are as a
rule included. . . .'

But Hofmannsthal had already seen that this time he had let his
temper get the better of him and wrote again immediately in quite
profuse apology:

'Please forgive my outburst: I am really sometimes very
vehement, even more so than I show . . . I ask you now to
expunge the whole thing from your memory. . . .'

Nevertheless in his rebukes there were many uncomfortable truths
and near-truths and, moreover, he had a real complaint over Strauss's
actions in appointing both the producer and designer without even
mentioning the matters to him.

In the end Strauss had his way and Rethberg gave the first performance which took place in Dresden on 6th June 1928. On the other hand
there was considerable compensation in the bringing forward of the
Vienna production from September to a date only five days later than
that of the Dresden opening. For Jeritza did sing in Vienna, which could
afford her immense fee, and the production was by the greatly gifted
Lothar Wallerstein, of whom more will be heard in due course. Strauss
himself conducted in Vienna, while the Dresden première was entrusted
to Fritz Busch.

The distinguished repetiteur and conductor Leo Wurmser was on
the staff of the Dresden State Opera at the time and has written amusingly
and pungently on what took place:

'In 1928 we gave the world première of *Die Aegyptische Helena*
conducted by Busch and produced by Erhardt. At that time
there were not very many first class singers on the staff of the
Dresden Opera. Strauss was very fussy about the casting, and
his wife even more so. Nevertheless there was still enough

importance attached to a Dresden première for him to agree
to have the first night there. Elisabeth Rethberg, who had
begun her career in Dresden, was brought across from the
Metropolitan to sing the title part in the first performances.
Aithra was sung by Mario Rajdl; Menelas by Kurt Taucher;
and Altair by Fritz Plaschke. The small part of Da-ud was
sung by a young Italian tenor, Guglielmo Fazzini, who had
a high tenor voice, whereas the part lies rather low, and here
Strauss showed that he did not insist on the notes he had
written being sung, and was willing to alter them to suit the
singer. Busch had been ill for some weeks while the opera
was being prepared, and had not taken part in the piano and
stage rehearsals. When he returned to work he was busy with
the orchestra and only took one or two piano rehearsals with
the principals. My colleague Ernst Richter and I, who had
prepared the opera, tried to indicate the tempi from the piano
and Busch, as was often his habit if he did not know an
opera very well, let us lead and more or less followed us.
But when he was at the rostrum we could not help him, and
things began to go wrong.

Strauss came to the final rehearsals, seemed on the whole
more interested in the production than in the music and
wanted several things altered. Pauline, who sat in the first
row of the stalls, to everybody's consternation, clamoured
for horses on the stage which had not been provided. At the
end of Act 1 she cried: "That isn't enough thunder! We
want more thunder here". After a whispered consultation
with her, Strauss called to Erhardt: "All right Dr Erhardt,
let's have more thunder" and added aside to the orchestra,
"Die Weiber sind immer für's Donnern". At the first
dress rehearsal he sat in the stalls following the score at a
lighted desk. I sat nearby taking notes. He listened patiently
to the end of the first act and then went forward and said to
Busch: "Wissen's 'was, lieber Busch, lassen's mich den Akt
noch a mal dirigieren!" So we had a break and then Act 1 all
over again with Strauss at the rostrum. It was like a different
opera; one big broad line from beginning to end, the right
tempi and rubatos, co-operation with the singers and many
of the $\frac{4}{4}$ passages beaten in 2. Busch now sat in the stalls
following the score and I sat beside him, trying tactfully to
point out what Strauss did differently.' [36]

[36] 'Richard Strauss as an opera conductor'. *Music and Letters*, January 1964. I
shall have occasion to return to Wurmser's articles when discussing Strauss's position and prestige as a conductor in Volume III. Wurmser was devoted to Strauss
and in his eulogies writes disparagingly of other world-famous conductors besides
Fritz Busch.

It would however be quite wrong to leave the impression that Busch was guilty of bad workmanship and insufficient knowledge of the score. He had studied it closely with Strauss personally and Karl Alwin who prepared the opera for Strauss's own Vienna production paid tribute to Busch's insight and understanding in, for example, suggesting improvements to the dynamic range of the closing duet, which Strauss readily incorporated into a revised ending.

The poor reception of the work was, on the contrary, due to its intrinsic shortcomings. Some critics sympathized with Strauss over the impossible libretto (it is touching to observe Strauss conciliating Hofmannsthal with extravagant praise when this happened), others included him in the general indictment, such as one reviewer who described the opera as 'ponderous, complicated and apathetic . . . its dreariness a libel on the vivacious Helen of Troy . . . [nothing] could hide the fact that neither Hofmannsthal nor Strauss was any longer anything more than mediocre'.

Such a judgement is savage but typical of widely held opinion. Even so loyal a follower as Strauss's biographer Richard Specht found the musical style dated.

The composer himself was by no means unaware of its faults. Stefan Zweig wrote:

'Once I sat alone with him at a private rehearsal of his *Egyptian Helena* in the Salzburg Festival Theatre. Nobody else was there, the place was completely dark. Strauss listened intently. All at once he began to drum inaudibly and impatiently with his fingers upon the arm of the chair. Then he whispered to me: "Bad, very bad! That spot is blank." And again, after a few minutes: "If I could cut that out! O Lord, Lord, that's just hollow, and too long, much too long!" A little later: "Look, that's good!" He appraised his own work as objectively and unconcernedly as if he were hearing the music for the first time and as if it were written by a composer unknown to him; and this astounding sense of his own dimensions never deserted him.'[37]

Yet Strauss was loath to leave the opera to its fate. Some years later he approached Wallerstein to help him revise the second act which he had always felt to be lame and messy. He no longer had to consider the inevitable protests from Hofmannsthal as in the meantime the poet had

[37] *The World of Yesterday.* Cassell, 1943.

died. It has been suggested that Hofmannsthal himself had some revisions of his own in mind, but there is no positive evidence of this and on the contrary he had described even the controversial second act as 'transcendental and subtle', commenting that admittedly after a great deal of hard work Strauss had succeeded in making it theatrically convincing.

Although now forced to rely largely on his own intuition, Strauss was at least able to turn to Wallerstein for advice in tidying up the obscurities of the action, and Wallerstein agreed to provide some extra lines of his own where nothing of Hofmannsthal could be found to fit the reorganized passages.

The first act was left untouched, but the alterations to Act 2 were considerable, involving an appreciable amount of fresh composition. The first emendation is relatively straightforward: it occurs at the turning-point of the act where Menelas flings off to the hunt leaving Helena with a short monologue before Aithra's sudden appearance. Hofmannsthal's text was certainly unfathomable here, though Strauss had got out of the difficulty by his effective use of the Wagnerian link (see above, p. 335) in which the enigmatic lines (e.g. 'how to return—this is the art! Aithra's goblet was too strong and not strong enough for Menelas' heart') were swallowed up by the musical design. He now decided, nevertheless, that this passage ought in some way to prepare the audience for Aithra's entrance.

Wallerstein accordingly changed Helena's monologue into a clearer exposition of Aithra's failure with the first potion and a plea for new aid to annul its effect. This revised text Strauss then set to fresh music actually some eight bars shorter than the original but unfortunately reverting to the stronger dramatic level of the preceding bars. Thus the gain in textual comprehensibility has to be weighed against the loss of an excellent musical moment of aftermath and gloomy repose.

The next alterations are more complicated. Strauss was worried by the way in which many of the events interrupted each other and had to return later in order to reach one by one their various conclusions: the potion brewing, Altair's courtship, the maid-servants' description of the hunt, and so on. How much better, he thought, to take out of their original contexts all the bits of each episode and lump them together at some point where their importance and relevance to the main action would be clearest and most effective.

So Strauss completely excised the first potion-brewing and transferred it to the middle of scene 4 (with some new lines for Helena and Menelas in place of Helena's original quarrel with Aithra) where it now altogether replaces the second potion-brewing (see p. 339). Altair's courtship scene therefore comes much sooner and is itself both abridged and also simplified by the removal of the bars describing the hunt, which all come together at the end of the same scene.

The loss of the second potion-brewing presented a difficulty, since it had been intermingled with the preparations for Altair's feast. This, by developing the Arab music, had led to an orchestral tutti via a striking and declamatory use of Helena's words about 'starting her own feast'. The sacrifice here was considerable and Strauss decided that Helena's words ought to be kept somehow, if perhaps incorporated later on. In the meantime the old potion-brewing music was linked to its new continuation by means of an entirely original trio for Aithra, Helena and Menelas.

This substantial insertion required a new section of text and Wallerstein began with an extended solo for Aithra featuring her appeal to Poseidon, for which Strauss, recognising his part in the weakness of the original, also took the opportunity of bringing Poseidon's Ex. 3 into unmistakeable prominence. As a result both the new solo and the succeeding trio are certainly amongst the positive gains of the revised version, both musically and dramatically, although the succeeding orchestral tutti follows less naturally than out of the music of the first version for which it had been planned as the climax.

The confused and ineffective passage describing the progress of Poseidon's cohorts had now been made redundant and Strauss's last task was completely to rewrite this so as to preserve only some brief reference in both text and music to Altair's activities, Aithra's warning of the sinister and misleading nature of these festive ceremonies (made directly explicit by Wallerstein in place of Hofmannsthal's subtle hints), and Helena's line about her own feast, which here found a suitable place for reinsertion.[38]

The alterations was complete by the end of 1932 and put in charge of Clemens Krauss who by this time had become Strauss's favourite

---

[38] These complicated revisions are very clearly set out in side by side comparison by William Mann in his study of the operas (Cassell, 1964) and are also described in close detail by Tenschert in a pamphlet (Fürstner, 1934) which latter, however, assumes too readily that every change is a masterstroke.

conductor and a close colleague. Krauss was not entirely happy about all the revisions, even preferring the original in some instances. He outlined his carefully reasoned objections and proposals in a letter to which both he and Wallerstein subscribed their names. But Strauss had lost interest, and in any case realized that no amount of patching would ever enable an audience actually to understand what the piece was all about.

The first performance of the revised score was given at the 1933 Salzburg Festival on 14th August, with Viorica Ursuleac, Krauss's wife, in the title role, and since that time this is the version which is normally heard in its periodic revivals. But it had been a vain idea that by transplanting or clarifying the work of his dead collaborator, against his certain wish, Strauss could bring the piece back to life. Apart from Munich, where nearly all of Strauss's operas are performed in rotation over the years, and Vienna, whose opera company gave birth to the new edition, *Die Aegyptische Helena* is hardly ever brought out of limbo.

However much Strauss might sardonically resent Specht's mild criticisms ('even ... my biographer, Herr Specht, considers it old-fashioned that nowadays I have *only* the ambition to 'make beautiful music'), the 'pretty tunes' he had taken a holiday in Greece to find had indeed been no substitute for the white heat inspirations of earlier days. The music, despite many beautiful and soaring passages, reflects all his manner and much of his skill but very little of his genius. Above all Strauss could not bring any of the characters to life, since he himself had never been able to believe in them.

As the poetic grandeur of the text is weighted down by Hofmannsthal's dialectics and symbolism, so the final effect of the opera is overloaded by the continual thickness of Strauss's polyphony at its most Wagnerian. Of his earliest intentions, the set pieces separated by light recitative, even spoken dialogue, nothing whatever remains. Finding Hofmannsthal's poetry so delightfully easy to set, Strauss had day by day clothed it in the gorgeous vocal and orchestral apparel which always flowed so readily from him.

And yet, although seen in the panorama of his output *Die Aegyptische Helena* must remain at one of the lowest ebbs, there are some elements within it which look forward to the pure ethereal beauty of his last period. The soaring soprano cantilena of Helena's aria at the beginning of Act 2, a long-established speciality of Strauss, has a new simplicity and quality of ecstasy. The duet of Helena and Aithra is an elaboration of the same device but is curiously enthralling in a way Strauss was able to develop magically in the next opera, *Arabella*. Even the banal Da-ud theme finds its sublimation in that far greater work in which Strauss was able, his feet once again firmly on the ground, to make capital out of the experience he had acquired with this ill-fated work, on the surface hardly more than the product of a great but facile mind.

CHAPTER XVI

AN AMALGAM OF VOCAL MUSIC

I

ALL THROUGH his long life Strauss produced a quantity of vocal music of all kinds, from arrangements of folk-songs and whole classical operas to original compositions for large choruses with or without orchestral accompaniment. The last of these to have been surveyed in chronological sequence was the setting of Goethe's *Wanderers Sturmlied*, composed in 1885 (see Vol. I, pp. 32–35) and it is now time to bring this category of Strauss's output up to date. The songs for solo voice however, remain outside the scope of this chapter as they require a section to themselves which will, in Volume III, round off the complete picture of Strauss's life work.

Apart from Lieder the period of Strauss's early maturity, that of the early tone-poems, produced little vocal music of importance. A four-part male chorus to words by Löwe, a setting of part of Kleist's *Hermannsschlacht* which will be discussed a little later in this chapter and a *Scherzquartett*, also for male voices, composed for a Swedish matchbox manufacturer, are separated by a curious group of pieces already mentioned briefly in Volume I.[1] Recently discovered in the archives of the Munich Nationaltheater, these are fragments of incidental music supposedly composed by Strauss for a production of *Romeo and Juliet* in 1887 when Strauss was 3rd Kapellmeister in Munich, and were published, together with a detailed commentary by Hermann Friess, in the Strauss Jahrbuch 1959–60.[2]

[1] See Vol. I, p. 51.   [2] Boosey and Hawkes. Bonn, 1960.

There are four little pieces, the first of which purports to come from Act 1 of the drama and consists of a *Tanzlied zur Moresca* ('Lasst sie tanzen, sie tanzt so bewegt', etc.) for two sopranos with accompaniment of small orchestra with harp in $\frac{6}{4}$ time. The second piece comes from Act 2 and, described as a *Träller-Lied*, is for unaccompanied voices in unison. The third, *Vor dem Hochzeitsbette*, is a bridal procession for female voices, woodwind and triangle ('In diesem Bett, mit Tüchern reich erlesen'). Lastly comes a short *Trauermusik* for woodwind alone, playing pianissimo throughout.

These sketches, for they are hardly more than that, are mysterious as well as disappointing since they show no vestige of Strauss's style, while the words of the three choral sections are not even by Shakespeare. In spite of the evidence of the manuscript their authenticity is doubtful, to say the least. In any case they are wholly unimportant and only interesting in the conjectures to which they give rise concerning the young Strauss's possible activities in the theatre five years before venturing into the field of opera with *Guntram*.

Yet *Guntram* did not initiate his creative contact with the theatre. In 1889 one of his first ventures on taking up his appointment at the Weimar Court Theatre was to prepare a full-scale revised edition of Gluck's *Iphigénie en Tauride*. In doing this he followed closely in the footsteps of Wagner, under whose spell he had by then completely fallen.

Wagner had made a complete revision for the German stage of Gluck's earlier companion-piece *Iphigénie en Aulide*, changing the end of the overture, revising the orchestration to a considerable extent, adapting and rewriting the recitatives, and actually introducing an entirely new character, Artemis, after the Euripides version of the myth.

Strauss imitated this august example up to a point, though he found no need for anything as drastic as either an extension to the cast list or to the orchestra as a whole (Wagner had added third and fourth horns and a third trumpet). On the other hand such resources as were available he used to a far greater extent than Gluck had done, enlivening by this means the opening storm music and the battle towards the end of the opera, while he also used the full orchestral range to vary the texture and emphasize the dramatic impact of the recitatives, many of which he completely rewrote. He made a number of cuts, sometimes of no more than a few bars in order to tighten the musical scheme, but often of a more radical nature.

The most extensive alterations are in the first and last acts. In Act 1 he changed the order of the numbers and actually used Iphigénie's aria 'O toi qui prolongeas mes jours' to end the act. Acts 3 and 4 he coupled together by means of a *Verwandlung* (quick scene-change) while the finale of the opera he revised considerably, changing Orestes' 'Dans cet objet touchant' into a trio with chorus for Iphigénie, Orestes and Pylades. Many of these more elaborate revisions are linked by a new motif of Strauss's own invention,

Ex. 1

Appearing first during one of the initial recitatives, Ex. 1 can be traced through the opera in connexion with Iphigénie's instinctive sympathy for the stranger whom she is required to sacrifice to the gods and whom she eventually recognizes as her own brother Orestes.

In some places Strauss alters the words in order to clarify or intensify the action, and as a result his complete retranslation of the text becomes an integral part of the version which he describes as being specifically 'arranged for the German stage'.[3]

An outline scheme of the work will make clear the formal construction as presented by Strauss:

Strauss's score containing from	*Gluck's original*
Act 1	**Act 1**
Scene 1 'Ihr Götter, seid uns Armen hülfreich!'	Scene 1 No. 1 Introduction and Chorus: 'Grands dieux! soyez-nous secourables'
(No. 2 is telescoped with the recitative which follows it)	No. 2 Chorus: 'Ô songe affreux'
Scene 2 'Besänftigt ist der Götter Zorn'	Scene 3 No. 6 Chorus: 'Les Dieux apaisent leur courroux'[4]
	Scene 2 No. 5 Aria (Thaos): 'De noirs pres- (part) sentiments'
Scene 3 'Blut sühnet alle Schuld'—the repeat of the chorus linking directly (by means of a diminuendo and Ex. 1) into:	Scene 4 No. 7 Chorus: 'Il nous fallait du sang'
	No. 8 Ballet
	No. 9 Ballet
	Scene 5 No. 10 Ballet, Scene and Chorus: 'Malheureux! Quel dessein'
Scene 4 'O du, die mich in Aulis schützte'[5]	Scene 1 No. 3 Aria (Iphigénie): 'Ô toi, qui prolongeas mes jours'

---

[3] The previous standard German translation was by Peter Cornelius, the well-known friend of Liszt and composer of the opera *The Barber of Baghdad*.

[4] Strauss ingeniously presents this chorus off-stage with a stage band of wind and percussion only.

[5] This reference to the other Iphigenie opera was Strauss's invention, though he did not accompany it by any appropriate musical quotation.

Strauss's score	containing from	Gluck's original
Act 2		Act 2
Scene 1 'Welche grau'nvolle Stille'		Scene 1 No. 11 Recit: 'Quel silence effrayant!' No. 12 Aria (Orestes): 'Dieux! qui me poursuivez' No. 13 Aria (Pylades): 'Unis dès la plus tendre enfance' Scene 2 (Recit: 'Étrangers malheureux')
Scene 2 'Ihr, die das Land des wilden Volkes schützet'		Scene 3 (Recit: 'Dieux! protecteurs de ces affreux rivages') No. 14 Aria (Orestes): 'La calme rentre dans mon coeur' Scene 4 No. 15 Chorus: 'Vengeons et la nature'
Scene 3 'Welch ein Graun fasst dich an'		Scene 5 (Recit: 'Je vois toute l'horreur') Scene 6 (Recit: 'Ô ciel! De mes tourments')
Scene 4 'O armes Land' (Nos. 17 and 18 both slightly abridged)		No. 16 Chorus: 'Patrie infortunée' No. 17 Aria (Iphigénie): 'Ô malheureuse Iphigénie!' No. 18 Chorus: 'Contemplez ces tristes apprêts'

Act 3		Act 3
Scene 1 'So sei es denn gewagt'		Scene 1 No. 19 Recitative and Aria (Iphigénie) 'D'une image hélas! trop chérie'
Scene 2 'Die Fremden, die du befahlst'		Scene 2 (Recit: 'Voici ces captifs malheureux') Scene 3 (Recit: 'Ô joie inattendue!') No. 20 Trio: 'Je pourrais du tyran'
Scene 3 'Welche selige Wahl' (No. 21 greatly cut down, though there is more music in the full score than in the vocal score and orchestral parts)		Scene 4 No. 21 Duet: 'Et tu prétends encore' No. 22 Aria (Pylades): 'Ah! mon ami, j'implore ta pitié'
Scene 4 'Wie du auch flehst'		Scene 5 (Recit: 'Malgré toi, je saurai t'arracher') Scene 7 No. 23 Aria (Pylades): 'Divinité des grandes âmes'

Verwandlung		Act 4
Scene 5 'Weh'mir, der Abend naht' (Strauss composed an entirely new introduction to the recitative)		Scene 1 No. 24 Recitative and Aria (Iphigénie): 'Non, cet affreux devoir' ('Je t'implore et je tremble')[6]
Scene 6 'Grosse Göttin' (No. 25 is linked to No. 24 through the omission of the ritornello)		Scene 2 No. 25 Chorus: 'Ô Diane, sois nous propice' No. 26 Hymn: 'Chaste fille de Latone'
Scene 7 and final scene: 'Erbebt! Deine Tat ist entdeckt' (Nos. 27–8 greatly altered, Orestes' arietta 'Dans cet objet touchant' converted into the Trio 'Iphigenie, O welch' ein holdes Glück!')		Scene 3 (Recit: 'Tremblez! On sait tout le mystère!') Scene 4 ⎱ No. 27 Aria and Scena (Thaos): Scene 5 ⎰ 'De tes forfaits la trame est Scene 6 ⎰ découverte' Last scene No 28 Final Chorus: 'Les Dieux longtemps en courroux'

---

[6] This aria is one of the most remarkable features of Gluck's score, being derived directly from the Gigue of Bach's Clavier Partita No. 1 in B flat.

At various productions ballet music was added before the second and during the last act, but this was the individual concern of the different conductors and never formed part of Strauss's score. The music for this purpose was generally drawn from other Gluck operas such as *Orfeo* and *Armide*.

Some mystery attends the first performance of Strauss's work. It seems highly improbable that the new musical director of the Weimar Court Opera would have celebrated his appointment by preparing so thorough and elaborate a transcription and not carry it through to performance. Yet records are lacking to show that it was given in Weimar until 1900 (six years after Strauss had left) when it is known that it was produced on 9th June under the baton of Rudolf Krzyanowski. By that time, however, Strauss had been including it in his Berlin syllabus for at least two years in conjunction with Wagner's version of *Iphigénie en Aulide* and was now writing disconsolately to his parents to say that it had been temporarily dropped, though 'it would come back at the first favourable opportunity'.

Such opportunities did certainly occur and it has been fairly regularly revived at intervals. Nevertheless it cannot be said to have served its original purpose of bringing Gluck's work up to date and hence into the standard current repertory any more than Wagner's *Iphigénie* had done. As Dr Hermann Abert wrote, rather touchingly:

> 'The number of performances of the two works has not been
> significantly raised through their arrangements. That Gluck
> has generally become so rare a visitor to the stages of today
> may be regrettable but also very understandable. Gluck's
> works are no repertoire pieces, but festival art for people of
> good will and pure in heart.'

2

In 1897 Strauss felt he wanted to pay some practical compliment to his friend Ernst von Possart. Possart was an eminent actor who had two years before replaced Strauss's old enemy Perfall as Intendant of the Munich Court Opera, and had been influential in confirming Strauss's promotion to chief conductor after Levi resigned in 1896.

Possart had for many years specialized in the art of recitation and Strauss determined to write a work in which he could accompany him on the piano, a scheme which might lead to some agreeable concert tours

and cement a valuable and cordial friendship. His choice fell on Tennyson's *Enoch Arden*, a substantial piece of Victoriana which would give
Possart ample scope. An adequate translation had been published by one
Adolf Strodtmann some ten years previously and on this Strauss based
his setting which was completed on 26th February and first performed
within the month by Strauss and Possart.

Exactly as they had hoped, the Munich première was followed by tours
round the theatres of Germany and it was in fact during one of these that
Strauss received the news of the birth of his son Franz. Slight as it is,
Enoch Arden seems to have been an inordinate success, and had the
gratifying consequence of adding considerably to Strauss's reputation,
surprising in so unrewarding and problematic a medium.

Whether in order to avoid obscuring Possart's performance with the
distraction of too much music; whether because Strauss wanted this
affecting narrative verse tragedy to create its own effect; or whether
simply because he found the sentimentality of the extensive poem stimulating to only a limited degree, at all events, Strauss's contribution is
remarkably scanty, leaving immense passages entirely unaccompanied.

On the whole it is just the corner-stones of the story that are pin-
pointed: the childhood triangle of Enoch, Philip and Annie; Enoch's
successful courtship and Philip's self-effacement; Enoch's farewell and
departure to sea; Philip's own subsequent courtship of Annie; Annie's
dream and marriage to Philip; Enoch's lonely and discouraging years on
his south-sea island; his return, bent and aged, to spy unseen upon the
domestic bliss of Philip and Annie; his despair and saintly vows of
abnegation; and finally his last gift to Annie and death.

In between come the long dramatic details of the narrative, often up
to fifty, a hundred or even more lines at a time, of pure declamation, in
view of which Strauss's method of applying *leit-motifs* to link the utterly
disconnected fragments gives the all too necessary unity to the piece as a
whole. Here, for example, is Annie Lee:

Ex. 2   Philip: Ex. 3

24

and Enoch Arden himself: Ex. 4

The three themes are oddly memorable and endearing, especially bearing in mind the limited opportunity Strauss allows himself to develop them. They are also undeniably soft-grained to the point of sentimentality but this is in keeping with the period of the drama, in which every character behaves impeccably from beginning to end.

None of the more vivid events in the story are outlined in music—Enoch's wedding, his broken limb, above all his shipwreck. The only atmospheric music is the rolling of the breakers which are so strong a feature of Enoch's home village with its cliffs and little port. This is portrayed in the theme with which the work begins and which is recalled poignantly by the parallel sea-noises as Enoch waits year after year to be rescued from the isolation of his tropical island.

Ex. 5

The melodrama is divided into two parts, each with its miniature prelude and each with a more extended musical section as the end is approached. Part 1 ends with Annie's dream, her wedding to Philip and the birth of their child, while Part 2 takes up the thread of Enoch's adventures from the moment he sets sail on his ill-fated voyage. It makes a well balanced scheme, the relative paucity of music in Part 2 (even by its own rigorous standards) being to some extent offset by the fervour of the passage describing Enoch's sufferings on witnessing the happiness which should by rights have been his.

Enoch Arden is still occasionally performed though by its very nature this can only be a rare event. Melodramas have never been a highly favoured form though constantly recurring as an operatic device or especially as part of incidental music in the theatre (viz. for example, Mendelssohn's *Midsummer Night's Dream*, or Strauss's own *Bourgeois Gentilhomme*). The problem of hearing the words in the spoken voice over music is acute, but has fascinated composers up to the present day, whether with piano, instrumental or even orchestral accompaniment. Strauss's models range from examples by Schubert and Schumann to the outstanding concert melodramas, Berlioz' *Lélio* and Grieg's *Bergliot*, the latter written in 1870 and orchestrated in 1885. In more recent years experiments combining speech and music on a number of different lines have been made by Schönberg, who was especially attracted to the form, by Walton in *Façade* and—best known of all—by Prokofieff in *Peter and the Wolf*. Even so, it has never been able to establish itself as a wholly successful medium.

Strauss produced one further example in 1899, two years after *Enoch Arden*, though on a far smaller scale: a setting of Uhland's *Das Schloss am Meer*. In contrast with Tennyson's poem, Uhland's is quite short and the music runs consecutively. The idea of the verses is a single tableau presented in a series of questions and answers. The interrogator asks after the majestic castle, painting a bright sunlit scene by the cheerful waves, the proud king and queen and above all the radiant princess. But the answers are uniformly gloomy and reach their climax as it emerges that the royal pair are mourning the recent death of their beautiful daughter.

There is plenty of scope for varied music full of contrasts, and Strauss dutifully goes through all the motions. The style strongly recalls Liszt:

Ex. 6

and achieves a warm lush climax when the princess is described, which
turns to an interesting moment of harsh polytonality as the grim truth is
revealed.

Ex. 7

Das Schloss am Meer was also written for Possart who first performed
it with Strauss in Berlin on 23rd March 1899. It was obviously composed
in order to make up the programme for these 'Recitation Evenings'
which otherwise contained similar pieces by composers such as Max
Schillings, a contemporary of Strauss and once highly thought of. But
like the works of Schillings, *Das Schloss am Meer* has long since disappeared. It may perhaps be indicative of its secondary purpose that
Strauss delayed its publication for twelve years and even then allotted it
no opus number.

3

In 1897, the same year as the composition of *Enoch Arden*, Strauss published his first music for a large unaccompanied mixed chorus, two part-
songs which appeared together as a pair: 'Der Abend' to words by
Schiller, and 'Hymne' on a Rückert poem.[7] Both divide the voices into
no less than sixteen parts but the distribution is different. In 'Der
Abend' each of the four conventional groups (Soprano, Alto, Tenor,
Bass) is itself subdivided into four lines, providing a variety of
resources from antiphonal blocks of sound to intricate polyphonic
weavings.

The style is a cross between Strauss's Lieder and the *Wanderers
Sturmlied* of thirteen years before, with the instrumental textures adapted
for voices with extraordinary ingenuity of invention.

[7] In his *Thematisches Verzeichnis* Azow makes the curious mistake of saying that
this is the same Rückert text as in the later *Deutsche Motette*, op. 62.

Ex. 8

The Rückert 'Hymne' suggested to Strauss a new arrangement of the voices. There are still sixteen parts but these are divided between two distinct choruses, the second approximately twice the size of the first. But whereas the first chorus is in the four main voice parts S.A.T.B., the second subdivides these again into three parts each, thus making up the sixteen but in slightly different proportions from the straightforward grouping of 'Der Abend', and with an entirely new lay-out with enhanced technical possibilities of antiphonal effect.

The motivating purpose lies in the refrain line of Rückert's poem which is echoed at the end of each verse, 'O gräme dich nicht', ('O do not sorrow'), and which is given entirely to the first chorus. The verses proper are therefore handled by the twelve-part second chorus, which is treated in a more genuinely contrapuntal manner than is to be found in 'Der Abend', though the alternation of block passages with polyphony can be found equally in both songs. Apart from their technical differences the two pieces are nicely contrasted in mood, the magical description of sunset in the first being offset dramatically by the enthusiastic opening of 'Hymne', as it hails the return of the prodigal son.

These *Gesänge* are all too little known and both their inherent difficulty, which is considerable, and the rarity of performances in the concert world of the present day by *a cappella* choruses of such mammoth proportions as they require, militate against them. Yet they represent an important facet of Strauss's output, and one he was to return to at intervals during his life.

The year 1899 saw the appearance of two further groups of unaccompanied male-voice choruses (op. 42 and 45) based entirely on the collection of folk-songs which are amongst the best known work of the eighteenth-century German poet Johann Gottfried von Herder, who lived for much of his life in Weimar. Although obviously minor compositions, these are by no means devoid of interest. The following passage, for instance, strongly suggests Schönberg's treatment of male voice choruses in the third part of *Gurrelieder*:

while the extreme range of the bass line a few bars later in the same song ('Lied der Freundschaft' from the op. 45 group)[8] reinforces the idea of Strauss's influence on the young Schönberg in his vocal writing.

Ex. 10

ver - lach'.___ ich Pein und Not,   geh' auf den Grund der Höl - len

The composition of so many choruses of this kind seems to have stemmed to some extent from Strauss's participation as adjudicator in choral competitions, an unexpected assignment, one might think, for a figure of such eminence as he had long since become. He added, however, a further half dozen folk-song arrangements in the same medium at the specific instigation of the Kaiser, the fruits of this labour being included in a large collection published by Peters in 1906.

4

In the summer of 1903, during the transition period after the completion of the tone-poems and *Feuersnot* but before Strauss fully found his feet in opera with the production of *Salome*, he received a commission to compose a work for the Centenary Jubilee of Heidelberg University, in acknowledgement of which 'thesis' he was to receive his doctorate.

It so happens that he had by now on the stocks a setting of Uhland's Ballade *Taillefer*, the sketches for which were far advanced and were thus drafted at the same period as those for *Sinfonia Domestica*. So obviously ideal for the purpose was this gigantic piece for chorus and orchestra that it would in a way be true to say that the work indirectly sponsored the commission.

It was a year earlier than the Heidelberg approach, during the April of 1902, that the first hesitant ideas for *Taillefer* had been jotted down. Strauss had been passing through a barren period caused by an exceptionally heavy conducting season, but the subject—the Battle of Hastings —amused him and once he had got back into the swing of composition

[8] Strauss's father accepted the dedication of these part-songs as a birthday present in preference to the Rückert Lieder, op. 46.

it had progressed more and more easily. By September he had begun the orchestration on 40-stave paper specially ordered from Paris, and from then on it was plain sailing.

The following April saw Strauss playing the work through to Siegfried Ochs, the conductor of the Philharmonic Choir in Berlin, in the hopes of a performance there during the autumn. But there were already other irons in the fire through Strauss's friend Philip Wolfrum, an influential choral composer and conductor in Heidelberg to whom Strauss had four years before dedicated the *a cappella* 'Hymne', op. 34, no. 2. Wolfrum not only suggested the idea of an August première for *Taillefer* in the newly built Heidelberg Town Hall, but went on to make himself personally responsible for coupling the occasion with a University commission and Strauss's doctorate.

At first Strauss doubted whether the 'fossilized old professors' at the University would approve his award *honoris causa*. However, towards the end of June the invitation duly came through,[9] though a slightly later date was fixed for the actual première, which took place on 26th October 1903.

If it were not for the irrefutable order of events in the above time-scale one would have thought that the work could only have been conceived for such a commission, so frankly does it savour of a festival *pièce d'occasion*. Uhland was always a most stirring writer and many of his poems have over the years taken on the character and popularity of folksongs. This particular ballad describes in heroic terms the Norman Conquest and especially the courageous part played in it by Taillefer, Duke William's favourite minstrel.

It is apparent from first to last that Strauss thoroughly enjoyed making the most of the gay text. There are beautiful and exciting solos for baritone, tenor and soprano representing respectively Duke William, Taillefer himself and the Duke's sister who is greatly taken with the young man. The chorus acts as narrator and commentator while the orchestra comes into its own with a graphic description of the Battle of Hastings in a splendid interlude which even outdoes the battle scene of *Heldenleben*. The whole score is carried forward impetuously and with a most infectious *élan* verging at times on the hilarious. At the half-way point the poem describes the effect upon the Normans of Taillefer's singing and Strauss matches this with a heroic song which for all its

---

[9] Strauss was enjoying his sea-side holiday in the Isle of Wight at the time. See Vol. I, p. 182.

obvious Jingoism is pleasurably unforgettable; it would make a marvellous National Anthem.

Ex. 11

From its first entry until its culminating restatements at the close of the work Ex. 11 recurs constantly in the texture suggesting the dauntless Taillefer leading the Duke and his warriors into the thickest fray. The other dominating elements in the score are first the flowing ¾ melody of the noble Duke with which it opens, and then the battle music headed by an energetic rhythmical theme treated in elaborate imitation as the whole work progresses:

Ex. 12

This long-drawn-out subject contains a number of useful motivic fragments which supply much of the material for the battle music. From the technical point of view it is here that the main interest lies and Strauss's vast orchestra[10] is treated with virtuosity and imagination. The

[10] He stipulates 145 players although, as in the *Festlisches Praeludium*, he uses no harps. He also adds in his foreword that the piece is clearly only suitable for large halls.

analogy with *Ein Heldenleben* is apt, and although the earlier tone-poem rates higher for its greater musical distinction the two passages are closely related.

The chorus is directed to be as large as possible in view of the orchestration and is handled throughout with bold simplicity, much of the time even in unison. There was no opportunity for intricate or subtle choral subdivided effects in so frankly flamboyant a work. It is of course this aspect of *Taillefer* which has caused it to lapse into a neglect which it shares with far inferior works. Although outrageously expensive for its sixteen minutes, it might well justify being brought back and dusted for special occasions.

5

Strauss's interest in the Bardic chorus from the Battle of Hermann dates from as early as 1886. Hermann, or Arminius, was the German chieftain who, in the beginning of the first century A.D., won a great battle against the Romans. His exploits were dramatized by two great poets, Kleist and Klopstock, writing—strange to say—within a few years of each other. The Kleist *Hermannsschlacht* was played in Meiningen in January 1886 and the performance was attended by the young Strauss in company with his mentor, Bülow.

A letter had just reached Strauss from the Grand Duke of Meiningen expressing dissatisfaction with the existing setting of the Bardic Song in the Kleist representation and asking Strauss to take over the task of re-composing it. Writing to his parents, Strauss commented ironically that perhaps if his work went down well with the Grand Duke he would be decorated.

Within the space of a month the chorus was complete. It was tried out on the stage and His Highness was well satisfied, though no decoration ensued that time. Strauss himself clearly thought less of the piece, as he withheld it from publication and it has since vanished. Nevertheless it remained at the back of his mind, and when in 1905 he wanted some larger offering for the Prussian Kaiser (for whom he was before long to write and arrange all those military marches) it occurred to him to try a new setting of the Bardic Song.[11]

[11] In the event, permission was not granted for this royal dedication although Strauss wrote to Count Hülsen asking for the Intendant's intercession on his behalf. The imperial ice was not broken until the incident of the marches a year or so later (see p. 268).

To work a second time with the identical words was, however, an uninteresting proposition, and for his new *Bardengesang* Strauss turned to the Klopstock drama which was in one respect eminently suitable. It is not only a much more ambitious scheme, being a trilogy, but is in prose interspersed with Bardic Choruses (called by Klopstock 'Bardiete') which, being detachable, might be said to cry out for music.

The fact that these impressive lines by the great Klopstock are, as Strauss's biographer Steinitzer acknowledges, almost empty and meaningless, deterred Strauss not at all and they provided him with a work which is, to quote Ernest Newman, 'magnificently barbaric, though it slightly tries one's gravity as the chorus thunders out the names of the tribes:

> Ha, ye Cheruseans! Ye Chattees! Ye Marsians! Ye Semno-nians! Ye Brukterians! Ye Warnians! Ye Gothonians! Ye Lewovians! Ye Reudinians! Ye Hermundurians! Ye Nehmetians! Ye Wangtonians!

and so on'.

The entirely male chorus is divided into three large groups of tenors and basses which themselves each subdivide into two, three or even, at times, four parts. Once again the accompaniment is for large orchestra with the extra effect of offstage horns, trumpets and trombones which herald the supposedly approaching tribes with fanfares in a variety of different keys.[12]

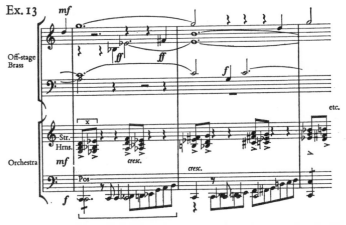

Ex. 13

[12] It is amusing to note that at the first performance the orchestra was augmented by the band of the 2nd Royal Saxon Grenadiers, Regiment No. 101. (Authorities differ over the date of the event.)

The treatment of the multi-part chorus, like the instrumentation, is of the simplest, giving a first impression of unashamed banality. Yet there is something in the immense show of theatrical energy together with a certain distinction underlying the deceptively simple motivic germs out of which the single extended movement is built up, which strikes a vivid chord of recollection. For here is the origin of the granite-like substance of Strauss's masterpiece *Elektra*, which germinated so soon after the conception of *Bardengesang*. The Agamemnon motif, Elektra's dance, the nostalgia and fulfilment themes (see Vol. I, Chapter VIII b, Exx. 13(d), 23 and 38), the savage closing chords of the opera so clearly developed in the figure ⌐ x ⌐ in Ex. 13 above, all appear unmistake-ably in embryo in this extraordinary piece the value of which must ulti-mately be conceded as purely historical.

6

A further collection of small-scale *a cappella* male voice choruses (includ-ing a number of folk-song arrangements undertaken once more at the suggestion of the Kaiser) follows the extrovert orchestral ballades *Taillefer* and *Bardengesang*, and it was not until 1913 that Strauss turned again to a substantial choral setting. This was another anthem for a large unaccompanied mixed chorus divided, as in the op. 34 settings, into six-teen parts though with the addition of four solo voices. This *Deutsche Motette*, op. 62, as Strauss designated the work, is based—again like one of the op. 34 pieces—on a poem by Friedrich Rückert, 'Die Schöpfung ist zur Ruh gegangen' ('All creation is at rest').

Rückert, who died in 1866, was a well-known romantic poet whose works inspired some of Mahler's finest music such as, in particular, the *Kindertotenlieder*. Strauss had, apart from the choral setting of 'Hymne', turned to Rückert for a number of his Lieder, even devoting the whole of the op. 46 group to his verses. This new text is distinctive for its atmosphere of rapt dedication, not a quality which normally recom-mended itself to Strauss. It has even been cited as the nearest approach to a religious subject Strauss had made since the metaphysical conflicts of *Guntram*. Certainly the absence of any sacred works in Strauss's entire output should not be overlooked.

The formal plan of the *Deutsche Motette* strongly resembles the earlier large-scale *a cappella* pieces. that is to say, an impressive opening section based on antiphonal harmonic effects is followed by a contra-puntal central passage which builds up to a climax in which the two are combined. A long coda concludes the work containing wistful references to the chief motifs of each section.

Technically there are advances on even the spectacular virtuosity of Strauss's earlier multi-part vocal writing. With the number of strands risen to no less than twenty, the variations of colour and the degree of light and shade are markedly greater than before. The word 'orchestra-tion' has justifiably been used to describe Strauss's handling of his unusual forces. Moreover, true to type he extends his palette by writing his

sopranos up to and his basses down as far as  .

The formidable difficulty of the work is apparent, and the complex harmonic shifts contain clashes of passing notes and chromatic false relations which, although in no way comparable with the acute choral dissonances which bristle in a work such as Stravinsky's *Zvezdoliki* (composed two years earlier), present real problems for a wholly unac-companied choir of such dimensions.

The *Deutsche Motette* is to some extent hybrid in style; the striking somewhat instrumental motif of the opening section, announced by the solo voices against a soft chordal background, strongly recalls the *Alpensinfonie*, which was being sketched at the same time:

Ex. 14

On the other hand many of the subsequent ideas reflect a much earlier Strauss, such as the imitative transition theme:

Ex. 15

'O laß im feuch-ten Hauch der Näch - - - - - (te)'

and the subject of the relatively conventional and less interesting central fugal section. The theme of this owes its shape—as so often in Strauss's choral music from as long ago as *Wanderers Sturmlied*—to the sheer diction of a catchphrase in the text.

Ex. 16

There are, as one would expect, however, passages of considerable beauty, especially in the closing pages which bring to mind moments in the recently completed *Rosenkavalier* and *Ariadne*.

It is surely remarkable that Strauss's operatic librettist of this time, himself a poet in his own right, supplied no texts for Strauss's vocal music other than a tiny Cantata for unaccompanied male voices. This was a tribute by Strauss and Hofmannsthal to Count Seebach on the occasion of his 20th Anniversary as Intendant of the Dresden Opera. Hofmannsthal's text has been praised as artistic, but it can scarcely be said to have evoked any correspondingly meritorious music from Strauss. Set in four simple parts, much of the time in unison, it is entirely undistinctive both thematically and harmonically and must have taken Strauss quite ten minutes to jot down.

7

On 1st May 1924 the Schubert Society of Vienna, a male voice choral society of great distinction and long standing, serenaded Strauss outside his Vienna home in the Mozart-platz in honour of his forthcoming 60th birthday, and the society's conductor Viktor Keldorfer took the opportunity of asking Strauss to write a work for them. At first Strauss was dubious and spoke deprecatingly of his choral technique. 'It never sounds', he said, 'as I would like it to!' But when Keldorfer suggested the popular romantic poet Joseph Eichendorff as the possible source for a choral work Strauss was tempted. Eichendorff's poems had provided texts for some of Hugo Wolf's finest Lieder and Strauss himself was to turn again to this poet for the profoundly moving 'Im Abendrot' from the Four Last Songs.

For three years Keldorfer heard no more on the subject, but during the autumn of 1927 an invitation from Garmisch suddenly arrived together with the news that three out of four projected movements were complete. The work was to be a song cycle from the *Wanderlieder*, descriptive of the different times of day—*Tageszeiten*—with 'Der Morgen' and 'Mittagsruh' followed by 'Der Abend' and 'Die Nacht'. Only 'Der Abend' was still lacking and this was completed before the end of the year.

The *Liederzyklus* had originally begun with a brilliant orchestral introduction leading to a setting of the first poem 'Fliegt der erste Morgenstrahl' ('The first ray of morning flies, [through the still mist of the valley']) but Keldorfer suggested that it could be very attractive to preface this orchestral opening with a few bars for the male chorus *a cappella* and proposed the addition of an isolated stanza depicting daybreak at the first cock-crow 'Wenn der Hahn kräht auf dem Dache...' from Eichendorff's short poetic story *Die Glücksritter*.

It so happened that Pfitzner had already used these very lines for a cantata *Von Deutscher Seele*, and Strauss was by no means sure that he wanted to tread the same grounds as this lesser contemporary.[13] However, Keldorfer allayed his doubts with a few well-chosen words of adulation and the *a cappella* opening bars were duly inserted.

Thematically this first movement is built on two contrasted elements, a lively passage full of declamatory and sweeping figures:

Ex. 17

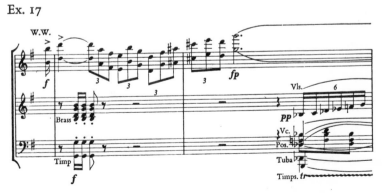

[13] Pfitzner had also written a *Gesang der Barden*, using the Kleist text.

and a lyrical second subject similar in character to Sophie's theme from
Rosenkavalier:

Ex. 18

The fact that both the above examples are taken from the orchestral
rather than the vocal passage-work is no chance circumstance. Although
the shape of the piece arises from the form of the Eichendorff poem, the
style of the music depends predominantly on the instrumental textures,
and except for a brief section at the words 'Und sein Hütlein in die Luft
wirft der Mensch vor Lust und ruft' ('Man throws his cap in the air and
cries out for joy') the vocal lines occupy a relatively subordinate role.

The peaceful second movement has its roots firmly planted in German
folk-song though its conventionality is leavened by Strauss's calculated
indifference to the rules of strict part-writing.

Ex. 19

Such apparent gaucheries of counterpoint would cause little or no comment in music of more advanced idiom, but obtrude when the prevailing genre is otherwise so traditional. In the same way Strauss's characteristic habit of extricating himself from an ostensibly perplexing moment of harmonic progression by an unprepared leap into some new key emerges as a slightly stylized mannerism.

Despite some moments of deep beauty this portrait of a summer noon-day is arguably the least interesting of the cycle. The chorus part is to a large extent in block formation, and apart from some attractively soaring horn and string writing even the orchestration is inclined to be thick and unimaginative. Nevertheless the movement both conjures up the required atmosphere of sultry heat and provides an attractive contrast to the more vivacious movements which flank it.

The last two songs run continuously, 'Evening' appropriately merging into 'Night' with haunting suggestions of more or less distant storms, as hinted at in the text (upward flicks on the piccolo with drumrolls in *Alpensinfonie* style). 'Der Abend' is a relatively short but telling piece based for the greater part on variants of the rising figure given by the chorus in the opening bars:

Ex. 20

This motif also appears in the colourful central section of the final song, a peaceful and attractive Nocturne which opens with a horn solo:

Ex. 21

25

The simplicity of the thematic content in this song is remarkable and harks back in flavour and manner to early works such as *Aus Italien*. On the other hand there is a sophistication which together with the frequent use of extremes of compass, seemingly taken for granted in voices and instruments alike,[14] betray the mature Strauss.

The music is broadly ternary in form, the bird-calls and atmospheric orchestration of the middle passage leading to a broadly lyrical return of Ex. 21 in which the figure ⌐ x ⌐ is now expanded in augmentation to a flowing melody, while the quaver arpeggio motif provides the harmonic background.

The work ends with a hymn-like treatment of the closing stanza which is quietly enunciated against the new version of Ex. 21. Originally the orchestra had accompanied this somewhat four-square final chorus throughout its two statements but Keldorfer begged Strauss for a further alteration on the grounds that there were 'too many notes, and the repetition would have a more solemn effect if the verse were first sung by the chorus alone'. Once again Strauss obliged good-naturedly though perhaps unwisely, as the exposed choral setting is revealed to be uncomfortably humdrum.

Altogether the *Liederzyklus* leaves one a little nonplussed. There is admittedly so much that lacks the true spark of inspiration, but there are also pages which are vintage Strauss and hardly deserve the almost total obscurity into which the work has fallen. The first performance was given by the Schubertbund during the Schubert centenary year, 1928, but since then *Die Tageszeiten* has only rarely been revived despite a misguided arrangement (not by Strauss) for full mixed chorus made, no doubt, precisely to facilitate performance.

One more short work for male voice chorus falls within the orbit of this chapter—the *Österreichisches Lied* written for Strauss by Anton Wildgans in 1929 and published under the title of *Austria*. This wholly occasional piece is set for a large but not outsize orchestra against which the men's chorus declaims the patriotic anthem in unrelieved unison. There are some splashes of Straussian orchestration and towards the end two amusing references to Haydn's famous hymn (and Austria's first National Anthem) *Gott erhalte unsern Kaiser*; but the score reflects none

---

[14] The persistent low F's in the violin parts raised a worried comment from Keldorfer, but Strauss assured him that if the players *thought* these notes intensely enough the audience would be misled into believing that they had actually been played.

of the gay enthusiasm which gives the big tune in *Taillefer* its infectious
and memorable quality. Strauss's heart was not carried away and a potential National Hymn was still-born.

8

It was at the time of the composition of *Aegyptische Helena* that Strauss
came to know the Czech producer Lothar Wallerstein. During the years
when Clemens Krauss was musical director in Frankfurt Wallerstein
was the Generalintendant, and when in 1927 Wallerstein moved to
Vienna it was not long before he called Krauss to join him in continuing
their highly successful partnership in the Austrian capital. Hofmannsthal
was a great admirer of Wallerstein's work and had long since drawn
Strauss's attention to its outstanding quality. For his part Wallerstein
was a warm devotee of Strauss and endeared himself especially to the
composer by his high regard for the opera *Intermezzo*. Wallerstein also
knew through Krauss of Strauss's passion for Mozart and Gluck, and
at Krauss's suggestion eagerly proposed a collaboration in preparing
for the Viennese stage that most Gluckian of Mozart's operas,
Idomeneo.

Certainly to occupy himself directly with the music of Mozart was for
Strauss a major incentive, for his was no superficial devotion. He was
once asked to write a preface for a book on 'Mozart and Munich' but
actually replied, 'I cannot write about Mozart, I can only worship him'.
Towards the end of his life he even dedicated a work to the 'spirit of the
divine Mozart'. He took every opportunity when conducting to include
a Mozart symphony in his programmes, and in the great E flat and G
minor Symphonies was in the habit of returning a second time to the
Trios after the *Menuetto da capo* because 'such music should be heard
more than once'.

All the same, he remained for a time unsure whether he should again
dress up a classical opera as he had done nearly forty years before with
Gluck's *Iphigénie en Tauride*; but when the venerable publisher Hugo
Bock, of the Berlin firm of Bote & Bock, heard with delight of the
scheme and exerted pressure with a substantial commission, Strauss
capitulated.

Idomeneo is not only one of Mozart's greatest works but also
one of his least known. Until its revival after the Second World

War it had fallen into almost as complete a limbo as the operas of Gluck, known only to the scholar and the historian. To rescue it and bring it up to date, so that it would be an acceptable repertoire piece for the modern German stage, must have seemed a genuine act of faith.

Work on the score temporarily interrupted the composition of *Arabella* and the first performance took place on 16th April 1931 at the Vienna State Opera under Strauss's personal conductorship.

With a producer such as Wallerstein at his elbow, apart from his own enormous experience in the theatre, it was inevitable that Strauss would make far more extensive changes and adaptations than he had done to *Iphigénie* in his Weimar days. On the surface the most startling alteration is the metamorphosis of Elektra, Ilia's passionate rival for Idamante's love, into the far less convincing Ismene, a malignant high priestess, jealous lest the purity of Grecian blood be tainted by the threatened alliance with a Trojan princess. It is difficult to sympathize with so drastic a change, but Strauss recoiled against working again with Elektra whom he had, after all, already disposed of otherwise in an earlier opera.

The actual name of Ismene comes from a different Greek myth in which she is the daughter of Oedipus, sister of Antigone. Nevertheless there can have been no intention to link the two myths as there is a considerable divergence of period between them.

The importance of Strauss's version is twofold: in the choice and rearrangement of numbers into acts and scenes, and the great amount of entirely new music which he composed for every recitative and for some additional numbers such as an Interlude in Act 2 and an elaborate closing ensemble in the last act. In every case this new matter contains themes or passages drawn from Mozart but reworked amidst material which Strauss supplied himself.

In so doing he drew attention to one of the most remarkable features of this wonderful and all too neglected opera. Mozart's use in *Idomeneo* of interrelated thematic references is almost unique in his own work and was far ahead of its time. It was, of course, a source of continual fascination to Strauss who, in the course of turning all the *secco* recitatives into continuous symphonic structures, transformed many of the more prominent themes into something verging on Wagnerian *leit-motif*. For example phrases such as the following from the scene between Idomeneo and his son Idamantes:

Ex. 22

contain two such ideas capable of independent development to depict the suffering of Idomeneo on account of the dreaded secret of Idamantes' identity as Poseidon's[15] intended sacrificial victim. (An anticipation of the figure ⌐ x ⌐ can even be found in the closing bars of the Overture.)

Another phrase much used in various ways by Mozart is:

Ex. 23

To these Strauss adds a theme from the closing scene of the whole opera, using it as a motif for Ilia and her love for Idamantes:

Ex. 24

In broad outline the action and scheme of Strauss's first act is fairly close to Mozart. Ilia appears first alone bewailing her fate, after which she is joined by Idamantes who, happy in the safe return of the Greek fleet from the Trojan wars, enthusiastically declares his love.

He sings an aria, 'Endlich dürfen Worte sagen' (Wallerstein supplied a German text to which Strauss worked throughout), but in place of the original, 'Non ho colpa', Strauss substituted the concert aria with violin obbligato, 'Non temer, amato bene' K.490,[16] which Mozart composed five years later, in 1786, for a new scene at the beginning of Act 2. This contains a phrase which Mozart had already used for a second version of the Act 3 duet No. 20, 'Spiergarti, non poss'io':

Ex. 25

---

15 Strauss uses throughout this Greek name for the original Nettuno (Neptune).
16 The preceding recitative is, however, omitted.

The resemblance of this melody to a phrase from his own *Ariadne auf Naxos* is hardly likely to have escaped Strauss (cf. Chapter X, Ex. 23).

Idamantes next frees the Trojan prisoners in token of his desire to re-unite the Greek and Trojan people. Already in the original text there is a reference to Helen of Troy and Strauss whimsically decided to retain this, matching it with an appropriate quotation from his *Aegyptische Helena*, the Burning of Troy motif (Ex. 26 from Chapter XV).

Idamantes' magnanimity is strongly resented by Ismene. She tells of a punitive storm at sea sent by Poseidon, which has wrecked another Greek Armada including, unknown to Idamantes, the ship of his father, Idomeneo.

Then follows the impassioned chorus in which the people appeal to the gods for mercy. Its motif Ex. 22(y) is no addition by Strauss for it is strongly in evidence in Mozart's score; Strauss, however, changes the male voices to female and considerably expands the vocal textures. This chorus leads to Idomeneo's appearance, his recitative and aria, his duet with Idamantes, and the latter's aria of despair at being so abruptly abandoned by his distraught father.

As in the original, the act ends with the March and choral Chaconne in which the Cretan troops, having at last reached land with Idomeneo, are fêted by the populace.

9

It is in the second act that the more striking and involved changes begin. The scene in which Idomeneo confides in Arbace is only retained in embryo as an interpolation after the opening bars of the giant aria 'Fuor del mar' (translated here as 'Gott! Du strafst mit harten Händen') with which essentially Strauss begins the act.

As instructed by Idomeneo, Arbace has summoned Ismene and Idamantes, and told them to prepare for a journey to Greece. In escorting the Priestess to her homeland, Idamantes may perhaps escape from Poseidon's wrath. They accordingly come now to Idomeneo, Ismene jubilant but Idamantes noticeably downcast, and after a fragment of what was once the introduction to an aria for Elektra they sing with Idomeneo the trio (No. 16) from the later part of Mozart's Act 2.

Idamantes commends Ilia to his father's care and her scene with Idomeneo, transplanted from the beginning of the act, finds a logical new niche here.

The stage now reveals the harbour with Idamantes' ship ready to sail. After the ⅜ chorus 'Placido è il mar' ('Wasser und Wind versöhnend') Strauss aptly brings forward Ilia's aria from Act 3 'Zeffiretti lusinghieri' ('Sanfte Winde'). No sooner, however, has she finished praising the weather than, as if proverbially tempted, the gods send another violent storm (Mozart's chorus, No. 17), sea-monster and all, causing the terrified people to clamour for the name of the culprit who has thus provoked Poseidon's wrath.

Strauss replaces the dramatic recitative in which Idomeneo tries to bring the catastrophe down upon his own head with a short but important passage for a Representative of the People, who tells of the monster's activities. A new motif describes the universal horror at this dreadful manifestation:

Ex. 26   Lento

After the succeeding chorus of alarm which ends Mozart's Act 2, Ex. 26 is elaborated into an extensive *Interludio* in which Strauss also incorporates a few bars from Idomeneo's aria from Act 3, 'Torno la pace al core', not otherwise included in this version.

The curtain now rises again to reveal Ilia alone as at the beginning of Mozart's third act. But instead of bewailing her ill-fated love (for we have already had the aria 'Zeffiretti' which originally belonged here) she expresses her own horror at the evil monster raging about the city, and her bewilderment over the enigma of the unknown sacrificial victim (Ex. 22(y)). Idamantes enters to say farewell before engaging the monster in mortal combat (Strauss introduces a motif from the aria 'Non temer amato bene' on the solo violin—this section is full of motivic allusions of the kind) and he and Ilia sing the duet 'Spiegarti non poss'io' ('Es fehlen mir die Worte', see Ex. 25).

They are next joined by Ismene and Idomeneo, and the Quartet follows. At this point, however, Strauss and Wallerstein rearrange the drama so as to concentrate all Ismene's remaining action in a final solo scene. As the other characters leave the stage she overhears Idomeneo's words of fatherly affection to Ilia, whom she can still only see as an enemy princess. Filled with alarm she finishes the second act of the new version by venting her rage in the great recitative and aria 'D'Oreste,

RICHARD STRAUSS

d'Ajace ho in sensi tormenti'. She announces her intention to commit suicide and thus, after this supreme moment in which she has the highly dramatic curtain to herself, we see her no more.

10

Since Strauss's third act begins so much later than Mozart's it is very short. The temple scene is completely rewritten, making motivic use of a variant of Ex. 22, but dramatically it follows the general course of the original. The chorus 'O voto tremendo' is retained and leads to the solemn march to which Idomeneo had entered. In the new version, however, Idomeneo is already on stage and Strauss therefore labels the music 'Sakraler Tanz' which does less than justice to its sternly ritualistic character. It is indeed an early example of the March of the Priests from the second act of *Die Zauberflöte*, which it strongly resembles.

The magnificent scene of Idomeneo and the Priests follows unchanged, and is interrupted as in Mozart by the off-stage fanfare and chorus announcing the overthrow of the monster at Idamantes' hands. This is again followed by a section in which Strauss replaces Mozart's very varied accompanied recitative by one of his own, using bits of arias, fragments of the original and a host of motivic references to the Quartet and other passages.

At last the dramatic climax of the opera is reached with Idomeneo on the point of sacrificing a willing Idamantes, Ilia drawing a dagger to sacrifice herself in his stead, and the voice of Poseidon interrupting all these self-sacrificings with a traditional happy ending. Mozart supplied three versions of this *deus ex machina* section but Strauss provides yet a fourth, containing elements from the others, before continuing with an elaborate and extended ensemble derived from Mozart's *Scena Ultima* though enormously adapted and recomposed. It would not be too much to say that with the Interludio from Act 2 this gorgeous ensemble is Strauss's major contribution to the whole work. Idomeneo's last aria is cut (except for its previous instrumental appearance during the Interludio) and nothing remains except the closing Chorus, described as 'Schlussgesang mit Tanz', a little oddly since Strauss omits the dance-like middle section (and hence the *da capo*) as well as the few bars of coda. He also makes no use of the outstandingly fine ballet music (K.367).

Complicated as it is, an outline scheme showing the Strauss and Mozart side by side may (as in the Gluck above) clarify the comparative formal construction of the two versions:

Strauss, *c.* 1930

Mozart's score	Strauss's score	Movements retained from original
Overture	**Overture**	**Overture (unchanged)**
Act 1	**Act 1**	**Act 1**
Scene 1 Recit: 'Quando avran fine omai', No. 1 Aria (Ilia): 'Padre, Germani', Recit: 'Ecco, Idamante, ahimè'	Scene 1 Recit: 'Wann enden meine Leiden', 'Aria der Ilia': 'Vater und Brüder'	Scene 1 Recit (with some alterations), No. 1 Aria (Ilia)
Scene 2 Recit: 'Radunate i Trojane', No. 2 Aria (Idamante): 'Non ho colpa', Recit: 'Ecco il misero resto di Trojani'	Scene 2 Recit: 'Frohe Botschaft bring ich, Ilia', 'Rondo' (Idamantes): 'Endlich dürfen Worte sagen'	— Rondo (only) from K.490 'Non temer' (Idamante), originally intended as part of alternative Act 2 Scene 1 (Anhang XIII)
Scene 3 Recit: 'scingete le catene', No. 3 'Coro de' Trojani e Cretesi'	Scene 3 Recit: 'Nicht reize der Götter Zorn', 'Chor der Trojaner und Kretenser'	Scene 3 No. 3 'Coro de' Trojani e Cretesi' (practically unchanged)
Scene 4 Recit: 'Prence signor'	Scene 4 Recit: 'Höre mich, Fürst!'	—
Scene 5 Recit: 'mio signore, de' mali'	Scene 5 Recit: 'so starbst du, Idomeneo?', Aria (Ismene): 'In meine tiefen Schmerzen'	
Scene 6 Recit: 'Estinto è Idomeneo?', No. 4 Aria (Elettra): 'Tutto nel cor vi sento'	Scene 6 Chor: 'Du seht! Götter, O helft!'	Scene 6 Recit (practically unchanged), No. 4 Aria (Elettra)
Scene 7 No. 5 Coro: 'Pietà! Numi pietà!'	Scene 7 Recit: 'Gerettet! Dank dir, Gott!', Aria (Idomeneo): 'Schon war ich ein Opfer'	Scene 7 No. 5 Coro
Scene 8 Recit: 'Ecco ci salve alfin', No. 6 Aria (Idomeneo): 'Vedrommi interno l'ombra dolente', Recit: 'Cieli! che veggo!'	Scene 8 Recit: 'Gottheit, wie grausam!'	Scene 8 Recit (with considerable alterations), No. 6 Aria (Idomeneo)
Scene 9 Recit: 'Spiagge romite'	Scene 9 Recit: 'Was bedeutet dies Wort?', Aria (Idamantes): 'Wohl ist er gerettet'	Scene 9 (Part of accompanied recit retained with alterations)
Scene 10 Recit: 'Ah qual gelido orror', No. 7 Aria (Idamante): 'Il padre adorato ritrovo'		Scene 10 Recit (unchanged), No. 7 Aria (Idamante)

Mozart's score—	*Strauss's score*	*Movements retained from original*
Scene 11 No. 8 Marcia	Scene 10 Marcia	Scene 11 No. 8 Marcia (unchanged except for altered repeats)
No. 9 Coro 'Ciaccona': 'Nettuno s'onori!'	'Ciaconna' (!): 'Poseidon verehret!'	No. 9 Coro (central 4 completely omitted)
Act 2	**Act 2**	**Act 2**
Scene 1 Recit: 'Siam soli, odimi Arbace'	(Orchestral Introduction)	Orchestral opening of No. 12 Aria (Idomeneo) (unchanged for eleven bars—last two bars adapted for new continuation)
No. 10 Aria (Arbace): 'Se il tuo duol'		
Scene 2 Recit: 'Se mai pomposo apparse'	Scene 1 Recit: 'Nun weisst du das Geheimnis'	—
No. 11 Aria (Ilia): 'Se il padre'	Scene 2 Aria (Idomeneo): 'Gott! Du strafst mit harten Händen!'	
Scene 3 (Recit): 'Qual mi conturbi i sensi'		Scene 3 No. 12 Aria (Idomeneo) starting at voice entry. Text as in Anhang V (some changes and cuts). Alternative coloratura version—from main body of score—also included together with introductory orchestral bars already played by Strauss at beginning of act. The whole of this original version presented unchanged apart from the indication of optional cuts
No. 12 Aria (Idomeneo): 'Fuor del mar'		
Recit: 'Frettolosa e giuliva'		
Scene 4 Recit: 'Sire, da Arbace intesi'	Scene 3 (Recit): 'Die Freude spielt in deinem Aug',	Scene 5 Recit (greatly adapted and altered)
Scene 5 Recit: 'Parto, e l'unico oggetto'	Terzett: 'Muss ich von dir mich trennen'	
No. 13 Aria (Elettra): 'Idol mio, se ritroso'	Recit: 'Darf ich dir, Vater'	Scene 7 No. 16 Terzetto (practically unchanged)
No. 14 Marcia (Elettra): 'Odo da lunge'	Scene 4 Recit: 'Dir, König, neigt sich die Verwaiste'	—
	Aria (Ilia): 'Wie lang schon beweinich'	—
		Scene 2 No. 11 Aria (Ilia)
Scene 6 Recit: 'Sidonie spende'	Scene 5 Recit: 'Wie unerwartet!'	Scene 3 (Recit): 'Qual mi conturba' with considerable alterations

Mozart's score	*Strauss's score*	*Movements retained from original*
Scene 7	**Scene 6**	Scene 6 No. 15 Coro (altered and abbreviated)
No. 15 Coro: 'Placido è il mar'	(Chor): 'Wasser und Wind versöhnend'	Act III Sc. 1 No. 19 Aria (Ilia)
Recit: 'Vatene prence' 'O ciel!'	**Scene 7**	Scene 7 Adapted to 'Tempesta-più Allegro'
No. 16 Terzetto: 'Pria di partir' (Tempesta—Più Allegro)	Aria (Ilia): 'Sanfte Winde' Recit: 'Ist dieser Donner deine Antwort'	
No. 17 Coro: 'Qual nuovo terrore!' Recit: 'Eccoti in me, barbaro Nume!'	**Scene 8** (Chor): 'Das Meer ist in Aufruhr' Recit: 'Weh, neues Unheil entsteigt dem Meere'	No. 17 Coro (unchanged) —
No. 18 Coro: 'Corriamo, fuggiamo'	(Chor): 'Aus Tiefen des Meeres'	No. 18 Coro (unchanged)
Act 3	**Interludio**	**Act 3**
Scene 1 Recit: 'Solitudini amiche' No. 19 Aria (Ilia): 'Zeffiretti, lusinghieri' Recit: 'Ei stesso vien'		Opening theme of No. 31 Aria (Idomeneo) 'Torno la pace al core' quoted in central 'Poco più mosso'
Scene 2 Recit: 'Principessa, a tuoi sguardi' No. 20 Duetto: 'S'io non moro'	**Scene 9** Recit: 'Würgend verbreitet Tod das Untier in der Stadt!' Duetto: 'Es fehlen mir die Worte'	Scene 2 Recit (greatly adapted and altered from accompanied recit) Duetto: 'Spiegarti non poss'io' Anhang VII (alternative to No. 20)
Scene 3 Recit: 'Cieli! che vedo?' No. 21 Quartetto: 'Deh resta, ò cara'	**Scene 10** Recit: 'Idamantes!' 'Mein König!' Quartett: 'Nein, du sollst bleiben'	Scene 3 Last five bars of accomp. recit Quartetto (virtually unaltered apart from indication of optional cut)
Scene 4 Recit: 'Sire, alla reggia tua immensa turba'	**Scene 11** Recit: 'Du armes Kind!' 'Erbarmen'	—
Scene 5 (Recit): 'Sventurata Sidon!' No. 22 Aria (Arbace) 'Se colà ne' fati è scritto'	(Recit): 'Was hörte ich? Trost sei sie ihn?) Aria (Ismene): 'Orestes und Ajas'	Scene 10 Recit (Elettra). Unaltered as from 'Oh smania! oh furie!' No. 29 Aria (Elettra): 'D'Oreste, d'Ajace'

Act 3

Scene 6	No. 23 (Scena): 'Volgi intorno lo sguardo, O Sire' No. 24 Coro: 'O, o voto tremendo!'	Intr. and Scene 1: 'König, wir müssen dich fragen'
Scene 7	No. 25 Marcia No. 26 (Scene): 'Accogli, o rè' Coro dentro le scene: 'Stupenda vittoria!'	Scene 2 'Sakraler Tanz' (Marcia) Scene 3 (Scene): 'Von dir, O Gott' Chor hinter der Scene: 'Heil dir, Idamantes'
Scene 8	Recit: 'Qual risuna qui intorno'	
Scene 9	Recit: 'Padre, mio caro padre!' No. 27 Aria (Idamante): 'No, la morte' Recit: 'Ma, che piu tardi?'	Scene 4 (Scene): 'Idamantes? Gerettet ist die Stadt' Scene 5 (Scene): 'Halt ein, Fürst, ich sei das Opfer'
Scene 10	Recit: 'Ferma, o Sire che fai?' No. 28 (Scene): 'Ha vinto amore' Recit: 'Oh ciel pietoso!' Recit: 'Oh smania! oh furie!' No. 29 Aria (Elettra): 'D'Oreste, d'Ajace'	(Scene): 'Die Treue siegte'
	Scena Ultima No. 30: 'Popoli! a voi l'ultima legge' No. 31 Aria (Idomeneo): 'Torna la pace' No. 32 Coro: 'Scenda Amor'	(Ensemble): 'Erlösung!' 'Gnade verkündend' 'Schlussgesang mit Tanz': 'Eros führt'

Notes (right-hand column):

Scene 6   No. 24 Coro. Retained only in part and with alterations

Scene 7   No. 25 (unaltered)
No. 26 (unaltered)
Coro dentro le scene (unaltered)

Scene 9   Some excerpts from No. 27 Aria and succeeding recit preserved in through-composed section also containing allusions to earlier numbers
No. 28 considerably altered

Scena Ultima: Themes from No. 30 used in composition of new extended ensemble

No. 32 Coro (greatly abbreviated and orchestral middle section omitted)

Strauss's handling of Mozart's score varies enormously in degree. Where the music is either unchanged, as for example in the Overture, or only slightly so, the revisions in orchestration and dynamics are far less than Strauss had made in Gluck's score, and it is significant that the publishers were able to make considerable use of the plates of the Breitkopf & Härtel *Mozart Gesamtausgabe* in preparing the new edition. There are, however, a great number of cuts, hardly a single aria escaping from continual excisions ranging from two or three bars to large chunks of thirty or forty,[17] a surprising treatment from a composer who so resented cuts being made in his own operas.

The originally castrato role of Idamantes Strauss retained for the soprano voice, an unexpected purity of style rarely emulated today but one obviously in line with Strauss's personal taste.

The orchestra is also exactly that prescribed by Mozart, only the keyboard continuo being replaced throughout the recitatives and dispensed with. In this respect, as in his supplying of new numbers in a late-romantic style so very far removed from the classicism of the original Mozart, Strauss misjudged the trends of future taste, his well-intentioned work accordingly paying the inevitable penalty of rejection. Nevertheless his reconstructions are uniformly fascinating as well as unerringly dramatic and theatrical, whilst his high-lighting of the genius and originality of Mozart's score may well have contributed to its return to the stage after a period during which it had been set aside as a museum piece of no more than academic importance.

For Strauss himself, moreover, this preoccupation with a favourite opera of his beloved Mozart provided a freshening of spirit during a period of discouragement whilst working on the last libretto of his dead friend Hugo von Hofmannsthal, *Arabella*.

---

[17] Idomeneo's Act 2 aria 'Fuor del mar' is given by Strauss in two versions, following Mozart's example. The shorter, more usually performed text he cuts still further but gives the extended coloratura version in full as an 'Ossia'. This question of different versions abounds in *Idomeneo*, the original full score containing no less than thirteen appendices of the highest importance. On the whole, Strauss chooses his texts from amongst these Anhang variants.

CHAPTER XVII

SWANSONG OF A POET

I

AS the plans for *Die Aegyptische Helena* took shape Strauss realized he would have to face the truth that Hofmannsthal would never again provide him with a libretto on the lines of *Elektra*. In the hopes of such a work he had followed bravely for over ten years along the tortuous paths of philosophical dialectic and mystical symbolism; but in vain.

This was not to say, however, that the poetic spring which had supplied their other major successes had dried up. There was no denying that their venture into period comedy had been a triumph and Strauss had long noticed with sharp awareness that suggestions of a second *Rosenkavalier* did not produce the abrupt rebuffs suffered by his wistful requests for some lurid drama.

At the same time he also realized that, distasteful as it had been to Hofmannsthal, the development of his own *Rosenkavalier* idiom in *Intermezzo* had been genuinely fruitful and was well worth still further exploitation—as he himself put it: 'I haven't spoken my last word yet in that genre'. A Voltaire comedy, a tale of intrigue from medieval Verona, a latter-day *Meistersinger*, a subject out of Turgenev (either gay or sad)— these were some of the subjects Strauss proposed to Hofmannsthal at intervals even while *Aegyptische Helena* was still on the stocks. The *Meistersinger* idea, though it came to nothing, is interesting both because of the ethical discussion it provoked (including two of Hofmannsthal's best letters on the subject of opera in general) and because it represented a further strand of the autobiographical thread in Strauss's work. He had never forgotten Bülow's remark labelling him Richard III ('there is no Richard II'—see Vol. I, p. 204) and tried to apply it to some possible *Meistersinger III.*

Oddly enough Strauss came nearer the mark when referring to one of Hofmannsthal's scenarios, *Achill auf Skyros,* which Egon Wellesz had just set as a ballet. Perhaps this might be turned into a pretty little one-act play, he ventured. But whilst it was clear that a previously composed libretto was out of the question, it now emerged that Hofmannsthal had indeed been searching for ideas amongst his own earlier sketches. One of these, concocted fairly recently, was almost pure burlesque and evoked shades of Johann Strauss's *Zigeunerbaron.* Entitled *Der Fiaker als Graf* it was to have been played in contemporary dress in the Viennese ballrooms of the 1860s. Its focal point would have been the traditional annual cabbies' festival in which a Carnival Queen was chosen and fêted. The feature of the occasion was the relaxing of all social barriers, and the proceedings were presided over by a Cabby-mascot, a well-known tavern singer known as the 'Fiakermilli'.[1]

Hofmannsthal had at one time projected this light entertainment on a substantial scale with three acts, but had remained undecided how to handle it. It's chief drawback for operatic purposes was that, having curiously little action for such a piece, it depended once again almost entirely on dialogue.

The other sketch to which Hofmannsthal had given serious reconsideration was a short story, only partially worked out, written as long ago as 1909. He had actually allowed it to be published the following year, but had emphasised its unfinished state by adding the subtitle 'Characters for an Unwritten Comedy'. In putting it forward to Strauss, Hofmannsthal wrote:

> 'One of the chief motifs [is] that of a younger sister whose love for an admirer of the older one grows in proportion to the increasingly unkind treatment he receives from the latter, until finally to console the unhappy lover she grants him an assignation in the name of her sister, in a completely dark room, speaking only in a whisper.'

Here was a subject full of much deeper feeling, yet Hofmannsthal believed it might also have possibilities of a lighter, almost Vaudeville character, taking place 'among young people and ending in a multiple wedding'.

[1] This 'Fiakermilli' was a historical character who lived from 1846–74. She was in fact for many years a popular Carnival Queen but died in poverty.

He had at various times considered redrafting the story for the theatre; even before the war Reinhardt had encouraged him to make a musical work of it, while a more recent and particularly grotesque version had made use of 'up-to-date' ideas such as psychoanalysis and spiritualism. All this was nothing more than scribbling, however, and it was on an entirely different level of intention that he managed subtly to fuse his original basic conception together with the *Fiaker als Graf* fragment into a single scenario which he proposed for

> 'a three act comic opera, indeed almost an operetta (I would describe *Rosenkavalier* as an operetta too!) which in gaiety does not fall short of *Fledermaus*, and without any self-repetition is related to *Rosenkavalier*, contains five or six very lively roles and above all a very strong second act and a third which does not in any way fall off. . . . The characters of this new Comedy for Music are dancing about almost too persistently under my very nose. The spirits which I summoned for your sake now refuse to leave me alone. The comedy could turn out *better* than *Rosenkavalier*. The figures stand out very clearly in my mind and are beautifully contrasted. The two girls (sopranos) could turn into glorious (singing) roles. They stand to each other roughly in the same relation—as characters—as Carmen and Micaëla (one very dazzling, the other softer and more humble). As lovers a high tenor and a baritone. This latter is the most remarkable character in the piece, from a half-alien world (Croatia), half buffo and yet a grand fellow capable of deep feelings, wild and gentle, almost daemonic. . . .'

Here, clearly recognizable, is the ground-plan of what was to become the new opera, *Arabella*.

2

Lucidor, the 1909 short story on which Hofmannsthal built his new comedy, is an affecting little tale of an eccentric widow of high birth living in a Viennese hotel during the latter half of the nineteenth century together with her two children. The elder is an extremely beautiful girl of nineteen called Arabella, while the other—nearly four years younger —is shown to the world as a boy, Lucidor, but is in fact a second girl (Lucile by name), the family circumstances and Arabella's matrimonial prospects being greatly enhanced by such a masquerade.

The plot revolves around the prospects afforded by a rich uncle a notorious woman hater) and a young suitor Vladimir who arouses the devotion not, as he hopes, of Arabella but of Lucidor, who sends him love-letters in Arabella's name and (strangely) handwriting. The climax of the story comes, as in Hofmannsthal's résumé, when in desperation at their impending departure from Vienna Lucidor seduces the suitor in Arabella's bed, deputizing for her sister in total darkness.

The deception is successful and leads naturally to a highly involved situation which the sudden self-revealing of Lucile in her true feminine guise does little to disentangle. The story ends with the tantalizing but touching words: 'Life may create the dialogue which followed, comedy might imitate it, but a story cannot . . . in any case the whole beauty of a soul so devoted as Lucile's could only have been revealed in circumstances as strange as these'.

It was a sure instinct that led Hofmannsthal back to this story, and with one or two additions to the basic cast, such as a dissolute father and a further suitor to Arabella, this time rich and highly eligible, the substance of the plot was far enough advanced to be read to Strauss, a plunge which Hofmannsthal took on 16th December 1927.

For the first time for seventeen years Strauss found himself with a subject he could really understand, which he could criticize from a secure standpoint and in which he knew himself to be collaborating once more on an absolutely equal basis.

The new suitor was the first important change to the Lucidor story, since only through him could the character of Arabella herself be developed as Strauss insisted it must, though he was anxious that the lover should not acquire too much emphasis in the way Ochs had once threatened to do. He pointed out to Hofmannsthal how it had been the Marschallin who had captured the audience's hearts, to whom indeed the whole success of *Rosenkavalier* was due, even though she was off the stage for a whole act and a half. The new plot seemed to lack that kind of warm human interest. Perhaps some flirtations with the mother who was still young and attractive might be what was needed.

But Hofmannsthal knew that such a close parallel amounted to self-repetition, always a mistake. It was, however, quite correct that the action should lean towards the girl rather than the man and this had always been his intention, *vide* his provisional title: *Arabella oder der Fiakerball*. The value of the new suitor was twofold; not only did he throw Arabella into sharper relief as a personality, but he would bring an altogether new and local colour into the drama. Hofmannsthal saw

26

him as a rough Croatian landowner, whose bluff honesty would contrast well with the corrupt Viennese society of the 1860s which was to supply the background of the basic plot. He was also to be accompanied at all times by a retinue consisting of Welko a dragoon, Djura a gypsy, and Jenkel a Jew. These extraordinary individuals were originally made to introduce themselves in turn by comically putting their heads round the door in the first scene in order to reassure their master that the beautiful Arabella really lived in this hotel room, a piece of buffoonery later abandoned.

Strauss had lighted upon a collection of South-Slav folk-songs which interested him greatly and, believing that a little support in the way of Croatian folk melody was a welcome idea, Hofmannsthal encouraged such researches. On the other hand he took fright when Strauss started to talk of 'knocking up some colossal ballet based on Slav songs and dances'.

'For heaven's sake!' he wrote, '. . . we are at the Vienna Cabbies' Ball and on such an occasion there can be no more question of a Croatian dance than of a Persian or an Indian one.

At a Court Ball one might find a perfectly good excuse for a czardas or a kolo or a mazurka, but not, for goodness sake, at the Cabbies' Ball, that would jar intolerably. By now I have come to regret my premature description which had led your phantasy, busy and active as it is, along the wrong track. If these things please you so much, I don't mind making you a ballet later on out of some Serb ballad material. But for the Cabbies' Ball itself, that ought not to give you any trouble whatever. The action of the comedy which is highly concentrated and lively, takes place at the front of the stage; down stage one descends into the ballroom and for my own part I rather thought of the ball as more or less invisible, only of course the characters join the dancers now and then and return again. I felt that to a master like you this hint of a ball in the background would be welcome, this touch of the ballroom atmosphere, and at the same time of an animated pulsating crowd, this flash of a dance rhythm now and then, while the foreground is entirely given over to *parlando* and to a sentimental-lyrical mood.'

The fact is that having turned the Arabella story over again in his mind he was greatly taken with it but saw that it could so easily go wrong if the contrasting element of operetta were allowed to become too brash for the delicate Lucidor motif. It was this which now affected him most deeply together with the new possibilities of a situation in which Arabella herself was the main figure.

This was all very well, but in the first act (the only part Strauss had received so far) the characters scarcely substantiated so much promise. Even the title role seemed a shadowy figure, a mere coquette; while viewed as a whole the scenes were all too fragmentary and the end ineffective. The first curtain would profit by a solo scene which would make an interesting shape and at the same time deepen Arabella's personality. This was something he continued to press for right through to the end, thereby once again showing his sure theatrical instinct.

The early draft of the first act certainly had many failings. The altogether appealing and unselfish little Lucidor had been turned into Zdenka, seventeen years old[2] and deeply malcontent. Repeatedly she begs her parents, and Arabella also pleads in vain on her behalf, that her masquerade in boy's clothes be brought to an end. At this intermediary stage Zdenka appears a far less convincing foil to her sister, and her disgruntled conduct is rather less sympathetic than Lucidor's had been. Zdenka has a series of scenes (too many, Strauss thought) with Arabella's original suitor who is changed from the conceited Vladimir into a pathetic little subaltern, Matteo, though her relationship with him remains as in the story.

In order to symbolize Arabella's rejection of her previous flirtatious existence Hofmannsthal introduced a group of further suitors, three Counts whom he called Dominik, Elemer and Lamoral. They made a somewhat ridiculous first entrance in a scene in which they arrive at the hotel already in full fancy dress as cabbies in anticipation of the evening's Fiakerball. Admittedly their purpose was merely to serve as prototypes, but at present they were too intangible to be more than cardboard figures.

Now that the girls' eccentric and scatter-brained mother is no longer to be a widow, Hofmannsthal changed his mind over the kind of man the father would have been. In *Lucidor* he had been 'proud, disappointed and irritable, very handsome . . . prone to contempt but able to conceal it under excellent manners, respected and envied by men, loved by many women, and deficient in feeling'. Arabella had been described as the image of her father, but as her own character was now to undergo immense changes it was clear that his must also change. The Count

---

[2] Zdenka's age is once more diminished in the final draft, to the considerable advantage of the character.

Waldner of this first draft is already that of the completed opera, a ruined, dissolute cavalry officer and an obsessive gambler. His scene with the rich Croatian suitor, now christened Mandryka and also fully drawn, is the only one which remained to the end virtually unchanged.

Hofmannsthal recognized that the charge of diffuseness was justified though he stressed that this first act was far more in the nature of a dramatic exposition than that of *Rosenkavalier*, which was complete in itself. Hence also the lack of set pieces, for Hofmannsthal refused to consider Strauss's suggestion that since it was so episodic it might just as well be broken up altogether into a series of vignettes like the style of *Intermezzo*. Such a plan was contrary to his methods and in particular he regarded a comedy in this 'looser' form to be ephemeral and so quite impossible.

He did, however, try very hard to meet Strauss's carefully reasoned views by writing an elaborate ensemble for the scene following Mandryka's exit and a revised ending giving more prominence to Arabella. These were incorporated into a fresh draft which Hofmannsthal read to a number of his colleagues in the literary and theatrical worlds, including Roller, his old friend and stage designer, and Lothar Wallerstein. The reactions, he reported hopefully to Strauss, were uniformly favourable, and he outlined the *mise en scène* in terms which throw considerable light on the finished work as we know it:

> 'What is vital is to find the right atmosphere for the whole, a certain general atmosphere in which that whole will live. In *Helena*, for instance, this is somewhere between the elegant and the solemn (and infinitely far from the sombre massive tone of *Ariadne*). The atmosphere of *Arabella*, again, differs greatly from that of *Rosenkavalier*. In both cases it is Vienna, but what a difference between them . . . the atmosphere of *Arabella*, quite close to our own time as it is, is more ordinary, less glamorous, more vulgar. The three Counts in frivolous pursuit of anything in a skirt, Waldner that cashiered cavalry captain and his whole shady *milieu*, these figures are tainted by vulgarity tangled up with a rather vulgar and dubious Vienna—it is this background which sets off the courageous and self-reliant Arabella and the touchingly impulsive Zdenka. Above all, this pleasure-seeking, frivolous Vienna, where everybody lives on tick, is the foil for Mandryka; he is steeped in his world of unspoilt villages, his oak forests untouched by the axe, his ancient folk-songs. With him the *wide open spaces* of the vast half-Slav Austria enter Viennese comedy and let a totally different air rush in.'

Once again the character of Mandryka had risen in his mind to a position of paramount importance, and although he slyly credited Strauss with this discovery ('that is why I was so delighted when, with your sure artistic instinct, you saw the figure of Mandryka as the key to the whole piece') he failed to convince him that this could make up for 'an uninteresting almost unattractive Arabella' as Strauss saw her. The setting in itself provided no incentive; a 'putrescent Vienna of 1866' was plainly unpalatable to Strauss, and he doubted whether he would have either the patience or the talent to maintain an artificially degenerate style over three acts. Everything depended on the verisimilitude of the people, and Strauss again made a series of propositions, some more, some less apt and tasteful: flirtations between the three Counts and Adelaide the mother; between Mandryka and the Fiakermilli; a more serious affair between Arabella and Matteo, even an awful Building Contractor, once mooted as a potential solution to the family problems. Strauss's mind teemed with possibilities which might restore the conflict at present so woefully lacking in Acts 2 and 3.

Hofmannsthal's reply, far from the ill-humour of earlier days, or still perhaps in the aftermath of having so obviously gone too far in the recent outburst over *Aegyptische Helena*, was as wise as it was tolerant. With all its birth pangs, he knew he had found an ideal subject and was resolved not to let it go. To him, the librettist not of *Fledermaus* but of *Rosenkavalier*, the characters really were 'imbued with life in its most serious aspect'. In one respect he saw his way clear, which was in the reconstituting and working out of a scene, previously suppressed for reasons of conciseness, between Arabella and Matteo.[3]

But much as Strauss appreciated this concession it was not enough, and all his efforts to begin the actual task of composition came to a dead end. Reluctantly he arrived at the decision, unusual for him, that he would have to delay 'embarking on the job until the whole thing was absolutely ready'. A number of suggestions concerning the outline shape of Act 2 followed and were in turn well received by Hofmannsthal.

During the autumn of 1928 Hofmannsthal addressed himself seriously to these two later acts, and by December was ready to read them to Strauss. Much depended on this meeting; in a sense the libretto was finished but Hofmannsthal knew that Act 1 had not reached its final

---

[3] All these early supplanted scenes, as well as the entire original draft of Act 1, are printed in full in *Die Neue Rundschau 65 Jahrgang*, Vol. 3/4, S. Fischer, Frankfurt, 1954.

shape and was still for Strauss a stumbling block. If only they could reach agreement over Acts 2 and 3 he would then try to rethink Act 1 completely. On Saturday 29th December Hofmannsthal accepted a lunch invitation at Strauss's Vienna home and the reading took place.

It was a most happy occasion and, Hofmannsthal's confidence fully restored, he determined to accomplish the total redrafting of Act 1. At first the work went slower than he had hoped; a series of irksome bouts of ill-health dragged him back and when spring came he feared that Strauss's enthusiasm had waned. Sadly he wrote that 'over this comic opera we have got ourselves into an awkward spot for the first time in our lives'.

Nevertheless he persevered, and after the restorative effect of a holiday in Florence he completed the revised first act early in July 1929. It is clear from his account of how he had set about the task that he had fully understood Strauss's points and requirements:

> 'My purpose in the revision has been twofold: (1) to place the character of Arabella more definitely in the centre, to throw her into every possible relief, but with soft, not harsh outlines; (2) to eliminate from the first version of the act that string of so many scenes of varying tempo, varying purpose and varying mood which proved unacceptable to the composer.'

Strauss was delighted; only one thing was lacking—Arabella's aria for the end of the act, and this Hofmannsthal willingly added, virtually by return of post. Strauss wired his congratulations—but Hofmannsthal was dead.

3

On 13th July 1929 Hofmannsthal's elder son Franz committed suicide. The shock was more than the sensitive poet could sustain; the funeral was fixed for two days later but before he could set out for the terrible ordeal Hofmannsthal collapsed and died of a stroke. He never read Strauss's telegram, which remained on his desk amongst the countless messages of condolence which he could not bring himself to open.

It goes without saying that Strauss was profoundly upset. Though he and Hofmannsthal had never very much liked one another personally, seldom met, and had quarrelled bitterly over almost every work, their mutual respect and—above all—loyalty had been enormous. The sudden loss of his colleague in such circumstances constituted so great a threat to the ageing composer that Pauline took it upon herself to protect him by every means in her power.

In the first place she threw a series of tantrums so formidable that they camouflaged the terrible news which had been delivered by phone and had somehow to be broken to him. She then refused to allow Strauss to go to the funeral (she herself and Bubi representing him) and gave it out that he was undergoing a vital cure which could not be interrupted. Finally she absolutely forbad Strauss to utter his dead friend's name in the house, so that he was only able to release his pent up emotions during a reading of *Arabella*, Hofmannsthal's last libretto, which he arranged abruptly at the house of his friend Karl Alwin.

For the appalling prospect was suddenly borne upon him that he would have to carry on without this partner of over twenty years standing. In particular there loomed the inescapable responsibility of completing alone this opera they had been currently hammering into shape. The new draft of Act 1 was an improvement beyond Strauss's most sanguine hopes; but some things which he had pressed for and successfully obtained—the ensemble after Mandryka's exit and the Ara-bella/Matteo scene—had again disappeared. The renewed rejection of the latter had actually been sound instinct on Hofmannsthal's part. The interpolated scene had greatly weakened Arabella's first entrance as well as confusing Matteo's standing in their waning relationship.

If there were losses in the final text, the gains more than outweighed them and, left irrevocably to his own devices, Strauss shrank from tampering with Hofmannsthal's latest scripts the minute death intervened to prevent the poet from protesting. As he wrote to his friend Anton Kippenburg: 'it is Hofmannsthal's last word—one has no choice but to follow', and with a sense of dedication he quickly applied himself to composition.

For a time the music flowed easily; by September the new first act was almost completely sketched out. But gradually the unaccustomed isolation of his position slowed the work. During 1930 it stopped altogether while Strauss turned his attention to *Idomeneo* and it was not until this was launched the following year that the piano sketches neared completion. Even then he lacked the incentive to carry on with the orchestration, cloaking his inertia in gloomy remarks like 'now is absolutely not the time for such works. . . . Until the charming public are half way to understanding a bit about *Frau ohne Schatten*, *Intermezzo* and *Helena* they don't need to hear anything else'. It so happened that Kippenburg, who was director of the famous Insel-Verlag, was the friend and publisher of Stefan Zweig. Accordingly he encouraged Strauss, who was feeling stale and depressed, to approach Zweig for a libretto.[4] After all, to interrupt *Arabella* yet again with some new work would perhaps be the best plan, 'provided', as Strauss wrote to Fritz Busch, 'my powers of invention continue to function reasonably well as my 70th birthday approaches'. However, Busch and his Intendant at Dresden, Alfred Reucker, pressed him to persevere with *Arabella* and while the first meetings with Zweig were in fact coming to fruition he managed to complete his last setting of a Hofmannsthal libretto, the score being finished on 12th October 1932.

4

Hofmannsthal had at first intended to begin the action with a violent scene showing a distraught Zdenka trying hopelessly to keep a pack of irate creditors at bay. In his revised draft this is reduced to a mere background, and when the curtain rises the attention is concentrated on Adelaide and the Fortune-teller. The reason behind this change of emphasis (in the first version the Fortune-teller is only hinted at during a later scene) is to focus the action from the very start on Arabella and her forthcoming marriage. In fact the cards tell, with astonishing accuracy though in veiled and mysterious terms which are sometimes misinterpreted by the foolish mother, the whole complicated course of the forthcoming drama. Firstly Graf Waldner's disastrous gambling losses are revealed, and Strauss opens the opera with music descriptive of these:

Ex. 1

---

4 It has sometimes been suggested that Zweig's first collaboration with Strauss was in a revision of the text of *Arabella*, but all the evidence is against this.

There follows some rapid string figuration intended to depict the play with the fortune-telling cards which is amusingly reminiscent of the card-shuffling music in *Intermezzo*.

Adelaide's feverish anxiety and the family financial straits have their own motif:

Ex. 2

to which is added a wailing passage on the woodwind illustrating Adelaide's over-excited outbursts of which more will be heard later. Her main concern is for Arabella's future, since only a successful marriage can save them from ruin. As she speaks of her beautiful elder daughter one of the main themes of the opera is heard:

Ex. 3

Ex. 3 symbolizes Arabella's power of inspiring devotion through her beauty, and the exploitation of that power both by her desperate parents and, at first, by the coquettish Arabella herself. The transformation of this theme as Arabella's character deepens is one of the opera's most striking features.

Various suitors are alluded to, more or less obliquely: Graf Elemer, one of the three attendant Counts:

Ex. 4

the young officer Matteo, who is far too small fry to merit Adelaide's approval:

Ex. 5

and a third suitor who is favoured by the cards. They foretell that he is to be summoned by a letter from far away, from amidst deep woods, to become the bridegroom. A number of his themes are touched upon against the fluttering of the cards-music:

Ex. 6

This complex of motifs contains presages of greater things to come, as the suitor referred to will be the hero of the opera. The excitable Adelaide, however, scarcely listens to the significant details given by the oracle. Assuming that the successful suitor can only be Elemer, she listens with horror to the tale of the obstacles through which his courtship must pass. The danger comes not only through Matteo but through the apparently unlikely agency of a second daughter.

Throughout this *entretien* Zdenka (dressed up, of course, as a boy) has been unobtrusively coping with the endless delivery to the door of creditors' bills. Until now the music has ignored her, but when the Fortune-teller, who had been deceived like everyone else, looks up with surprise from the all-wise cards Adelaide lets her into the secret, and the clarinets softly give out one of Zdenka's motifs:

Ex. 7

Adelaide explains the masquerade with the briefness exacted by an operatic libretto and there is no doubt that some knowledge of the original *Lucidor* story would make the situation more credible. For it is

only there that the physical details are given—short hair on account of a
bout of typhus, slender hips and so on, without which the impersonation
could never have been convincingly accomplished. There too we learn
of the young girl's shyness, unselfishness and above all her patience,
sorely needed for the suppression of her true nature. In the opera Adelaide merely says that Zdenka was such a tomboy that she has always
been allowed to run about wild in boys' clothes, and that in their
straitened circumstances it was cheaper and simpler to let this continue
rather than spoil Arabella's chances of a good marriage through unnecessary competition. Zdenka's compliance is attributed in part to her
overwhelming affection for her sister, but other reasons emerge as the
act progresses. The important consequence is that her discontented
behaviour, which had made her less attractive in the first Act 1 draft, has
altogether vanished and the Zdenka of the opera is an immensely
appealing character.

Embarrassed by Zdenka's obvious interest in what is going on,
Adelaide whisks the Fortune-teller off to her room and Zdenka is left
alone to puzzle over the turn of events. Her two great fears are that the
threatening creditors may force them to leave Vienna and that Matteo,
with whom she has fallen in love, may lose favour not only through
Arabella's indifference but through the antagonism of their parents,
which the Fortune-teller seems to endorse. Her despair soon gets the
upper hand and she bursts into a highly excitable tone of voice, an
'exaltierten Ton' which, as Arabella later shrewdly observes, she has
copied from their mother. The wailing woodwind passage of Adelaide's
outbursts now blossoms into an important pair of themes, much used
throughout the opera.

Ex. 8

Ex. 9

In either event, whether they leave Vienna or Matteo is rejected, Zdenka would never see him again, a prospect she cannot endure. She longs for a change in the family fortunes, referring to a rich aunt (a parallel figure derived from the uncle of the *Lucidor* story) and declares that she will sacrifice her life and remain a boy for ever if only her beloved Bella will make Matteo happy.

At the end of this touching little aria, Zdenka's Ex. 7 is declaimed in a broad unison by violins and woodwind in the guise of a kind of *Valse Triste*. This is the first of the many waltzes in which the opera abounds, underlining, undoubtedly to its disadvantage, the comparison with *Rosenkavalier*. Despite the daring anachronism of the waltzes in the earlier opera, they had become one of its most popular and memorable features. When Hofmannsthal had mooted the idea of returning to a Viennese setting for the new work Strauss had intended to vary the dance-rhythms by employing a more colouristic vein. The fixing of Mandryka as a Croatian landowner was of value in this respect and Strauss probed ever deeper into his four-volume encyclopaedia of South-Slav folk-music in which there are indeed an enormous variety of songs and dances of every kind.

Typically, however, the keener Strauss became the more Hofmannsthal retracted from this line of approach:

> 'It would be appalling if this figure were to become a music-box for Croat folk tunes. . . . Here I shall have to make a firm stand, for it is precisely the point that everything must be *authentic*, the authentic Vienna of 1860 . . . the kind of dances people would in fact have danced around 1860 were waltzes, waltzes above all, then fast polkas and at the end a jaunty can-can. But this does not concern us in the least, and the action will certainly not lead up to a finale *à la* Offenbach. That is not my line at all and I don't even know whether the can-can is much your style.'

So waltzes were once more the order of the day and Strauss had to concentrate his efforts on giving the new examples a pronounced unmistakable character of their own.

5

Zdenka's soliloquy is interrupted by Matteo, who comes in anxiously, hoping for an interview with Arabella or at least a letter from her. He little knows that the letter he received only three days ago was written in her forged handwriting by the being he takes for his young friend, her brother Zdenko, and who continues to assure him that he is deeply loved by Arabella despite outward appearances. He plies Zdenka with jealous questions over Arabella's whereabouts—she has been for a walk, she has been to the opera (Strauss quotes a motif from *Lohengrin*), today she is going tobogganning, and so forth. Zdenka's parrying of his questions is haunted by the nagging knowledge that it is hopeless, for Arabella is tired of Matteo and has little patience with even the bare mention of his name. Her frown or displeased toss of the head, all too clear in Zdenka's recollection, occurs again and again in various parts of the orchestra:

Ex. 10

Pouring out his ecstasy at receiving the letter (the origin of which is clearly indicated by Ex. 7 in the orchestral background) he too breaks into an 'exaltierten Ton' (Ex. 9). Zdenka tries hard to explain Arabella's apparently two-faced behaviour in terms of her own so very feminine heart, and promises another letter within a day or two. Unsuspecting, Matteo affectionately calls the sweet 'boy' his dearest and only friend and, threatening to shoot himself unless he (she) helps him more successfully, rushes off leaving the poor girl to wonder who indeed can help *her*. This remains her only twinge of self-pity and, simply expressed, is very affecting.

She has a few more brief moments to herself in which she ponders on all the letters she could so easily write (Exx. 8 and 9) before Arabella at last makes her now well-prepared entrance. Both the timing and the setting for so poised, so serene an appearance are admirable and at one stroke solve Strauss's pangs on his heroine's behalf. Instead of the shallow haughty minx of the first draft, we are at once conscious of the gentle warmth lying behind her calm, beautiful exterior.

Strauss catches this change in Hofmannsthal's view of Arabella to perfection. The oboe phrase which accompanies her as she quietly dismisses her chaperon is far from cold in its beauty, while Arabella's own words—words of mere practical instruction to a servant—are sung to the same charming phrase.

Ex. 11

The little triplet figure ⌐ x ⌐ becomes a motif of her gayer moods, but it is her self-possession that the theme as a whole reflects, and this characteristic immediately makes the strongest impression, especially in contrast with the wilder emotionalism of her younger sister. She quietly puts aside Matteo's roses, though with disappointment, because she had hoped they were from a mysterious stranger whom she has noticed watching the house. At the same time she knows that it is required of her to come to a decision about her future after the evening's festivities when she is to be Carnival Queen. For all their many and varied qualities she feels that none of her suitors has so far touched her heart. She has moreover complete confidence in her own judgement and, unlike the 'proud irritable' Arabella 'prone to contempt' of the *Lucidor* story, she is too honest and kind to have knowingly raised false hopes in any admirer.

With the final rejection of the Arabella–Matteo scene, which would have occurred at this point, we know very little of their love-affair but clearly some time has elapsed since it cooled, so that Matteo's persistence, annoyingly abetted by Zdenka, is both foolish and troublesome. Although Arabella cannot suppress a frown (Ex. 10) as she turns from Matteo's roses (the true nature of her hopes had been reflected by Ex. 6) her music remains unruffled and a new lyrical melody enters while Zdenka pleads Matteo's cause:

Ex. 12

One of the more endearing qualities of Hofmannsthal's new conception of Arabella is her elder-sisterly concern for Zdenka, who is rapidly giving herself away. After making the cautionary remark about the 'exaltierten Ton' already mentioned (Ex. 9), Arabella suddenly realizes that Zdenka is in love with Matteo herself and by inference that she is

quickly growing up; it is high time to stop this silly masquerade. But to
the half-fledged tomboy Arabella's attitude is incomprehensible, and
Zdenka cries out that rather than perform antics of frigidity and haughty
coquetry she will remain a boy for life. Unquestioningly as she adores her
sister, her own simple directness cannot begin to understand Arabella's
more reserved and cool-headed nature. She is, like Lucidor, 'nichts als
Herz' (nothing but heart), and such a nature can neither calculate nor
fathom such detachment in others.

Arabella makes no attempt to argue with Zdenka on the latter's own
terms; it would lead nowhere. Instead, quietly and composedly, she talks
with great seriousness of herself. It is not with malice that she flirts suddenly with one young man after another and as suddenly drops them; it
is the way she is made. Just as she knows that Matteo is not the right one
for her, so the questions which still torment her day and night will
vanish when the right man does come along.

This all-important exposé of Arabella's nature is the great significant
gain of Hofmannsthal's redrafted Act 1, for the idea from which it
germinated was originally disposed of in a few lines passed off with no
great emphasis. But Hofmannsthal unforgettably and with great human
perception now brings Arabella fully to life in just the way Strauss
wanted. The passage ranks with the Marschallin's 'Die Zeit sie ist ein
sonderbar Ding', and Strauss rose to it in the same way. For Arabella's
serious talk of the nobility of love, which she is certain exists though she
has yet to experience it, Strauss composed a melody of distinction and of
dignified beauty:

Ex. 13

while in setting to music the verses in which Arabella foretells the magical
moment of which she dreams, when 'Der Richtige'—the right man
whom she will recognize instantly—will come and claim her, Strauss
had an illogical idea amounting to purest inspiration: since the one letter
from Hofmannsthal back in December 1927 when he had promised to
make his Croatian hero 'strike up now and then a line or half a verse from

some of his native folk-songs', no more had ever been said on the subject, and the utterly final libretto on Strauss's desk gave very little indication of anything of the sort. One or two of the folk-songs Strauss had ear-marked, however, seemed to him too good to waste, and so he used them as he needed them, without necessarily having regard to their original purpose or Croatian context.

The first of these tunes is the motif of Arabella's 'Richtige'. As it occurs in Volume I of Kuhač's collection of South-Slav folk-songs[5] it is No. 34 and appears under the title of 'Ljubomorna' as follows:

Ex. 14[6]

Ti mla - dju lju - biš, mene se tu - djiš, ti se š njom še - ćeš, a mene ne - ćeš,

In Strauss's hands this became one of the finest and most moving operatic melodies of all time:

Ex. 14a

'aber der Richtige—wenn's ein-en gibt für mich auf dieser Welt—der wird einmal da - stehn, da vor mir'[7]

It develops gradually and naturally into an arched sentence to which Zdenka contributes as she in turn pours out her creed—she has no idea if Arabella is right in what she believes; all she knows is that she loves her and wants her to be happy, even at the cost of her own future, as the Fortune-teller seems to have suggested. It is this nostalgic expression of love and the desire for happiness which comes across so movingly as the two soprano voices combine in a soaring restatement of Ex. 14a which is the quintessence of late Strauss.

[5] Albrecht, Zagreb, 1878. Strauss found a copy in the Vienna Hofbibliothek.

[6] As an illustration of the universality of folk-music this quotation of a Baptist Hymn from Virgil Thomson's *Four Saints in Three Acts* (1928) may be of interest:

Begin to trace   begin to race   begin to place   begin and in

[7] 'But the right man—if such a one exists for me on this earth—he will stand there one day, there before me.'

27

6

The song comes to an end and sleigh-bells are heard announcing the approach of Graf Elemer. There is the faintest touch of bitterness in Arabella's reaction to the three Counts, in her mockery of their attentions. Presents from all three come by the same delivery and they themselves always band together in an absurd troupe so that there is some justification in her banter. But she fears that she may be thrown by circumstances into the arms of one of them and just a vestige still remains of Hofmannsthal's first conception of her as 'a mature and beautiful girl who has probed too deeply into certain aspects of life, a little seared by cynicism and resignation, and who is ready to enter into an arid *mariage de convenance*'.

Zdenka cannot believe that Elemer is the 'Richtige', but Arabella thoughtfully tells of how she must make her decision that very evening and it may have to be in favour of Elemer. In a flight of adolescent romantic fancy Zdenka paints to herself the dramatic scene of Matteo's suicide if Arabella should choose Elemer, but Arabella is not listening. Walking over to the window she describes the stranger she has seen, a large impressive man with a very serious look in his eyes. She has become more and more certain that he was looking straight at her, and could have sworn that through his *Leibhusar*[8]—who is always in attendance—he would have been the one to send her flowers, flowers which more than any other she feels she would be glad to receive.

This, her first mention of Mandryka, is accompanied on the orchestra by the relevant fragments of his motifs as they occurred in Ex. 6. The little horn and trumpet fanfare ⌈ x ⌉ is especially in evidence and was in fact discreetly present in the background during the duet 'Aber der Richtige'.

Zdenka has one last despairing outburst on behalf of Matteo, but she has overplayed her hand and Arabella is on the point of losing patience when Elemer appears, so that Zdenka has no choice but to make herself scarce.

The emergence of Elemer as a character in his own right is another product of the revised act. Hofmannsthal wrote that he had it in mind to 'concentrate the *three* Counts into a single figure in the first act as well as in the farewell scene; as a result this single figure will become more significant and Arabella's attitude towards him more interesting. I will,

---

[8] i.e. 'personal hussar', in effect a glorified batman.

however, keep the actual appearance of that triad of noble admirers, because in this case three is less than one—three admirers compromise her less than one serious suitor—but what I shall do is to make two of them mere shadows, mute or almost so, and only one (Elemer) a genuine lover.'

The appearance in the flesh of the shadow-Counts, Dominik and Lamoral, was kept in hand for Act 2 by having them draw lots for Arabella's companionship on this important day. She greets Elemer's bumptious arrival (much play with the motifs of Ex. 4) extremely coolly, especially when he claims to be her overlord for the day as the result of the lottery, a cavalier treatment of her person which by no means meets with her approval. He tries to cover up his tactlessness but she is unimpressed (Ex. 10) and he has to work hard for the privilege even of taking her out for the afternoon. His hasty recollection that she is to be Carnival Queen brings with it a new motif symbolical of that role.

Ex. 15

Much of Elemer's courtship in the scene which follows is dominated by Ex. 15, but whereas to Elemer it signifies his hopes of winning for ever this queen of women, to Arabella it stands for her last evening of careless gaiety before having to make an irrevocable choice. She damps his ardour by informing him that if he wants to take her out in his beautiful sleigh drawn by Russian horses he will have to put up with Zdenko as chaperon.

Greatly disconcerted as he is, Elemer has no option but to agree and she dismisses him promising to be down in half an hour. Zdenka, on returning, is as dismayed as was Elemer to hear of her enforced role during the sleigh-ride, but Arabella is adamant. Their quarrelling breaks off as Arabella again spies Mandryka with Welko, the Leibhusar,[9] in the street outside (Exx. 13 and 6(y)) and the two girls are then bustled out of the room by their parents, for Graf Waldner is in a very depressed frame of mind.

---

[9] Like the three Counts, Welko is the only survivor of Mandryka's three curious attendants in the revised Act 1, Djura and Jenkel making relatively minor appearances in the later acts.

Certainly the father of these two adorable girls presents a sorry picture. Rather than Mandryka, it is Waldner who calls to mind the boorish Ochs, but an Ochs dismally deflated and without the bluff assurance which gave that key figure its distinction. To repeat oneself at a lower level is always hazardous and Strauss found it impossible to portray the vulgarity of a small personality and still write good music. Waldner's tale of the absurd extravagances of the quasi-millionaire Mandryka he once knew as a fellow cavalry-officer is clumsy rather than witty.

To this comrade of the past he has sent Arabella's picture in the hopes that, veteran though he now must be, the girl's beauty will cast its customary spell (Ex. 3) and he will come, whisk her off and marry her.

Such a solution to their problems appals his wife who, rather than sacrifice her first-born to such a fate, would sooner they all went as servants to her old aunt's castle. Zdenka can perfectly well remain a boy and as for Arabella, Adelaide still has faith in the Fortune-teller's prophecies of a rich marriage (Ex. 6(z)).

After a short duet for the wretched parents, Adelaide goes off, leaving her husband to his misery (Ex. 2). An unwise call for a glass of cognac is received with contempt by the waiter who has been instructed to insist on payment in advance, but just when Waldner is in the depths of gloom a visiting-card is presented. At first he naturally takes this to be another account for payment and tells the waiter to say that he is out. When he comes to examine the unfamiliar-looking card, however, he suddenly spots the name of Mandryka. At the same moment the waiter returns yet again: the caller has been insistent. Joyfully Waldner now changes his tune and rises to welcome the very man whose arrival he has been longing for.

7

But it is not the Mandryka he expected who stands before him, tall, young and heavily impressive (Ex. 13 on four horns). Waldner's greeting 'Ciao,[10] comrade' dies on his lips. With the utmost courtesy and dignity the newcomer advances, with Waldner's letter outstretched, and on completion of the formal introductions immediately embarks on an explanation of the letter's blood-stained appearance. So grotesque and improbable is his account of being wounded on a bear-hunt, letter in

[10] It is amusing to see the familiar Italian expression rendered in German: 'Tschau'.

hand, that it can only have been inserted as part of Hofmannsthal's intentions to establish Mandryka's image there and then as an unsophisticated sporting country squire.

Waldner agrees that he wrote the letter, though it was to his regimental comrade. Now at last Mandryka introduces himself: he is the old man's nephew and namesake. His uncle is dead and he, the surviving Mandryka, took it upon himself to open the letter. Abruptly he comes to the point and commands Welko to bring forward the photograph he had found enclosed. In so doing Welko, who adds local colour by addressing his master as 'Gospodar' (an equivalent of the Scottish 'Laird'), confirms that the young lady 'with the face' does indeed live here.

There is an upsurge on the violins beginning with an anticipatory outline in rapid diminution of the melody which is soon to represent Mandryka's courtship. As this fervent theme becomes particularly prominent during the scene to come it is quoted at once in its fully-developed form.

Ex. 16

Mandryka: 'So gib das Mä - del mir zur Frau' [11]

Mandryka establishes to his satisfaction that Arabella is not only Waldner's daughter but unbetrothed. He then proceeds to disentangle the situation for himself strand by strand, thereby laying bare Waldner's plot, the significance of which he has some difficulty in understanding. In his perplexity Mandryka paints with the most glowing colours an imaginary picture of his dead uncle in rude and lusty health receiving the latter with the ravishing portrait and, being—as he puts it—'ein ganzer Mann' (i.e. altogether manly), taking the only reasonable step upon seeing such beauty (Ex. 3 in augmentation) of making an immediate proposal.

Mandryka is entirely carried away by his little drama and the vignette takes up and elaborates Ex. 16 in various ways, culminating in the final shape as it is quoted above.

Turning to Waldner, Mandryka asks quite frankly what in such circumstances would have happened, but the old man dares not admit the

[11] 'So give me the girl for wife.'

truth, and hedges. Mandryka, who has seen through him, now speaks ardently for himself with an exuberant affirmation of his inheritance, wealth and position which is proclaimed to a new theme combined with an equally motivic embroidery on the first violins.

Ex. 17

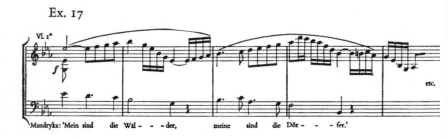

He speaks of the sincerity of his love, and references to Ex. 13 appear in the orchestra, for his is just the kind of permanent and deeply-intentioned love of which Arabella has been dreaming. At the same time his passion has been inspired by a mere picture and in this respect Hofmannsthal's outstanding precedent in the operatic field was, of course, Tamino's love for Pamina in *Die Zauberflöte*, expressed in the famous aria 'Dies Bildnis ist bezaubernd schön'. But Schikaneder's symbolic fairy-story is not particularly noteworthy for the plausibility of its action and Hofmannsthal recognized the need to concoct a stronger degree of verisimilitude within the terms of his own more realistic drama.

Hence the adventure of Mandryka and the she-bear who, he now tells Waldner, broke no less than four of his ribs within an hour of his receiving the portrait, so that he had twelve full weeks in bed during which to admire Arabella's features with ever-increasing ardour.

The romantic yearning music accompanying this narration (which resembles one of the 'exaltierten Ton' motifs of Adelaide and Zdenka, Ex. 8(x)) breaks into a vivacious movement as Mandryka describes the perturbed reaction of his many retainers to his impulsive decision to sell one of his large forests and with the proceeds make the pilgrimage to Vienna. He shows his wallet, bulging with bank-notes, and Waldner joins him in an enthusiastic duet.

Two new themes are introduced during this vigorous passage, the first an important variant of Ex. 13.

Ex. 18

Ex. 19

Lju - bi, lju - bi, ne dan - gu - bi....il ak' hoćeš baš i me - ne

Ex. 19 is another South-Slav folk-song (No. 1001 from Kuhač's Volume 3, entitled 'Vanjkušak (jastučak)'). Here Strauss is nearer to his original purpose, for although it is hardly a case of Mandryka 'striking up a verse of one of his native songs', he certainly is reflecting something of his life in Croatia as he tells of issuing instructions to his retainers, planning his visit to the capital, and so on. Hofmannsthal had in fact recommended just this passage to Strauss:

> 'May I make a suggestion?! Why don't you occupy yourself a little with the ballad-like passage of Mandryka's beginning ... 'Kommen meine Verwalter ...' as if these were the words for a song. Perhaps in this way this highly important figure will begin to take on style and shape.'

In his excitement Mandryka offers Waldner the loan of unlimited thousand-gulden notes. The phrase to which he repeats his invitation quickly acquires the status of a motif:

Ex. 20

Mandryka: 'Teschek, be-dien'dich!'[11a]

The little turn, Ex. 6(w), is also prominent, identifying itself with Mandryka, the saviour of the family. Waldner is shamed into taking no more than one bank-note, followed with a certain amount of genuine hesitation by a second. There is a moment of embarrassment and Mandryka broaches the question of how he is to be introduced. Waldner at once suggests this can be done on the spot, but to his surprise Mandryka

[11a] 'Help yourself, old chap' (a Croatian word: dječak = chap, lad).

refuses. In a beautiful passage based on the themes of love and courtship (Exx. 13 and 16), through which Mandryka's Ex. 6(z) winds continuously, he becomes very serious. He speaks of his wooing in sanctified tones, begs to be presented on a more formal occasion, and with the utmost courtesy he bows himself out, the nobility and depth of his character firmly established.

8

Waldner is left wondering whether he has dreamt the entire incident. In a short scene dominated by Mandryka's themes (and especially by that of his generosity, Ex. 20) he tries to come to terms with the fantastic change of fortune which has so abruptly transformed his entire outlook.[12] He is interrupted in turn by a waiter—who rapidly drops his insolence when he sees the thousand-gulden notes—and by Zdenka, who cannot fathom what has come over her father. But Waldner can do nothing but repeat the words 'Teschek, bedien' dich' in ever more jubilant tones, and his bewildered younger daughter is left standing in the middle of the room with her mouth open as he dances out waving an enormous bank-note, with which he will clearly try his luck at the gambling table in a matter of minutes.

Poor Zdenka, in terror that her father has gone out of his mind, has scarcely time to recover her composure when Matteo bursts in. He can think of nothing but the next promised letter which he believes Arabella is about to write to him, and he exacts a promise from Zdenka that he will receive it at the latest during the Fiakerball that same evening.

He rushes off again just as Arabella herself returns, chiding Zdenka for being so long getting ready. Zdenka loses her temper at last and storms out, jeering at Arabella's precious Elemer.

Ex. 21

Zdenka: 'Die Rappen und dein E - le-mer!'

Her scornful phrase becomes the starting point for Arabella's aria with which Strauss had been so eager to close the act. It must have been a sad

---

[12] It was for this moment that Hofmannsthal drafted a quartet for Adelaide, Waldner, Zdenka and Arabella as one of his projected revisions. In view of the paucity of ensembles in this act it seems a shame that it found no place in the final scheme.

task to set it to music, for these were Hofmannsthal's last lines, written only a couple of days before his death. But they are beautiful lines and for Strauss a genuine fount of inspiration.

Ex. 21(x) is combined with Exx. 10 (Arabella's frowns) and 12 (Zdenka's appeals) as the effect of her sister's gibe makes itself felt upon the pondering Arabella. The whole aria is given a colour of its own by the use of a solo viola, a particularly fine idea. Arabella is sobered by the idea of 'her Elemer', and the ghost of Mandryka's themes confirms her intuition that the words have a curious ring to them. She is yearning for love (Ex. 13) but senses that Elemer cannot fulfil her need (Exx. 14 and 15). Her thoughts next pass to Matteo but the boyish earnestness of his calf-love arouses no more than her pity.

Throughout this and the following sections the beautiful Ex. 12 appears and reappears in combination with the other themes. Zdenka's unconscious influence upon her sister and the course of events is omnipresent, and at this point her motif even hints prophetically at the future outcome.

The music now passes to Ex. 14, for the first time close to its Croatian form, and Arabella bursts into an exposé of her desire that the stranger might come and claim her. Suddenly the idea of marrying Elemer comes back vividly and makes her shudder. In trying to reason with herself why this should be so (Ex. 13 on solo viola) she allows herself to ruminate further upon the stranger. She considers the likelihood of his being already married and Ex. 14 undergoes a rich and extended development, gradually turning into a lively waltz.

Arabella's coquettish motif reappears in the gay style of an operetta and she remembers the evening's carnival ball at which she is to be queen. Her spirits rise and philosophically she prepares to put aside her worries while she enjoys her final fling. The orchestra whirls up to a frenzy and pauses; Zdenka is at the door in full masculine attire, top-hat in hand. The girls go out together and sweeping strings proclaim the waltz form of Zdenka's Ex. 7. This quickly gathers pace and as it turns into a Molto Allegro with rushing semiquavers it carries Ex. 15 with it.

For the moment Elemer is in possession, but Arabella's thoughts are more on what the evening's festivities are to bring, and as the curtain falls an atmosphere of excited anticipation is created. The brilliant coda thus serves the dual purpose of providing a splendid climax to Arabella's aria and to the whole of the first act.

9

Act 2 takes place at the actual Fiakerball. The curtain rises during the opening bars and discloses a vast ballroom dominated by a central flight of stairs.[13] Staircases are to play a significant role in the denouement and Strauss at once gives pride of place to a staircase motif of majesty and distinction:

Ex. 22

Waldner and Mandryka are standing at the foot of the stairs watching Arabella and her mother descending. Typically the lover comments on Arabella's angelic appearance, the father on her unpunctuality. In his fervour Mandryka presses Waldner's hand so hard that the latter jocularly fears for his ability to hold his cards (Ex. 1).

The moment has come for the formal introduction (Ex. 16) and both Mandryka and Arabella are, all of a sudden, smitten with nerves. Each draws back, pale and momentarily ill at ease, and the parents are visibly disconcerted. Arabella recovers herself however, and to a soft repetition of Ex. 22, the significance of which emerges later, comes forward to be introduced to her romantic stranger. A tender, expressive form of Ex. 3 also accompanies this decisive moment; Arabella is entering a phase in which coquetry plays no part but deepens to a more subtle deployment of her charms.

At a wink from Adelaide, Waldner joins her in making their escape. The lovers are left, for the first time, alone in each other's company. It is a

---

[13] Ludwig Karpath wrote in the Vienna *Neue Freie Presse* (13.7.30) that there was reason to suppose Hofmannsthal had in mind the ballroom of the 'Sperl' Hotel in the Leopoldstadt. This was where the actual Fiakerball was held during the 1860s, and a popular venue amongst the aristocracy of that time. Moreover, Karpath puts forward the conjecture that for the action of the first and third acts Hofmannsthal was thinking of the Hotel Munsch in the Neuer Markt (long since demolished) or possibly the Hotel Erzherzog Karl. Karpath pointed out that both hotels stood in the district of Vienna inhabited by refugees of the Polish nobility from which, in the *Lucidor* story, Arabella's family was descended.

familiar situation of agony and uncertainty, and one which is brilliantly satirized by Mozart and Da Ponte in *Così fan Tutte*. There it is the men who break the ice, but Hofmannsthal, with insight, gives Arabella the opening gambit, albeit with a remark of mere small talk. Strauss found this naïve and in any case was unhappy about Arabella's show of reticence and faint-heartedness on meeting Mandryka, referring to it as 'a bit trivial'. But Hofmannsthal was sure of his ground and expressed surprise at Strauss's comment.

'That Arabella is taken aback at the sight of Mandryka—her fear of experiencing yet another disappointment and with just this very man—this whole feature strikes me as arising naturally out of the character of this young girl who has already arrived at danger point. . . . It would actually not be too difficult to substitute some other opening for this conversation, but I would like to defend the present one strongly to you. It is, as it stands, the result of much thought, i.e. of thinking with the figures and in their situation, and coming from Arabella, it is anything but naïve. Mandryka has for weeks been deeply in love with her picture; a meeting at the hotel has made a strong, a striking impression on her (Act 1, *new*): her father, what is more, has naturally told her that this gentleman has arrived from the furthest corner of Slavonia expressly in order to marry her. Both are very nervous. (Beginning of the act, when Mandryka practically crushes Waldner's hand, and when Arabella for a moment is on the point of fainting with excitement.) Now they are face to face, alone, Arabella is in the stronger position, for she knows how he feels towards her—he has not the slightest notion how she will receive him and his suit. He stands before her, elegant, strong, heavy—and visibly ill at ease. She possesses the greater self-control, and since she is also the lady and therefore the superior of the two, it is up to her to open the conversation. He has pleased her from the outset and so she is eager to hear him confess his love. But to begin, say, with the words: "I am told you want to marry me!"—that would be most unladylike. Therefore, just because she knows perfectly well that he has come to Vienna and to the Ball for her sake alone, she asks this question, not naïvely, but most deliberately and a little *coquettishly*: "And what brings you here?—for you don't look like a habitué of the ballroom, but rather like a solid country squire accustomed to solitude." This question throws him into some slight confusion, but sets him going nonetheless. The poet (librettist) had to aim at bringing the two figures as rapidly as possible, and in a psychologically convincing, not operatically trivial manner, to the point where they express their love for each other, where they actually sing. I fancy I have succeeded in doing this naturally and attractively by mixing retarding phrases and motives ("delayers") with the desire of both to speak of love as soon as possible (that means to become lyrical), and I consider this passage of three and a half pages one of the best I have ever done as a librettist.'

This quite admirable summing up of the situation Strauss received warmly, thanking Hofmannsthal for his 'beautiful letter'.

The halting attempts of Arabella and Mandryka to come to the point are interrupted by first Dominik and then Elemer, each asking Arabella to waltz with them (the orchestra interpolates brief fragments of dance music which, during Elemer's invitation, naturally include his Ex. 15). She composedly puts them off till later and turns her attention calmly once more to Mandryka. She pretends that her father has said nothing of Mandryka's intentions or background, and this forces him to speak. He knows no better than to start by telling her of his first wife, which he does in terms recalling the aria 'Pura siccome un angelo' from Verdi's *La Traviata*.[14]

Arabella receives this gauche tale non-committally and Mandryka, realizing that he is making but an indifferent impression, changes his tactics. In an aria punctuated by self-deprecation as a mannerless peasant he extols her breathtaking beauty with such vehemence that he now scares the poor girl into jumping up from her chair.

Mandryka's awkward behaviour is reflected in the orchestra by a development of the motif (Ex. 20) which in the first act signified his unbridled generosity to Waldner. Its present reappearance shows that this was in itself no more than symptomatic of his sterling if unpolished character, and the motif should now be interpreted in the more general sense.

Many of Mandryka's and Arabella's themes are interwoven during this passionate section and a new ardent motif also arises.

Ex. 23

14 Mandryka originally gives Waldner a fuller account during Act 1 of Maria, this angelic first wife, but Strauss cut the lines which are, after all, unnecessary and even indiscreet.

The music changes abruptly once more to a quick waltz as the lovers are interrupted by the third of the Counts, Lamoral, who receives the same polite refusal as his predecessors.

Arabella now takes the initiative. She sits down and invites Mandryka to sit by her as she at last reveals that she knows from her father of his intentions. The music combines her serious theme, Ex. 13, with those of Mandryka (Exx. 14 and 16) while her worried consciousness of her family's insecurity is portrayed by Ex. 2 and also in her frowning expression as she sings (Ex. 10). As she sees it, Waldner's disgrace and their financial embarrassment must make her a less desirable match.

Mandryka waves aside her qualms. In accents ever more fervent and burningly sincere he presses his suit, revealing as he does so—yet without tasteless boasting—his enormous wealth and position. Very quietly Arabella repeats to herself her creed of love at first sight, which Strauss accompanies with a suave reprise of the *Richtige* melody, Ex. 14.

The character of the music matches Arabella's simile of 'a clear stream shining in the sun' and Mandryka seizes upon her phrase to draw a comparison with the river Danube which flows past his home. His Exx. 16 and 23 now lead not only to a rapturous reference to Arabella's Ex. 3 but to a new melody which Strauss once more found in Kuhač's collection (No. 19 in Volume 1, 'Ono je moja djevojka'):

Ex. 24

Či - ja je_____   o - no__ dje-voj - ka,_____

Strauss keeps this Herzegovinian tune unaltered apart from its unusual mode (and key signature) which he puts into the major.[15] Ex. 24 is followed by another, and extremely beautiful, theme:

Ex. 25

etc.

---

[15] Curiously enough as a result of the change of mode Ex. 24 strongly resembles the Da-ud theme from *Aegyptische Helena* (Ex. 34) though with none of the banality of that much-criticized melody.

Both Exx. 24 and 25 find their origin in the spiritual depth of Mandryka's love, but Ex. 25 symbolizes that love in a specific way. To the calm lines of the music he tells Arabella of a quaint custom by which any girl of his village would set the seal of her betrothal by offering her beloved a glass of fresh water drawn from the well behind her father's house.

The appearance of yet another *Trank*, after all the controversy of the potions in *Aegyptische Helena*, threw Strauss into complete consternation. He expostulated with Hofmannsthal: 'I am getting less and less keen on that drink of pure water! Just think: we are being accused already that there's nothing but drinking in *Helena*: but there at least it was a case of interesting magic potions! The joke 'Hofmannsthal must have got water on the brain' is too cheap to be passed over by a single 'witty' journalist'. But Hofmannsthal insisted: 'I can't get it into my head that I should not be allowed to introduce even a glass of water on account of the magic potions in *Helena*. Nor do I think that I should be able to find anything better . . . either in my imagination or in any collection of Slav popular customs.'

In fact Hofmannsthal had additional reasons connected with the end of Act 3 to support his conviction that he was incontestibly in the right.

Arabella echoes the Glass of Water theme, Ex. 25, as she acknow-ledges that she finds Mandryka's unalloyed personality, his very view of life, a new and refreshing experience. Sensing her capitulation he drives home his advantage and in a triumphantly passionate phrase formally 'chooses her for his wife'. The themes of love, seriousness and nobility build to a soaring climax and then descend to a hushed statement in full of the Slav melody, Ex. 24. With the most profound sentiment, yet utter simplicity, the two plight their troth, Arabella to the words, so moving, derived in their form and expression from the famous passage in the Book of Ruth: 'And you shall be my master, I your subject. Your house shall be my house, in your grave shall I be buried. I give myself to you for all time and eternity.'

10

There is a glowing after-phrase based on the Glass of Water theme (solo trombone with cantabile strings) and Arabella changes her tone as she begs Mandryka to return to the hotel and leave her; she wishes to dance her last farewells to her childhood. This is so strange a demand that, not unnaturally, Mandryka demurs. To the staircase motif (Ex. 22) which is to symbolize their union in absolute and mutual confidence, he states that from henceforth his place is at her side. Her frowns at being crossed (Ex. 10) bode ill for their future relationship but the compromise is reached by which Mandryka has her permission to remain, though he will in no way interfere with her, nor even speak to her.

A crowd of coachmen and revellers headed by the three Counts now approaches Arabella with an enormous bouquet; Mandryka gives his formal consent to her dancing with them and, as the dance music takes over, she leaves him. The spell is broken.

But the thread of Strauss's musical thought was also broken, and it is here that Strauss acknowledged himself hopelessly stuck for many months, interrupting the work with lighter tasks, such as the *Idomeneo* reworking. For the first time he missed Hofmannsthal's intellectual opposition and the ruthless criticisms to which he had become so accustomed that he could scarcely remember how to apply them to himself. Equally he desperately missed the ability to fire back criticisms at Hofmannsthal, resulting in an interplay of ideas out of which, as in *Rosenkavalier*, some entirely new and successful solution sometimes emerged. He knew the remainder of the second act was still in an unpolished state and that the very style of the music was the subject of an argument that could now never be resolved. Ultimately he steeled himself to complete the act as it stood, but there was never any reasonable prospect of the end matching the very high artistic level of the preceding scenes.

Strauss based the music of the Fiakerball on two themes: a waltz derived from Arabella's Ex. 3 and a Polka in unashamedly popular idiom:

Ex. 26

Ex. 27

Ex. 27 provides the setting for the Fiakermilli who, in a series of coloratura cavortings and yodellings, invites Arabella to be Queen of the Ball. In mock vulgar doggerel she likens Arabella to a new star in the firmament:

> 'Die Wiener Herrn verstehn sich auf die Astronomie:
> die könnten von der Sternwart sein und wissen gar nicht wie!
> Sie finden einem neuen Stern. . . .'[16]

and so on.

Strauss's decision to return to the coloratura voice which he had used to such good effect for the subtle light-heartedness of Zerbinetta was a good one, in principle. To apply it in practice to the Fiakermilli, a character of deliberately unadulterated superficiality, was a hazardous undertaking requiring the taste and wit of an Offenbach or a Johann Strauss. However much he may have wished to be, Richard Strauss was no born composer of operettas and his direct emulation of the style lacks the fineness and elegant manner of his models.

The chorus takes up the refrain (Ex. 15) and, after a yodelling cadenza by the Fiakermilli, Arabella distributes her flowers amongst the thronging crowd, accepts Dominik's arm and plunges into the festivities. The orchestra elaborates Ex. 26 as a symphonic waltz in the style of the *Intermezzo* waltzes, while the mingled Counts and coachmen disperse gaily into the ballroom.

A quartet follows formed of two independent pairs of characters. Mandryka is joined by Adelaide and, across the stage, the despairing Matteo by Zdenka. Adelaide guesses by Mandryka's expression what has taken place, and when she asks after Arabella he explains that she has gone off to fulfil her duties as Carnival Queen. In his enthusiasm he showers Adelaide with compliments, while she rushes off to share the good news with Waldner, who is, naturally, gambling somewhere behind the scenes.

Zdenka tries pathetically to raise poor Matteo's spirits but he is inconsolable and increases her own distress with talk of going far away in his attempts to forget. She is frightened off the stage by the appearance of her father (Ex. 2) who, however, goes straight up to Mandryka and embraces him warmly (Ex. 20). The latter orders a sumptuous supper with champagne for everyone, thirty bottles at a time, so that none should know which are Counts and which coachmen in the prevailing hilarity. On

---

[16] 'Viennese gentlemen understand astronomy:
they could be from the observatory and simply don't know how!
They find a new star. . . .'

being pressed, Adelaide ventures a suggestion for more flowers, and Mandryka gives Djura flamboyant instructions to order them by wagon-loads. He is riding the crest of the emotional wave and upsurgings of Ex. 8 support his extravagant exuberance. Adelaide takes his arm and they go down to the ballroom together.

Next comes the scene in which Arabella formally takes leave of her *Jugendzeit*, her youthful days, symbolized by the three Counts. This is a scene requiring a consummate actress if Arabella is not to appear an in-sufferable prig in need of a good hiding. Dominik, with whom she has just been dancing, is the first to get his *congé*. He was the first man to declare his love for her, she tells him, yet they were not the right ones for each other. He clearly has other views but Arabella does not allow him to speak, dismissing him as Elemer approaches. At no time has Dominik come to life in the smallest degree, and the music of his scene with Ara-bella is a curious mixture of ideas from earlier operas recalling, for example, Zerbinetta and Barak.

As soon as he is alone with her Elemer senses that Arabella is in a transcendental state. He tries to bulldoze his way through it but she is past master at handling him. She earnestly tells him that he is right in thinking that something has happened to change her (Exx. 13 and 16), and as a result it is time to say good-bye for ever. When he refuses to accept this treatment and begins to refer disparagingly to Mandryka she simply leaves him standing, despite his proposal of marriage, and passes to Lamoral who is awaiting his turn.

Poor Lamoral is treated like a little boy (at one point she even says to him 'Geh, du Bub!'). At the end she bestows on him, as if it were an order of knighthood, his 'first and last kiss'—on the forehead. Lamoral is instantly transported into a seventh heaven and Arabella further rewards him with a last waltz before 'never seeing him again'. So juvenile an impression does Lamoral leave behind that it is perplexing to find Strauss giving him a deep bass voice, the lowest, in fact, of the three Counts. He also, like Dominik, is too insignificant a character to possess themes of his own and the music of his scene is a flowing non-motivic section which glides easily into his 'last waltz', based once again on Arabella's Ex. 26.

The interest now centres again on Zdenka and Matteo, who return from opposite sides. Exx. 8 and 9 are followed by Zdenka's Ex. 12 as she makes furtive signs to him. What she has not seen is that Mandryka has entered unobserved and is concealed behind a pillar. Hofmannsthal was in some difficulty to find an adequate reason for his presence there as an

28

eavesdropper, but as the plot stood this old-fashioned theatrical device was indispensable.[17]

According to the scenario then, Mandryka has crossed the stage in order to speak with Welko. The behaviour of Zdenka and Matteo 'is so striking', as Hofmannsthal puts it, 'that Mandryka, who is no eavesdropper, finds himself intrigued by these strange goings-on and in stepping forward overhears. . . .'

Zdenka, completely overcome by Matteo's unhappiness, has been pressing upon him an envelope purporting to be a love-message from Arabella. Matteo is unwilling to take the letter which he feels sure signifies the end to their relationship, but Zdenka forces it upon him. As he takes it he feels the outline of a key and his incredulity is such that Zdenka is obliged to say out loud that it is the key to Arabella's room, which revelation Mandryka has the misfortune to hear.[18]

II

The knife is now turned in the wound. Mandryka signs away the approaching Jenkel and draws near to the unsuspecting pair at the very moment when Zdenka overcomes her shyness and promises Matteo that, if he will only trust her and use the key, Arabella will come softly and silently to him in the room. Zdenka's own love pours out, could Matteo but see it through her boyish get-up, in a passage of passionate sincerity which looks forward thematically to the Prelude to Act 3. The combination of Zdenka's and Matteo's themes (her Exx. 8, 9, 12 and his

---

[17] One earlier suggestion by Strauss had been that Jenkel should be a spy, but Hofmannsthal rejected this as bearing too obvious a similarity to Valzacchi in *Rosenkavalier*, Act 2.

[18] In the libretto the distribution of lines is quite clear, viz:
    'Matteo: Das ist der Schlüssel? (That is the key?)
    Zdenka: Zu ihrem Zimmer! (To her room!)
    Matteo: Der Schlüssel zu Arabellas Zimmer! (The key to Arabella's
        room!)
     He holds out the key in front of him.'
Unfortunately, in leaving Matteo's last line to be spoken for the sake of clarity at this crucial moment, Strauss wrote the words carelessly into his score with the result that they now appear in Zdenka's part and are always spoken by her in every performance. The effect on top of her previous line is as if she (or Strauss) is making absolutely sure that Mandryka cannot possibly miss a single syllable, thus creating an intolerably artificial situation. Matteo's spontaneous ejaculation together with his gesture with the key is, on the other hand, perfectly plausible and could be overheard quite credibly by Mandryka.

Ex. 5) with wisps of Arabella's Ex. 3, drawn tantalizingly but mislead-
ingly across the canvas, give advance indications of the love drama to
come. The fatal key itself is characterized by a brusque little figure:

Ex. 28

Matteo's agony of mind at a stroke of fate he cannot understand receives
a composite theme, the second part of which—the figure⌐ y ⌐—
acquires prominence during Act 3.

Ex. 29

Her mission completed, and terrified of being seen, Zdenka makes off
to lie in wait back at their hotel for the successfully deluded Matteo,
whom she will receive in Arabella's name and in Arabella's bed. The
bewildered Matteo, muttering under his breath about the mysteries of
the female sex, rushes away after her and Mandryka is left alone on stage,
confused and out of his mind with bitterness and disillusionment. We
now see a different Mandryka, one who (as Hofmannsthal put it) 'turns
on occasion rather wild and savage, without, however, losing his essential character as a noble-minded and unsophisticated fellow'.

In his rage his first thought is to summon his servants to catch Matteo,
who is of course unknown to him, and bring him back. But the young
officer has already vanished and Welko, who rushes up to his master
with Djura, cannot understand what Mandryka is shouting about and
looks vaguely round at Dominik, who has entered in company with
Adelaide.

Mandryka now storms up and down in utter fury. He sees himself as
the country-bumpkin made to look a complete ass in the unfamiliar
over-civilized world of Viennese society. He raves about the key and
sardonically comments on Arabella's methods of saying farewell to the
time of her youth.

Meanwhile, on the other side of the stage, the disappointed Dominik has been making a pass at Arabella's mother. In the libretto there is a good deal more of this faintly ridiculous incident in which they talk sentimentally of Chopin, of Lenau, and fantastically of the combined threat to Austria from the Prussians and the Russians. It had been Strauss who originally suggested that Adelaide could be made into a kind of Marschallin figure. 'Could she', he wrote, 'be one of those mothers-in-law who are themselves in love with their sons-in-law and jealous of their daughters?' Hofmannsthal replied:

> 'The mother is definitely still a young and pretty woman, and I had already thought of her as a little bit in love with her daughter's admirers herself. She is a gay and original figure, very necessary to the whole action and by no means an altogether insignificant part. But to involve her in serious scenes of love and resignation, to make of her a sort of sham Marschallin, to introduce a kind of "quotation" of the Marschallin's fate—no, for God's sake not that; that really would be a damaging improvement.'

Strauss was still not fully convinced, feeling that more should be made of the role:

> 'How would it be if the three Counts . . . were now to conspire . . . to make a pass at the mother since the daughter has been denied them ?. . . this ballroom flirtation with one of the Counts . . . which starts as a joke, might develop into something a little more serious (even on both sides) and might likewise end in a kiss.'

Hofmannsthal was doubtful but promised to do his best. After a couple of months' interval he hazarded:

> 'It has . . . become possible to introduce . . . a few lyrical passages for Adelaide which help to bring out this part gracefully as that of a woman still young and affectionate who all too suddenly finds herself in the position of mother-in-law, but who can also still easily attract an admirer (in Count Dominik). . . .'

Yet, ironically, when Strauss saw the result his every instinct was to cut back Adelaide's flirtation to the barest minimum. It showed great good humour for Hofmannsthal to write:

> 'You would rather, I gather, cut the flirtation between the mother and Dominik. That I shall do with pleasure! Your

letters of last summer seemed to ask for something of this
kind and there was certainly nothing impossible about it,
since the woman is still young; but I willingly give it up.'

The Fiakermilli now comes up on Elemer's arm and not noticing that
Mandryka is in a temper asks him to give Arabella back to the ball. This
is the first indication we have that she has disappeared and it naturally
confirms Mandryka's every suspicion. He grasps a chair with his hands
so clenched that its back snaps (cf. Octavian who in a similar moment of
rage snaps a wine-glass) and, in a tirade punctuated by violent interjections of Arabella's Ex. 3, angrily refutes the implication that he has got her
under lock and key (Ex. 28). At the mention of the key, poor Zdenka's
Ex. 12 screams out against his own Ex. 20, which now acquires more
than an element of brutality. He tries for a brief moment to remember his
manners, adopting a lighter tone based on the Fiakermilli's Polka, Ex.
27, though the depth of his real feelings can be discerned in the growlings
of Ex. 8 in the basses and bassoons.

Unfortunately Elemer maliciously adds his word to the Fiakermilli's
request, saying that of all people Mandryka will certainly know where
to find Arabella. At this Mandryka explodes and showers vulgar abuse
upon Arabella, the Fiakermilli and high society in general. He is just
offering champagne to the Fiakermilli as a gesture of deep irony when
Jenkel hands him a note from Arabella.

But this too is equivocal, though we, who know both the truth and
her complex brand of sentiment, can understand what she has really
meant. She is going home, she writes, and will be his from tomorrow.
Even her use of a single small letter 'a' by way of signature seems to the
enraged Mandryka indicative of her insincerity.

His tirade breaks out again and becomes wilder and more abandoned
every minute. Even the most sacred themes are churned into coarseness
after the example set by Liszt in his *Faust Symphony*. He sings vulgar
songs to the Fiakermilli who joins him in the refrains with yodelling and
bursts of coloratura, while on his instructions servants pour out endless
quantities of champagne. Mandryka's folk-song, Ex. 19, joins in the
furore and the beautiful folk-song love-duet, Ex. 24, is subjected to every
kind of variation and desecration.

At last he stands up in front of everyone, kisses the Fiakermilli and
publicly insults Arabella and her mother, who has suddenly been
shocked out of her little tête-à-tête. She sends Dominik, now reduced to
a mere dogs-body, for her husband (Exx. 1 and 2) and bravely confronts

the semi-delirious Mandryka. Waldner appears and, called upon to protect his wife and daughter, joins Adelaide in a dignified request that Mandryka produce Arabella. They can make no sense, however, of his bitter replies full of double meanings, and Waldner turns on Adelaide. To the audience the orchestra reveals by means of the Staircase motif, Ex. 22, that Arabella has escaped to enjoy a little quiet solitary self-communion on the threshhold of happiness, but the characters in the drama can naturally have no inkling of this. They are accordingly in complete perplexity over what can have become of her.

Waldner decisively cuts short his gambling and summons his wife and Mandryka to follow him back to the hotel. Mandryka accepts his challenge to a duel, at the same time inviting the company of revellers to continue the festivities of the Fiakerball at his expense. The Fiakermilli takes over Arabella's role of Carnival Queen (Ex. 15) and the act ends with a brief burst of forced hilarity in which she is joined by the chorus.

12

Whilst it was natural and appropriate for Strauss to write an Act 3 Prelude descriptive of the passionate love-scene in the darkened hotel room, it invited yet further inevitable comparison with *Rosenkavalier*. Moreover it is based on the same musical pattern as the Introduction to Act 1 of that opera, with Matteo's Ex. 5 corresponding to Octavian's similar (but superior) motif and Zdenka's Ex. 7 providing the equivalent feminine counterpart to that of the Marschallin. The new Prelude is almost pornographic in its illustrative wildness but lacks shape and formal direction, wasting away eventually in hopeless exhaustion.

Hidden in the texture are countless repetitions of Ex. 3, for Matteo believes that it is Arabella he is embracing. Strauss told Leo Wurmser that the appearance of Zdenka's Ex. 12 later in the Prelude meant that 'now in his heart Matteo knows it is really Zdenka', but this is inconsistent with Hofmannsthal's plot, even though Matteo later says: 'ist mir, als hätt'ich es ge-ahnt von Anfang an', ('It seems to me I sensed it from the first'), a classic instance of wisdom after the event.

The Prelude subsides into the *Valse Triste* version of Ex. 7 (or Ex. 9(x)) which itself gives way to echoing strains of dance music. The curtain has risen to disclose a vast hotel entrance-hall dominated, much as in the décor to Act 2, by a monumental double staircase from which corridors can be seen leading off to the rooms on the different floors. During the *Valse Triste* Matteo appears at the first-storey level. As he looks down over the balcony the doorbell rings and is answered by the night-porter. Matteo disappears and Arabella enters (Ex. 11(x)). She seems to be walking on air, enveloped by the gentle dance music which centres round the *Richtige* melody, Ex. 14. She goes to the foot of the stairs and sits on the bottom step.

Softly, in lilting tones, she sings of her new-found love with snatches of folk-melody including Exx. 19 and 24. That the apparent levity is only veneer is shown by the serious Ex. 13 which confirms this as the love of her life. Her thoughts have just reached Mandryka's tale of the symbolic glass of water (Ex. 25) when Matteo reappears. He is quite understandably dumbfounded to see her fully dressed in an outdoor cloak and his confusion is represented by the simultaneous presentation of Zdenka's Ex. 12 and Arabella's Ex. 3. Suddenly she becomes aware of him and, her train of thought broken, she wrinkles her brows (Ex. 10).

An extended duet follows which gives Matteo his first and only important part to sing in the opera. He is bewildered both by finding Arabella fully dressed and by her extremely offhand behaviour, and all too unwisely he presses for some sign that she is still the adoring mistress whose ardour he has enjoyed barely ten minutes ago. In so doing he breaks his promise to the tearful Zdenka, from whom he has just parted in total darkness, that he would go away immediately, releasing her, i.e. Arabella, from his attentions from that moment forth. The exact situation that Zdenka had dreaded and tried so hard to avert has thus been produced. The more heated Matteo's passion grows the colder Arabella becomes, the more convinced that he is out of his mind. Ex. 29(y) is built up here in an extended development, for not a word he says makes any sense to her. Worse still, she can find no way of stopping his torrential flow of words, or of brushing past him to find refuge by going upstairs to her room. Finally the worst thing possible happens: the front door is once more answered by the night-porter and they are discovered by the returning Waldner, Adelaide and Mandryka, seeking an explanation for her conduct and finding all kinds of misleading circumstantial evidence.

To her parents Arabella is quietly self-possessed but to Mandryka her bearing contains more than a hint of reproach. As she sees it he has broken their bargain that they will not see each other until the new day has dawned. What is taking place is none of his concern; Matteo is an old friend of the family and she is on her way to bed.

But Mandryka views the matter entirely otherwise. He has recognized Matteo as the man with the key (Ex. 28) and he gives Welko instructions to pack their bags in time to catch the next train home. While Adelaide flounders about uselessly, Waldner tries to summon some of his one-time dignity and authority. He cross-examines Arabella directly and a new pathetic motif is heard representing the agonizing suspicion under which Arabella now lies:

Ex. 30

Since Arabella has no idea what she is being accused of, she can give no satisfactory answer, but asks her father in return if everyone has gone mad. Waldner's demands for an explanation evoke from her no more than a quiet disavowal accompanied by the motif of her betrothal (Ex. 16). Very quickly satisfied that the whole affair is a storm in a tea-cup, he kisses her on the forehead and turns to his gambling partners who have followed him, suggesting that they continue their game (Ex. 1) in the hotel.

One more outstanding theme now enters as Mandryka tries to help Arabella to gloss over the shame of the incident by any means in his power—short of his intended role as her fiancé. Within these bounds he tries to forgive what he believes to be her faithlessness and duplicity.

Ex. 31

Arabella is bitterly hurt that he should find anything to forgive. Any forgiveness, she says, should be on her side, on account of the tone of voice in which Mandryka has addressed her.

But Mandryka, glancing sideways at Matteo, alludes to him in words containing a plain insult. Against repetitions of Ex. 12 (the motif of Zdenka, who is the unconscious cause of all the trouble) Matteo, who knows nothing whatever of Arabella's betrothal, declares that if it be true that Mandryka holds rights in the matter he will accept the

challenge to a duel. Arabella quickly puts him in the picture by announcing her engagement (Exx. 6(z) and 16 combined), at the same time
repudiating Matteo's claim to the merest shadow of a right. Thoroughly
embarrassed, he assents in stammering syllables punctuated by phrases
of Ex. 7.

Mandryka is no fool however; he has grasped the significance of
Matteo's hesitation and pounces on it. Again with repetitions of Ex. 12
he completes Matteo's thought for him—'except for the right the events
of this night have lent him'.

Arabella is stricken. She had never thought so ill of Matteo as to believe that he would willingly harm her, yet here he is, compromising her
publicly and destroying her marriage prospects. Arabella's despair takes
the form of a widely chromatic motif which accompanies her conviction
that life is no longer worth living:

Ex. 32   or Ex. 32a

Adelaide adds her own rebuff to Matteo who, finding everybody against
him, shuts up like a clam. Waldner decides that Mandryka's sarcastic
insults justify positive interference, though the wind is taken out of his
sails when he realizes that his duelling pistols have long since been sold.
The scene develops into an ensemble which is heightened by the voices of
other inmates of the hotel. Disturbed by the uproar, these have come out
of their rooms and are looking down from the upstairs balconies enthralled by the drama being enacted below. Curiously enough Strauss
maintains a strictly male chorus of hotel guests, although Hofmannsthal
made no such stipulation and it seems unlikely in the extreme that the
wives would have shown such self-control in mastering their curiosity.

Overwhelmed at dragging Waldner into the quarrel, Matteo tries to
shoulder all the blame, but this only makes matters worse. Waldner rebukes him sourly and Mandryka, rather touched by Matteo's gesture,
turns on Arabella. The least she can do is to stand by Matteo and acknowledge that he is her lover. But although she protests her innocence
with all the fervour she can command, Exx. 14 and 25 reinforcing the
sincerity of her words, she cannot overcome Mandryka's memory of
the ballroom episode with Zdenka, Matteo and the key (Ex. 28) and at
last he plays his trump card, revealing all he has seen and heard.

But she still fails to understand, and, deeply offended, replies to Mandryka's direct accusation in cold speech, refusing to answer his questions and going away from him.

13

There have been various lines in the spoken voice during the opera, a device which Strauss had used many times in his earlier *durchkomponierte* scores. But the longer section of dialogue which now occurs, entirely unpunctuated by music, is unique and highly dramatic.[19] Mandryka succinctly and sternly gives Welko peremptory orders to knock up a swordsmith in the city, at whatever cost, for two heavy, freshly-sharpened sabres. Otherwise nothing is required but a doctor. Half turning to Matteo he requests his presence in the adjacent winter garden; he stipulates no witnesses. He then takes out a cigarette and smokes silently, awaiting the fulfilment of his commands. There is a long general pause with everyone standing dismally around.

Suddenly the hiatus is cut through with Zdenka's voice crying out to her parents. As everyone looks up she rushes out from upstairs and careers all the way down, throwing herself on her knees in front of Waldner. The orchestra bursts in with the utmost vehemence, the music recalling the passionate Prelude; Zdenka is in a négligé, her hair loose, unmistakably a girl. Her scatter-brained mother can think of nothing but the scandal and tries to hide Zdenka in her cloak; Arabella, however, perceives that something is very wrong and speaks comfortingly, protectively, to her. Zdenka talks wildly of last farewells before throwing herself in the river and in the confusion the hotel guests and Mandryka can be heard wondering who this ravishing young girl can possible be; Mandryka thinks he has seen that face somewhere before, another over-close similarity to the equivalent place in *Rosenkavalier*.

Waldner is completely nonplussed and Adelaide's absurd admonition to Zdenka for 'silence to the grave' (Ex. 2) is certainly no help. It remains for Arabella to take her sister under her wing. Zdenka, tormented with the need to confess, tells her beloved Arabella the truth she would never have dared to reveal to anyone else, least of all her parents. As she shyly, but with a touch of pride in her own new-found womanhood, says that Matteo still does not realize who it was he seduced she calls out instinctively to him with anguish in her voice.

[19] One recalls Britten's parallel use of the effect in the third act of *Peter Grimes*.

Finding that he responds to the unmistakeable fondness with which she utters his name, Zdenka reveals her identity to Matteo. That loyal, that only friend, Zdenko, was a girl all the time, a girl who is now hiding her face in her hands and begging for forgiveness.

To Arabella, Zdenka's only fault has been an excess of love and, as she expresses this, something of her own restored peace of mind shines through the music with a tender derivative of her Ex. 3:

Ex. 33

Vls. & Fls.

She has learned the meaning of true forgiveness through love, and Ex. 33 reflects her warm-hearted acceptance of the Forgiveness motif, Ex. 31.

Complete realization of the truth comes to both Matteo and Mandryka. To the one the knowledge of Zdenka's boundless devotion inspires love, to the other deepest humiliation. How can he who had no true forgiveness in his heart (Ex. 31) expect in his turn to be forgiven?

At this moment Welko and Djura enter with sabres, pistols and doctor, all complete. Waldner cuts a slightly ridiculous figure by trying to impress his gambling companions with his resolution to press on with the duel in spite of everything. (A father must, after all, avenge a daughter's honour; Ex. 32 in aggressive diminution.) Mandryka simply ignores him. He has only one thought—his prospects of making peace with Arabella. With rough statements of Ex. 20 he stops his servants in their tracks and turns to her. His abysmal self-abnegation is accompanied by a combined development of Exx. 30 and 31, through which Ex. 13 and a gravely beautiful augmentation of Ex. 3 entwine to denote Arabella's serious and sympathetic reception of his apology. Nevertheless she does not answer him directly but turns back to Zdenka. Humbly she acknowledges the opera's central theme; it is Zdenka who has the sweeter and more loving character, Zdenka who must now follow her own heart, for she has taught her all too complacent elder sister an enduring lesson on the sanctity of love and unselfishness.

Zdenka finds it hard to absorb the volte-face around her. She only knows that she has a deeper faith in her sister than Arabella herself, and she is confident that Arabella will never abandon her, come what may. The phrase 'come what may' now becomes a refrain, taken up by the different characters. To Mandryka it signifies his own uncertain future, to Waldner the forthcoming duel. But Adelaide cannot see beyond the family disgrace which the Fortune-teller seems to have overlooked, while Matteo is deeply conscious of having sinned against a veritable angel.

Mandryka is about to drift off in despair when Arabella calls to him softly over Zdenka's shoulder and fervently he kisses her hand. He has been forgiven (Exx. 31 and 33) although she will allow no more to be said tonight about the rights and wrongs of the past. In a warmly melodic passage built on many motifs but dominated by a gently transformed Ex. 23, she emphasizes that what matters now is that they all bear good will to one another during the 'come what may'. The music rises to a climax and there is a brief pause.

With immense nobility Mandryka provides the solution; come what *must* is the courtship of little Zdenka. He grasps Matteo by the hand, thus signifying the termination of their quarrel, and leads him over to Waldner. With an outstanding show of courtesy and breeding he pleads Matteo's case in terms that brook no refusal. Moreover, in Hofmannsthal's text Mandryka adds the following lines:

> 'Do not deny him that which great love has given him!
> And the lordship of two villages, two of my own,
> between the mountains and the quiet Danube,
> I make it my privilege to lay at her feet,
> with a castle as well;
> that she may possess the place where she is mistress
> and need not feel her sister puts her to shame.'

Apart from the altogether heart-warming nature of this gesture, it has considerable practical importance since it removes the penniless Waldner's qualms over giving his blessing to Zdenka's betrothal to a mere impecunious subaltern. Yet Strauss found himself in difficulties over the whole speech, cutting all but the first of the lines quoted above and setting the preceding lines (unquoted) to music of empty pomposity.

Poor Zdenka is still unable to grasp that so much happiness can really be hers, and Waldner, whose turn it is to be moved, kisses away her tears. Owing to Mandryka's generosity (Ex. 20) all has come right. He also embraces Adelaide who is weeping for joy (Ex. 2), and then turns again to his fellow gamblers, with whom he departs to continue their game which has been disturbed by the crisis. The hotel guests, disappointed, also drift back to their rooms since it is clear that the entertainment is over.

Mandryka approaches Arabella hopefully, but her resolution is intensified to begin their intimate relationship afresh on a bright new day. She tries to encourage him with a naïve 'don't you think so', but he is dismayed and stands irresolute. Adelaide takes Zdenka off to bed, the latter encouraged to let herself be led away by Arabella's assurance that Matteo will return in the morning to be hers for ever. The Marriage theme (Ex. 6(z)), now applied to Zdenka, floats up through her motifs, Exx. 9 and 12.

Matteo obediently disappears; what he is feeling we can only guess. He has lost Arabella, who had become for him hardly less than an obsession. In gaining so sweet and devoted a substitute he will need an infinity of tact and understanding. But Strauss has no further interest in him and lets him vanish without a passing thought or musical phrase, leaving the focus now exclusively on Mandryka and Arabella. On her way upstairs, she pauses and turns, asking Mandryka, to the gentle strains of Ex. 25, whether he will instruct Welko to bring to her room a glass of water from the hotel spring. Welko rushes off to comply, and, with a reference to Ex. 32a on the oboe and violins signifying her conciliatory intentions, she too departs. Miserably, racked with uncertainty, Mandryka stands by himself in the darkened, deserted hall. The stage is set for the final scene.

14

In an impassioned monologue Mandryka persuades himself that Arabella has deserted him and indulges in masochistic self-chastisement for his lack of trust. In the middle of his introspective outpourings Welko appears carrying the water on a tray, and Mandryka motions to him to go upstairs with it.

Strauss is now firmly back into his stride and Mandryka's outburst is a magnificent piece of symphonic thinking in which many of the motifs coalesce to give a sure psychological picture of the unhappy man: Ex. 32 both direct and inverted; the Slav tune, Ex. 19, developed in ill-humoured bursts; the *Richtige* theme, Ex. 14, reduced to a timpani figure; Arabella's Exx. 3 and 11(x) in rapid string rustlings; above all, the Forgiveness motif, Ex. 31, the repetitions of which contain the theme of Arabella's displeasure, Ex. 10. There is a glowing modulation which springs naturally out of Hofmannsthal's deeply beautiful and poetic text and the music dies away to a held horn note over a soft brass chord.

The Staircase music follows, a most justly famous passage, and one which Hofmannsthal foresaw when he insisted on retaining the idea of the Glass of Water. In writing to Strauss that this was the best solution he could think of, he added:

> '. . . and at the same time equally simple for the quiet lyrical close of Act 3. . . . For it must, after all, be something that can happen in the village and can be copied quite fittingly on the staircase of a hotel. If on the other hand one takes something more complicated, it may easily look forced, intentional and almost theatrical if staged by Arabella at midnight. Instead of any ceremony at this point, one could of course have the still outstanding engagement kiss. Yet this simple ceremony of carrying the filled glass down the stairs has immense mimic advantages. A kiss she cannot *carry towards him*, she would simply have to walk up and give him the kiss; the other implies the most bridal gesture in its chastest form, and it can be followed by the kiss which thus gains solemnity, something that raises it out of the ordinary; from this final moment after such a lot of fracas I expect much.'

Nor were his expectations betrayed. Arabella is seen slowly descending the great staircase to a gravely beautiful exposition of Ex. 22, followed by other themes of love and forgiveness. In her hands she holds the tray with the glass on it still full. Very quietly, as she reaches the last step, she commends Mandryka for remaining. In a melody combining Exx. 25 and 33 she tells him that she had wanted to drink the glass of water in solitude, to the cleansing of all the evening's ills, and to think no more of their union until the 'bright new day'.

Now, however, sensing him standing there in the dark, she has been so moved—as if by a power from above—that the draught has become superfluous. As she sings of her experiences alone upstairs there is a cumulative development of the Forgiveness motif, Ex. 31.

So she has come to the decision (surely in point of fact the obvious purpose of her request for the glass of water) to bring it 'untouched to her friend on the evening which ends her girlhood'. She elects in this way to enact Mandryka's symbolic ritual in place of her own, the supreme gesture of surrender, and this decision is appropriately accompanied by the Slav melody, Ex. 24, to which she had sung the great Book of Ruth words at the moment of her betrothal.

Mandryka jubilantly completes the ceremony by drinking the water in a single draught and dashing the glass to pieces on the stone floor.

As no one will ever drink again from that glass after him, so too is he the ultimate possessor of Arabella's person. Ex. 25 encompasses Arabella's Exx. 3 and 11(x) now firmly united into a single strand and leading naturally to wide statements of Ex. 13, capped in its turn by Ex. 33. The Arabella he has won has truly left her childhood behind and stands before him a mature woman.

With the *Richtige* theme (Ex. 14) in its waltz rhythm, as in the monologue at the end of Act 1 which it recapitulates, she confirms her acceptance. They are henceforth united in betrothal, in joy, in sorrow, in hurt and forgiveness. Cheerfully he accepts the allusion to forgiveness in a passage combining Ex. 14 with Ex. 31, but she whimsically queries once more his belief in her, and Zdenka's Ex. 7 passes like a shadow over the canvas. He is unperturbed, however, and at last she throws herself into his arms fully and without reserve. Her final phrase reiterates Ex. 13 and after a brief embrace she disengages herself and rushes upstairs.

Mandryka gazes after her rapturously as the orchestra joyfully peals out a theme from Act 1 in which he had proclaimed his substance and position to Waldner (Ex. 17, 'Mein sind die Wälder' etc.) followed by rising sequences of Exx. 16 and 23. One grand proclamation of the *Richtige* theme on brass and timpani and the curtain falls on this tenderest and happiest of love dramas.

15

Before *Arabella* could be launched, the Nazis had taken control of German political life, and both Busch and Reucker, to whom jointly the opera was dedicated, had been relieved of their posts after an appalling series of degrading incidents. Busch himself described Strauss's reaction:

> '. . . we had a conference in Berlin with Tietjen, the Intendant of the Prussian State Theatres, to discuss the affair of *Arabella*. Tietjen was watching over the interests of his absent colleague and friend, Reucker. Strauss declared it was to be taken for granted that the première of the work, dedicated to us both, would only be allowed if produced by Reucker and conducted by me. My remark that he was not to take me into consideration he put aside with decision. If I positively refused to conduct in Dresden then it should be somewhere else. There was no question of any other solution, as far as he was concerned.

When Strauss said this there is no doubt he was quite sincere. Many years later common friends assured me that he
really tried to keep his word and withdrew the work in due
form. Nevertheless, in the end he had to give way to the
claims of the contracts he had signed.'

Accordingly the première, which took place at the Dresden State
Opera on 1st July 1933, was produced by Josef Gielen and conducted by
Clemens Krauss, with Viorica Ursuleac in the title role. Eva von der
Osten, the original Octavian, had in the meantime married Friedrich
Plaschke, who was creating the part of Waldner. At Strauss's request she
was given the unusual position of artistic adviser for stage direction and
presentation (Regie und Vortrag).

Leo Wurmser, who was still the chief repetiteur at the Dresden opera
house, has written of his experiences with *Arabella* in terms which
vividly recall Strauss's manner towards those to whom he entrusted his
first performances:

'I had naturally prepared the work with strict adherence to
the indications and metronome marks in the score. But when
Krauss came and took some ensemble rehearsals with the
singers, with me at the piano, he altered many of them. He
was very much a man of the theatre, always keen on bringing
out the drama or the comedy, and he believed that this purpose was often best served by numerous rubatos, pauses,
commas, ritardandos, etc. even if the composer had not indicated them. When Strauss came we had another piano rehearsal with Krauss also present. Much to my gratification,
he removed practically all the rubatos, breaks and pauses that
Krauss had inserted. He kept saying, in his quiet way: "Nein,
kein ritardando", or: "Keine Fermate", or more often:
"Einfach. Im Takt".'

The interest in this once again rather caustic reminiscence lies in
Strauss's typically bland attitude towards his own music which, for all
its frequent extravagance and romantic fervour, he used himself to perform with remarkable dead-pan expression, both facially and interpre-
tatively.

The opera was at first fairly well received but quickly suffered under
the very stigma of being an inferior sequel to *Rosenkavalier* which its
creators had anticipated. Despite more regular revivals than any of
Strauss's later operas, it has taken *Arabella* all too long to shake itself clear
of that damaging comparison.

For when it comes to the point, of far greater importance is its own particular quality of warmth and glowing beauty. Even the orchestration has a timbre unique amongst Strauss's operas up to this time, and it is interesting that with masterly restraint Strauss uses no percussion throughout the work other than timpani.[20] Fortunately in recent years the opera has begun to occupy a position of popular prestige in its own right as a heart-searching character-study clothed in a gay and attractive comedy, despite some far-fetched situations and occasional weak moments, especially in the latter part of the second act. Strauss recognized the poorer inspiration of this section of the score and agreed to a proposal of Rudolf Hartmann that for the Munich performance the second and third acts should be dovetailed by means of a cut in the Fiakermilli scene. This proved no more than a half measure however, and although sometimes adopted it has not supplanted the original version.

16

Arabella brings to an end an episode in Strauss's life and work which began over a quarter of a century before. The span from *Elektra* is incredibly wide and varied and, for all its temporary set-backs, marvellously fruitful. In the face of such productivity, with two undoubted and three near masterpieces to its credit, it seems almost petty to disparage the long relationship Strauss maintained with Hofmannsthal. Nevertheless the suggestion cannot be avoided that in outstaying its original purpose the collaboration actually reached the point of doing harm to Strauss, who lost his initiative and with it his position of pre-eminence in the avant-garde of contemporary composition. Yet at no other time did he find libretti of a remotely comparable stature to which he could apply his instinctive gift of characterization and sense of the theatre. He was well aware of the beauty of Hofmannsthal's language, and where the subject-matter was congenial and comprehensible to him it sparked some of his finest inspirations.

Hofmannsthal was a poet of wide erudition and great sensitivity. He occupies a position of major importance in Austro-German literature and in his work with Strauss this is both his strength and his weakness. For even the greatest poet and dramatist cannot be an ideal librettist if he

[20] The sleigh-bells announcing the arrival of Elemer's carriage in Act I are no exception, as they are essentially a stage effect.

29

fails to understand the requirements of his composer or forces him along paths for which he is manifestly unsuited. History knows of no other instance of an author of the highest rank acting unaided as the librettist to a great composer, for the subjection of personality must always be a stumbling-block. But Hofmannsthal's self-sufficiency as an artist in his own right was always battling with his confessed need—the need of his work—for music, his love for which was real and deep, although he had no illusions about his technical knowledge. A year before he died he wrote to Strauss:

> 'I . . . am a non-musician and a stranger to musical tastes and education, but at the same time almost frighteningly free from ephemeral judgements, scales of value etc. My appreciation of music might almost be called barbaric, but still, with great attentiveness and with the sensitivity of the artist, I listen and try to get right inside all the music presented to my ears by an orchestra, by a piano or by a gramophone, whether Beethoven or Lehár, a scene by Verdi or one of yours, gipsy music or *L'Après-midi d'un Faune*. And somehow, in my barbaric manner, I do know what it is all about; I am open to all that is creative and have always, even amid the clamour of enthusiasts and sycophants, refused to countenance what is heterogeneous, hybrid and vague aspiration rather than solid achievement.'

It was this self-assured point of view which led Hofmannsthal utterly to reject Mahler's work; even Strauss's music all too often offended his sensibilities. He once wrote in 1914 to Bodenhausen that 'his hair stood on end' when the latter compared Strauss to Beethoven. Such a comparison undoubtedly makes little sense, but Hofmannsthal's instinctive revulsion gives the clue to what was wrong with his liaison with the eminent composer. He could never forget his conviction that Strauss was a being of inferior calibre, both as artist and as man. After a meeting in 1928 with Strauss and Count Harry Kessler, Hofmannsthal actually wrote to Kessler apologizing for the 'rubbish Strauss talked'. There is no doubt that Hofmannsthal's feeling of intellectual superiority had always been underlined by his consciousness of the social difference between their backgrounds. It is sad that his overriding snobbery further damaged a partnership which achieved so much but might have been far more beneficial had not Hofmannsthal held Strauss in too low an esteem to accommodate him at whatever temporary sacrifice of his own plans or development.

It should not be forgotten that whereas at the beginning of the collaboration Strauss had been enjoying a period of genius and greatness, at the point where this volume ends we leave Strauss in a slough of self-repetition, despite a partial upsurge of inspiration for his colleague's swansong. This state of affairs would be depressing if it marked the final deterioration of Strauss's powers, but fortunately such is by no means the case. As the last volume of this astonishing story will reveal, the great composer in Strauss was no more than dormant.

INDEX